D1594319

DISCARD

Declarations of Dependence

Declarations of Dependence

THE LONG RECONSTRUCTION OF POPULAR POLITICS

IN THE SOUTH, 1861–1908 **Gregory P. Downs**

THE UNIVERSITY OF NORTH CAROLINA PRESS • CHAPEL HILL

This book was published with the assistance of the Fred Morrison
Fund for Southern Studies of the University of North Carolina
Press.

Designed by Jacquline Johnson
Set in Janson
by Keystone Typesetting, Inc.

The paper in this book meets the guidelines for permanence and
durability of the Committee on Production Guidelines for Book
Longevity of the Council on Library Resources.

The University of North Carolina Press has been a member of the
Green Press Initiative since 2003.

Library of Congress Cataloging-in-Publication Data
Downs, Gregory P.
Declarations of dependence : the long reconstruction of popular politics
in the South, 1861-1908 / Gregory P. Downs.
p. cm.
Includes bibliographical references and index.
ISBN 978-0-8078-3444-2 (cloth : alk. paper)
1. North Carolina — Politics and government — 1861-1865. 2. North Carolina —
Politics and government — 1865-1950. 3. Reconstruction (U.S. history,
1865-1877) — North Carolina. 4. Dependency — Political aspects — North
Carolina — History — 19th century. 5. Patron and client — Political aspects —
North Carolina — History — 19th century. 6. Political culture — North
Carolina — History — 19th century. 7. Populism — North Carolina — History —
19th century. 8. North Carolina — History — Civil War, 1861-1865 — Social
aspects. 9. United States — History — Civil War, 1861-1865 — Social aspects.
10. North Carolina — Social conditions — 19th century. I. Title.
F259.D69 2011
975.6'03 — dc22   2010029301
15 14 13 12 11   5 4 3 2 1

FOR DIANE, *from whom all blessings flow*

Contents

Illustrations

Declarations of Dependence

Friends Unseen

The Ballad of Political Dependency

THE CIVIL WAR transformed the relationship between the American people and their government. As war shifted the boundaries between the political and the personal, women and men pressed previously private, intimate needs onto states they embodied into patrons they could beg for favors. In the process, democracy and wartime exigency turned dependence from a personal condition into a political style. In strange and seemingly un-American ways, the war sparked a revolution not just in what the American state could do but in what people believed it could do. In the decades following the attack on Fort Sumter, people spoke of politics not just through classic American languages of independence and autonomy but also through a vernacular vocabulary of dependence. The popular politics that flowered from the dialogue between crowd and politician was a calculated, often selfish, frequently extravagant set of appeals. This politics emerged from the particular circumstances of the Civil War and Reconstruction, flourished through the 1880s and 1890s, and was seemingly, if not completely, buried by progressive rationalization and disenfranchisement at the turn of the century.

The development of a politics of dependence — what I call an American patronalism — undermines several basic American myths: that political history can be told largely through the centrality and contested expansion of citizenship rights, that Americans deeply resist relationships of dependence, that the United States possessed a weak government, and that its people, by and large, expected nothing more, at least not before the New Deal. Much of American political history might be summed up in the observation of South

Carolinian David Ramsay more than two centuries ago. Because of the Revolution, some Americans had been transformed from "subjects to citizens," and "the difference is immense." In praise and in critique, scholars affirm the importance of citizenship rights and narrate much of the nation's history through struggles over the extension of those rights to previously excluded groups. These guiding assumptions lead even the best historians to miss the importance of other types of claims that have been central to politics, including those rooted in a fantastic, temporary reconstruction of subjecthood.[1]

This book explores the sometimes grand, sometimes delusional expectations of government that the Civil War created, and that postbellum politicians tried simultaneously to manage and to exploit. It is a story about the dynamic, often surprising way that American people interact with their government, and it is also a story therefore about democracy and public opinion. The letters and pleas in this book demonstrate that many, many people acted as if they had a right to depend on government for food, shelter, even love in the allegedly laissez-faire nineteenth century. As scholars have long recognized, the expansion of American democracy in the nineteenth century did not create a government that perfectly reflected the popular will; it did, however, open up a permeable politics where eccentric popular ideas could influence candidates' self-presentation. Brisk campaigns made politicians keen listeners not from choice but necessity. They learned to respond not just to party platforms or organized pressure or discursive shifts, but also to a less-studied, less easily identified but nonetheless real foundation of popular politics, the mad swirl of ideas circulating among political consumers in the proverbial crowd. Thinking about rights claims, state development, and American political languages in these ways reminds us of now-familiar but still easy to forget lessons that liberal ideology is a complex grab bag of aspirations, that rights are defined not absolutely but contextually, that citizenship and state-building occur in fits and starts and reverses, and that teleological assumptions about an exceptional American politics of independence or autonomy can obscure as much as they reveal.

Although historians have long examined dependence as an epithet or a structural condition in American politics, few have asked whether, when, why, and how Americans treated dependence not as an insult but a strategy, a tool to mediate politics for their own benefit. While historians frequently, if often in critique, define American political aspirations through the "ideal of independence," "individual freedom," or "autonomy" — views that have, in the words of one scholar, a "conceptual lock on the historiography" — those aspirations were also expressed through voluntary claims of dependence.

This political development has largely eluded historical notice because of its erratic, irrational nature. Unlike the movements that fill most works of history, this transformation seemed disorganized, transitory, even delusional. At moments of strain and need, people creatively combined old languages and new conditions to make innovative, bewildering claims, appeals based not upon legal or citizenship rights but upon need and loyalty and love. These innovative, often aggressive popular appeals — what one scholar calls "upstart claims" — push the boundaries of political expression, exposing the thin, tenuous hold of candidates and editors over the language of politics.[2]

To see these claims, and to reach beyond untenable and often untested assumptions about the dominance of republican independence, we have to look past the normal contours of electoral and grassroots politics, the world of party caucuses, campaign orations, local organizing, and elite discourse, and to examine the vast, if strange and often difficult to analyze, reservoir of individual appeals to the various forms of the American state. In the peculiar but influential interactions between politicians and individual people, a separate set of transactions attempted to bind people and nation to each other. We also have to conceive — in ways foreign to modern, educated understandings — that government can be interpreted not just as policy but patron. Under this interpretation, its largesse may be distributed — not as a flaw but a feature — through favors not programs. Together, these presumptions — or at least hopes — reduced the state-citizen relationship to that of an embodied patron and his particular, personal subject, who might be rewarded individually, without creating an obligation on the part of the state to take care of all the other people in the same condition. This unsystematic, even antisystematic, personalistic view of governance served simultaneously as both obstacle and spur to the development of a more powerful, more rational liberal state. At once, people exposed the unfinished nature of the modernization of the state and inspired reformers to stigmatize dependence.

In North Carolina, which sits at the center of this study, thousands of "suffering" people writing from "the depths of black and awful ruin" portrayed themselves as "poore and unnoticed," "remediless," a "Lilliputian," a "poor mortal," a "mean + shaim faced" "subject" who was "beneath you" and "so lonely in this world." The letters that poured into the state capital — at a rate double that of the prewar years — remade a succession of mostly prosaic governors and congressmen into a "friend to the poore and a farther to the fartherless," a "friend unseen," a "listening ear," and a "refuge." In return for "some money" or a "small mite" or for someone to "come to my rescue," people with "no claim upon you whatever, but my helplessness and need"

promised loyalty and praise, or, as one put it, to be "your mule." And at critical moments in national politics, Carolinians, like many other Americans,
turned from Raleigh to Washington to make figures like Grover Cleveland,
William Jennings Bryan, and Franklin Roosevelt into fictive friends. No
mere Tar Heel anomaly, these appeals were part of what reformer Charles F.
Adams Jr. called a "popular hallucination" that made of each new presidency
a "new millennium." From "talk heard on the streets" about a "new and
brighter epoch," Adams commented, a stranger might suppose each new
president a "species of arbitrary monarch."[3]

Because this politics of dependence grew from wartime and postwar experiences, it allows us not just to sketch a new political story but to reassess the
impact of the war more broadly. The Civil War exposed the political nature
of dependent relationships by shifting many previously private obligations
onto the state and by empowering disenfranchised people to make new types
of claims. For the sixty-five years between the American Revolution and the
Civil War, dependence had been a political liability, a reason to be disenfranchised and ignored. Typically, dependence was sheltered under private
relationships between husbands and wives, fathers and children, masters and
slaves, employers and employees. By drafting away husbands and fathers and
brothers, by throwing harvests into chaos, by breaking down slave control,
and by opening up new opportunities for escape and self-reinvention, the
war seemed suddenly to make those previously private needs public responsibility. In response, politicians learned to play to these new expectations. In
North Carolina, the dominant politician of the latter half of the nineteenth
century, Zebulon Baird Vance, performed the role of a distant but powerful
friend over more than thirty years in the spotlight. During wartime, the "cry
of distress" that came up "from the poor wives and children" prompted
Governor Vance to create the state's first large program for poor relief, which
he cast not simply as good policy but as a personal promise from "your Chief
Magistrate." Soon he was overwhelmed by people, especially white women,
who took his words as a pledge that he would care for them individually. A
decade later, Vance reemerged in the state's momentous Redemption campaign of 1876 as the self-styled "friend" of "every poor man in North Carolina." In 1885, now in the U.S. Senate debating the civil service acts, Vance
led a nationwide defense of patronage. Against reform, Vance proclaimed the
"birthright" of every American to ask for favors. "If a man's friends take him
up and enable him after a great struggle to arrive at the point coveted by his
ambition he owes something to them," Vance said. "They believe that . . . in
the bestowal of favors that man should give preference to his friends over his

enemies; and so do I." In response, Vance received hundreds of grateful letters from women and men across the country. *"God speaks to you,"* one wrote. The mutual construction between citizens and figures like Vance laid the groundwork for national politicians like William Jennings Bryan, who called up hopes that he was a silvered savior, and Franklin Delano Roosevelt, who sparked fantasies that he was not just the first great liberal but also the last good king.[4]

Patronalism emerged from the interaction of politician and crowd. Most commonly applied to Latin American politics, and closely related to the idea of clientelism, patronalism describes a belief that services are distributed by big men on behalf of favored clients. Mimicking patterns of both hierarchical friendship and familialism, patronalism encompasses much more than simply the well-known facts of patronage and corruption; it describes the way people imagined what government was and what democracy could accomplish. Once defined as an aspect of underdeveloped or backward societies, patronalism is now understood to be found — to different degrees — in most countries. As democracy and expanding markets break down older systems of cartels or personal mastery or kin-group domination, patronalism emerges as a way to manage the problem of delivering new state services to a heterogeneous population. In the American Civil War, novel but limited intrusions through relief, conscription, protection, and patronage, as well as the thinness of state control over large sections of its territory, produced both new hopes for and grave skepticism of government. A politics of fictive friendship therefore helped explain a government that suddenly seemed able to do anything but incapable of doing anything thoroughly, much less doing everything that it promised. Instead of inspiring revolts or widespread resistance, patronalism was tamed and nourished by democracy in the United States, as in parts of South and Central America and Europe, producing not rebellions but a complex dialogue in public campaigns and private petitions, and at times helping fuel the development of the welfare state.[5]

Because their language can sound rustic, it is easy to mistake these appeals for a romantic, separate, anti-liberal politics. Rather than opposition to or ignorance of liberal governance, this politics of patronalism was a moment, if perhaps a strange one, in the development of liberal politics. American liberalism inspired and was constructed within these intimate appeals. Women and men vested the obligations of fathers and masters and gentlemen upon the state partly because of their exposure to the classically liberal idea that the government was responsible for their pursuit of happiness. Popular pleas illustrate an understudied conundrum of liberalism. As modern states expand, they inspire expectations that elected officials cannot possibly fulfill. Patronalism emerged as one way to deflect those hopes without destroying faith in government. By promising that a favored few could share in the state's bounty, governors developed ways to say no without destroying their own credibility. In turn, people used patronalism to claim what they could from a state with important but sometimes scarce resources. Patronalism — and those unrealistic desires — became one way to build support for a stronger state among Americans who had good reason to be skeptical of universal promises or broad-based programs. Intimate appeals reveal a lost trajectory of American liberalism, a version more pervious and responsive than many modern variations, full of fluidity, passion, and complication. American liberalism was not inherently as programmatic, individualistic, or expert-driven as both its celebrators and its critics have claimed.[6]

People broadcast their appeals using the vocabularies available to them: family paternalism, biblical mercy and grace, gendered honor and chivalry, traditional claims of the weak upon the strong, and friendship. Like many people, nineteenth-century North Carolinians spoke of power in part by naturalizing the presumed powerlessness of women. Therefore, the legitimacy of authority was tied to the leader's gentlemanly obligations to weak and dependent women. But what is most striking about these gendered appeals is not their traditionalism but their creativity. People applied entrenched languages easily to innovative government programs, and men used gendered, feminine appeals for their own ends. Instead of segregating men's behavior from women's, gender provided a way for women or men to assume the mantle of the needy. Through languages of gender, women and men learned to make use of dependence, not just as a victimized status imposed by the state but as a tool for state expansion. Religion, which also provided much of the vocabulary of dependence, proved a supple mode of appeal. In the words of their preachers in the pulpits, and in the songs they sang in the pews, and in the prayers they recited at their bedposts, North Carolinians — like many Americans — practiced a language of supplication and subjection. These pleas conveyed double messages, at once denigrating and aggrandizing the petitioner. Frequently, women and men warned governors and congressmen that God would judge them for failing to take care of the meek. Mercy and grace became not virtues but obligations of the state. Through seemingly old languages of gender and faith, Carolinians remade dependence into a tool they could use for their benefit. People turned to patronalism because it confirmed some of their judgments about how politics and power actually worked. Through experience with intense power invested in local magistrates, Americans learned that rights were meaningful only when affirmed by someone both sympathetic and powerful.[7]

Women and men personalized government not because they were naive but because they were paying attention. Nevertheless, leading historians have often presumed that a desire for autonomy naturally defines modern political behavior. This presumption grows from teleological views of politics, social stigmas against dependence, and historians' well-intended but sometimes misplaced preference for granting agency instead of assessing the powerlessness created by social conditions. Voluntary claims of dependence therefore are often portrayed as vestigial or insincere. Scholars used some of the very letters quoted here as proof of pre-political, perhaps even premodern, "political inexperience" and "utopian hopes" or a timeless set of "grievances" about "suffering" and "injustices," in which "always their needs were the same." If one views the nineteenth-century South as backward, it is particularly easy to misread the petitions in this book as proof that an illiberal South produced an illiberal politics. This misses the dynamic nature and national scope of these pleas. Claims of dependence, no matter how venerable their language, were innovative efforts to take advantage of new government powers. In the process they both narrowed the state into an accessible human figure and expanded its potential reach into every conceivable aspect of life.[8]

The suppleness and complexity of patronal appeals become more evident the more closely you look at them. In 1872, a carpenter named Williamson Buck tried to divorce his wife, who was "afflicked" by the "white swelling" and "can't do a thing for herself." Buck sought aid at his desk, where he pleaded to Tod Caldwell, the newly elected governor of North Carolina. He called "the Ruler of the state" a title that seemed out of place in American politics: "your magisty." At that moment, frozen in time, Buck might appear to be a monarchical subject trapped in the wrong century, an American who had somehow not received the news of the Revolution. Upon closer examination, Buck becomes much more complex. In his letter, Buck quickly shucked the garb of a subject for that of a partner, claiming, "I hav stuck to you like a leach and dun a heap to keep you whare you are and I want you to stand By me in this case if you Pleas." Then Buck shifted again, transforming himself into a neighbor promising to build Caldwell a "fine house Eny time you will let me no that is if you should want one . . . if you will get me out I will never no when I do anuff for you I am in so much trubble I doant no what to do." Having tried contractual bargaining and republican friendship, Buck ended by calling himself Caldwell's "umble sirvent." In the confusion of his own situation,

Buck drew upon as many tactics as he could to get the help he wanted. Instead of a naive belief, dependence was a canny strategy born of a judgment not about how the government should work but how it did. Aware of the state and yet unsure of its form, people who wanted things from government tried to mold casts atop something they could not see or find, atop a power that was not even a tangible thing at all but an intangible force that could descend upon them like rain or pass by them like drought. Paying attention to the vertical relationship between ruler and ruled does not diminish the power of more commonly studied horizontal connections between people organizing into interest groups or political parties. The largely unwritten history of the imagined relationship between Americans and their state helps us understand the imaginative field upon which both high politics and social organizing took place. Examining these pleas helps open up the mysterious, often peculiar relationship between Americans and their governments.[9]

American patronalism transcended state lines; nevertheless, its nineteenth-century manifestations are best studied at the state level. Presidential elections continued to stir passions among the electorate, but local candidates were much more proximate and important figures for the shaping of the political imagination. Until Franklin D. Roosevelt's inauguration, letters from citizens to the government often ended up in state capitals for the simple reason that local officials were more likely to be able to listen and provide assistance. North Carolina works especially well for a study of patronalism because of its combination of rich postwar archives and turbulent politics. As a central place for Confederate state expansion, Union contraband camps, military Reconstruction, Redemption, anti–civil service sentiment, Populism, Progressivism, prohibition, and segregation, North Carolina opens a window into almost every important postbellum political movement. As a slave state that also encompassed mountainous regions with very few slaves, North Carolina allows for careful examination of the role of slavery in forming ideas of power. Although slaves made up about one-third of the state's population on the eve of the Civil War, 72 percent of white families owned no slaves at all. In large part this was due to the limited role of cotton, cultivated mostly in far eastern Carolina and near the modern city of Charlotte. In the piedmont near the Virginia border, small-scale plantations grew bright tobacco, while large sections of the state were given over to general farming and livestock. Compared to other Southern states, North Carolina hardly had a Black Belt; only fourteen of the state's eighty-seven counties were majority slave, and most of those by only a slight margin; some counties in the Appalachian western region had almost no slaves. The growth of a guardian government in a state with so few large planters, so little evidence of antebellum paternalism, and such a strong postwar commitment to economic development suggests that it was not solely a strange offshoot of Southern plantation slavery.[10]

The centrality of dependence to American politics would not have surprised the men who founded the nation. In fact, they might well be more surprised at our willful insistence that voluntary dependence does not play a constitutive role in politics. They worried constantly about the impact of dependence upon political behavior, and tried to resolve the problem by excluding dependent people — including wage laborers — from voting. They feared that need inherently produced loyalty toward those who helped ameliorate it. Rational politics therefore functioned only among those who, in the words of English radical John Toland, could "live of themselves." Everyone else, he added, "I call *Servants*." As the colonies rebelled against British taxation, John Adams, Thomas Jefferson, James Madison, and many others used this British vocabulary to denounce the colonies' dependence on England. There are only two "*sorts* of men in the world, freemen and slaves," John Adams wrote. As modern feminist scholars discovered, independence was constructed upon power over dependent slaves, children, women, and apprentices. The solution to the problem of dependence lay in excluding dependents from politics, and many Revolutionary states barred propertyless white men from voting because they were "so situated as to have no wills of their own." As suffrage expanded in the nineteenth century to include first poorer white men, then African American men, and, in a few states, women, activists pushed the boundaries of suffrage by declaring that these groups were not in fact dependent at all but just as independent as merchants and planters. Some radicals went further, arguing that even dependents deserved the vote, but most expansive movements confirmed the importance of independence. Workingmen deserved "independent equality" based upon their freedom of contract, African American men upon the "manly independence" they showed at war, women upon their "love of freedom and independence." By expanding the meaning of independence, activists argued that the inclusion of people previously considered dependent would not alter the fundamental nature of a political system premised upon independence. In their celebration of independence, democratic activists made dependence anathema, something no one would freely choose. Instead of a diagnosis of a human condition, it became an insult. The enduring queasiness around dependence made them, and many modern scholars, unable to think through the role of voluntary claims of dependence in politics.[11]

As he watched the first stages of democratic expansion, John Adams was not sure that the United States had succeeded in saving democracy from dependence. Calling a "democratic republic" a "chimera," Adams in 1814 prophesized that personalized power would persist in the United States, perhaps in the form of an "oligarchic" republic. Whether they rose by "virtues," "talents," "wealth," "birth," "fraud," "violence," or "treachery," aristocrats were "visible, and palpable, and audible, every day, in every village, and in every family of the whole world," not in spite of the people's will, but because of it. "The shortest road to men's hearts is down their throats," Adams wrote. "Humane" and "generous" landlords acquired political power through "attachment," while cruel employers settled for fear. Instead of abolishing aristocracy, the American Revolution made it possible for people to choose their own aristocrats. About fifteen years later, Alexis de Tocqueville made a similar observation about American politics. Although the thought provoked less anxiety for de Tocqueville than it did for Adams, the French aristocrat diagnosed a paradox: the very independence at the center of American ideology created a reservoir of personal dependence upon the state. The presumption of "equality" meant that each person had no compulsion to help "his fellow men" nor "any right to expect much support from them," so "everyone is at once independent and powerless." Therefore, "the citizen of a democratic country" was filled with "Self-reliance and pride," yet his

> debility makes him feel from time to time the want of some outward assistance, which he cannot expect from any of them. . . . In this predicament he naturally turns his eyes to that imposing power which alone rises above the level of universal depression. Of that power his wants and especially his desires continually remind him, until he ultimately views it as the sole and necessary support of his own weakness. . . . This may more completely explain what frequently takes place in democratic countries, where the very men who are so impatient of superiors patiently submit to a master, exhibiting at once their pride and their servility.[12]

Decades later, the Civil War accelerated the popular dependence Adams and de Tocqueville observed by revolutionizing the relationship between personal needs and politics and transforming American attitudes about the role of the state in everyday life. Placing the personal, unequal relationship between citizens and statesmen at the center of politics opens up a new way of seeing postwar America by directing our attention to the peculiar nature of the state the Civil War created. In Governor Zebulon Vance's efforts to deliver state relief to starving women and children, in Confederate conscription, and in Union occupation and emancipation, Americans experienced monumental transformations in governance. On local levels, the war and the ensuing Reconstruction placed Confederate and Union military officers and Freedmen's Bureau agents in positions of unusual authority over the people they encountered. As a social phenomenon, a hope that rich men would act benevolently toward poor neighbors, personal patronalism surely functioned to some degree within all Southern and Northern societies, as Adams noted. But as an expression of the relationship of state to subject, it was much more widely expressed after the Civil War trained people to believe government could and would intervene in all sorts of intimate arrangements. While scholars argue over the line between the political and the personal, the boundary is not a transhistoric fact but a creation of particular power arrangements. Desires that might have seemed private at other moments become political because events and candidates move them into public arenas.[13]

Wartime governments could not create clearly definable, abstract rights because Reconstruction state expansion was intensely personalized and localized. In the peculiarly chaotic and anarchic world of the postwar South, the natural tendency for on-the-ground actors to retranslate (or forget or ignore) broad policies was exaggerated. Intense local struggles for power made basic rights meaningful only with the assistance of a powerful ally. In Buck's Alamance County, the Ku Klux Klan murdered elected officials, terrorized a Northern schoolteacher, threatened African American voters in their homes, and paraded through town to scare off their enemies. In response, locally organized and armed African American Union Leagues marched to claim their own authority over the land. As decrees from Washington and Raleigh reached Alamance County, they landed on the laps of Freedmen's Bureau agents and magistrates who freely confessed they could not enforce laws even if they wanted to. Of necessity, these agents picked and chose, working within pockets of state control. In the process they conveyed the message that a right became meaningful once a patron recognized it. This simultaneously expansive and constrained view of rights made almost anything possible, but nothing reliable. It is no wonder that Williamson Buck, like many other North Carolinians, looked at the violent and anarchic world around him and came to the conclusion that his pathway to a divorce lay not in making his case but in making a friend.

Therefore, the Civil War sparked a revolution not just in what the state did but in what people believed it could do. By seeing Reconstruction as literally the reconstruction of American authority, historians can explore the gaps and weaknesses within this postbellum American state. Corruption and personal systems of patronage shaped politics because the war simultaneously flooded the country with government spending and produced local anarchy. Even the central fact of Reconstruction, the emancipation and enfranchisement of the freedpeople, was partly defined upon those terms, as freedom sparked a search for reliable patrons who could make their abstract rights felt.

Although the extraordinary transformation from slavery to freedom steered Southern politics in particular directions, it would be a mistake to see these as solely a Southern phenomenon. After the war, Northern and Western cities were riven by conflict, and white men, including decommissioned Union soldiers, attacked rival political gangs, police, militia, city officials, even occasionally the army. At the same time, Indian wars in the West both extended state-building projects and reminded Americans that the national project of territorial control was incomplete. In the face of urban riots in the 1870s, it was no wonder that so many Northerners and Westerners spoke of anarchy. Engaging with dynamic, expansive, and also fragile governments, people across the country, in a variety of political systems, developed ways of using real and fictional patrons to mediate between their needs and the alluring if also distant state. The intimate, hierarchical, sometimes affectionate relationship between urban bosses and needy constituents frequently, if not always, mirrored the dynamics at play in North Carolina and other Southern states. Cities were, in the words of Tammany Hall's George Washington Plunkitt, "a sort of Garden of Eden, from a political point of view." The resources of expanding city and state governments and the intense, unmet needs of the poor provided extraordinary political opportunities. "What tells in holdin' your grip on your district is to go right down among the poor families and help them in the different ways they need help," Plunkitt said. "The poor are the most grateful people in the world, and, let me tell you, they have more friends in their neighborhoods than the rich have in theirs. . . . The consequence is that the poor look up to George W. Plunkitt as a father, come to him in trouble — and don't forget him on election day." In Plunkitt's self-interested telling, this system not only benefited Tammany Hall but also built close attachment between people and their government, an attachment that civil service reform threatened to sever. As many scholars have shown, urban machines functioned as primitive welfare states, distributing goods and jobs to their members. Northern reformers, like Southern Progressives, ran against this largesse not merely as a critique of tax-and-spend policies but also because it seemed to create dependence. Their reform efforts aimed to purify politics (and increase the supply — and therefore decrease the value — of labor) by expunging voluntary dependence.[14]

Urban bossism and Southern patronly rule were distinct, interrelated aspects of a greater, nationwide patronal politics, one that exerted a strong hold upon the imagination both of its practitioners and of its critics, a signal moment in the development of modern democracy. At the same time, however, further examination may well find important distinctions between them. The greater distance between rural people and their would-be patrons probably encouraged a particularly literary form of dependence, since words had to stand in for personal interaction in tenement apartments and on sidewalks. Without overstating the overlap between these forms of patronal government, however, their evident similarities suggest that scholars anomalize Southern claims of dependence at their peril.[15]

Understood not simply as a project of emancipation or racial readjustment or sectional reunion but as a style of governance that arose from the transformations of the Civil War, Reconstruction lasted well past the mid-1870s. Instead of ending with the violent Democratic takeover of Southern states in Redemption campaigns in 1875 and 1876 in North Carolina, South Carolina, Louisiana, and Mississippi, or with the withdrawal of federal troops from the South after the 1876 presidential election, the political style of Reconstruction, like the incorporation of freedpeople, lasted deep into the 1890s. Although scholars have traditionally called the years following 1876 the Gilded Age, after Mark Twain's satirical novel about corruption, this division between Reconstruction and the Gilded Age is easier to justify as tradition than practice. Worse, it obscures more than it reveals about enduring patterns. Gilded Age corruption, political patronage, and national economic development reached back into the earliest days of the republic but especially into Reconstruction; Reconstruction's limited but essential federal oversight of certain African American public rights stretched into the early 1890s. Defining the era around a patronal style, a constant stream of complaints about corruption, and an unsteady but occasionally intrusive state reveals a set of practices that ran smoothly from the 1860s through Cleveland's second term. By stripping away the framework of American exceptionalism, this book treats Reconstruction as part of a global transformation of state authority, a project of nationalization and legitimization concurrent with national formations elsewhere around the world, as states as different as France's Third Republic and Mexico's Porfiriato worked to extend government power over the hinterlands and foster a binding, national politics, culture, and market. In the United States, the politics of dependence became one way of attaching people to a state, a popular form for producing stability.[16]

Placing this politics of protection at the center of Reconstruction also makes it possible to rethink the movement that killed Reconstruction, Progressivism. Partly in opposition to this politics of dependence, educated men worked diligently in the late nineteenth century to rationalize the state. Despite Progressives' varied approaches to education, public health, and personal morality, their political aims often centered upon the creation of a dispassionate, abstracted government with an obligation not to individual persons but to "the people." With their success in turn-of-the-century political campaigns, these reformers reconfigured the language and practice of politics. Progressivism opened up the state's capacity to deliver programs while at the same time emancipating the state from an obligation to listen to people's particular wants. At its most extreme, Progressivism inspired the nation's most significant retraction of suffrage in American history. In this constriction of voting rights, the South again was the leading but not sole voice, as Progressives worked in tandem to restrict immigrant and poor voters in the North and West in what the leading scholar of American voting tellingly called the "Redemption of the North."[17]

I

Hungry for Protection

The Confederate Roots of Dependence

IN JUNE 1861, five days after he enlisted, a Confederate private named Harrison H. Hanes knew "nothing a bout the war only there are many men here" at his drill camp in Garysburg, North Carolina. Writing to his friend Nancy Williams, Hanes asserted, "[I] still feel that I will get to see you before long," if not through a furlough then "the probability is that I can any how after the 4 of July for it is thought congress will setle the mater but if they fail to [do] this it will be don by the bulet cirtin unless the north will let the south a lone." Even those who might have known better had little inkling of the revolutionary impact of the Civil War. During North Carolina's secession campaign, a leading proponent promised that he would "wipe up every drop of blood shed in the war with this handkerchief of mine," and South Carolina U.S. senator James Chesnut offered to personally drink all the blood spilled for secession. Across the South, people said the war's blood would not fill a thimble.[1]

The war that Hanes thought might end within two weeks instead lasted four years, a time that profoundly transformed the state and the nation. Begun in haste, the Confederacy repented at length, if not at leisure. The fight that Confederates initiated had its roots in long-simmering political conflicts over the expansion of slavery into the West. The Mexican-American War and the annexation of Texas raised simmering tensions to a boil. Throughout the 1850s, increasingly divided Northern and Southern politicians fought over the management of the territories, the Fugitive Slave Act, and the *Dred Scott* decision. When the Democratic Party fractured into regional pieces in the 1860 conventions, and the Northern Republican Party captured the

White House, fire-eaters in South Carolina and Mississippi led other Deep South states to secede in the winter of 1860–61, on the grounds that Republican control of the federal government would eventually spell the doom of slavery. After the attack on Fort Sumter prompted Abraham Lincoln to call up troops in April 1861, four Upper South states—Virginia, Arkansas, Tennessee, and North Carolina—joined the original seven members of the Confederacy. Over the next four years, more than two million Americans fought for the Union, one million white Southerners served the Confederacy, and more than 600,000 lost their lives.[2]

The impact of the war could not be summed up in the death toll. Wartime necessities pushed both governments toward extensive, novel interventions in the lives of their citizens. Southerners particularly experienced a new world, as the Confederate government conscripted their white men and impressed their slaves. Over those four years, white Confederates like Hanes waited months, even years, between furloughs home. In farmland emptied of men, and sometimes of slaves, white women like Nancy Williams wrote to their husbands and brothers and sweethearts and friends about the deprivations of the home front, of lost crops, of unmanageable slaves, of rampaging mobs of deserters, even of starvation. From the happy gossip of the spring of 1861, the letters turned increasingly to pleas for help. The intensity of their need and the obvious connection between their problems and Confederate enlistment policies soon pushed these complaints onto the desks of political and military officials, the only people with the authority to send the soldiers home or to provide for the women and children left behind.

For Confederate North Carolinians, the Civil War was full of ironies. The state that lost the most men for the Confederacy was among the last states to join it. The war that redefined North Carolina was a war sparked elsewhere, especially in South Carolina and Mississippi, and fought on other terrain. North Carolina was, arguably, the final and most reluctant member of the Confederacy. When South Carolina led Deep South states from the Union, North Carolina did not follow. North Carolina unionists, who included diehard mountain loyalists, skeptical small tobacco belt farmers, and Whiggish eastern planters, turned back the secession tide at a February 1861 election. Only after the Confederate attack on Fort Sumter and Lincoln's April 15, 1861, call for troops did North Carolina join the Upper South states of Virginia, Tennessee, and Arkansas in the Confederacy. If North Carolina was last to join, it was in some ways first in sacrifice. With its relatively large white population, North Carolina provided 125,000 Confederate soldiers, of whom 40,000 died in service, the largest number of fatalities of any Confederate state.[3]

One of the war's unexpected outcomes was Southern governments' response to these needs. After September 1862, when Zebulon Baird Vance was elected governor, the North Carolina state government not only listened but responded by fashioning a small welfare state to quiet those cries. Instead of silencing the people, however, Vance's initiatives only encouraged their sense of what he could do for them. As the need for food and protection grew over the course of the war, more and more Carolinians projected their wishes and hopes upon the distant man who might possibly fulfill them. Although often treated as simple statements of fact or uncomplicated pleas for justice, these wartime pleas, and Vance's complex response, are much more revealing. By examining the way North Carolinians called upon the state, we can see the roots of a newly expansive politics of dependence, one of the war's significant, if understudied, outcomes. From the age-old cry of distress and the modern claim of conscripts' wives upon the government, public and private North Carolinians created a state patronalism that would shape politics for the next generation. If Carolinians began to demand more of their government during the Civil War, this was partly because the government demanded more of them; in educating people about the power of governments, the Confederacy inadvertently taught them to ask for more in return. In the process, needs that had previously been private became public. The dishonorable and disreputable condition of dependence became normal under new conditions of wartime deprivation. Absent local men to receive these pleas, the cries flooded the state government in Raleigh.[4]

For much of the war, North Carolina Confederates lost lives but not much land to the Union. While Virginia and Tennessee and Mississippi raged with battles, North Carolina's ground was relatively untouched. The major exception lay on the far eastern coast. Between August 1861 and April 1862, the Union invaded a narrow band of ports, islands, and towns on the eastern shore to block maritime trade. For the next three years, until Sherman's final drive into North Carolina in March 1865, there were few battles in the state, other than small expeditionary skirmishes. Although Union occupation of the east provided an avenue for thousands of slaves to escape to contraband camps in Roanoke Island and New Bern, in much of the rest of the state, life continued apace. Many North Carolinians therefore felt the war not through the presence of armies but through the intervention of state and Confederate governments, which enlisted, conscripted, and exempted white men, impressed supplies and slaves for military use, scoured the countryside for deserters, and, eventually, provided food and support for soldiers' wives and children. At the same time, white Carolinians felt the war through the chaos and anarchy in many of the state's counties, unpoliced, unprotected, and governed in part by bands of deserters. Together the combination of state intervention and state absence would produce a hope for a powerful patron who might deliver his friends from want.

The war's transformations were almost immediately evident in the bodies of a thousand slaves impressed from the plantations of eastern Carolina to work on the fortifications at Wilmington, the state's main port and only major city. At once, these impressed slaves were proof of the Confederacy's strength and of its vulnerability. While the defenses constructed around Wilmington saved the city from invasion until the war's final months, the slaves drawn away from their home plantations began running almost immediately to a Union military that at first was not sure of what to do with them. Over time, slaves' increasing flight to Union lines and the Union's growing utilization of those ex-slaves created innumerable strains upon the Confederate state. If the military fought to defend the principle of slavery, local and state governments — and informal patrols — were charged with making sure that slavery continued to exist in practice. Across the South, and particularly in North Carolina, whites asked the government that disrupted slavery to take on the responsibility of maintaining it.[5]

Among the first to run were impressed slaves working on fortifications in tidewater Virginia and coastal Carolina, and their destination was Fortress Monroe, a Union-held base near Hampton, Virginia. At the so-called Fortress Freedom, Massachusetts general Benjamin Butler decided in May 1861 not to return slaves who fled from forced work on Confederate fortifications. Quickly, Butler's decision reverberated in two directions. Up the military and political ladder, Butler's actions spurred Lincoln and his subordinates in Washington to fix their policies toward the contraband. In tidewater Virginia and coastal Carolina, word of Butler's actions spread quickly, drawing in seventy more slaves in two days and a thousand in two months, including some who had run from North Carolina to gather information before traveling back home to spread the word.[6]

These early experiences with Union soldiers helped prepare the foundation for the greater flight to Northern lines in February 1862, when Union general Ambrose Burnside's force invaded coastal North Carolina and captured Roanoke Island, New Bern, and Beaufort. Union troops were "overrun with fugitives. . . . It would be utterly impossible if we were so disposed to keep them outside of our lines as they find their way to us through woods & swamps from every side," General Burnside wrote. One of them was William Henry Singleton, a twenty-seven-year-old slave from near New Bern who had served under his master in the Confederate army. During the war's first months, Singleton had watched events carefully, waiting for a chance to escape. When Burnside captured New Bern, Singleton "ran away from the regiment and made [his] way to Burnside's headquarters." Another was Allen Parker, a slave in northeastern Chowan County, who in August 1862 "began to form plans" over "many conferences" with neighborhood slaves who witnessed Union gunboats moving up the river. Hearing gunfire one day, they crept down at four in the morning, found a boat, and paddled to a Union vessel. In the morning, when their owners massed on the riverbank, the Union captain fired a shell over the masters' heads. Not all freedpeople ran, and not all who did were happy with their decision. Nevertheless, the Union's steady presence along the coast and the occasional expeditionary raids into inland North Carolina opened up the possibility of escape for thousands of slaves, many of whom ended up in massive settlements on Roanoke Island and near New Bern.[7]

The problem of controlling slaves in a chaotic environment worsened as more and more white men left for the Confederate army. White men's departures accelerated dramatically in the spring of 1862. The Confederacy's wholesale conscription, the first in American history, depopulated the countryside of adult white men and transformed life for both slaves and the white families left behind. Like many Confederate innovations, it was the offspring of necessity. Although the Confederacy, like the Union, relied at first upon voluntary enlistments, in April 1862 the new nation faced a crisis of manpower. Approximately 150 Confederate regiments were prepared to muster out at the expiration of their one-year enlistments. At the same time, the Union army under General George McClellan massed for an attack on Richmond, and the Confederates suffered a serious and bloody setback in western Tennessee at Shiloh. To forestall disaster, Jefferson Davis signed the conscription act "in view of the exigencies of the country" and the "advancing columns of enemy now invading our soil." Under the law, all white men between eighteen and thirty-five (eventually raised to forty-five and then to fifty) years old were presumptively in military service unless explicitly exempted, and all current soldiers' terms were extended for another three years. Although frequently called a draft by both historians and contemporaries, Confederate conscription was actually a forced enrollment of all white men of age, while Union conscription (which followed a year later) worked more like a modern draft, in which the state selected particular men through lotteries. As soon as the law was passed, Confederate officers like Colonel Zebulon Vance used the threat of conscription to shame men into enlisting "like white men" before they were forced by "the sheriff." This shaming worked. Just before the conscription law went into effect, nearly 45,000 additional Carolinians volunteered.[8]

Each Southern solution, however, created its own problems of enforcement. To make sure that drafted men actually enrolled, the Confederate government created a new bureaucracy of state conscription bureaus and deployed state militias to hunt down evaders and deserters. This new face of the government inspired grave mistrust and was "very distasteful to our people," North Carolina's governor wrote. Late-arriving volunteers, who thought they could select their units, complained to Raleigh and to Richmond that they were instead treated like conscripts and apportioned out to whatever regiments needed men. Additionally, Carolinians protested that laws on substitution and exemption — which excepted ministers, teachers, telegraph operators, railroad officials, and, with certain restrictions, one adult white man on plantations with more than twenty slaves — disproportionately aided the well-to-do, fueling the complaint of a rich man's war and a poor man's fight. This discontent with the long arm of the state was not peculiar to the South. In July 1863, two days after the implementation of the Union conscription law, the New York City Draft Riots began with an assault upon the provost marshal's office, site of the first draft lottery. Southern, and particularly Carolinian, responses to conscription were more profound and long-lasting because enlistment was more extensive in the South. Of approximately 180,000 white adult men in North Carolina in 1860, 125,000 served the Confederacy, more than half of whom either were conscripted or volunteered shortly before they were to be drafted.[9]

With the enlistment and conscription of so many white men, the control over slaves that once had fallen under the personal authority of masters now increasingly became a problem for the state. Police control over slaves evaporated, even in interior counties far from the Union lines. The enlistment of so many white men drained away the support system upon which slavery depended, what Frederick Law Olmsted called the "constant, habitual, and instinctive surveillance and authority of all white people over all black." This collective policing, not just legal rulings, was what Stephen Douglas had referred to in his famous 1858 argument that "slavery cannot exist a day or an hour anywhere, unless it is supported by local police regulations." Although slavery was in essence a property relationship of master over man, it relied upon the broad, semigovernmental commitment of white men in the community either through formal slave patrols—the nation's first large-scale police force—or informal surveillance. Without this commitment, slaves were "not afraid of the slaveholders," a Union officer reported. "They said there was nobody on the plantations but women and they were not afraid of them." A vacuum of control at home and an influx of rumors about Fortress Monroe, Roanoke Island, and New Bern primed slaves to run for freedom. "The news went from plantation to plantation," Mary Anderson, a slave in Wake County, remembered. When Union troops approached, "the grown slaves were whisperin to each other," discussing the best way to seize the situation. Charity Morris recalled the confusion of the war's early days. "We couldn' make out" all that was happening; nevertheless, she added, "we begin tub move erbout." Soon, according to Jane Lee, "de woods was full of runaway slaves."[10]

To many white Carolinians, government actions created an untenable chaos in the countryside. Slaves were "lirking about through the woods. . . . Nearly all of our white mails are in the Servis which leaves no one to control our negros," North Carolinian N. P. Pope wrote. "They can Runaway to stay out as long as they pleas and no one to hinder them. . . . We need something like a polleace on duty." In eastern Greene County, one woman noted, "there is not white man to do any thing for any of us . . . the niggers want do nothing only as the plea." When the Confederate government conscripted a home guard in southeastern Duplin County, slave owner Jere Pearsall protested that "the said Patrol have been 'the ounce of preventive in place of the pound of Cure.' We are here not far distant from the Yankee lines; and you well Know a good watch should be Kept. Since the organization of this Company, there has been *no* attempt of escapes by the Slaves *but one*, (save in the Raid in July) and the whole number of negroes (save one, & he was shot & killed *near* the Yankee lines) were Captured & returned to their owners." As some petitioners argued, and as the policy of impressment suggested, the Civil War made slaves almost government property and therefore government responsibility. In the language of letters and petitions, this expanded relationship between state and slave was expressed in the state's efforts to assume what were formerly the duties of white masters: to protect white people from slave uprisings and force slaves to work the fields.[11]

The problem of controlling slaves without adequate numbers of white men produced a flood of appeals to the state governor in Raleigh, asking him to fulfill the duties of the men he and the Confederacy had called away. People reasoned that if the state took men, then surely the state must have the power to send them back. Early on, these appeals arrived on the desk of Henry Toole Clark, who had ascended to the governor's office in July 1861, following the death of the governor who had presided over secession. The appeals baffled Clark for the simple reason that the gubernatorial powers they described did not match the actual powers of the office. From the beginning of statehood, occasional Carolinians asked governors to interpose on their behalf, but a governor's power was tightly circumscribed; except in the realm of pardons, the most he could usually do was refer the writer to a legislator who might consider introducing a private law to ameliorate the case. Faced with a flood of these appeals, Clark responded with confusion, hesitancy, and references to the limited actions of his antebellum successors. When more than fifty people in Chatham County asked for an exemption for the local blacksmith whose services were necessary to produce tools to "make bread" and "feed our families," Clark stonewalled. For the women who wrote for food in the summer of 1862, he could do nothing because the legislature had not authorized him to do anything. To those who asked for help in procuring a legal substitute, Clark replied, "The Conscript Act is a law of the Confederacy and the State authorities have no control over it, consequently appeals to me are useless — all the information I have is what has been published by Richmond authorities."[12]

By September 1862, these appeals arrived on the desk of Zebulon Vance, a far more innovative politician who understood immediately that these pleas presented him with an enormous challenge and opportunity. Although he could not meet all of the requests, Vance recognized that he could use these letters' imagined powers to expand his actual authority. First, however, he had to create an image of himself in keeping with the hopes invested in him. Although Vance had served one full term in Congress before the war (and had been reelected to a term he would not serve because of secession), he was not especially well known outside of western Carolina until 1862. In the campaign of 1862, Vance, then a colonel in the Confederate army, emerged less as a candidate than as a symbol. While Vance stayed with his troops and delivered few speeches, his backers, especially editor William W. Holden, portrayed him relentlessly as the "soldiers' candidate" and their friend. As governor, his allies promised, Vance would feed and clothe both troops and their families. Vance himself was an unlikely symbol of masterful power. While many Southern leaders emerged from coastal or tidewater plantation belts, Vance grew up in western Buncombe County, a place that inspired a self-portrayal not of a young master but of a young mountaineer. Years later, when Vance entered the University of North Carolina with the help of personal loans, he struck the other students as a "rough and uncouth mountain boy," "quick and rough at repartee," an "inveterate boaster," and a rube with his "homemade shoes and clothes, about three inches between pants and ankles, showing his sturdy ankles." Nevertheless, Vance charmed and impressed the university's leading figures and left Chapel Hill with important connections to the state's Whigs, but without losing his down-home manners. In 1862, and in the campaigns he waged over the next thirty years, Vance proved adept at precisely those kinds of cultural translations, maintaining support from the state's most-educated men while portraying himself as a rustic from the mountains, the people's friend.[13]

Vance managed the crisis of popular dependency by fueling people's abstract hopes and denying most of their concrete demands. Despite his interest in maintaining his popularity, Vance was constrained by the needs of the army and the Confederate government in Richmond. Even though he rejected many individual claims, Vance worked to augment the sense of his power by waging several popular fights against Confederate president Jefferson Davis. Although Vance accepted the legality of the unpopular conscript law, he resisted the use of the state militia to enforce it, lobbied for exemptions and furloughs, demanded state control over enlistment and assignment, pardoned many deserters, and opposed Confederate efforts to suspend habeas corpus. This adroit political maneuvering helped Vance shift the blame for impressments, conscription, crop shortages, and the capture of deserters to Davis and the Confederate government. In one of his most explicit efforts at generosity, Vance granted more than 14,675 exemptions, a rate that dwarfed that of most other Southern governors. When Confederate officials complained about Vance's generosity, Vance argued that only he "must judge" the "necessity" of each employee he exempted. Were the state's militia and magistrates called to service, he added, "I am at a loss to know what would be left of the power or sovereignty of this state."[14]

Along with his actions, North Carolinians learned from Vance's words. Vance claimed that he acted in response to the "cry of distress" that "comes up from the poor wives and children of our soldiers . . . a subject which distresses me beyond measure, the more so as I feel powerless to remedy any of these evils." In April 1863, as deserters and evaders terrorized some parts of the state's backcountry, Vance issued a proclamation promising personally "to protect the citizens of the state." Distressed Carolinians turned their pleas to him, and in so doing they transformed him from "powerless" to powerful, even iconic. From the first days of his administration, Vance drew upon the presence of women in political space, using their need to expand his authority and to portray himself as the agent of the people's will. Although Vance could only receive the votes of men, "lady as well as gentleman" flocked to his speeches. A group of "respectable ladies" in Wilson County wrote "begging [Vance] for protecion. . . . We know if we don't have some men left to protect we are ruin." Where personal relationships of dependency failed, they sought the state's intervention, putting the duties of those husbands, fathers, and neighbors upon the governor. At the same time, they also provided Vance with an easy escape. He could fulfill his obligation by exempting a group of men (many of whom were likely boyfriends and husbands of the writers) who "has kept the negroes under better subjecion." In the common interplay of requests from the weak to the strong, thirty-five "good women" promised Vance, "If you will we shall be under many obligations to you." Seventeen women from Mallard Creek, "dimly populated by whites and a large number of the Slaves," turned to Vance with a "Prayer." As the state called away the last two young men, the women were left with men "entirely worthless and unfit for Patrolers" and so would be "entirely destitute of that Valuable Protection." Like others, this claim probably masked personal needs in political languages; six of the signers shared a last name with one of the men they hoped Vance would exempt.[15]

Although these pleas for protection from slaves largely came from women, they grew from a gendered language that men, too, could use to explain their new dependence upon the state. In November 1863, seventeen male justices of the peace of one county asked Vance to suspend the conscript law in eastern counties vulnerable to Union expeditionary raids from the coast. After the fall of Roanoke Island in February 1862, "the slaves, especially the laborers amongst them, left suddenly and almost in a body." Since then, the magistrates wrote, "we stand in hourly fear from the incursion of the enemy. . . . He has already taken all the laboring slaves, he has robbed us of the best portion of our stock, private homes time and again have been entered, robbed of their contents and deprived of every particle of food. Bands of armed negroes" entered the "home of their masters and spread terror over the lands." All of this was due, the letter implied, to the "absence of our young unmarried men. . . . Those now at home subject to conscription are men upon whom women and children are entirely dependent for food clothing, fuel and protection from insult." In telling the story of "the many dangers which surround the people of this county," these public men recast their pleas as the "entreaties of the helpless wife and child" to be "weighed by your Excellency." Their fear turned the men into women, at least for the moment, and gave them the "excuse for wearying the ear of your Excellency with cries for relief." By cloaking themselves as women and children, they gained a woman's right to beg.[16]

The prolonged absence of men from farms during 1862 and 1863 fueled a grave crisis of hunger and need among the families they left behind. Their pleas and the need to maintain soldiers' morale inspired Vance's most significant welfare program for soldiers' wives and widows. The Civil War decimated North Carolina's economy and its everyday life, drying up cotton and food crop production and overturning slavery as freedpeople ran toward the Union lines. The Union naval blockade, solidified by the 1861–62 seizure of ports along the eastern Carolina coast, dramatically slashed supplies in North Carolina, leading to wildly inflated prices for simple but necessary household goods like sewing needles and farming tools. Confederate impressment of food and slaves made the scarcity even worse. The crises of feeding and protecting a population under these strains, left without a hundred thousand of its white men and an increasing number of its slaves, shifted from a challenge for local families to a dilemma of the state. It was the "hardest times we have ever seen," one white farmer wrote in his diary. The "suffering among the poor . . . is dreadful to contemplate," another claimed. If "more men are called to the field," another Carolinian wrote, "many *must* starve."[17]

Shortly after his inauguration, Vance asked the state's constitutional convention to answer the "cry of distress" from the "poor wives and children" by allocating money to relieve them. To Vance's dismay, the convention adjourned without acting upon his request, so Vance then set about lobbying the legislature. In a series of appropriations, the legislature over time allocated $6.5 million to buy provisions that could be resold at cost to soldiers' families. In 1863 alone, the state sold 17,000 bushels of corn and 125,000 pounds of bacon to county governments for distribution. In some counties, more than a third of the white women were on relief. As hunger wildly outstripped assistance, however, women complained bitterly that county agents handed out money unfairly, or not at all. In response, women and men turned their pleas to scarcity-driven efforts to get for themselves what little there was to be had. In this competition for attention from overwhelmed state actors, the only way to advantage seemed to be through a personal connection. Barring the good luck of having an actual personal relationship, many North Carolinians — like Sarah L. Johnston — tried to imaginatively create one by turning to Vance "as a friend for a Little advice."[18]

Vance himself personalized the delivery of relief. In a January 1863 proclamation about the state's crisis, Vance finished with a statement of his individual obligation and responsibility. "As your Chief Magistrate," he pledged, "I promise you that the wife & child of the soldiers who are in the Army doing his duty, shall share the last bushel of meal & pound of meat in the State." In reply, these wives and children held Vance to his promise. They asked the governor for a more permanent interposition, not to transfer masculine obligations to some committee but to assume those obligations himself. After the death of her husband at Fredericksburg in December 1862, Mary F. Andrews wrote in a fit of "boldness" to let Vance "know my situation." Andrews blamed her need for her unfeminine assertiveness. "I don't know what else to do," she wrote. Andrews's husband, "a hard working man," sent her money during the war, but with his death she alone was responsible for their three young children. At the same time, Andrews critiqued the state's program, which paid her seven dollars a month. "I can't live at that," she wrote, since wartime shortages drove the price of corn to twenty dollars a barrel and meat to a dollar a pound. "I do think that it is hard and not fare my little children to perish after my husband went and lost his life to defend his country." Instead of eliciting Vance's assistance, such complaints could inspire a gentleman to defend his reputation. Like needy people the world over, Andrews navigated these narrows by carefully (and perhaps inaccurately) blaming the county officer, not Vance, for her troubles. When she "told the man that sees to me that 7 dollars was not enough," he "told me he could not do no more that it never was intended" to cover all of a woman's expenses. Women had to fend for themselves.[19]

Andrews recast the independence the county agent celebrated as a prettier name for starvation. "But sir," she wrote, "what am I do when I have not got nothing to find with and there is no employment that I could do to get my living. . . . [I am] willing to do all I can to earn my living but there is nothing to do that I can do." To Andrews, this independence was a curse: "It almost breaks my heart for my little children to ask me for bread and I cant give it to them." Confused and desperate, Andrews sought advice from men in her community, and one of them suggested writing to Vance: He "knew you and said you would help me to get bread for my children to eat." This man told her that Vance "had the power" and "was a good man" and therefore "would do something for me." Andrews's burdens were Vance's, she claimed, because she lacked a family to turn to. She transferred these family obligations — a man's presumed willingness to accept dependent kin — onto the fantastic family of the state, with the governor as the father. "If you don't do something for me I shall have to starve," she wrote. "I have no folks to do nothing for me I have no father no mother no money and no friends. . . . [I hope] to

God that you will be a friend to me." Instead of a friend or a father, however, Andrews found an administrator. Vance's notes on her request indicate that he told his secretary to tell the "lady" that she "must" present her claims to the county commissioner, who is "amply supplied with money from the state of North Carolina."[20]

Writers like Andrews used the language of friendship and state familialism to leap the most significant hurdle they saw, the problem of gaining Vance's attention. These appeals reflected their awareness that the governor could not interpose on behalf of all women; being human, he was not omnipresent even if he was (they hoped) omnipotent. Therefore the language of friendship invoked a special, intimate consideration, one that transcended merit. Although she was a "stranger," Sallie C. Crandell of Oak Grove hoped Vance would "condescend to read these few lines and lend a helping hand." The widow of "as true and brave a soldier as ever fell upon the field of battle," Crandell "heard that you were a friend to the suffering daughters of the South" and so "I thought I could well approach you on this subject, feeling assured that you would sympathize with me in my afflictions and do all you could to keep me and my little ones from starvation." Crandell tried to avoid invoking the bad dependence of the lazy by telling Vance that she "always tried to support" herself but was still "suffering." Anabella Davis was less optimistic. Instead of apologizing or humbling herself, Davis snapped that if Vance "cant condesend to read it you can only treat it with contemt." Davis had reason to suspect she might be mocked. When she told her local relief agent that she "would complain to the govner," he "laught at" her. Some, she added, "will say that is foolishness the govner cares not a fig for you . . . but I tell them I think he is a good southern man."[21]

This desperation, along with a growing skepticism about the war, opened new public roles for women. Instead of precluding organized activity by women and soldiers, the vertical relationships of patronalism became intertwined with more familiar, horizontal forms of political activity. Acting both from need and from moral outrage at speculators, women across the Confederacy led bread riots against local stores. In the spring of 1863, women raided warehouses in Mobile, Milledgeville, Richmond, Atlanta, Columbus, and Augusta, among other places. In March of 1863 in Salisbury, North Carolina, a desperate "mob of females, accompanied by a number of men," marched on Michael Brown's shop. When he refused their demand for flour, they took hatchets to the door and burst inside. Only when Brown promised to give them ten barrels did the women disperse. In response, both Brown and the women turned to Vance. Brown expressed outrage at local authorities who witnessed the scene and did nothing. The women tried a different strategy. Women's organization and their assertiveness against certain men were intertwined with an enduring public profession of dependence upon others. In a petition signed "Soldiers Wives," a writer from Salisbury admitted their actions were "not at all pleasant" but were an "absolute necessity" to "obtain something to eat." Turning to Vance they "humbly pray" that he would "inform us whether or not we are justifiable in what we have done — and if not for Heavens Sake tell us how these evils are to be remedied." The writer, whether one of the "Soldiers Wives" or simply someone hiding behind that identity, defended them on several grounds. At her meekest, the writer claimed desperation. "Sir we have to live," she pleaded as she listed the high prices of flour, wood, and eggs and the low wages for sewing. "Many of us work day after day without a morsel of meat . . . how We ask you in the name of God are we to live?" More assertively, she defended their actions as soldiers' wives whose husbands had gone "not only to defend our humble homes but the homes & property of the rich man." She also argued that they had done nothing wrong. They sought not "charity" but simply "fair and reasonable prices." "To whom else can we go but to you our highly esteemed and cherished Gov to redress these evils?" she asked. In return for his "prayerfully considering our letter," she called down "Heavens richest blessing" upon him.[22]

Confederate defeats at Gettysburg and Vicksburg in July 1863 deeply undermined faith in the war effort and prompted new waves of appeals upon the state. Writing from an inauspicious place called Clay Beat, Ann E. Hodges was heartily sick of the fighting by September of 1863. No longer confident in her husband's speedy return, Hodges looked to Vance for help. "My situation is indeed a pitiful one," Hodges wrote. "Confined to [her] bed a good part of the time," she was unable to take care of her children or herself. Hodges wanted her husband sent home, and she believed Vance had the power to help her. To appeal to him, Hodges fashioned a Vance who would be receptive to her pleas. "I know you have a kind feeling heart and if in your power will do all you can for me," she wrote, although there is no reason to believe she knew much about Vance at all. Blaming her troubles on speculators who drove up the price of food, she told Vance, "This dose not seem right to me," and then added, "and I know you do not think it right." Establishing, at least fictionally, Vance's morality, she then appealed to what must lay beneath it, the cultural values that connected Hodges and Vance, especially Christianity, and deemed government help a "great blessing." Having aggrandized Vance, Hodges quickly transformed herself from a helpless, feeble woman into someone with access to God through her "feeble petitions" to the "throne of grace." Hodges quoted from Hebrews 4:16, where the "throne of grace" was the place where "we may obtain mercy . . . in time of need." Simultaneously helpless and demanding, Hodges perhaps relied upon two other lines of Hebrews, the one often used as a justification of power: "Salute all them that have the rule over you," and the other the book's famous definition of faith, "the substance of things hoped for, the evidence of things not seen."[23]

Confederate defeats, "homesickness, fatigue, hard fare," and the withdrawal of promised furloughs, along with the need for men at the spring planting, shattered morale among soldiers in 1863. Many soldiers were poorly equipped and "ragged and dirty," suffering from "itch vermin and disease," an observer wrote. "Many a sick soldier lies for weeks in rags & filth and actually rots away with disease." One who looked to Vance for assistance was a private named Archibald Curlee. Sick and discouraged, Curlee hoped "there is sompthing i Can do that i Cold live out of the army for i assure you i Cant live there long." If it is tempting to discount letters like Curlee's as mere stabs in the dark, and his language as simple overstatement, he gave visible proof of the letter's importance to him. With his note he mailed ten cents to pay for Vance's answer. In his effort to get his dime's worth, Curlee performed a wide range of roles. For part of his letter, he was the inquisitive legalist, acknowledging that he was "young and green about" the law and asking whether Vance could discharge men "or, no." At the beginning, Curlee played the part of the meek subject begging for the attention of "One i never have seen." Curlee attempted to preserve both his worthiness and his need through his "Bad health." Despite Curlee's dime and his promise to "thank you a thousand times," Curlee received disappointment. In response, Vance noted only, "No power to detail him."[24]

Angry over a lack of furloughs, worried about missing another planting season, and despairing of a war that would not end, North Carolinians deserted in large numbers in the spring of 1863. North Carolina may have suffered more desertions than most states simply because, as Vance noted, "our troops" in Virginia "are nearer their homes and therefore more tempted." Some of these deserters returned for visits or to plant crops. Other hid out in the woods or gathered in massive camps for self-defense. Vance's control over them was limited; he attempted to use the state militia to round up deserters, but in March of 1863, the chief justice of the North Carolina Supreme Court barred the state militia from enforcing national laws. This judgment in turn provoked more desertion, as rumors "went abroad to the army in a very exaggerated and ridiculous form." Led to believe that the conscript law was unconstitutional and that they were entitled, if they came home, to the protection of the civil authorities, soldiers deserted "worse than before." Against this "fearful evil," Vance reorganized the militia and asked "the people to assist [him] in the arrest and return of deserters." By September, a Confederate inspector in North Carolina warned that in western and central North Carolina deserters "organize in bands" of fifty to one hundred armed men who in some counties occupied towns, drilled regularly, and fought off the state militia in armed skirmishes. According to a Confederate inspector, peace meetings in North Carolina, inspired by editor William Holden, produced letters "inviting the men home, promising them aid and comfort. . . . There is danger of marked political division and something like civil war if the military evils reported be not at once met by strong measures of military repression." In response, the assistant secretary of war warned the Confederate government that "the condition of things in the mountain districts of North Carolina, South Carolina, Georgia, and Alabama menaces the existence of the Confederacy as fatally as either of the armies of the United States." Over the next year and a half, desertions ebbed and flowed with military success and failure, but by 1865, a large proportion of North Carolina troops — perhaps as many as a third — had left their regiments.[25]

Despairing of the anarchy at home, deserters placed their masculine obligation to their family above theirs to the state. "A mans first duty is to provide for his own household the soldiers wont by imposed upon much longer," one wrote. James W. Stricklen, a "humble Private," complained that his "wife and children was to be supported" but that "never has had one cent given to her." Without help, he added, "my family must suffer." At this point, Stricklen shed his humility, proclaiming himself fit to judge his own obligations. If his family suffered, Stricklen promised, he "shall know longer be in the Service" but would desert in order to defend his family. Stricklen therefore placed the burden of resolving this crisis of masculinity on Vance. In January 1864, J. E. Robertson explained to Vance that his fence rotted away. Without his help fixing it, he went on, his wife could not plant corn, and "my wife + poor little children must awl starve to death." Robertson wrote that he had not had a single furlough, while richer soldiers had been home multiple times. "It is not Rite and I Aint willing to" be put "down under the Big Men." Having made his case in dramatic terms, Robertson became much more deferential at the end of his letter. "Pray studdy on it," he asked, "and look at my pittifull case" and "I will give you awl the honer that Belongs to the human Rase of men."[26]

Those soldiers who did not desert tried other methods to gain Vance's attention and win a legal pass home. Soldiers knew that the right kind of friendship did indeed create mutual obligations. One soldier who succeeded was Moses O. Sherrill of Cabarrus County. In August 1863, Sherrill was suffering. He had been wounded in December 1862 at the battle of Fredericksburg. Now, back home and in bad health, he turned to Vance. Unlike many of the letter writers, he had an actual relationship to call upon, one rooted in a type of mutuality, though not equality. Vance and Sherrill's relationship dated back to Vance's days in the Confederate army. In March of 1862, at the battle of New Bern, Vance had made his reputation for courage. During that battle, however, he also fell from his horse into Bryce's Creek. As Vance struggled to the surface, Sherrill helped him out of the creek, perhaps saving him from drowning. The next day, according to Sherrill, Vance told him he owed Sherrill a favor. "Now is the time that I need healp if I ever Did in this world," Sherrill pleaded. "I have a wife and small children and my wife is weakley." Therefore, Sherrill asked for "a little sum thing for me in the way of money." In return, Sherrill would be "a thousen times A Blige to you." Unlike many others, Sherrill's request was honored. Vance asked his secretary to "send him some money & write" to the commissioners of his county on his behalf. Sherrill's triumph suggests why so many Carolinians made their claims on intimate terms. In the world they understood, only intimacy could gain the help of a powerful patron. If they did not have Sherrill's good luck to have saved Vance's life, they tried, fantastically, to create the same obligations on the page.[27]

Vance's performance as the "soldier's friend" in his campaign inspired appeals that nudged him to live up to that promise. Otis Porter drew directly upon Vance's words in his request for a furlough. From the beginning, Porter understood that his simple request was personal. "Feeling that I mirited a favor as much as any one in the Co," he asked his commanding officer, but was denied. Therefore, Porter turned to Vance, the "soldier's friend," with a question about the "meaning and justice of sutch treatment." Even as he framed his request as a favor, Porter also declared it as his right, reminding Vance, "I believe I hav ben as patriotic as any man." In September 1863, the 26th Regiment Band told Vance that he had "upon a certain occasion" promised "us that if we ever got into any difficulty we should apply to you + if in your power you would assist us. . . . Circumstances have arisen which impel us to seek your advice, perhaps your assistance."[28]

Men quoted Vance's own words back to him as part of their complex effort to avoid dishonoring themselves. By turning the request into a simple delivery of a promise, they tried to turn their plea into a right, and make the potential dishonor not theirs but Vance's. In March 1863, a Newton man named Michael Bollinger framed his plea as a manly effort to comply "with the request of the poor soldiers women in my Neighborhood." They wanted to know "what the are to doo for Bread. . . . These women look to you as there chief magistrate for protection." Their complaint (or Bollinger's voiced in their name) was about speculators who held on to corn and other foodstuffs in 1863 in order to sell them later at higher prices. Like many other writers, Bollinger quickly turned his ventriloquism in another direction, no longer speaking for women but "in the name of God." Having played God and women, Bollinger then became the voice of soldiers "riting home now that if there familes cant get bread the will come home and die at home befor there little ones shall starve." The last, and most striking, voice that Bollinger assumed was Vance's own. Near the end of his letter he turned Vance's words from a January 1863 proclamation back on him. "You Proclaimd to them in your Proclamation to the soldier in the army doing his Duty that the Wife and child should share the last bushel of meal + last lbs of meat but when men have it and wount let them have it for there money what will the do." Perhaps recognizing the danger of assuming Vance's voice, Bollinger at the end retreated to a safer position, blaming not Vance but a local merchant for the suffering.[29]

To explain why Vance should be, as one Carolinian wrote, "the earthly source for a redress," Carolinians often portrayed themselves as kinless. The particular loneliness of the kinless person became during the war a free-floating dependence that should settle upon the government. Like many societies, especially agrarian ones, the American South functioned through extended families with complex, sometimes contested ties of obligation and deference. In many small towns and plantation districts, prominent white men distributed gifts, loans, food, and the services of slaves to their literal kin or to neighbors who created a type of kinship bond; this pattern was reproduced within the household, where a patriarch at least in theory dispensed justice and mercy to his family, free and slave. In drawing upon broad definitions of kinship, writers analogized the relation between stronger and weaker kin to state and subject. Men like John D. Hudson asked for discharge on the grounds that without it, their families would be left kinless and defenseless. "I am all the Son my father has got," Hudson wrote, "and him and mother is a sufern for the want of me at home." Nancy Speaks asked Vance to "place your self in my condition, an old helpless widow with all her children gone, with no relations to care for you." Dependence upon kin could stretch far beyond actual families. A woman named Mary E. Shearin of Brinkleyville begged Vance not to take away a hired "mulatto" who was "my last Dependence of making a support for me and my little children" now that her husband, two brothers, and five step-brothers were in the service. "It is said that the government will support the women and children but if the poor women was to throw their entire dependence on the government they would soon perish," she wrote. "I think you are gentleman enough to let me know what to do."[30]

The politics of dependence also opened a small window of space for free people of color. Daniel Locklar, a man with almost no rights, turned his letter into a complex performance of power and deference, independence and dependence. Until the winter of 1862–63, Locklar supported his large family in Laurinburg "very well" by working for neighbors as a laborer. But during the winter of 1862–63, a man "living near me," claiming to be an "Agent of the State Salt-workes," took "all we colored men . . . to make Salt." Now, in July of 1863, the impressment agent returned "after us to make Barrels for the state Salt-workes." Locklar acknowledged the state's general right to press him into service but sought help in judging whether he was being fairly treated. "If this be a law and he is ortherised by law to use that power I am willing to submit to his calls," Locklar wrote, "but if there be no such law and this Agent-taking this power within himself perhaps speculating . . . I am not willing to submit to such." In laying out the distinc-tion between proper and improper service, Locklar appealed to fairness, making a petition of right. For part of his letter, Locklar sounded very much like any man seeking to know his legal obligations, and Vance responded in part to this, noting, "He" (presumably the agent) has "no such authority." And yet Locklar could not be any man seeking his rights, for he was a particular man, a free person of color in a state hostile to him. If he sought to defend his abstract, legal rights, Locklar found their defense not in a legal system but in a distant figure. To excite Vance's attention, Locklar tried to personalize his situation, complaining that the agent came at the "Dead hours of night" and paid them only $1.50 a day. "I cannot support my family at that rate." Finally, Locklar called Vance "your highness" and hoped he would "condesend to reply to my feble Note" and "confer a great favor on me." In his short letter, Locklar simultaneously played the role of aggrieved citizen (a status he held in only the most tangential way), put-upon mascu-line head of household, and dependent subject. In the brief light of his let-ter, Locklar appears to us as someone completely recognizable — the citizen poised to sue — and also someone hardly recognizable at all — the supplicant poised to beg. In the doubleness of his role, in his strange combination of strength and weakness, Locklar interwove the abstract with the intimate, the rights of a citizen with the pleas of a subject. As a subject, as a particular, fleshed human being, perhaps Locklar could find a receptive ear.[31]

Like Locklar, many other Carolinians asked, in similarly creative spellings, for Vance to condescend to their level. Drawn from biblical notions of Christ's condescension to earth, the term "condescend" (like its sibling, "patronize") rings more negatively to modern ears than to nineteenth-century ones. The word "condescend" carried connotations of acquiescence, of deferring, or giving way. More frank about acknowledging power distinctions, these Carolinians seem to have used the word in its scriptural context, as praise for a graceful act, not as an affront to social equality. Christians believed that Christ literally "condescended" into human form on earth, and the word rang with notions of sacrifice and mercy. In the book of Romans, condescension was a veritable commandment to "rejoice with them that do rejoice, and weep with them that weep." Rather than holding to "high things," a Christian should "condescend to men of low estate." This voluntary assumption of equality with an inferior did not erase all distinctions; in fact, Locklar and others very much wanted Vance to maintain, at least for the moment, the powers of his position, so he could use them to their benefit. By condescending, by lowering himself, Vance would see people like Locklar. Operating from an assumption that superior and inferior positions existed (whether rightfully or not), this theory of condescension celebrated those who could see beneath them, and, in seeing, act in a benevolent way upon their dependents.[32]

These needs grew more intense in the summer of 1864, after the fall of Atlanta wrecked Southern confidence and prompted grave fears of invasion in North Carolina. By October, Eliza A. Thomas was near to giving up. Throughout the war, she attempted to raise six small children, five of them sick, by herself. "I cannot attend to them," she wrote to Vance, "my health is so feeble, I can get no one to stay with me, I can only sit over them and cry god be merciful. . . . I have no relations that is able to help." Thomas therefore begged Vance to discharge or at least furlough her husband. When Vance did not reply, in her next letter she made her faith into a weapon against him. Supposing that Vance had turned "a deaf ear to all of [her] entreaties," she claimed a biblical warrant for criticizing Vance, quoting Proverbs 21:13: "Whoso stoppeth his ears to the cries of the poor he shall cry himself and not be heard." Thomas told Vance what to expect if he refused her request: "I fear when Judgement shall be laid to the line and righteousness to the planet. There will be a fearful reckoning sometimes." Despite the intensity of her call, Thomas did not succeed. Vance asked his secretary to "assure the Lady that I have no power to relieve her." At about the same time, a man named P. J. Sinclair turned his wife's status as a Northerner into proof of her dependence. "Should I go as a private who would look after her and my children what would be her situation when all her kindred are north?" he asked Vance. When Vance wrote a noncommittal response, Sinclair tried to turn his words against the governor: "You say 'it would afford' you 'much pleasure' to give me 'any assistance which' you 'can in the matter.' There is but one way of doing it, Governor."[33]

Over the course of the war, Vance became increasingly aware of the impossible demands placed upon him. No matter how many men he exempted, others would desert. No matter how much he lobbied to increase funding for wives, some would go hungry. Constrained by the state's limited bureaucracy, small budget, and necessary deference to Confederate policy, Vance found himself the author of expectations he could not meet. Despite his own eagerness to be munificent, Vance began to publicly aggrandize the power of Jefferson Davis and the Confederate government in Richmond. As the war dragged on, and Vance deflected more and more requests, Carolinians turned to their president in Richmond. Ironically, the Confederacy, established in the name of states' rights, produced a president who was the subject of intense fantasies. These letters were not inspired by Jefferson Davis's charisma but by the revolutionary experience of Confederate governance. A legislator named William Alexander Smith complained on behalf of the "people of Johnston County" about widespread impressments by "would be Aristocratic and demanding Horse leeches of the Confederate Service." Because he owed allegiance "first to *North Carolina* secondly to the Confederate States," he turned for protection to his state, but Vance reminded him that North Carolina might be first in his heart but not in its powers. Help would have to come from Richmond.[34]

As his frustrations with Jefferson Davis grew, Vance found in Davis's power a necessary scapegoat, a way of holding himself blameless. When Iredell County residents petitioned for the discharge of William Davidson so he could serve once again as the "natural protector" of his two sisters and his widowed sister-in-law, Vance granted their favor by passing it along to the Confederate secretary of war with his own personal request to "oblige" him by listening to the plea. In Pitt County, a mother and four aunts had been "dependent" on Frederick J. Bryan "ever since he has been old enough to aid them and have always lived together." Poor, propertyless, diseased, and decrepit, they "must surely suffer seriously" now that Bryan was off with North Carolina's Third Regiment. "Many hard cases must occur in the general operation of any law, but we regard this as one of such destitution and dependence as to claim consideration," they wrote. Vance quickly forwarded the petition and, he hoped, the obligation, to Jefferson Davis in Richmond. This time, however, Vance's gambit failed miserably. Not only did Davis's staff in Richmond decline the request "for the usual reasons," they also declined to answer the Bryan family directly, instead answering "thro Gov Vance."[35]

By the spring of 1864, Vance's attitude toward the Confederate national government hardened. Outraged by Jefferson Davis's suspension of habeas corpus against deserters, Vance wrote a bitter, personal letter to the Confederate president in early February 1864. Among his many complaints was Confederate unresponsiveness. "The files of my office are filled up with the unavailing complaints of outraged citizens to whom redress is impossible," Vance wrote. Vance meant to demonstrate his state's loyalty; their requests were not answered, "yet they submitted" to Davis's rule. Davis, however, took personal umbrage. "I am at a loss to conceive how you can assert that these complaints are 'unavailing' and that 'redress was impossible' if you kept the papers in your files in Raleigh," Davis wrote. "I know that no complaint has ever been received from you on any subject, without meeting respectful consideration and redress, so far as it was within my power to have justice done." Vance did not back down, stating, "I *have* sent up to the Secretary of War's office many complaints of wrong and outrage and, to my knowledge, no case whatever has been redressed." This failure did "add to the discontents in North Carolina." Responding with "prompt efforts to redress . . . would cause these poor people to love their Government and support its laws more than the terrors of the suspension of the writ of *habeas corpus* and a display of force." Davis was incensed. In his response, he claimed that Vance had "so far infringed the proprieties of official intercourse as to preclude the possibility of a reply." "In order that I may not again be subjected to the necessity of making so unpleasant a remark," he concluded, "I must beg that a correspondence so unprofitable . . . may end here."[36]

After this break, Vance turned his petitioners toward Richmond with such dispatch that it seemed almost like glee. While he previously tried to cull some powers for himself, or to sustain his role as a patron, he now directed request after request to Jefferson Davis. Whether he hoped to bury Davis in pleas or merely to obey Davis's order, Vance worked to shift the direction of Carolina pleas toward a new friend in Richmond. In the midst of his bitter exchange with Davis, a Davidson County man named Johnson Boner asked Vance for help exempting a local man from the service. "I know of no way to relieve him except a direct appeal to the President," Vance wrote his secretary. "If such application is sent me I will welcome + forward it." At the same time, Vance told Sarah A. Barden to write to Davis. Even if he could not personally deliver favors, the chance to reach distant leaders was itself a form of power. Barden wrote in reply, "I take you to bee a nice man and of course you should be." By June of 1864, Evey S. Jackson of Rowan County knew enough to beg Vance and "mr Davis" to "send home the poor solgers to cut the wheat. . . . I hope that you and mr Davis will help ous all you can fer yous are all the wones that can done any thing . . . and I beleve you are Christen harted men and that you wonte sufer to say the poor wimens wheat fall to thee ground."[37]

Carolinians adeptly integrated their knowledge of the new government in Richmond into their already developed modes of appeal. Rather than collapsing in the face of a burgeoning Confederate bureaucracy, claims of dependence fit this new world. Carolinians continued to present their own need in the stark terms of dependence, a state that could easily define women or children or, with a little imagination, men (especially sick ones) and entire communities who could become "dependent" upon blacksmiths or tanners or shoemakers or slave patrollers. In pleading for a blacksmith in Martin County, ten men and three widows stated that he was "Invaluable" in making tools and farm implements. "In him was our dependence," they wrote. For Mrs. Charles H. Howcott of Brinkleyville, Jefferson Davis was the man who could relieve her sick husband from duty, and so she prayed with a "heart . . . bowed down with grief" for his release and that "the blessing of Heaven may be showed on my President and my Country." While Carolinians appealed to Davis and his subordinates as "feeling men" and friends, they did not often aggrandize them in the same terms or to the same degree that they did Vance. Perhaps this was because Davis's administration, based firmly upon the forms of the federal bureaucracy, was known to be adept at saying no. When many of A. H. Boyle's friends petitioned for his discharge on the grounds that without him his wife would be a "Bed ridden object," a bureaucrat used their claims of friendship against them, noting, "It is hoped the numerous signers of this petition and friends of the family will see to the wants of Mrs. Boyle." If Boyle had that many friends, then why did he need the state?[38]

By early 1865, the war was about to come home to central and western North Carolina. The final days blurred even more thoroughly the boundaries between personal and public dependence, between the intimate and the political. From December 1864, when General William Tecumseh Sherman captured Savannah, it was clear that South Carolina and North Carolina would be next. A whole region of slaves, including those who had been refugeed from the eastern seaboard, suddenly looked vulnerable. The final pleas to Vance were panicked. On New Year's Day, 1865, a man named M. S. Wiggins asked Vance to come to the aid of two white "helpless females." In 1862, after Union troops drew near their plantation in eastern Carolina, these women had fled to the relatively safe interior of the state. In December 1864, their overseer had been called off to the home guard, and, according to Wiggins, the "negroes have become alarmed and run off and everything they have is likely to be destroyed" unless Vance discharged the overseer. Over the course of his letter, Wiggins transformed his words into "their . . . petition." Wiggins's own absence demanded explanation. "If I could aid them myself I would most cheerfully do so," he wrote, "but I am nearly" worn "down myself, having no one to assist me in my old age." A group of North Carolina "Soldiers of Lee's Army," perhaps purposely cloaking themselves in the power of anonymity, warned Vance in January 1865 that "those at home must look to the wants, and ameliorate the suffering of our wives and little ones there." If the government would help, "there will be less desertion." Without assistance, "it is impossible for us to bear up under our many troubles."[39]

In February 1865, two months before the surrender at Appomattox, J. Felton wrote of her faith in a Vance she could not see. Calling herself a "weak woman," Felton placed Vance momentarily in the role of her dead husband but then immediately pointed him toward an easy exit. Simply by absolving her son from service, Vance could ensconce the boy in the husbandly role, and free himself from responsibility. To gain his attention, Felton flattered Vance relentlessly, calling him "one of the old North State's most gifted, and intellectual Sons." Humble and full of "reluctance" about writing such a great man, she appealed to his generosity: "I'm sure your heart is warm and very kind, you will excuse mistakes." As she flattered, she also insisted that he would attend to her wishes. Felton claimed her dependence not only upon her feminine weakness but upon her specific need, as she did not know how to support herself. In exchange, she would reward Vance with a prayer that "you may live a long, a happy life, that success may ever crown your efforts. The people of the glorious old North C. almost worship you, they say you have given satisfaction, that you have done more for soldiers familys than any other Gov in Confederacy." In Reidsville, a woman named Mary Windsor had plenty of problems of her own, with fifteen daughters and three sons at home. In February 1865, her forty-nine-year-old husband had been gone for three months, leaving her and her oldest son to fend for the family. Windsor's eldest son was twenty-three years old but had "fits" and "can't go to the mill by himself." Her next-eldest boy was only twelve. Windsor therefore asked that Vance detail her husband home. Cloaking herself in her weakness, she called upon his Christian obligation toward the meek: "May God now teach you too look on helpless infancy and delicate females with tender mercy." The melodic phrase "tender mercy" played through Psalm 25, which praised the Lord's "tender mercies" and "lovingkindnesses" to loyal subjects who were "desolate and afflicted." Psalm 25 also spoke of the importance of seeing and being seen, an idea that troubled many letter writers. "Mine eyes *are* ever toward the Lord; for he shall pluck my feet out of the net," the psalmist wrote hopefully, if God would only turn His eyes "unto me." Those who turned to Raleigh, like those who turned to heaven, worried constantly about how to gain the notice of a powerful, distant figure who might deliver them from need or pass by them altogether.[40]

As the war turned toward North Carolina in 1865, Union victory raised the possibility not only that all slaves might become free but that white Carolinians might, in some way, become slaves. In describing their future servitude, white Carolinians did not seem to mean a literal slavery but instead a denial of access, the transition from subjects of to subjects to the state. As they wrestled with this problem, some white Carolinians developed elaborate fantasies about Vance and the state, rooted in analogies between biblical and present time. An anonymous writer in January 1865 begged Vance "for they sake of suffering humanity" and "for the sake of surfering women and children" to "stop this cruel war, here I am without one mouthful to eat for myself and five children and God only knows where I will get something." The writer despaired of victory: "Now you know as well as you have a head that it is impossible to whip they Yankees." The writer pleaded with Vance to at least preserve families. "If we poor women and children are to be slaves let they rest of they men come home to try and take care of there poor women and children. . . . Let us be slaves together." By framing slavery as inaccessibility, the impossibility of reaching patrons, she drew upon important antebellum ways of thinking about power. At the same time, she recognized the changes in the world around her. "I believe slavery is doomest to dy out that god is agoing to liberate niggars and fighting any longer is fighting against god," she wrote. In terms used by peasants across the world, Vance had lost the mandate of heaven: Whether or not God was just, God was mighty; as they were weak, God had surely abandoned them.[41]

Five days later, the Union army launched a massive amphibious assault on Fort Fisher, which provided cover for the state's main port of Wilmington. A few days after the Union captured Fort Fisher, C. D. Smith from Haw River used the Bible to argue against the possibility of surrender. During the conflict, he had "studied and collected the Bible history of the Jewish wars" and of "eclipses and disasters of the reigning Princes for over five hundred years." "I have not found," he wrote, "a single instance in which a war conducted on the principles upon which this war is conducted against us ever had any permanent success." Smith did not believe God would "abandon" the Confederacy, and he asked to speak to the legislature "for the sake of the widows and orphans" to beg it "by every sacred sentiment and by every noble + generous impulse not to sanction anything that may in the remotest way lead to the delivering up of my children and thine to future slavery."[42]

For both writers, talking about political power meant talking about the divinely sanctioned institution of slavery, even as they recognized that the enslavement of African Americans was over. Therefore, they traced the assumptions that underlay their different arguments about surrender. Power lay with a mighty God. Enslavement was distance both from God and from his merciful agents on earth. Between the states of godly power and abject slavery lay a ladder of people dependent upon powers above them. What was untenable was not dependence but the condition of abandonment. These ideas became by the war's end a creative, free-floating, and generative discourse for discussing how political power worked and for whose benefit.

These political claims developed in the heat of the Civil War — made by people writing from their desks — inspired a new mode of politics. As the social structure broke down around them, and as once-thriving plantations were taken over by Union soldiers and slaves, some white Carolinians turned their hopes for proximate help to distant figures in Raleigh and Richmond. The way they constructed those powerful men provided tools that Vance used to augment his power and his popularity. Programs to exempt men and to feed wives established the intimacy of the state's relationship to its people, while the limitations of those programs reinforced the notion that help would come idiosyncratically. This combination of novel war experiences, slavery-based ideals of paternalism, day-to-day chaos, and biblical views of grace would not just survive but thrive in the hardships and chaos of postwar Reconstruction. In part this was because people like Vance and the women who appealed to him continued to play important roles in shaping state politics. In part it was because the people excluded from this public system, the 330,000 people who had been slaves before the war, themselves developed a parallel, if often oppositional, view of politics that would make of Reconstruction a war over patrons.

Weeks after Fort Fisher fell, the Union occupied Wilmington, at last sealing off the Carolina coast. In early March, Sherman crossed into North Carolina, taking the towns of Fayetteville and Goldsboro. Days after Lee surrendered the Army of Northern Virginia at Appomattox Courthouse, the Union captured the state capital of Raleigh, and soon began negotiating with the last Confederate army left in the east. On April 26, Confederate general Joseph E. Johnston surrendered 90,000 troops — the largest of the war — to Sherman near Durham. Vance, now governor of a state that did not exist, turned himself in to Union general John M. Schofield, who sent Vance back to his family. Defeat would make Vance the object, rather than subject, of petitions. Although wartime writers had cloaked Vance's power in personal terms, his power was based not in his physical body but in his status, and that status, to his dismay, became inextricably tied to the Confederacy. Although Vance had opposed secession before Sumter and had lobbied for peace negotiations during the war, he was a high-ranking officer of the rebellion and so, in the eyes of the Union, a traitor. On his thirty-fifth birthday, Vance was arrested and dispatched to Washington, D.C. During his forty-seven days in the Old Capitol Prison, Vance's close friend Cornelia P. Spencer, a companion from the University of North Carolina, organized a petition from the "Ladies of Chapel Hill" to President Andrew Johnson. In it "they beg that he may receive his pardon." Despite the begging tone, however, Spencer and her friends sought Vance's pardon as a matter of fairness, since others who committed similar acts had "long since been pardoned," and since Vance had been a "faithful and ardent supporter of the Union as it existed before the war." Finally, they claimed that this "act of simple justice" would "help attach" people to "your Government." After several delays and some political maneuvering, Vance himself applied, while in prison, for a pardon, which he received in 1867.[43]

Slaves and the Great Deliverer

Freedom and Friendship behind Union Lines

IN APRIL 1865, not long after the Confederate surrender at Appomattox, a "dispatch boat, with drooping flag shrouded in mourning" carried the news of Abraham Lincoln's assassination to the massive Union colony of ex-slaves on Roanoke Island in North Carolina's Albemarle Sound. The message "brings us down to the valley of humiliation," a missionary on the island wrote. "Old and young were alike bowed down . . . moaning and weeping near my school house." When the teacher reminded the ex-slaves that God would not "desert you in the wilderness," one of them answered gloomily, "I knows it honey, but 'pears like I cant see de light anywhere. I cries might hard to de Good Lord, to have pity on us, now wese no friend on earth." Across the South, Yankees described ex-slaves' reaction to Lincoln's death as a widespread panic that their rights had died with their president. At the end of June, the Union officer in charge of North Carolina ex-slaves reported that "bewildered" African Americans "scarcely" knew "whether they were or were not free," in part because of "the untimely death of their great Deliverer, Abraham Lincoln." For reassurance and protection, they flocked to Northern military officers, African American soldiers, kinsmen, teachers, and missionaries. This panic was not an idle fear. For those far from Union lines like Granville County–born Charity Austin, who lived on a southwest Georgia plantation during the war, Lincoln's death in fact did temporarily forestall their freedom. "Boss tole us Abraham Lincoln wus dead and we are still slaves," she remembered. "Our boss man brought black cloth and made us wear it for mourning for Abraham Lincoln and tole us that there would not be freedom. We stayed there another year after freedom. A lot o' de niggers knowed nothin' 'cept what missus and marster tole us."[1]

Lincoln's death did not, of course, end emancipation, but the panic that followed his assassination casts light upon the way freedpeople understood politics. Their personalistic view of rights was something that Horace James, the Union Superintendent of Negro Affairs in North Carolina, counted as one of the war's most significant, but also most troubling, outcomes. On New Year's Day, 1865, months before Lincoln's assassination, James described the seventeen thousand ex-slaves then under Union control as "hero worshippers." Although, as James put it, they "strongly aspire to the common rights of citizens," ex-slaves counted those rights in part as a gift from a distant patron. "The eternal progress of ideas they comprehend not, but Abraham Lincoln is to them the chiefest among ten thousand, and altogether lovely. They mingle his name with their prayers and their praises evermore." James believed this "great reverence for the 'head men' and for all in authority" grew from freedpeople's own limitations. Slavery and racial inferiority made them "simple children of nature"; therefore, the federal government "should stand god-father . . . and throw the strong arm of its protection around them" until they had the knowledge to understand their world and the power to defend themselves.[2]

James's conclusion looks at first glance like simple racism. Freedpeople's assertive political organizing belied James's judgment of their capacities, but it did not always contradict his verdict about their attachment to patrons. Beyond his racist explanation, James's account provides an entry into the complex question of how slaves made sense of a political world full of both promise and peril. On those terms, James's story fits in easily with petitions and pleas from ex-slaves during the war and with stories told long after. Ex-slaves frequently made Lincoln a biblical saint, a savior, and a good king, a necessary patron in a world where rights seemed not abstract but embodied in particular leaders. This mythic Lincoln represented not what James considered the transition state between slavery and freedom but a series of judgments made by freedpeople about the capacities and limitations of the Union government.

For North Carolina's slaves, the Civil War represented both revolutionary possibilities and grave danger. Although some Northern orators proclaimed the war was an effort solely to save the Union, many slaves knew better. From the beginning, they understood that their freedom lay in the balance, and that their actions could help shift the outcome of the war to their advantage and the Union's. Despite placating rhetoric by Northern politicians,

Southerners—white and black—judged the Republican Party a threat to the long-term survival of slavery. Even if most Republicans had no intention of directly attacking slavery where it existed, most of them intended to put the institution on a path to extinction. Once the war expanded from small skirmishes to full-scale armed conflict, and once the Union established control over parts of the South, slaves attempted to pressure the Union to fulfill this promise. From the war's early days, slaves called upon the Union for protection, enlistment in the military, fair wages, food rations, access to land, and, first and foremost, freedom.

In the complex interplay between state and subject, ex-slaves' increased expectations of government grew not from thin air but from the very actions, small as some were, that the Union took on their behalf. The more the Union did for them, the more it trained them to request, and the more it ended up disappointing their hopes. Often ex-slaves began by asking for their rights upon the broadest, most liberal terms imaginable. Almost immediately, however, freedpeople learned that Union patrons were both necessary and unreliable, so they organized to protect their interests and to make pleas rooted in dependence.

This was especially true for slaves' most basic need, for food. James's anxieties about dependence led him to withhold rations, thus sparking a fear of starvation that inspired the very politics of dependence he hoped to avert. Therefore, in another of the war's enduring ironies, ex-slaves' political claims of dependence came to resemble the simultaneous appeals of white Confederates to Zebulon Vance and Jefferson Davis. Directed at different patrons and for different purposes, white and ex-slave Carolinians' appeals illuminate a common problem of governance in wartime America, a mix of expectation and disappointment that emerged from the expanded promises but limited delivery of wartime governments trying to maintain support without emptying the treasury. This did not mean, however, that emancipation was a failure. Even this diminished promise protected freedpeople's family relationships, gave them space for political organization, ensured self-ownership, and offered them an enormously important opportunity to recast their relationship to white Southern planters. Wartime Reconstruction offered not a patronless world but the chance to compete for favors. By gaining access to new patrons, freedpeople altered local balances of power.

Reading the encounters between freedpeople and the Union army through the lens of dependence casts new light upon the actions of ex-slaves and Union officers, and reconfigures important debates about the Civil War, emancipation, and slave politics. Over the last thirty years, historians explained emancipation's creation of legal and political, but not economic, equality largely through the lens of free-labor ideologies and the reconstruction of labor practices. Union officers' contempt for slavery, mistrust of slave laborers, and eagerness to revive a Southern cash crop economy emerged from a coherent capitalist ideology that celebrated freedom of contract, not equality of condition, and predisposed many of them to defend freedpeople's civil but not economic rights. White Northern racism, even among solidly antislavery officers, also helped explain the quick transition from slavery to an exploitative free labor system. More recently, historians have explored the way ex-slaves in Union-controlled camps and plantations reshaped the particular labor patterns that arose after emancipation. Resisting work arrangements that hewed too closely to slavery, African Americans organized, sometimes successfully, for access to land and the right to control the terms of their labor. The freedpeople's politics that emerged from these fights for self-determination and self-sufficiency pushed emancipation in surprising, more radical, directions but ultimately could not create economic equality.[3]

While broadly accurate, this portrayal of white Union reluctance and ex-slave assertiveness risks detaching labor struggles from judgments about the power of the government. Between the elevated language of ideology and the gritty practice of labor negotiations, experience with various, often competing, forms of the state shaped the moments of contact between Union officers and ex-slaves. Understanding slaves' transition to freedom on these terms helps recover the dynamic, practical aspects of African American politics. As the Civil War rendered slaves legally visible to the government, they used their new access not just to lobby for autonomy but also to build patrons they could call upon to protect their rights. This was not because they misunderstood the meaning of freedom but because they understood it all too well. Many ex-slaves simultaneously claimed self-determination and dependence upon distant rulers — built assertive political groups and appealed meekly to leaders — because in the small-scale, local struggles that defined emancipation, autonomy from immediate oppressors, whether planters or Union officers, might well be contingent upon support from a distant figure.

Viewing these encounters through the lens of dependence also complicates the meaning of free-labor ideology among white Union officers. Conflicts between Northern officers and ex-slaves emerged prior to labor disputes and had their roots in Union officers' denial of food to needy ex-slaves. Part of the same civilizing impulse that inspired schools and even land for ex-slaves, this aversion to charity was not solely the product of racism or of personal failings but an expression of a coherent, regional- and class-based ideology of independence. This discomfort with dependence had several sources, including the anxiety-provoking disruptions of an expanding market economy, a profusion of visible beggars in the nation's Northern cities, and the early-nineteenth-century expansion of voting rights. When previously excluded groups like white male workers and renters demanded inclusion on the grounds that they, too, were properly independent, they stigmatized dependence in a new way, transforming it from a sometimes unavoidable condition into a deeply personal weakness reserved for women, children, Native Americans, African Americans, and paupers. In abolitionist Boston, the same celebration of freedom of contract that was a useful cudgel against slavery also justified "enforced labor" for "vagrants and vagabonds." The New York State Board of Charities treated beggars as "criminals," while many states disfranchised men who lived in almshouses or received public relief.[4]

Northern middle-class family life and friendship patterns also fostered a distinctly different definition of paternalism among Northern officers than among the Southern planter class. Vance played a fatherly role to suggest an archetypal (if almost never realized) Southern view of an inclusive, hierarchical family, one where children and dependents might linger forever in a state of attachment. By contrast, James and his fellow officers often used the language of paternalism to suggest a child-raising process meant to train, or even force, ex-slaves toward independence from government. While appeals to Vance centered upon pleaders' inclusion in the family of people entitled to beg, conflicts between James and ex-slaves focused upon the definition of proper dependence, the question of when a man might be entitled to food or charity. Union officials and ex-slaves interpreted their encounters in distinct ways, not just as whites and African Americans, or as middle-class men and agrarian slaves, but also as Northerners and Southerners trained by class and regional cultures to view need, family, and friendship differently.[5]

The encounters began in May 1861 about thirty-five miles north of the North Carolina border, when three Virginia slaves ran to the Union-controlled Fortress Monroe. Less than a month after the attack on Fort Sumter and a month before the First Battle of Bull Run, these runaways forced Union officials to spell out their policy toward slaves. Earlier that day, a Union private wrote, federal soldiers marched through the neighboring town of Hampton and "the negroes gathered around our men, and their evident exhilaration was particularly noted, some of them saying, 'Glad to see you, Massa,'" and passing information to the soldiers. To the private, the "first communication between our army and the negroes" in the area revealed the hopes that many slaves invested in the Union soldiers. That evening, when three slaves presented themselves at the camp, their appearance put profound questions to General Benjamin Butler, the fort commander. Should male slaves "employed in the erection of batteries and other works by the rebels" be returned to their masters? Or should they be protected by the Union and used "in aid of the United States?"[6]

Three days after the first arrival, Butler's dilemma was compounded when another "squad" came, "bringing with them their women and children." Forty-seven slaves, including six "entire families" ranging from toddlers to octogenarians, arrived en masse, and "then they continued to come by twenties, thirties, and forties," eventually including North Carolinians. Edward L. Pierce, a private at Fortress Monroe who penned an essay on the runaways for the *Atlantic Monthly*, wondered at slaves' confidence in the Union: "There was no known communication between" the first three runaways and the ones who arrived days later, "and yet those comrades knew, or believed with the certainty of knowledge, how they had been received." When soldiers asked these new runaways if more were coming, Pierce reported, "their reply was, that, if they were not sent back, others would understand that they were among friends, and more would come the next day. Such is the mysterious spiritual telegraph which runs through the slave population." By early June, Pierce wrote, "a squad of negroes, meeting our soldiers, inquired anxiously the way to the 'freedom fort.'" Although local masters "had been most industrious" in their attempt to persuade them that the Yankees were coming down to "kill the negroes and manure the ground with them, or carry them off to Cuba or Hayti," slaves "still believed that the Yankees were their friends." This judgment was based on a logic of opposition; slaves who heard their masters denounce Black Republicans as abolitionists "thought their masters could not hate us [Republicans] as they did, unless we were their friends."[7]

Slaves who ran in family units presented Butler with the question of how to treat children and the elderly, dependents who did not work for the Confederate military. Butler decided to employ the able-bodied adults, "issuing proper food for the support of all, and charging against their services the expenses of care and sustenance of the men laborers." Within days, Butler's questions reached Washington, where Postmaster General Montgomery Blair lobbied to protect only "working people, leaving the Secessionists to take care of the non-working classes of these people." Secretary of War Simon Cameron, however, approved Butler's actions, ordering him to employ slaves, "keeping an account of the labor by them performed, of the value of it, and of the expenses of their maintenance. The question of their final disposition will be reserved for further determination."[8]

In the absence of a "final disposition," Union actions often looked arbitrary and "irregular." While Butler agonized at Fortress Monroe, in Washington, D.C., General Irvin McDowell excluded runaway slaves from other army camps. "Sometimes officers assumed to decide the question whether a negro was a slave, and deliver him" to a master even when "they had no authority," Edward Pierce wrote. "Worse yet, in defiance of the Common Law, they made color a presumptive proof of bondage," turning over free people to white men who claimed them. This ambiguity persisted for the next eighteen months. While Lincoln edged closer to emancipation and the arming of slaves, the president also encouraged officers in Missouri, Kentucky, and Maryland to return slaves to loyal masters and recanted emancipatory orders from military commanders in Missouri and South Carolina. Despite a great deal of talk, Congress's effort to clarify matters in its 1861 Confiscation Act was inconclusive. Slaves near Fortress Monroe therefore, wrote Pierce, "were somewhat perplexed by the contradictory statements of our soldiers, some of whom, according to their wishes, said the contest was for them, and others that it did not concern them at all and they would remain as before."[9]

By the end of July 1861, nearly 900 slaves had arrived at Fortress Monroe, and their intense need prodded Butler toward a final disposition. These exslaves included a large group of dependents, including about 400 children, 175 adult women, and 30 elderly men. Many of them settled a couple of miles from the fort in the town of Hampton, which had been abandoned by most of its white residents. Union officers hired ex-slave men to build breastworks for defense, paid women to wash clothes, and provided them with rations for the "support of the children." In this way, Butler managed the problem of dependence by tying the provision of women and children to male labor and by keeping most of the ex-slaves out of official Union lines. Pierce, a Massachusetts lawyer and politician, assumed the job of supervising the sixty-four ex-slave workers, a task he began by creating the first documentation of their presence and then by training them to work. Pierce told the ex-slaves that "their masters said they were an indolent people" but that Pierce "did not believe the charge" and "should be glad to report" to his friends in Massachusetts that "they were as industrious as the whites." Pierce's judgment was favorable but mixed. In the end, Pierce wrote in the *Atlantic Monthly* that the ex-slaves were "less vigorous and thrifty" than the Yankees but "quite equal to the mass of the Southern population." Pierce's engagement with ex-slaves did not end at Fortress Monroe. Later, he helped oversee a key Union experiment in free labor with the ex-slaves on the Sea Islands of South Carolina.[10]

Butler's plan collapsed in late July when commanding general Winfield Scott recalled four and a half regiments from Fortress Monroe. Short of men, Butler withdrew his soldiers from Hampton. Exposed to Confederate counterattack, "all these black people were obliged to break up their homes in Hampton, fleeing across the creek within my lines for protection and support," Butler wrote. "Indeed, it was a most distressing sight to see these poor creatures, who had trusted to the protection of the arms of the United States, and who aided the troops of the United States in their enterprise, to be thus obliged to flee from their homes, and the homes of their masters who had deserted them, and become fugitives from fear of the return of the rebel soldiery, who had threatened to shoot the men who had wrought for us, and to carry off the women who had served us to a worse than Egyptian bondage." Chastened by his failure to protect these needy people, Butler wrote: "The questions which this state of facts present are very embarrassing. *First*. What shall be done with them? and, *Second*. What is their state and condition?" If children and the elderly were not contraband, then were they the property of the United States? If the United States did not desire to hold them, then "have they not become, thereupon, men, women, and children?" Therefore, Butler believed he "should take the same care of these men, women, and children, houseless, homeless, and unprovided for, as I would of the same number of men, women, and children, who, for their attachment to the Union, had been driven or allowed to flee from the Confederate States." The secretary of war affirmed Butler's judgment, but his support did not constitute actual assistance. Butler found himself scrounging for donations of clothing, eventually turning to the American Missionary Association to meet needs beyond the army's capacity or will.[11]

These first encounters at Fortress Monroe revealed the revolutionary possibilities and practical limits of early contact between slaves and Union soldiers. Over and over, slaves ran to the Union out of confidence that their masters' enemies must be their friends, and would therefore protect them, settle them within Union lines, provide them with food and work, free them from slavery, and arm the men to fight against their masters. Over and over, Union troops proved themselves to indeed be friends, but not always reliable ones. The terrifying weakness of the Union and its inability to hold its ground or to command enough supplies to meet its own promises created grave fears among freedpeople. The problem of dependents that Butler wrestled with would also pose serious challenges for both Union officers and ex-slaves. When, and for how long, might slaves be worthy of support and rations? And when and under what terms should they be forced toward self-sufficiency?

Although some North Carolina slaves ran to Fortress Monroe, more slaves encountered the Union army in early 1862 after General Ambrose Burnside launched a major amphibious invasion of the North Carolina coast to cut off the state from foreign markets and supplies. In February 1862, after skirmishes along the Outer Banks, Burnside's men took Roanoke Island, an eight-mile-long fishing community home to Sir Walter Raleigh's failed "Lost Colony." The next month, the Union seized New Bern, once the state's capital and now a key port at the confluence of the Trent and Neuse Rivers. For the duration of the war, the Union held a narrow band of tidewater territory, successfully blockading most maritime trade, but it was unable to penetrate deep into the countryside. Although Union soldiers occasionally raided the interior of the state, and Confederates launched several counterattacks, Union and Confederate control remained generally stable, with the vast majority of the state in Confederate hands. Within the thin band of Union-controlled territory in coastal Carolina, the army eventually established one colony at Roanoke Island and two large, initially temporary, camps for housing ex-slaves, one at Beaufort and the other across the river from New Bern in a settlement named Trent River and later re-christened James City.

The slaves who ran to those Union camps acted upon a belief in the power of Union friendship to deliver them freedom, a faith worked out in group discussion and through information transmitted along the famous grapevine telegraph. This world of gossip was not solely a site for naive speculation or wishful thinking; in the life-and-death decisions of wartime, it functioned as a space where slaves could judge contradictory pieces of information, debate the meaning of the war, and refute malicious myths spread by their masters. Two years into the war, the Superintendent of Contrabands reported that slaves frequently traveled two hundred miles or more from North Carolina to Fortress Monroe in order to gain information about the progress of emancipation, then returned home to spread the news. A superintendent of contraband noted, "Some men who came here from North Carolina, knew all about the [Emancipation] Proclammation and they started on the belief in it; but they had heard these stories" that ex-slaves were being shipped to Cuba for reenslavement "and they wanted to know how it was. Well, I gave them the evidence and I have no doubt their friends will hear of it."[12]

As Union troops marched into plantation districts in eastern North Carolina, their proximity presented both opportunities and dangers to slaves. While Union soldiers maintained control, slaves could count on some degree of protection and access. Once Union troops marched on, however, Confederate planters often reasserted their power violently. Despite geographical and familial ties, therefore, many slaves — like those portrayed here entering the town of New Bern, North Carolina — packed up and followed Union troops as they marched, hoping to stay close to the individual figures who could make their new rights felt. Harper's Weekly, *February 21, 1863, p. 116. North Carolina Collection, The University of North Carolina at Chapel Hill.*

In a common inversion, slaves defined the freedom they sought from the Union as the antithesis to the slavery they experienced under their masters, but the independence they celebrated could be communal or familial, not just personal. If the "yoke of oppression" under slavery was a denial of family formation, property ownership, bodily autonomy, adequate living conditions, choice over work conditions, and liberty of movement, then freedom would be in part the right to build families, protect their persons, choose their work, travel where they liked, and live in a manner comparable to whites. William Henry Singleton, a twenty-five-year-old slave near New Bern at the beginning of the war, understood slavery as a refusal of his basic humanity. "It was believed I had no soul," he wrote. "I had no rights that anybody was bound to respect. For in the eyes of the law I was but a thing. I was bought and sold. I was whipped." Like many ex-slaves, Singleton particularly denounced the destruction of families through sales. "[At age four] I had been sold off the plantation away from my mother and brothers with as little formality as they would have sold a calf or a mule," Singleton wrote. "Such breaking up of families and parting of children from their parents was quite common in slavery days and was one of the things that caused much bitterness among the slaves and much suffering."[13]

Beginning in 1858, Singleton began to connect his individual acts to a broader political context. That year, he heard a rumor that his master's wife told a group of slaves on her deathbed that "the time will come when you will all be free. The North is not satisfied with slavery." From then on, Singleton and his fellow slaves talked frequently about Lincoln (who was, his master said, "a bad man and that he had horns"), Wendell Phillips, and William Lloyd Garrison. "We only knew, of course, what we were told. . . . So we learned little about the outside world." But they knew enough to doubt their masters when they "kept talking against the North." When a local free man of color prayed in church that "Ethiopia should stretch forth her arm like an army with banners," Singleton's master and other owners whipped him severely and fired the church's white minister. By watching his master, Singleton learned to attach the cause of freedom to the Civil War before some Union leaders or soldiers did. When a young neighbor withdrew from West Point and "commenced to organize" soldiers, Singleton volunteered to be his servant because he "wanted to learn how to drill." A year later, Singleton was with a Confederate unit at New Bern when General Burnside's men attacked, and he took advantage of the disorder to flee to Burnside's headquarters.[14]

The very family that slaves sought to defend could also limit slaves' pursuit of freedom. In coastal Chowan County, twenty-three-year-old Allen Parker, "in common with all the Negroes," had "imbibed a very strong yearning for freedom," but he did not wish to leave his sick mother. On her deathbed, she told her family that she believed freedom was coming. "Although our masters tried to keep all matters relating to the war from their slaves, the slaves managed to get hold of a good deal of news, and the idea was fast gaining ground, that in some way they were soon to be free," Parker wrote. After his mother died, Parker fled the plantation. His first move was to the surrounding woods, a middle ground of territory where slaves frequently disappeared for temporary, or sometimes permanent, escape from their masters. For a week, Parker hid in the daytime and spent evenings with a poor white woman, then turned himself in and was beaten with a cowhide. The next spring, when Yankee boats appeared on nearby rivers, slave owners cracked down by increasing patrols and sending some slaves to Richmond for safekeeping. Parker and other slaves organized together to find a way to escape. "Those of us that were left on the plantation, felt more and more restless," Parker wrote. "We did manage to get away quite often and many conferences were held, in which the doings of the 'Yankees' were talked over, and ideas in relation to freedom exchanged by the slaves." Finally, in August 1862, after hearing of the escape of slaves from "the neighboring plantation," Parker and some of his fellows sailed out to a Yankee gunboat on the Chowan River.[15]

It was often easier to make of their masters enemies than to understand the Yankees as friends. Even as slaves critiqued their owners, many were skeptical of the Union. This was especially true in their first encounters with the Union troops, a process that began in 1862 in the coastal portions of the state but did not occur until 1865 in the central and western regions. In the inland piedmont, Elias Thomas remembered, "the white folks had told me the Yankees would kill me or carry me off, so I thought when I saw them coming it was the last of me. I hid in the woods while they were there." For Mary Barbour in the foothills of the Smoky Mountains, "We wuz skeered of de Yankees ter start wid, but de more we thinks 'bout us runnin' way from our marsters de skeerder we gits o' de Rebs." After her father decided to "jine de Yankees," the entire family fled, eventually landing in the camps near New Bern, almost three hundred miles away. When Dilly Yellady's mother saw the Union soldiers, she and her friend "just went flyin'. When dey crossed a creek my mother lost her shoe in de mud, but she just kept runnin'." At her house, she relayed the news that the Yankees were "ridin' up de railroad just as thick as flies," and her grandmother dismissed her fear, telling her, "Well, I has been prayin' long enough for 'em now dey is here." Squire Dowd's shift in feelings toward the North was not a revelation but a process. At first he "did not like the Yankees" and was "afraid of them. We had to be educated to love the Yankees, and to know that they freed us and were our friends."[16]

The moments of first contact between slaves and Union soldiers often produced intense scenes of both joy and hunger. Here, Union officers witnessed the excitement and the dire need that drove slaves toward Yankee lines. As slaves staggered under "huge bundles of bedding and clothing," they were "usually both hungry and tired from their oftentimes long journeys and fastings." Along with protection, one of the first gifts a soldier could offer was "food and hot coffee, which they seemingly relished highly." In this moment, slaves and Union soldiers experienced freedom as high ideals and practical wants, a moment of both independence and intense need.[17]

Ongoing contact with Yankees educated slaves toward broader expectations of freedom and of friendship, especially the hope that they would

Squire Dowd, shown here in a picture taken in the 1930s when he was eighty-two, was a young slave in Moore County during the war and remembered the slow process by which slaves learned to make sense of the new force of the Union army. "We were afraid of them," he recalled. "We had to be educated to love the Yankees, and to know that they freed us and were our friends. I feel that Abraham Lincoln was like a father to us" (Rawick, American Slave, *11 [1] 268). Library of Congress, American Memory, LC-DIG-mesnp-111263a.*

achieve not just legal emancipation but a sense of economic security. In rumors passed along by soldiers and in the land allocation at camps like Roanoke Island and Trent River, many ex-slaves attached their freedom to rural people's common dreams of a farm of their own. In Clayton, about eighty-five miles northwest of New Bern, a soldier told Caroline Richardson and her parents "dat dey'd git some land an' a mule iffen dey wus freed." In coastal Enfield, John Hunter's family expected to "get a home" when they were "freed. . . . They said that the President and the Governor was going to give land to the niggers — going to take it off the owners that they worked for. But they never did get it." When Union troops occupied the Wake County plantation where Tanner Spikes lived, Spikes recalled, he and his fellow slaves "ain't knowed nothin' 'bout freedom," but the Yankees told them that freedom meant not just liberty but sustenance and that they "ort ter have meat an' stuff in de smokehouse."[18]

Slaves learned the transitory nature of Union soldiers' friendship when troops marched on and left them behind. Instead of a permanent occupation, Union power outside of the coastal band was fleeting, and so too seemed the newfound freedom slaves experienced in the presence of Union soldiers. This sense that freedom marched away with slaves' powerful friends was a precursor to the panic over Lincoln's assassination in 1865, a reminder that their rights were not abstract but embodied in particular patrons. In the sand hills of south central Harnett County, Ambrose Douglass recalled, "I guess we musta celebrated 'mancipation about twelve times. . . . Every time a bunch of No'thern sojers would come through they would tell us we was free and we'd begin celerbatin'. Before we would get through somebody else would tell us to go back to work, and we would go." As troops left, slaves feared their masters would reassert power, so "lots of the slaves went with them."[19]

When slaves followed the Union lines, they frequently ended up at one of the camps and colonies on the state's eastern coast, where they learned new lessons about friendship, rights, and freedom. The first large-scale camp was opened in February 1862 at Roanoke Island near North Carolina's Outer Banks. As at Fortress Monroe, slaves interpreted the Union's invasion as proof of friendship even before General Burnside and the victorious Union officers laid their plans. Soon, according to Vincent Colyer, the Superintendent of the Poor and future notable painter of the American West, a "party of fifteen or twenty of these loyal blacks, men, women and children, arrived on a 'Dingy,' " from "up the Chowan River," where, "as they were passing they had been shot at by their rebel masters." The "calm trustful faith with which these poor people came over from the enemy, to our shores; the unbounded joy which they manifested when they found themselves within our lines, and *Free*; made an impression on" Colyer. Many officers "gathered around the tent to hear them sing the hymn, 'The precious Lamb, Christ Jesus, was crucified for me.'" While slaves treated the Union arrival as a promise of emancipation, white Carolinians were convinced they witnessed a revolution, and some believed the Union troops would "massacre the inhabitants generally." Union occupation was not nearly so revolutionary, at least at first. Burnside ordered his men to follow the "laws of civilized warfare" and avoid damaging property. When Burnside's men offered white residents a loyalty oath, many took it and went back to fishing. Meanwhile, slaves from the mainland arrived in larger and larger numbers, 100 within the first month, and 250 by early April, spurred by rumors that they would soon be free. Over the next several years, the Union transformed Roanoke Island into a large, semipermanent "colony" for ex-slaves. By "giving them land, and implements," Union officials at the Roanoke colony hoped to lay "the foundations of new empire," the basis for a "NEW SOCIAL ORDER IN THE SOUTH."[20]

The next month, Burnside's men took the large town of New Bern and created what was originally meant to be a temporary camp but became a massive settlement of slaves who ran from tidewater plantations. Immediately, two slaves hiding in the swamps rushed to Burnside's men, believing them to be deliverers of freedom. To Burnside, this looked less like republican independence than like anarchy. "*Nine tenth* of the depredations" at New Bern, he reported, "were committed by the negroes. . . . They seemed to be wild with excitement and delight — they are now a source of very great anxiety to us; the city is being overrun with fugitives." Burnside had no illusions that he could keep slaves out. "It would be utterly impossible" since "they find their way to us through woods & swamps," but he hoped to reach a "Definite policy to govern them." Dealing with the great need among the ex-slaves raised Burnside's fears that he was creating a permanent dependence upon government. Although Burnside issued "provision to the poor," his generosity must have puzzled slaves, for he defined the poor to include ex-Confederates who were recently "in affluent circumstances, but who now have nothing but confederate notes . . . and negroes who refuse to acknowledge any debt of servitude." Shortly after the occupation, the quartermaster general informed an officer in New Bern that the six hundred contrabands there who were "dependent upon the Army for a support" should be denied their requests for aid and only be rewarded for "public work, not for charity."[21]

This conflict over food rations in New Bern established a precedent that shaped many ex-slave/Union encounters during the war. By the spring of

After the Union occupation of much of North Carolina's eastern seaboard in early 1862, ex-slaves flocked to the contraband camp on Roanoke Island and the distribution center in New Bern. Pictured here, needy ex-slaves line up in front of the office of the Superintendent of the Poor, Vincent Colyer, hoping for food and other supplies. These interactions fostered the politics of dependence that Colyer feared. Frank Leslie's Illustrated Newspaper, *June 14, 1862, p. 164. North Carolina Collection, The University of North Carolina at Chapel Hill.*

1862, Burnside turned the oversight of ten thousand African Americans to a man with a similarly close grip on rations. Vincent Colyer, the first Superintendent of the Poor, was a Quaker who originally traveled south with the United States Christian Commission. Colyer intended to train ex-slaves into a workforce that would bolster Union efforts and elicit sympathy from Northerners. This intention often made Colyer a strong defender of the ex-slaves and occasionally a bitter scourge. To prove that ex-slaves were "not a Burthen," Colyer resorted to measures that looked to some ex-slaves like cruelty. In his three months at New Bern, Colyer distributed sixteen times as much food to poor whites as to ex-slaves, despite the fact that there were more than four times as many ex-slaves as whites under his control. While he dispersed 76 ½ barrels of flour and 116 barrels of beef to 1,800 whites, he gave only 19 barrels of flour and 4 ½ barrels of beef to 7,500 ex-slaves, two-thirds of whom were women and children. The generosity for whites helped Colyer win support from potentially loyal white North Carolinians and also let Colyer celebrate the fortitude and independence of the ex-slaves, who, as Colyer put it, "never became vagrants or objects of charity on our hands."

Colyer bragged that he, unlike superintendents in other states, never made an appeal for donations of money or books or clothing because his ex-slaves were not "paupers." Although Colyer recognized that the ex-slaves depended upon the government for an initial "place of refuge . . . on their first arrival within our camps," this support should be merely a temporary measure "to be abandoned, if possible, when the war is over." Colyer's commitment to training would endure, as he later served on missions to bring "civilizers" to natives in the West and Alaska, where he lobbied for education and the "Reservation system."[22]

Union policy in 1862 was driven by conflicting impulses to befriend both ex-slaves and loyal white Southerners. Eventually, the contradictions between these goals would force Lincoln to choose freedom over loyalists, but through 1862, slaves had good reason to watch the portents with grave concern. For part of the year, Lincoln and his advisers saw North Carolina, like other Upper South states, as a potential site for a Unionist awakening. By feeding white Southerners and working in their interests, Northern officers pursued a strategy of pacification. In North Carolina this fight over friendship came to a head in a confrontation between Colyer and the state's military governor in New Bern, Edward Stanly. At first Stanly appeared to be an ideal candidate to help Union forces gain allies in North Carolina. After terms as a congressman, Speaker of the state legislature, and attorney general, Stanly had left North Carolina for California in the 1850s and ran for office there as a Republican. Once Stanly was back in power in New Bern, however, his efforts to build up support from white North Carolinians came at the expense of slaves. To convince skeptical Southerners that the Union was not fomenting a "servile war," Stanly forbade exhortatory speeches, enforced antebellum laws on slave control, and closed schools for freedpeople. Along with securing Southern loyalty, Stanly also promised to save the North the "enormous" expense of caring for thousands of slaves by returning them to their masters. Ex-slaves in the camp around New Bern soon fled to the swamps in a "perfect panic" that they were to be "sent back to their old homes." Outraged, Colyer traveled to Washington, D.C., and, with the help of Senator Charles Sumner, protested directly to Abraham Lincoln. Lincoln supported Colyer, telling him, "I have always maintained, and shall insist on, that no slave who once comes within our lines a fugitive from a rebel, shall ever be returned to his master." Afterward Sumner told Colyer, "You have seen more of the real character of the President, and have heard a more important declaration than is usually seen or heard in a hundred ordinary interviews." When Colyer returned to North Carolina, he reopened the schools and forced Stanly to rescind his orders; the next year Stanly resigned in the wake of African American enlistment in the army. Stanly's efforts, however, taught ex-slaves in the area important lessons. Freedpeople in New Bern had reason to suspect they had entered a confusing world of competing power sources, not a world of perfect freedom. When seeking to defend one's rights, it made a great deal of difference whether one ran to a slave-catcher like Stanly or a sympathizer like Colyer.[23]

Over the course of 1862, the steady flow of ex-slaves into camps, their enthusiasm for serving in the military, the North's intense need for soldiers, and the enduring antagonism of many Southern whites turned the Union into a friend to the ex-slaves. None of this happened as quickly as some allies wanted. From the moment William Henry Singleton ran to Burnside's lines in spring 1862, he believed he would end up fighting for the Union. First, however, Singleton had to convince the soldiers that he was not a spy. Even a full year into the war, many Yankee troops were skeptical of ex-slaves' loyalty. After Singleton proved his worth by passing along information, he joined their attack on his old company as a scout but was not allowed to carry a weapon. Following the battle, a Union colonel swore, "We will never take niggers in the army to fight." But Singleton answered, "The war will not be over until I have had a chance to spill my blood." Over the next year, Singleton lobbied General Burnside and then Lincoln himself, promising the president he had a thousand men ready to fight "to free our race." Lincoln deferred Singleton's request but praised his courage, telling him that "there may be a chance for you." Well before the Emancipation Proclamation, abolitionist Massachusetts governor John A. Andrew pressed the army to enlist former slaves from occupied North Carolina and Virginia so that they might shore up the defense of Fortress Monroe and begin the "education of their manhood" in the defense of their rights. Andrew's early appeals floundered on opposition from North Carolina Unionists and some military officers like General John Foster. Although the black men whom Foster armed during attacks on the North Carolina towns of Elizabeth City and Washington "did their duty well enough," he "found they could not be trusted . . . probably owing to their lack of discipline." Foster was especially critical of black men who preferred to "live with their families" rather than with the soldiers, and some unsympathetic white officers saw the push to enlistment as simply another effort to get rations from the government.[24]

By early 1863, Abraham Lincoln's Emancipation Proclamation and a Confederate counterattack in North Carolina created new openings for North Carolina–based African American units. In April 1863, the secretary of war authorized what eventually became four brigades of African American North Carolinians under the command of Brigadier General Edward A. Wild. Soon nearly "every able bodied man" in the area served in the army, as either a soldier or a civilian employee. In May 1863, Corporal Zenas T. Haines of the 44th Massachusetts wrote, "Quite a recruiting fever has seized the freedmen of Newbern. . . . There is, perhaps, not a slave in North Carolina who does not know that he may find freedom in Newbern, and thus Newbern may be the Mecca of a thousand noble aspirations." Despite this widespread enthusiasm, the number of black soldiers remained relatively small due to Confederate control over the interior of the state and slave owners' success at refugeeing their slaves away from the front lines. During the war, approximately 6,000 black North Carolinians served in the army, a tiny fraction of the total number of nearly 180,000 black soldiers, and an additional 1,500 African Americans worked for the Quartermaster's Department in New Bern.[25]

In his orders encouraging the recruitment of ex-slaves, General Benjamin Butler articulated a stark view of freedom as independence: "Political freedom rightly defined is liberty to work . . . and no one with ability to work shall enjoy the fruits of another's labor: Therefore, no subsistence will be permitted to any negro or his family with whom he lives, who is able to work and does not work." Butler had a nuanced view of independence, one that could simultaneously penalize and defend freedpeople. Butler recognized that military enlistment posed significant questions about the "new rights" and "new obligations" of the freedpeople, and the complexity of the "claims their ignorance and the helplessness of their women and children, make upon each of us." Although Butler did not mean to see the army transformed into a charity, he fought against unfair treatment. African American soldiers, he noted, had "none of the machinery of 'State aid' for the support of their families while fighting our battles, so liberally provided for the white soldiers." To create some balance, Butler ordered a bounty of ten dollars to every "able bodied colored man who shall enlist and be mustered into the service of the United States," and "suitable subsistence" to "the family of each colored soldier so enlisted and mustered so long as he shall remain in the service and behave well." Butler also lobbied to equalize pay for black and white soldiers.[26]

Once enlisted, freedpeople found themselves with new friends they could turn to for protection and new ways of organizing to take advantages of their opportunities. When sixty troops from a North Carolina black regiment reported to a New York regiment at Folly Island, South Carolina, they were sent to pitch tents for the New Yorkers. Instead of submitting, they banded together to use their access to their commander and their commander's access to the officers above him to demand better treatment. "They have been slaves and are just learning to be men," their commander fumed. "It is a draw-back that they are regarded as, and called 'd——d Niggers' by so-called 'gentleman' in uniform of U.S. Officers, but when they are set to menial work doing for white regiments what those Regiments are entitled to do for themselves, it simply throws them back where they were before and reduces them to the position of slaves again." Brigadier General Wild, commander of the North Carolina Colored Volunteers, asked headquarters to eliminate "*all* such abuses," and a few days later, the commander of the Department of the South agreed. Other black soldiers used their access in more personal ways. Elijah Ives begged a Union colonel to investigate the poor treatment of African American volunteers left without clothing, shoes, or adequate medical facilities. "We thaught the Yankees to be our friends but we are nothing but A subgated people," Ives wrote. Over the course of his letter, Ives transformed his overall critique into a plea for a specific, individual favor, a half gallon of whiskey that he could use to care for his sick wife. Many black soldiers petitioned for furloughs and other rights granted to white soldiers. One soldier wrote all the way to the secretary of war, begging, "Please Pardon Mee for taking the liberty of Writing to you Without your permissions thoe i done it simpley th reason that i know that you had the Honnor of Holding the Most responsible Positions."[27]

As the Union army swelled with African American recruits, officers launched destabilizing raids into Confederate-controlled northeastern North Carolina. In a nineteen-day campaign in December of 1863, General Wild and 1,700 African American troops worked to "clear the country of slaves." During the raid, former slaves seized supplies from white masters, delivered the news of freedom, and drove off guerrillas. The most striking reversal of power probably occurred on May 10, 1864, when a "cruel Slave Master" named William H. Clopton was carried in by forces reporting to Brigadier General Wild, who reported, "I found half a dozen *women* among our refugees, whom he had often whipped unmercifully, even baring their whole persons for the purpose in presence of *Whites* and *Blacks*. I laid him bare and putting the whip into the hands of the Women, three of Whom took turns in settling some old scores on their masters back. A black Man, whom he had abused finished the administration of Poetical justice, and even in this scene the superior humanity of the Blacks over their white master was manifest in their moderation." The next month, a court-martial found that Wild broke army regulations by allowing the women the use of the whip, but Butler reversed the decision.[28]

Those raids into eastern Carolina also created new problems for the camp on Roanoke Island. Earlier in 1863, Union superintendent Horace James worked to make Roanoke Island an ideal colony for soldiers' dependents, where the government could "teach them, in their ignorance, how to live and support themselves" by "giving them land" and "making them proprietors of the soil." After laying out wide avenues, James apportioned acre plots to families for their own farming. The freedpeople and Northern missionaries established schools to teach reading, writing, and sewing, and students flocked eagerly to the classes. "Light has been flashed for the first time into hundreds of benighted minds, with an effect as electric, as inspiring, as beautiful, as when the Divine Spirit moved upon the formless void, and said, ' "Let there be light, and there was light,' " Horace James wrote. In an appeal for Northern support, James asked, "Let us fight with our right hand, and civilize with our left."[29]

The 1863 raids disrupted James's plans as Union excursions drove more than a thousand new contrabands to Roanoke Island, increasing the population by 50 percent in a short time. As the island's population exceeded three thousand, the colony's supplies were overwhelmed. "Those who are escaping from bondage are pressing in all directions," wrote Horace James's cousin Elizabeth James, a missionary on the island. "From one to two hundred arrive every few days, and it is a matter of no small moment to know where to shelter them. . . . There are many who escape literally 'with the skin of their teeth.' " Many lived in groups of up to ten people, cramped in brush and earth huts or under pine boughs. "Should not the government provide at least a temporary shelter for the crowds which come?" she asked. "Scenes of suffering are witnessed there which baffle description. . . . There are *hundreds* here ready to perish for lack of clothing, to-night." In December, after the arrival of boatloads of former slaves, Elizabeth James reported, "I see sights, *often, often,* that make my heart ache, & which I have no power to relieve." In the spring of 1864, Confederates counterattacked and regained control over the Roanoke River town of Plymouth. Hundreds of "forlorn, sad, and sick looking" freedpeople fled in a panic from the town to Roanoke Island. Rumors circulated that those left behind in Plymouth had been "cruelly murdered" or "sent back to their former masters." Those who arrived in Roanoke found poverty and confusion. By the spring of 1864, two-thirds of the island residents lived on government rations. "The destitution" was "truly frightful on the island," another missionary wrote. "Here are 3,000 bodies nearly naked, nine-tenths of them are women and children."[30]

The overwhelming need of the freedpeople created a dilemma for Horace James, the superintendent for much of the war. A Massachusetts minister from an old Puritan family, James preached against slavery from at least the 1840s, reminding his congregation of Psalm 82's injunction to "Defend the poor and fatherless; do justice to the afflicted and needy. Deliver the poor and needy; rid them out of the hand of the wicked." For James, this assistance was always meant to be temporary, delivering the poor not to a better condition but from the momentary "hand of the wicked" that kept them from exercising their independence. In his approach to the freedpeople, therefore, James was often simultaneously sympathetic and cold, eager to relieve them of their problems and to put them to work. Like Colyer, James cut off rations as quickly as he could. Also like Colyer, he used his reports to the North to celebrate the freedpeople's work ethic by comparing them favorably to the lazy and "helpless" white Southerners "totally unable to rally from the depression of spirits consequent upon their sudden change of life and their great deprivations" and "dependent upon charity." While ex-slaves built their own houses, whites had to live in the soldiers' barracks. Freedpeople worked with alacrity, "happy as larks in their toil," but white Southerners "know nothing" of labor's "processes, and are therefore incapable of self-support." Ex-slaves intensely desired private property "and ask nothing more than a decent chance to make themselves wholly independent of government aid, and be thrifty, wealthy citizens." James ascribed freedpeople's superiority to the power of labor, which "is honorable, and tends to independence." Despite his coldness and his own paternalistic racism, James could be a valuable ally to the ex-slaves. When the Union government was slow to pay its ex-slave workers, James defended them vigorously, even articulating a theory of unavoidable dependence caused by Union malfeasance. "The colored population of the island would have been much less dependent upon the Government, if the Government had more fully met its engagements with them," he wrote to a superior.[31]

The intense "suffering" on Roanoke Island and James's stinginess with rations created a politics of pleading for the freedpeople on the island. With Horace James busy at the other overwhelmed camps near New Bern, the responsibility for these pleas fell upon his cousin Elizabeth. When she received shoes or clothes, Elizabeth reported, "a crowd presses sometimes from before sunrise until nine at night, to buy, to beg, or to look on, & it exhausts my strength." When she rode on her horse, "they cluster about me." What the freedpeople needed was "friendly eyes to look after them, and friendly hands to aid." In response, Elizabeth James would talk "to them a little, and tell them what they must do, and what not to do." "My decisions," she wrote, "are not only gratefully received, but blessings from every side are showered upon me." Even as they "take severe colds from lack of *shoes* and stockings," freedpeople's very suffering made them "grateful for what has been done," Elizabeth James wrote in April 1864. Slaves are "aware *now* that the North *care* for them; that the 'Yankees' are indeed their friends, notwithstanding Southern teaching to the contrary, and they are *astonished* at what is sent." Under the burden of all these demands, and the nightmare of watching babies die from exposure, Elizabeth James turned toward her own forms of petition: "There is only one thing I *can* do that relieves my heart, and that is, what the disciplines of John the Baptist did, when their master was beheaded: they *went and told Jesus*. I do the best I can; then go to him and leave my burden there." Over the summer, as supplies thinned, and as shortages at New Bern limited Horace James's ability to help the islanders, some of the missionaries adopted a combination of fatalism and divine patronalism that mirrored the freedpeople's. After an empty boat arrived, missionary Sarah Freeman despaired that she could "not now even encourage the people to hope" for help from the North. "All I can do is to encourage them to hope in God." That day, a mother of five burst into tears, saying, "Honey, I is trusted and prayed since I was here to see you, and it seems like as God would never hear me, but dat my poor children must freeze this winter any way." Freeman could not say anything to the woman, but wrote subsequently, "Will not some of the benevolent at the North help us?" Other missionaries gave up on human aid and prayed that " 'Elijah's God' will send us food."[32]

Elsewhere across the state, experiences with independence were even more complex. While Roanoke Island remained safely in Union hands, some other parts of North Carolina were what Horace James called "debatable territory" or what General Wild called "neutral ground." There, freedom shifted like the sands, "on account of rebel raids and the incursions of guerillas." Many of these debatable territories lay outside of New Bern. The troubles began with one of the most exciting experiments of the war, a fulfillment of the much-wished-for dream of land. In May 1863, Treasury Department agent David Heaton seized a wide swath of abandoned lands for the federal government, permitted freedpeople to remain on plantations vacated by their masters, and leased out cotton farms and turpentine forests to one hundred North Carolinians. Soon, more than twelve hundred black people worked as renters or wage hands, supporting nearly another four thousand with their earnings. To Heaton and Horace James the experiment was a success. It "teaches the liberated slave, self reliance, and invests him at once with the responsibility of the support of himself and family, over any eleemosynary scheme which seems to regard him as a child or a pauper, and is too apt to encourage in him the old habit of dependence begotten in Slavery." Horace James proclaimed it proof that the "negro question" had been resolved: "Make them lords of the land, and everything else will naturally follow."[33]

The ex-slaves' very independence, however, also made them vulnerable. The "danger of guerilla raids has restricted the field in which this experiment could be tried, to a very limited area," Heaton complained. When Confederates attacked New Bern in February 1864, Union commanders pulled their troops from the outlying posts to defend the town. Freedpeople on settlements found themselves on an undefended space between the Union and Confederate lines. "Every man, woman, and child from these camps came rushing wildly into town, struck with fear, and feeling as keen a sense of danger as if they had been actually returned by force to their old masters," James wrote. "And why should they not?" James moved many of them across the Trent River into settlements that swelled to more than five thousand residents, only one-quarter of whom were supplied with rations. To Heaton the problem could only be resolved by sending ten thousand more troops to exert control over the land. Although Heaton lobbied for reinforcements, the soldiers and rations were needed elsewhere.[34]

Faced with distant, unresponsive, or ineffective local commanders, freedpeople learned both to organize for protection and to call for help from their superiors. In September 1864, forty-five freedmen from Roanoke Island looked to the ranks above their immediate officers in hopes of finding a friend in General Benjamin Butler. These men had been impressed from Roanoke Island in a grim, brutal way, "marched on board a steamer, at the point of a bayonet," while sick men were rousted "out of bed" and "men that had large familys of children and no wife or person to cut wood for them or take care of them" were also swept up, all sent to work on the Bermuda Hundred canal in Virginia. The men protested not the obligation to serve but the way their service was commandeered. If asked, the petitioners argued, "a large number would have gone without causeing the suffering that has been caused, we are willing to where our labour is wanted and we are ready at any time to do all we can for the goverment at any place and feel it our duty to help the goverment all we can." Blaming their mistreatment on bad local officers, the freedmen, perhaps optimistically, assumed that higher powers intended to protect them but simply "dont know the treatment we receive from Sup's of contrabands." They had not been paid in more than six months, and their families suffered. "No one knows the injustice practiced on the negro's at Roanoke," they wrote. "Our garden's are plundere'd by the white soldiers, what we raise to surport ourselves with is stolen from us, and I we say any thing about it we are sent to the guard house. . . . Its no uncommon thing to see weman and children crying for something to eat." In their petition they constructed Butler as a distant, well-meaning authority betrayed by inattentive underlings like James and malicious or corrupt ones like James's subordinates.[35]

Over time, freedpeople learned how to press their claims in broader fashion, extending their complaints to almost every aspect of their treatment. By January 1865, more than seventeen thousand black North Carolinians, not including the Union soldiers, worked for the federal government as military laborers, residents of one of the contraband camps, or agricultural employees on government-managed plantations. It was no surprise therefore that freedpeople's imaginations and hopes and frustrations were centered upon the federal government. Experience with the Union trained them not away from a politics of dependence but toward an assertive organization that helped them make effective claims of dependence upon distant officers. In March 1865, a black Roanoke Island schoolteacher named Richard Boyle gathered together a group of petitions to President Lincoln, who, Boyle commented, was "the last resort and only help we have got, feeling that we are entily friendless." Without Lincoln's help, they would be "stamp down or trodden under feet by our Superintendent." Signed "Roanoke Island," the petitions attempted to speak for "We Colored men of this Island" about "our present conditions and our rights."[36]

Freedpeople described their dependence not as their preference but as a choice they fell back upon after Union army actions prevented them from living independently. In this way, they advanced a politics of dependence rooted in wartime experiences with government. "We cant doe any thing with in our Selves So we Concluded the best thing we could do was to apply to you or Some of your cabinets," Boyle wrote. The petitioners understood that they had new rights, but they could not understand how to make those rights felt. "We want to know where our wrights is or are we to be Stamp down or trodden under feet by our Superintendent which he is the very man that we look to for assistants." While they accepted James's decision to cut off rations for able-bodied men, they protested vigorously against the government's failure to pay their salaries. "The next thing [James] said that he wanted us to work and get our living as White men and not apply to the Government and that is vry thing we want to doe, but after we do this we cant satisfie him," Boyle wrote. "Soon as he Sees we are trying to Support our Selves without the aid of the Government he comes and make a Call for the men . . . and if we are not willing to Goe he orders the Guards to take us by the point of the bayonet, and we have no power to help it."[37]

Without control of their own lives, they wondered how they could possibly escape a state of dependence. The government seemed to view their independence solely as an excuse to cut off support. They were not willing to be "haul a bout" by those who "treated us mean and our owners ever did they taken us just like we had been dum beast," Boyle asserted. They had "work faithful Since we have been on the Island" and built their own houses and cultivated their own ground "and have Tried to be less exspence to the Government as we Possible Could be." Their "head men have done every thing to us that our masters have done except by and Sell us and now they are Trying to Starve the woman & children to death." Although James "has promise to do Better," instead "of doing better he has done worst." In their desperation, their appeals quickly shifted toward assertions of loyalty and need: "We don't exspect to have the same wrights as white men doe we know that are in a military country and we exspect to obey the rules and orders of our authories and doe as they say doe, an thing in reason we thank God and thank our President all of his aids for what has been done for us but we are not satisfied with our Supertendent."[38]

In response, the Freedmen's Bureau referred the complaints back to Horace James, who answered with an unsurprising lack of sympathy, calling the charges "gross exaggerations." James critiqued the freedpeople as unworthy dependents. "It amounts just to this," he wrote to the Freedmen's Bureau. "The colored people who have been within our lines three years or more have been so long receiving aid from the government, as to count it their *right* to receive it, even when in many cases they might support themselves. . . . The truth is *they have had too much* given them." Instead of assisting the freedpeople, the government should put *"two thirds of its people upon plantations on the main land."* James considered Boyle and the other freedpeople "worthy of pity rather than of blame. . . . I look upon him, and others like him, as persons to be treated like children, who do not know when they are well used, and whose complaints should influence us but a little, while we do for them that which we know will promote their best good." By reaching above James to a Lincoln they presumed was sympathetic, freedpeople tried to find a distant power that could come to their aid. Instead they found more layers of unsympathetic bureaucrats. Eliphalet Whittlesey, state Freedmen's Bureau assistant commissioner, forwarded James's report with approval. "The Govt. has done and is now doing *too much* for that Colony," he wrote. In order to destroy "idleness," Whittlesey ordered the elimination of "gratuitous support." Later, when a black sergeant complained that freedpeople were dying for lack of medical care during a smallpox outbreak near New Bern, James's surgeon-in-chief attributed their deaths to their own reliance upon the government. "If perfectly well people are too lazy to cook the food *given* to them, I think they ought to go hungry," he wrote.[39]

These crises of dependence were exacerbated near the end of the war as General William Tecumseh Sherman turned north from South Carolina into North Carolina, and freedpeople followed in an enormous "dark tide" behind him. Ten thousand filled Wilmington, and five thousand landed in or near New Bern. Horace James found them "pitiable," "footsore and weary, ragged and dusty from travel . . . some of them emaciated and already marked as victims of death, afflicted with hoarse hollow coughs, with measles with malarial chills." Even James thought "it seemed like anything but a land of promise into which they had come." Again, they found their experience with Union power sharply mixed. Soldiers in the army, whom they looked to "with all confidence" as deliverers, treated them "not infrequently" with "rudeness and cruelty." Fearful of any kind of dependency, James expelled thousands of people from James City at the end of the war. Instead of independence, turning out these destitute people created new forms of dependence in the countryside as white landowners forced them into exploitative labor contracts. By 1867, James City, begun as an experiment in freedom, would be one of the most miserable spots in the South, home to several hundred starving, desperate people, left friendless and alone.[40]

After the Confederate surrender, conditions worsened on Roanoke Island. Horace James stopped giving rations to soldiers' families, a move one missionary called "heart sickening," as the commandant's doors were "besieged by starving helpless women and children." In June 1865, the Assistant Superintendent of Negro Affairs and several missionary teachers petitioned Freedmen's Bureau commissioner General Oliver O. Howard to alleviate the "suffering humanity which it is not within our power to relieve" on the island. Because "those whose duty it is to attend to, and remedy" these problems "disregarded" them, they appealed "to a Source more remote and out of the ordinary channel." Like the freedpeople, they blamed dependence on social, not moral, problems. Those able to work "have proved themselves industrious and would support themselves, had they the opportunity to do so," and there "are not many families on the island that have not furnished a father, husband or son" to the army. Nevertheless the government cut off rations to about twelve hundred of the twenty-seven hundred people who previously received them. These Northern petitioners acknowledged that "it is not the design of the government to support those who will not work, in idleness, nor is it the wish of those who make this representations as this would [be] an evil not Second to slavery itself." However, the "scores of women and children crying for bread, whose husbands, Sons and fathers are in the army today" created an obligation on the government to "prevent suffering" for the "infirm and the helpless," which "justice, humanity, and every principle of christianity forbids." Instead of choosing between independence and an immoral dependence, freedpeople had to either seek assistance from the Union or return "to their former masters to be supported and cared for by them." The freedpeople on the island "must have clothing and food," a teacher wrote. "Where the latter will come from after the *rations* are cut off, I do not dare to ask myself, and were it not that we *know* God can overrule all things for good, and will, in his own time and way succor the suffering and supply the needy, I should often yield to despairing thoughts that arise." Another missionary proclaimed that the scenes of "fearful" destitution in the winter of 1865–66 "so stir me at times, that I can only cry: 'Lord, help! or we perish!' "[41]

To explain the dangers and possibilities of this new world, some ex-slaves invented fantasies about Abraham Lincoln, even as they simultaneously organized into bands for self-protection. Drawing upon the incorporation of power in masters, some slaves imagined in Lincoln a stronger, more responsive master who would listen to their appeals. Lincoln's distance was also an explanation for the failure of their pleas; like many leaders, Lincoln could be distracted by other duties or betrayed by ill-intentioned subordinates. The perplexing variance in Union support therefore reflected the inconsistent access they had to their presumed champion. Rather than naive monarchism, such interpretations drew upon a somewhat sophisticated understanding of the power dynamics around them; being freed to become autonomous and unprotected individuals might be a dubious gift in a world that remained intensely violent and hierarchical. This was the type of negative freedom ex-slave Dilly Yellady recalled when she complained, "Yes, de Yankees freed us but dey lef' nuthin' for us to live on." Patsy Mitchner was even more critical, calling freedom a process where slaves "wus turned out wid nowhere to go an' nothin' to live on. . . . Slavery wus a bad thing an' freedom, of de kin' we got wid nothin' to live on wus bad. Two snakes full of pisen. . . . Both bit de nigger, an' dey wus both bad." By embracing Lincoln's distant mastery, these slaves did not reject freedom; they followed a path that seemed most likely to deliver a freedom they could survive.[42]

Freedpeople's fantasies about Lincoln grew from their religious practices; as much as a good king, Lincoln was a modern Moses. "They almost adore the persons who have brought them deliverance," Horace James wrote. Charles Jones, a former slave who enlisted in 1862 in New Bern, explained his freedom in intensely personal terms. "In 1861 the manspation had not taken place but I was in the protection By the youion Troops an Sat free by Presadence Lincon at the manspation." Jones's deeply personal affiliation with Lincoln was closely intertwined with the other authority he turned to, "My Lord and Savor Jesus Christ . . . who knows all Things and Shall Judge the world at the Last day." In stories told long after the war, Hannah Crasson called Lincoln "the Medicine man with grip in his han', cause he said every borned man must be free." Lincoln's powers were tied closely to God's. Tellingly, Crasson called God "the Great Marster dat got into Lincoln and the Yankees." The term "master" (transcribed by Crasson's interviewer as "Marster") presents some of the same difficulties as "condescend" or "patronize," words that ring more negatively in modern ears than they did at the time. Sometimes the biblical word "master" referred only to Christ as teacher, but at other times psalmists sang of lifting their eyes to the Lord "as the eyes of servants look unto the hands of their masters" in hopes that he would "have mercy upon us." Like many aspects of Christianity, the language of mastery was supple; at once it suggested resignation to the ways of the world and provided a standard for judging the world. If slave owners hoped to turn the mastery of God into a justification of slavery, at least some freedpeople found in the mastery of God a basis for judging their owners.[43]

Faced with Union actions that at times seemed arbitrary or malignant, freedpeople articulated their own politics through the figure of the Lincoln they wished they had. This Lincoln was personally accessible, visible in mythic but oft-repeated stories of his travels across the South prior to the Civil War. Annie Joyner Gavin's great-grandmother told and retold a story of seeing Lincoln "traveling alone . . . to this plantation where she was." Like many other ex-slaves in North Carolina, she described a long and ironic visit between Lincoln and the slave master's family, one that ended with the future president hiding a letter that revealed his plans. Most interesting, however, was her explanation for Lincoln's behavior. "He had a lonely life too and he said it wasn't right to have human beings as slaves like animals," Gavin remembered. "So he said when he got a chance to hit that thing he was going

Hannah Crasson, pictured here in the 1930s at age eighty-four, was born a slave outside of Raleigh. Although Crasson was afraid of the Yankees at first, she came to have faith in the Union: "I thought Abraham Lincoln wuz the Medicine man with grip in his han', cause he said every borned man must be free. . . . I thank de will of God for setting us free. He got into Abraham Lincoln and the Yankees. We are thankful to the Great Marster dat got into Lincoln and the Yankees" (Rawick, American Slave, *11 [1], 190–93). Library of Congress, American Memory, LC-DIG-111187.*

to hit it hard." Joe High, an ex-slave, portrayed Lincoln in similarly intimate terms as "like I wuz as a boy . . . he wuz like me jest the way he saw things." Charity Austin, a teenaged slave at the close of the war, described Lincoln as he passed through as "the raggedest man you ever saw . . . huntin' his people." But she added, "Soon we heard he wus in de White House then we knew who it wus come through. We knowed den it wus Abraham Lincoln."[44]

Lincoln's human traits and imagined proximity made him accessible; he was, Charlie Hunter said, "one of my best friends." A key feature of these stories was the moment when Lincoln saw the slaves as individuals. This humanizing touch conveyed Lincoln's sympathy. Lincoln "just learned ever'thing 'bout de folks," Amy Penny said. "He was 'guised so nobody knowed who he wus." Annie Joyner Gavin's great-grandmother showed Lincoln's compassion through a story in which the president visited the stables to see "for himself" whether the slaves had "enough to eat." Lincoln "had come to oversee what to do about the blacks. . . . He was looking over the area to see what was happening." Dilly Yellady's mother said that Lincoln and Grant "come through dressed like tramps," fooling the masters by pretending to be searching for "dere people." But, Yellady went on, "Mammy an' dad" knew Lincoln and Grant and they would "laf 'bout what de Yankees wus doin' 'bout Lincoln and Grant foolin' deir marsters so." The Lincoln in these myths had a double vision, looking up to God to see righteousness, and looking around him to see the individuals in need. Absent a belief in the efficacy of bureaucratic programs, people who hoped for revolutionary change turned those prayers toward aggrandized figures who still saw them in the flesh.[45]

Needing a Lincoln big enough to make changes and close enough to make sure those changes reached them as individuals, they simply created one. As important as Lincoln's accessibility was his power. Sarah Harris called Lincoln a man who could "cure or kill. . . . The Lord put it into Abraham Lincoln to do as he done." Along with Lincoln's loneliness and sensitive soul, the stories also emphasized his divine force. This was particularly true of tales of Lincoln as an epic wrestler matched against a demonic Jefferson Davis. Georgianna Foster, a young child during slavery, remembered her parents' stories about Lincoln coming "through there on his way to Jeff Davis." In a story told by other ex-slaves, including Ria Sorrell, Lincoln and Davis faced off. After Lincoln demanded that Davis "turn dem slaves loose," Davis "said nuthin." Angered, Lincoln declared war and wreaked vengeance upon his foes, hanging Davis "on a ole apple tree." Of course, this personalization of power was not only positive. As ex-slaves struggled through the disappointments of Reconstruction, some of them "cussed ole Abraham Lincoln" for failing to use the power he possessed. Harriet Ann Daves's mother "worshipped him, but he turned us out without anything to live or live on."[46]

By embodying their hopes in Lincoln, slaves invested in him the personal power to change their lives. The alternative perhaps was not an ideal liberalism but a fatalism, the sense that change was impossible in the American South. In making a Lincoln whose heart could be touched and whose hand was strong enough to turn the world over, freedpeople articulated a reason for hope, a source of necessary, visible power. It was no wonder that Lincoln's death sent shivers not just of sorrow but of fear through ex-slaves. The war taught them a profound understanding of their rights but also a grave sense that their rights had to be defended by a combination of assertive organizing and the intercession of distant friends.

3

Vulnerable at the Circumference

Demobilization and the Limitations
of the Freedmen's Bureau

 IN JUNE 1865, the face of government changed in North Carolina as Freedmen's Bureau agents opened offices across the state. Working with the Union's state military commander, the provisional governor, and the remaining Union soldiers, these officials were the front line of a piecemeal, tentative, and poorly planned occupation of the South. Like many others, North Carolina Freedmen's Bureau director Eliphalet Whittlesey encountered scenes of "much confusion" upon his June 1865 arrival in Raleigh as displaced whites and blacks clustered around bureau offices for food, and everyone watched for portents of the social order that would replace slavery. "The sudden collapse of the rebellion . . . was like an earthquake," Oliver O. Howard, the national bureau director, wrote. "It shook and shattered the whole social system. It broke up the old industries and threatened a reign of anarchy." As Whittlesey and others like him worked to create order, they found themselves up against the most intransigent and influential problem of postwar Reconstruction, a basic lack of manpower. In his first year, at least two-fifths of the state's bureau offices were vacant at all times; at the worst moments, only fifteen agents covered a state of roughly one million people spanning almost five hundred miles from the Atlantic Ocean to the Smoky Mountains. Across the former Confederate states, the bureau never was able to maintain more than nine hundred agents at any one time to cover 3.5 million ex-slaves and more than three-quarters of a million square miles.[1]

The immediate postwar period laid bare the intense need and stark power imbalances in the South. It also exposed the thinness of Union control and the uncertain nature of Northern authority and legitimacy in the former Confederacy. As Union political and military officials worried over the best way to reintegrate the states and reconstruct their emancipated society, Southerners — white and black — began making their own judgments about what the North could and could not, and would and would not, do. Even as white and black Southerners held to the war's central lesson, that the North possessed superior power, they also learned that this power would be deployed sporadically and sometimes eccentrically. White Southerners rushed to fill this power vacuum, acting not just through reconstituted state governments but as private actors as well, reclaiming part of the authority over blacks that they had possessed under slavery. Therefore, the early period of Reconstruction raised significant questions about the relationship between state and society in the South, the capacity of the Northern government to deliver timely and reliable assistance, and the type of social order that would arise in the postwar South. Many of these questions would be answered not by a lack of will on the part of Northerners, not by a failure of ideology or racism, but by a lack of planning and foresight.

Carolinians, like other Southerners, learned quickly that bureau agents and the remaining Union soldiers possessed profound but highly limited powers over a planter class that sought to restore as much of slavery as they possibly could. In August 1865, after an agent rode forty miles with a guard of six men to arrest a planter who beat, kicked, whipped, chained, overworked, and threatened to shoot his former slaves, he despaired of all the undiscovered wrongdoing that happened in the wide swaths of territory "far from garrisons and northern influences." Wrongs to the freedpeople "increase just in proportion to their distance from United States authorities," he reported. A Northerner traveling through the South in September described an "overworked" and "disheartened" officer in Greensboro who supervised seven counties with only one additional officer and no garrison. "A Negro who seeks redress for a real or imaginary injury," he reported, "must travel perhaps ten, perhaps fifty, miles." With no effective occupying force to pacify a society turned upside down, the first years of Reconstruction were chaotic, anarchic, and intensely violent. In the spring and summer of 1866, infamous massacres at Memphis and New Orleans shocked the nation's editors and lawmakers, but as early as May and June of 1865, some white Southerners launched a steady campaign of everyday violence against freedpeople. Soon, almost every report from Freedmen's Bureau officers included long lists of assaults and murders and rapes, some intended to intimidate laborers, some to quell political resistance, some a furious response to the overturned racial and labor order.[2]

Carolinians during the military Reconstruction from 1865 to 1868 developed a wartime politics of dependence in a period of supposed peace. Freedpeople learned to approach the bureau not as a rule-bound agency but as a body with "some mysterious power to serve them" and believed that they could "fall back upon it with a certainty of support." One freedman wrote, "Our only hope, under God, is in the bureau and the influence it throws around us." The intense need for protection, the spotty power of an understaffed bureau, and a devastated agricultural economy produced a deeply personalized and localized Reconstruction politics. Many Carolinians learned that government was capable of making itself available to particular friends within a narrowly defined radius but was unable to act systematically. Intruding into formerly private matters of servitude and education, the bureau at once defined both the postwar state's new powers and its dramatic limitations. In the confusions of the era, people turned to whatever friendly patron they could find, choosing among Union officers, bureau agents, magistrates of the new provisional government, and local men who exerted power in areas that were otherwise nearly stateless.[3]

At the root of Reconstruction's patronal politics lay a little-examined but defining aspect of the era, the federal government's massive and nearly immediate demobilization. Absent a force on the ground large enough to make itself felt, later efforts to reshape the South would be muted by an inability to create order. Historians frequently emphasize 1866 and 1867 fights among Democrats, Moderates, and Radicals about the future of Reconstruction, but by that time politicians debated a policy whose fate had largely been determined. Earlier, a series of uncontroversial, commonsensical decisions made the U.S. Army too small to govern the South. From this perspective, the common historical description of Reconstruction as a failed revolution grants the era both too much and too little. On the one hand, deep structural limitations of finance and manpower prevented Reconstruction from achieving a truly revolutionary outcome as early as the spring of 1865. On the other hand, by tying Reconstruction's virtues solely to its revolutionary potential, scholars at times understate the importance of the inclusion of African Americans in everyday politics as clients whom patrons had to listen to. This inclusion far outlasted typical endpoints of Reconstruction and meaningfully influenced Southern politics and African American life for nearly thirty years, until violent and legalistic assaults in the 1890s and 1900s drove African Americans from formal politics and closed the door on the gains of Reconstruction.[4]

Although ideological limitations and racism constrained Reconstruction, fundamentally Reconstruction was handcuffed by a common victor's blindness to the problems that follow victory. Union leaders almost universally failed to understand the need for a large occupying force to subdue the South. Instead, a consensual, uncontroversial plan for massive demobilization took hold over the winter of 1864–65 with consequences that endured for decades. It is likely that demobilization was actually not a decision at all, but an assumption set in place early in the war and never reexamined. By January 1865, three months before Lee's surrender at Appomattox, Lincoln was already at work scaling back war expenses. When the navy took Fort Fisher near Wilmington, Lincoln immediately ordered the secretary of the navy to cancel orders and cut costs. As Grant and Sherman faced off against Lee and Johnston in the fields of Virginia and North Carolina, the navy had already eliminated half its squadrons, and, by the end of 1865, 442 of its 471 vessels. Once Lee surrendered, Grant traveled immediately to Washington to plan demobilization with the secretary of war. In North Carolina, Sherman began plotting his muster out even before he and Johnston agreed on surrender terms. What followed, Lincoln's secretaries wrote, was the "quick and noiseless dispersion of the enormous host when the war was done. . . . The orders came as a mere matter of course, and were executed with a thoroughness and rapidity which then seemed also a matter of course." In his poem "Armies at the Peace," Herman Melville celebrated the speed of this demobilization by comparing it to the way stars fade into night. "What power disbands the Northern Lights / After their Steely play?" he asked at the beginning of the poem, then concluded with an image of the disappearance of "The million blades that glowed, / The muster and disbanding — / Midnight and Morn."[5]

Almost before the war was over, the very soldiers who might have helped to occupy and pacify the South were marching home. Two days after Johnston surrendered in North Carolina, the War Department issued general orders "reducing expenses of the military establishment" through an "immediate reduction of the forces in the field." By August 22, 640,000 of the Union's 1 million soldiers had been discharged; by November 22, the number was 800,000, and Sherman's army had disappeared completely. The final goal was to create a standing army of 50,000 to 60,000 troops, although some in Congress lobbied to reduce it still further. In North Carolina, the numbers were especially stark. In June 1865, there were almost 44,000 federal troops in the state, but by September more than 35,000 were gone. From 8,788 in September 1865, the federal presence dropped to 2,209 by January 1866, and 1,226 by October 1866; across the South, Union numbers fell from 202,277 in June 1865 to 17,679 in October 1866.[6]

Although this demobilization profoundly influenced the course of Reconstruction, it was not an effort at sabotage. Instead, Union decisions during the key months before and after Appomattox were determined almost exclusively by financial considerations and unconscious assumptions about the nature of authority. Fears of deficits and war fatigue created, as they often do, a seemingly nonpolitical momentum for decisions that would have grave political consequences. By the winter of 1864–65, many politicians, editors, and generals were concerned that the burden of taxation and federal debt payments would sink the Republican Party or even the nation's credit. To fund a million-man army in a two-front war, the Union budget had grown from $63 million in 1860 to nearly $1.3 billion in 1865. In part the Union met this gap by decoupling the currency from the gold standard and introducing a wide range of new excise and consumption taxes, including the nation's first indirect income tax, measures that were accepted for wartime purposes but were expected to be unsustainable in peace. The great bulk of the cost was covered by $2.4 billion in interest-bearing bonds. This debt saddled the nation not only with decades-long payments but also with a newly empowered class of finance capitalists in New York City who had a vested interest in debt collection.[7]

In the winter of 1864–65, as General Grant boasted that the Confederacy was a "hollow shell," the centrality of the debt took center stage. When the debt approached $2.5 billion, the secretary of the treasury warned that if it reached $3 billion, the Union might have to give up the fight or face default and collapse. The *New York Times* warned frequently of the "calamity" of "National bankruptcy" and the "destruction of the public credit," which was "improbable" but "within the limits of things that can happen." Because Republicans did not want to readjust the debt or raise taxes, the only answer was to cut spending, and the only place for savings lay — even in December 1864 — in "compacter armies." By January 1865, the secretary of war told Sherman of "the financial troubles that threatened the very existence of the Government itself. . . . There was danger of national bankruptcy, and he appealed to me, as a soldier and a patriot, to hurry up matters so as to bring the war to a close." Months before Appomattox, Lincoln began to take control of the postwar financial problem, calling a Troy, New York, chemist and self-taught government finance expert named David Ames Wells to Washington to help him plan systematic tax cuts and warning him that "great difficulties were yet to be encountered through the possible unwillingness or inability of the nation to pay the war debt, or the great increase in taxation which the war had made necessary." By the time Lincoln was assassinated, the president was associated strongly with the idea of retrenchment, a word that combined the discharge of the army and the leavening of financial burdens. Days after his death, eulogists from Norfolk to Providence praised Lincoln for his commitment to "retrenchment in our expenditures" and "some relief from the burden of taxation."[8]

Over time the Union's effort to contract the currency and establish the gold standard would become a vibrant, even bitter, political issue, but in the key moments of 1865 and 1866, many politicians and generals seem not to have considered any option other than a massive, cost-saving demobilization. As soon as the war neared its close, "strict retrenchment" was visible everywhere, in the shuttering of military hospitals, armories, and naval yards, in the sale of ships and supplies, and in the steady homeward march of Union soldiers, all at a savings estimated at a million dollars a day. "The question of finance now is the chief one," Sherman wrote in April, "and every soldier not needed should be got home at work." This was no anomalous, Sherman-esque conservatism; the army's quartermaster general wrote in similar terms that the "present danger and difficulty of the country is financial." Johnston's eventual surrender near Durham was celebrated by the *New York Times* as a prelude to "*retrenchment*," the "first duty of the government. . . . It is believed that within a week one hundred and fifty thousand men could be mustered out of the military service, without the least detriment to the public interest." The *Philadelphia Inquirer* agreed that "retrenchment is to be the order of the day." At the end of 1865, the Department of War, which spent $516 million in that fiscal year, cut its request to $33 million, the navy from $116 million to $23 million. In December, the secretary of the treasury's call for decreased spending and lower taxes passed the Congress by a vote of 144 to 6. That winter, Congress's Joint Committee of Reconstruction defended Reconstruction as a means of supporting the larger goal of the "disbandment of the armies, and the reduction of military expenses." Soon, the Senate and House established a Joint Committee on Retrenchment, dedicated to reducing military expenses, cutting taxes, and, eventually, enacting civil service reform. In a pairing that illustrated the relative importance of retrenchment and Reconstruction, the *New York Times* wrote, "Whatever provision it may be found necessary henceforth to make for maintaining the supreme authority of the Government in the districts recently occupied by the rebel armies, may be found in a greatly reduced military establishment."[9]

Although demobilization was in place before anyone could judge the Southern response to defeat, a faith in a Confederate "disposition" to "submit to the national authority" reinforced the decision to send troops home. Many Union officials deeply mistrusted the fire-eaters who led secession but were confident they could work with the conditional Unionists and reluctant secessionists who ran affairs in places like North Carolina. Near Durham, as Sherman negotiated surrender with Johnston, the Union acted as if the everyday affairs of governance would not be affected at all by Union victory. Fresh off his scourging of coastal Georgia and South Carolina rice planters, Sherman was more generous to North Carolina because he trusted its Whig leaders and because he believed, inaccurately but plausibly, that Lincoln meant to maintain continuous local governance in the South. Therefore, Sherman turned his victory into a moment of broad political planning, conferring with leading Carolinians, including Zebulon Vance's mentor David Swain, and inviting Vance himself back to Raleigh to continue to direct a state government charged with maintaining stability and "good order." When Johnston and the Confederate cabinet agreed to negotiate the surrender not just of the Confederacy's largest army but of the Confederacy itself, Sherman offered them extraordinarily lenient political terms, including general amnesty, protection of their right to vote, and the recognition of existing state governments. Days later, John Wilkes Booth shot Abraham Lincoln in Ford's Theater in Washington D.C. Even if Lincoln had lived, it is likely that Sherman's offer would have been withdrawn as Lincoln had already experienced second thoughts about his earlier engagement with the Confederate legislature in Virginia. In the darkened Union mood that followed Lincoln's assassination, Grant and the cabinet directed Sherman to accept nothing but unconditional surrender. Although Sherman bowed to their authority, he continued to argue that recognizing standing state governments was the "very best possible means" to maintain "the mere forms of law." Without a continuity of order, he asserted, "we will have to deal with numberless bands of desperadoes." For a moment, it appeared that the breakdown of negotiations would lead to more fighting, but eventually Sherman and Johnston finessed the situation in their own, telling way. Johnston signed an unconditional surrender, then wrote up a list of terms for postwar treatment that was accepted informally by the Union general who would command North Carolina.[10]

By 1865, everyone understood that the war had ended slavery, but no one had a clear sense of how the South would be governed. During the war, Lincoln had proposed readmitting Southern states after 10 percent of the voting population swore future loyalty and he pocket-vetoed a more rigorous congressional plan. Nevertheless, Lincoln, in what turned out to be his final speech, admitted that he would discard his original 10 percent plan as a "bad promise" if Southern states resisted. Although the Confederate state governments were not, Lincoln said, an "authorized organ for us to deal with," he held his other options open. In a private conversation on the day before his assassination, Lincoln echoed Sherman's concern about the continuity of "civil government. . . . There must be courts, and law, and order, or society would be broken up—the disbanded armies would turn into robber bands and guerrillas." Over the next days, Lincoln directed the secretary of war to draw up a tentative plan for military governance of North Carolina and Virginia but died before it could be completed. For the next month, as new president Andrew Johnson held his silence, various people tried to guide Reconstruction. Supreme Court chief justice Salmon P. Chase toured the South and urged the federal government to void North Carolina's current state constitution, throwing the state onto an earlier version that enfranchised free people of color, a move that would have given the state's freedmen the right to vote. The Union's state military commander dismissed the idea because it treated the Confederate states as "unorganized territories under the absolute sovereign authority of the United States." If North Carolina still existed, then its constitution was in force, and "no power on earth but the people of the State can alter it."[11]

At the end of May, President Johnson broke his silence with a series of proclamations that simultaneously asserted military control over the South and presented a mild plan for its readmission. Arguing that secession "deprived the people of all civil government," Johnson appointed provisional governments to ensure that "justice may be established, domestic tranquility insured, and loyal citizens protected." In order to maintain "peace, order, and freedom," the provisional governments would name temporary magistrates and call a constitutional convention to ratify the end of slavery and remake the states. Johnson's plan offered amnesty, pardon, and voting rights to ex-Confederates who took an oath of future loyalty but excluded fourteen classes of Confederates, including leading officials and the wealthiest landowners. For amnesty, they needed to appeal to Johnson directly. Instead of consolidating the provisional governments under the Union's military commander, as many generals expected, Johnson appointed a separate provisional governor with a promise of military assistance. In North Carolina, Johnson named the cantankerous editor and peace advocate William W. Holden and soon thereafter issued similar proclamations for other Confederate states.[12]

This early stage of Johnson's Reconstruction did not yet indicate his acquiescence to rebel rule. Although Charles Sumner and other Radicals critiqued the new president for missing a "golden opportunity," Johnson's actions were likely no weaker than any plan Lincoln would have endorsed and were notably harsher than Sherman's offer to Johnston. Johnson's plan did, however, create two important and enduring problems. First, the abrogation of civil governance and the establishment of new provisional governments created exactly the gap in civil law that Sherman worried about. Although provisional governor Holden scrambled to re-create a state as quickly as he could, it took months to assemble thousands of nominations from across North Carolina and wait for the nominees to take the loyalty oath. Over the summer and fall, Holden appointed about four thousand magistrates, but in the interim, parts of the state were left with essentially no civil law as the U.S. soldiers began to withdraw.[13]

More troubling was the response of leading Confederates. Many took Johnson's plan as a promise that they had a friend, even a patron, in Washington. This confidence and the absence of civil authority emboldened them to assert their power over their ex-slaves and their neighbors. Here, the ritual of pardon, with its promise of access in exchange for deference, conveyed a powerful message to white Southerners. Immediately, Northerners recognized a shift in Confederates' expectations. At the end of the war, one Northern traveler wrote, Southerners "expected to take the law from their conqueror. . . . Then, better than at any other time, the North might have reaped the fruits of the war." But by the middle of August, Unionists had begun "to wonder and fear if the secessionists were not more powerful at Washington and more in favor than the Unionists." At the end of the war, bureau commissioner Whittlesey later told Congress, Confederates "felt they were entirely in the hands of the United States government and they seemed ready to submit to whatever the government might be disposed to do with them; but, after receiving a great deal of liberality, they began to think they had a right to receive everything and to demand more." Many other bureau agents and Union officers confirmed this. "At the time of Lee's surrender they were ready to accept of any terms that might have been offered," a captain testified, but "they have been led to think that they have a friend in high station."

The "whole process of favors shown them seems to have worked badly as far as bringing them toward us," an inspector noted. "They have taken them as *rights*, and have been encouraged to demand more of the same sort."[14]

Emboldened by this access, many turned to Johnson not just for pardons but for a listening ear. Immediately after the end of the war, a white North Carolinian asked the president for "protection" against his former slaves and against bands of marauding whites. "At present I have no other means of being heard," he wrote to Johnson. At this point, however, Johnson was a figure many Southerners on different sides of the racial and political divides might invest hopes in. At nearly the same time, a former slave from Pasquotank County pleaded with Johnson for help, arguing that emancipation had made him "free but without a cent." He asked Johnson to allocate five acres to each freedman over thirty-five years old: "Is it too much to ask? Have strangers a better right than those who have tilled this soil?" Two years later, frustrated in his hopes, the ex-slave had apparently given up on President Johnson but not on the Union government. In 1867, having learned the virtue of both organization and dependence, he wrote a petition signed by about sixty others, asking Congress for "shelter and protection," for they were "subject to our enemies . . . they are driven from the Clover pasture to the barren Roads to root pig or die or to root and then die."[15]

With hopes of having a friend in Washington, ex-Confederates launched a campaign of violent, exploitative control over their ex-slave laborers. A bureau agent at Greensboro predicted in September 1865 that "the withdrawal of the Federal troops would be the signal for a reign of violence and terror." Another traveler described Southern efforts to whip and intimidate ex-slaves into submission. "In many counties slavery still exists as a fact even if abolished as a name," Sidney Andrews wrote in a postwar memoir. In November 1865 state elections in North Carolina, ex-Confederates turned out in force, especially in the eastern plantation belt, to defeat provisional governor Holden's bid for election, installing former Confederate state treasurer Jonathan Worth. Two months later, the new state legislature passed a "Black Code" that increased punishments for black criminals and banned blacks from testifying against whites or serving on juries and gave ex-masters preference in forcibly apprenticing black children. Vagrancy laws across the South criminalized unemployment, nudged freedpeople into exploitative labor contracts, and prevented them from renegotiating or seeking new jobs. In coastal Elizabeth City, ex-Confederates celebrated with "the swaggering air, the insolent look, the defiant manner and the reckless conduct" of people who had not surrendered. In wanton "acts of violence," whites assaulted black men on the street, shot at a black woman in her house, and beat a black former sergeant with a gun. "Instead of reciprocating the magnanimous trust of the President, they take advantage of the governor's loose construction of the law to exemplify their patriotism in abusing 'the inferior race' and in acts of insult to any and all who labor to elevate and improve them," a local lawyer complained. A bureau agent said that political success encouraged Confederates to believe they would receive their rights: "What they mean by rights is their power."[16]

Although African Americans quickly mobilized for self-defense, the only completely reliable safeguard against this overwhelming force was the Freedmen's Bureau and the remaining units of the army. One lieutenant testified that former owners spoke openly of their plans, if the army withdrew, to "make it worse" for freedpeople than before emancipation, "that is, to make their freedom of no avail to them. . . . There would, in my judgment, be no hope of freedmen's exercising any of his rights. He would have no chance in a court; he would have no chance anywhere." Without the bureau, Whittlesey predicted, "I think they would re-establish slavery just as it was before, if there was no fear of any evil consequences from the government. . . . They would enact laws which would make the blacks virtually slaves. I have no doubt of that." Without soldiers to protect ex-slaves, Southerners would "endeavor to reduce them to a system of peonage immediately. . . . By controlling wages and keeping them low, they would render the colored man helpless and dependent."[17]

The Freedmen's Bureau was itself a complex, paternalistic, and highly limited organization. Founded by an 1865 congressional act, the bureau was intended to take freedpeople "by the hand in their passage from the house of bondage to the house of freedom," in the words of Senator Charles Sumner, by "protecting them in the enjoyment of their rights, promoting their welfare, and securing to them and their posterity the blessings of liberty. The power of the Government must be to them a shield." A defender of the bill in the House of Representatives called it an effort to "organize them into society; we are to guide them, as the guardian guides his ward for a brief period, until they can acquire habits and become confident and capable of self-control; we are to watch over them. . . . If we do not, we will doom them to vagrancy and pauperism." The bill created a bureaucracy in each ex-Confederate state to manage the needs of freedpeople, defend their rights, rent out abandoned and public lands, readjust unfair contracts, adjudicate disputes, and provide rations to both freedpeople and loyal white refugees. In keeping with both the paternalistic metaphors and many Republicans' financial fears, the bureau was meant to be merely a "temporary expedient."[18]

Putting the bureau into action raised significant problems because of the challenge of creating a new bureaucracy overnight, the dire situation of many freedpeople, and tensions in many bureau agents' own views of freedpeople. The first person to try to impose order on this chaos was North Carolina Freedmen's Bureau assistant commissioner Eliphalet Whittlesey. When Whittlesey arrived in Raleigh in June 1865 to administer the bureau, he found "much confusion. Hundreds of white refugees and thousands of blacks were collected about this and other towns occupying every hovel and shanty." Immediately, Whittlesey plunged into the task of creating a functioning system of governance. In many ways Whittlesey was ideally suited to the task. A Connecticut Yankee, "as tough and dry as his name," Whittlesey was "intense almost to the point of being comic." The son of a state legislator and the grandson, great-grandson, and great-great-grandson of American soldiers, he had grown up around the military and the government. A former schoolteacher, pastor, and Bowdoin professor, Whittlesey joined the Union army during the Civil War and served on General Oliver Otis Howard's staff, where his "imperturbability" under fire impressed the general. After the war, Whittlesey followed Howard into the newly created Freedmen's Bureau, which Howard directed from Washington, D.C. After his time in North Carolina, Whittlesey returned to Washington to serve as the national bureau's adjutant general, where he helped oversee the founding of Howard University and developed a vast system of clerks and requisition vouchers. Later, he served for eighteen years as secretary of the federal Board of Indian Commissioners.[19]

If Southerners white and black were inclined to see governance as personal power, Whittlesey tried to reeducate them. He both fought vigorously to defend freedpeople and acted high-handedly in the presumption he knew their interests better than they did. This duality was embodied in his first guideline to his agents: "To aid the destitute, yet in such a way as not to encourage dependence." Characteristically, he started by divvying his state and his problems into measurable pieces. For the state, he created twenty-seven subdistricts and then went about trying to hire "a large number of efficient officers" to "investigate the conditions" and "minister to the wants of the destitute." Quickly he clarified the ration system, cutting food supplies to any "able bodied man or woman" who was not "utterly destitute." By "constant inquiry and effort the throng of beggars was gradually removed," and he slashed statewide rations by more than a third in two months. By May 1866, only two hundred out of fifteen hundred freedpeople on Roanoke Island received rations, and Whittlesey's primary goal seemed to be moving those freedpeople off the land and out of sight. By early 1866, only five thousand of the state's freedpeople received any relief at all, and many rations went to families of dead Confederate soldiers. Even when help was available, the bureau distributed it in "indiscriminate" ways, an agent complained, and the lack of "systematic manner" left the "really suffering . . . too weak to avail themselves of the opportunity to receive assistance." Even more egregiously, but like other bureau agents, Whittlesey intermixed his business and professional responsibilities, sharing ownership of a plantation with several partners, including wartime freedmen's superintendent Horace James. Although James and Whittlesey called their plantation an experiment in free labor, their personal and professional obligations conflicted when their white overseer shot and killed one of their black employees, and they did not pursue the matter. When word reached bureau opponents close to President Andrew Johnson, Whittlesey had to resign his position in North Carolina and return to Washington, D.C. Despite his limitations, Whittlesey was in other areas a fierce warrior against the "wrongs" committed against freedpeople. In the first six months, the bureau certified contracts for more than 5,300 freedpeople, helped establish 86 schools for 8,500 freedpeople, moved 50 criminal cases to trial, heard at least 5,000 complaints, oversaw several thousand sick people in hospitals, apprenticed 400 orphans, and rented out large swaths of abandoned lands to freedpeople.[20]

The primary problem facing the bureau was the practical question of how to improvise order without force. A new agent in Charlotte in June 1865 took over an office "without any rules, Laws or regulations where by to be governed." He found something like chaos. "The whole population of Blacks were completely wild," he wrote. "The Whites not being willing to yield their former right of Slavery used the lash quite freely." With "no instructions or authority as to this matter," he wrote, "I am at a loss to know what to do." Two weeks later, he was still stumped: "My District is a very large one + my labors are ardous And unless I have something to be Governed by I know not what to do." In desperation he turned to Whittlesey for help, but Whittlesey offered something less than reassurance. Although he sent orders and circulars, Whittlesey warned that "in many things your own good judgment will be your only guide." The agent's judgment, and his close observation of the people he was supposed to govern, led him to a personal vision of power. Soon, he reported, "I am often challenged as to my rights + Authority in

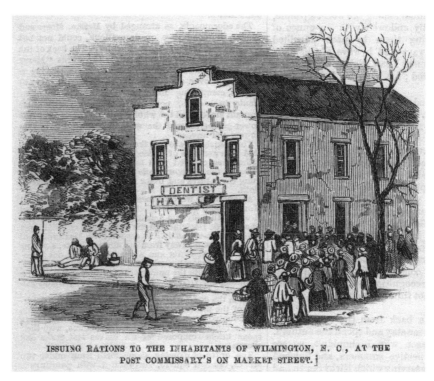

ISSUING RATIONS TO THE INHABITANTS OF WILMINGTON, N. C , AT THE POST COMMISSARY'S ON MARKET STREET.

Among the first, most intimate challenges presented to Union soldiers and Freedmen's Bureau officials were the intense needs of both freedpeople and whites, pictured here lining up for food rations in Wilmington, N.C., in the war's closing days. Demands for assistance prompted the establishment of large, if often haphazard, efforts to provide relief in the form of food and clothing, and Northern anxieties about providing too much assistance and engendering a spirit of dependence. Frank Leslie's Illustrated Newspaper, *April 1, 1865, p. 24. North Carolina Collection, The University of North Carolina at Chapel Hill.*

adjusting difficulties between the former Master and Servant. I have referred such persons to Maj Genl Howard or the President."[21]

Despite Whittlesey's efforts to create order, many freedpeople saw the bureau as less systematic than idiosyncratic. Primarily this was due to the extraordinarily thin nature of bureau coverage. The problem of enforcing the law "far away" from any "influence of troops and where the military power of the Government has been little felt" plagued Whittlesey and his successors' efforts to impose order upon the land. Although he planned for thirty-three military agents to govern the state, the largest number he had on hand in his first few months was twenty. As the Union discharged soldiers in the months after Appomattox, Whittlesey lost agents (many of whom were on loan from the military) in three more waves of musters. By the time he wrote to Howard in the fall of 1865, he was down to fifteen. "Thus more than half the State is still without an office or representative of the Bureau," he complained. In December 1865, Whittlesey described the necessity of force. "With an efficient office in each Sub District it would be possible I think to 'control all affairs relating to freedmen,'" he wrote. "The Bureau is hated as a representative of Federal rule, but it is respected as a representative of Federal power." Without an increase in federal troops, however, equal enforcement proved a chimera. Instead of an ideal, abstracted state, the federal government created pockets of control that were surrounded by chaos. "At points distant from any military force some gross outrages have been committed, by outlaws and desperadoes," Whittlesey wrote to Howard. He listed murders in Warren, Pitt, and Caswell Counties and a "serious disturbance" in Elizabeth City. These widespread attacks on freedpeople prompted General Grant to issue General Orders No. 3, which gave military authorities the right to intervene in civil prosecutions against freedpeople, loyalists, and military officers. Although Grant dispatched troops to arrest offenders and impose order, the bureau could not impose itself upon the state but instead was left to respond to events. In areas where the bureau could not maintain a serious military presence, disorder reigned.[22]

Set to expire in 1866, the bureau depended upon reauthorization from Congress. Anxiety about that reauthorization fueled desperate cries from freedpeople, Unionists, and agents for the continuance of the bureau. A freedman told the *Philadelphia Inquirer* that freedpeople did "well enough in town" but had "mighty hard times" in the countryside, where whites felt free to beat them for the "least little thing." The superintendent of the Western District claimed that "under the advice and authority of the Bureau" perhaps "two thirds of the Whites are willing to do well by their former slaves," but "there are not one hundred men that I know of in this District who would deal out what I call justice to the Blacks, unless for the bureau. The feeling of mastership, and the conviction that Blacks have few rights that a white man is bound to respect, have not yet been eradicated from the minds of the planters." Without the bureau, "the Blacks would be no better off than before the war." In Hertford County local militia confiscated guns from returning soldiers in December 1865. "We all as umble Servants of yours do ask of you to a vord any further privilege being taken from us and our guns if can be granted," one former soldier wrote to Whittlesey. If "there not be a stope put to it there will not bee any living in this Section." In May 1866, to "cries from all parts of the house," a Wilmington freedman told a visiting panel of generals that the bureau was their only hope. "Remove this refuge,

In the early days of Reconstruction, rural freedpeople caught in the chaos of masters' efforts to impose private authority in areas far from federal troops and Freedmen's Bureau agents fled to towns and cities where Union authority was more accessible and reliable. The freedpeople pictured here are traveling on the Cape Fear River en route to Wilmington. Frank Leslie's Illustrated Newspaper, *June 17, 1865, p. 205. North Carolina Collection, The University of North Carolina at Chapel Hill.*

and you will see that we have lost our protection. We might just as well be in the open field, and the hail beating down as big as hen's eggs on our heads." Another speaker stated that if the bureau were abolished, "in less than two weeks you will have to allay a riot in Wilmington." Freedpeople would be "at the mercy of those who hate" them.[23]

After a nine-month recess through most of 1865, Congress in December took up the problem of Reconstruction in a world that looked decidedly different than it had in the months before Appomattox. Appalled by the steady drip of reports of continual, everyday violence, Republicans returned to Washington ready to expand the scope of Reconstruction. Quickly they reauthorized the Freedmen's Bureau and expanded its jurisdiction over court cases involving freedpeople. Additionally Republicans in Congress passed a civil rights bill that invalidated discriminatory laws and made it possible to remove cases from state to federal courts. But the victory was short-lived. In April 1866, President Johnson proclaimed that the insurrection was over everywhere except in Texas and that standing armies and martial law were no longer necessary. The next day, the Supreme Court ruled against the use of military commissions in the case of *Ex Parte Milligan*, which raised questions about the constitutionality of bureau judicial acts. To the shock and dismay of moderate Republicans, President Johnson then vetoed both bills, calling the Freedmen's Bureau a bloated patronage machine that unfairly aided blacks over "our own people" and the civil rights bill a "Stride towards centralization." Appalled Republicans overrode the president's vetoes and moved to pass the Fourteenth Amendment. During the summer of 1866, bloody massacres at Memphis and New Orleans convinced many moderate Republicans that Southern violence was both widespread and partisan in nature. In reaction to the worsening violence in the South, including attacks on military personnel, General Grant in July ordered commanders to arrest and hold criminals until functioning courts could resume civil authority, but Johnson essentially nullified this order. Emboldened by victories in the 1866 midterms, Republicans returned to Congress in December 1866 with a plan to take control of Reconstruction. They refused to seat congressmen from the Southern states, carved the South into military districts governed by commanding generals with broad authority, disfranchised former Confederates, and required states to include black voting rights before petitioning for readmission into the Union. North Carolina was placed in the Second Military District, under the command of General Daniel Sickles. From the Black Codes, North Carolina and other states would move to black suffrage. It was a sweeping, even staggering transformation as a quiescent Reconstruction policy suddenly grew teeth.

Although black voting rights changed Southern politics dramatically, in the short run much of the promise of the military division of the South was lost in the absence of troops to enforce it. By the autumn of 1866, there were fewer than 18,000 soldiers left in the entire South, and almost one-third of them were stationed in faraway Texas. In all of North Carolina there were 1,226, almost 45 percent fewer than there had been at the beginning of the year. Although the Reconstruction acts gave more power to federal courts, blocked the retrograde efforts of Southern legislatures, and prevented Southern congressmen from hijacking Congress, by the winter of 1866–67, much of the potential for Reconstruction on the ground had already vanished.[24]

Far from Raleigh and Washington, in lonely offices in hostile towns across the state, individual agents experienced this stateless society in even more frightening and personal terms. There, the pockets of order seemed smaller and smaller, and the anarchy of society more apparent. One of the most acute observers of this problem was a man trained in a very different school of governance than Whittlesey's Connecticut. In Kinston and Greensboro, a bureau agent and true revolutionary named Hugo Hillebrandt worried that he managed not the birth of a new state but simply an isolated garrison in the wilds. Hillebrandt had reason to think broadly. The Civil War was his third revolution, and his experiences with governments from monarchies to republics were as broad as anyone's. Born in southeastern Hungary in 1832, Hillebrandt as a young man joined Lajos Kossuth's nationalist revolution, displaying "military genius and cool courage." From there Hillebrandt traveled to Turkey and the United States. Soon after hearing of Garibaldi's uprising, he left his job at the U.S. Coast Survey to fight in Italy. In 1860, Hillebrandt returned to the United States and in 1861 volunteered for the Union army. Wounded at Gettysburg and weakened by disease after the sleet and rain of the Mine Run campaign, Hillebrandt was mustered out in December 1863 and served in the Veterans Reserve Corps in Washington, D.C., for the remainder of the war. In 1866, he joined the Freedmen's Bureau and was stationed in North Carolina in the Kinston and Greensboro offices until the end of 1868. Later, President Grant appointed him U.S. consul to Crete.[25]

A hardened, determined, and courageous man, Hillebrandt nevertheless found himself frequently powerless. Without adequate support, no amount of personal valor mattered. In May 1866, a freedwoman ran into his office in Kinston to deliver the awful news that a Union soldier had been murdered nineteen miles away. Hillebrandt, a man who had fought in three wars on two continents, could do nothing but wait while his soldier's corpse rotted in the road. Hillebrandt wanted to rush to get the body but was horrified when he "was advised by the citizens not to go without ample force." When Hillebrandt asked these locals to come with him, he reported, "none of them was willing to offer his services." They "state that there is an organized band of horse thieves well armed ready to offer resistance." From a distance, the bureau not only failed to protect freedpeople; it could not protect its own officers, nor retrieve their dead bodies. A month later, Hillebrandt complained again about "horses and mules . . . mostly stolen from freedmen by white citizens." The "general impression is that a negro should not, and has no right to own property" in the "upper part of the county." There, "they are determined to carry out their purposes, the civil authorities and citizens do not act upon such cases the horse thieves are well known to them, but some are affraid to arrest or even report them for fear their life and property would be endangered." At his office Hillebrandt had four enlisted men and no rations. To "scour the country a little" and arrest the horse thieves, he needed twelve soldiers and horses. Trying to cover a twenty-four-mile range without them was impossible, he argued. "The rascals are all mounted we might meet with strong opposition or they run away."[26]

To a Massachusetts man touring the state in January 1866, the bureau was full of good intentions and "good and energetic" agents but not good effect because it lacked the "strong hand of power." Writing to U.S. senator (and eventual vice president) Henry Wilson, this visitor described the dramatic distance between the needs and the capacity of the bureau. In Goldsboro, the bureau office was "overrun with all sorts of applications," but the agent "is without any sufficient military force to do any thing for the adjoining counties." Therefore, neighboring Sampson County "is without protection." An old white man traveled forty-five miles to tell the agents that his life was in danger, and that "if he canot be protected he canot live." Recently, men had burst into his house, accused him of talking freely with freedpeople, and "put pistols to the head of his wife, sick in bed," "threatened death," and seized his guns. The man had an order of protection from a Union colonel, but without support, the order was meaningless. After he was threatened again, the man traveled to Goldsboro to "seek help," but the agent could not help him. To create order and safety and "subdue + protect the country," a "simple force of 25 men would be entirely adequate," the Northern traveler wrote. "The rebels are frightened at the very sight or name of Yankee. But they need to be kept in awe. The safety of the poor union whites as well as the Freedmen depend upon it."[27]

Instead of awe, however, the bureau inspired at best wariness, at worst contempt. In Caswell County's Yanceyville, soon to be the site of a full-fledged guerrilla war, agent and state legislator William B. Bowe had a bleak view of bureau power. Bowe, a native white conservative, was generally unsympathetic, apprenticing out black children to whites who would allegedly teach them to work, commenting unfavorably on the "fact" that the "affrican race are naturally lazy," encouraging the enforcement of vagrancy laws, and expressing support for white landowners. In 1870, Bowe would be arrested on charges of participating in the Ku Klux Klan. Nevertheless, Bowe was shocked by the disorder caused by some rough whites. Writing to Whittlesey in January 1866, Bowe complained about a white overseer who murdered a freedman and had "not been heard from" or brought to justice. The incident gave Bowe an excuse to remind Whittlesey that "our citizens are suffering very much for want of a civil magistracy scattered all over the county to deter all wrong doing." No matter how "vigilant an officer may be at a central point he cannot make his influence felt as it ought to [at the] circumference." Although Bowe likely argued for local justices of the peace on the grounds they would be fellow conservatives, his judgment of how force worked was telling.[28]

Powerful at its central point and weak at the circumference, the bureau was more like a patron than a bureaucracy. If its force was intense within its sight but irrelevant outside of its gaze, then the freedpeople were not wrong to personify the bureau into a powerful but distant friend. The narrow spatial limits of bureau power reinforced people's suspicion that rights needed to be invested in particular guardians who might be able to make them felt within particular regions. If power operated through significant persons who could act only upon proximate places, then patronalism was not an error but a diagnosis.[29]

No wonder then that a freedman named Peter Price begged for help not from a bureaucracy but from "Mr Freedmans Bureau." Price needed protection from his landlord, a local white man whom he worked for on shares. By 1867, when Price's problems began, many freedpeople had joined him in sharecropping. During 1865, many ex-slaves had resisted labor contracts from a futile hope that the government would deliver them land. By 1866, after the reappointment of conservative, even secessionist, magistrates by Governor Jonathan Worth, many freedpeople accepted highly unequal and unfair contracts. At the end of 1867, Price and a coworker decided to leave the farm in search perhaps of a better contract from a different planter. This raised a key legal issue. Would their employer honor the agreement by dividing still-unsold corn and tobacco with Price and his coworker? Price went to Hugo Hillebrandt for help, and Hillebrandt settled the matter in Price's favor. The planter owed them their share of the crop. As Hillebrandt acknowledged, right meant little without might. Hillebrandt had made his order, but he could not enforce it. A question of law had become a question of power. When Price returned to the farm, the planter told the freedman that he would see "Hilly Brand further in Hell than a Jay Bird could fly before we should have it," and claimed, "You might send ten thousand Yankees there and he did not intend to be governed by no such laws." This was almost certainly bravado. As Hillebrandt told his superiors, he did not need ten thousand troops; with even a few dozen soldiers he could enforce almost any act. But he did not have a few dozen, and therefore he could not help. "Almost upon starvation," Price desperately looked for help, first from a larger bureau office in Greensboro, then from General Nelson Miles, the new state military commander. "I would be glad that you would send some person down to Pelham to go with me there," Price wrote to the man he called "Mr Freedmans Bureau." Although Price carefully made his legal case, he also appealed in personal terms: "If you knew exactly my circumstances you would certainly take pity on me and do something for me without delay."[30]

Freedpeople needed the bureau because they feared being friendless, a condition not of loneliness but of powerlessness. To combat this condition, they simultaneously organized and sought help from above. By banding together, they magnified their voice. In the postwar South, association was not enough to yield results; they knew they also needed access. "We need sum Good frand to come down to hyde," Simon Handy and others pleaded to a bureau official. In Lexington, 106 freedpeople claimed on a petition that they did have a friend in the person of their agent, Col. W. F. Henderson. Calling him "our protector," the petitioners begged the bureau not to reassign him elsewhere. "Being in the midst of enemies to our race," they would "certainly have to suffer" without him. In making themselves visible, they hoped to make Henderson visible, too. What they sought was help not only from the bureau as an institution but from Henderson as a man. In a fascinating cover letter, a local white man named H. Adams presented the petition that he said was "gotten up by themselves in their own style, handwriting + the contents." The freedpeople had asked him to "transcribe the whole and put it in a more businesslike manner," but after contemplation, Adams wrote, he "prefered sending it in its original style and let you draw your own inferences." Adams hoped that letter's raw form showed that "these people not only speak their own sentiments + feelings, but they speak for other counties of the District." Another white man named H. L. Watson also vouched for the petition. "[It is] not exaggeration," he wrote, "for I have witnessed enough to satisfy me that the salvation of the colored race . . . depends materially upon the continuance of the Freedmans Bureau." Although Adams and Watson recognized the existence of another set of languages, ones more formal and legalistic, they chose to maintain the letter's intimate, personal appeal. More than a defense of abstract rights, these freedpeople needed recognition.

These personal pleas could easily be turned to personal advantage, not only for the petitioners, but also for the agents. A white man named S. H. Birdsall, who had previously worked for the bureau at Roanoke Island, forwarded a similar petition. "The people are Rebellious, insolent, and will not do right," it claimed. Birdsall was the "only Yankee living in this vicinity and they make a great many motions but do not strike." Although "scarcely a day passes but some colored person comes for advice," he could "claim no authority." In part the letter seems like an extended effort by Birdsall to get reinstated into the bureau as the local superintendent. He appears to have written the petition and to have jotted down the forty-five names that appear by the Xs the freedpeople presumably made. Even though Henderson and Birdsall may have orchestrated the petitions for their own ends, the letters still convey a sense of how they hoped to make their claims stick.[31]

In their letters freedpeople transformed generals and bureaucrats into little Lincolns, betrayed by bad local officers. In February 1866, a group of freedmen led by James Gilom begged the "gentel men of the freed man bureau" in "the naim of god and Abrum lincom for a protection" from apprenticeship, an extremely unpopular practice among the freedpeople. North Carolina permitted broad apprenticeship powers over children of both races, and the Black Codes gave ex-masters preference in the apprenticing out of children of their former slaves. As state officials broke up newly intact black families, freedpeople protested vigorously. In some counties, bureau agents helped; in others, agents encouraged apprenticeship as a means of reducing calls for relief. When Gilom and his fellow freedmen found their local officers unsympathetic, they wrote, "We are like a boat without a heulm or a captin and without releaf we must go to the destruction." Bureau officials reassured them that this problem would be resolved by a new agent. When George Hawley, that new bureau officer, also dismissed their complaints, their outrage turned against him. Two months later, twenty-one freedmen from Bertie, Gates, and Hertford Counties wrote to the "head commissioners of the freedmen Bureau." "Prayen you sir," they wrote, "Please do Saumthing for our trifling Race. . . . We are in your hands." The new agent, instead of being their friend, had "sould [their] children to they former marster." When the signers tried to reclaim their children, "the marsters" said they would shoot them. If they went to Hawley, the men complained, "he will not talk with us but will leave us + go to stand with the seces." All in all, "some of us will be worse of than when we was slaves" since the "ones that has our mothers + children are whipen . . . jest as bad as be four the war." The only way to make their "sad condison" better would be to send a company of soldiers to "go on every farm + in every villige + have our mothers + children set at Liberty + take this agent a way + a send a union man heare + not one that will take sides with the Rebs." Nevertheless, they had "confidence in you" (though they did not know or name the "you") that "you will seand + set maters all Right sir." If the commissioner only saw the actual conditions in the counties, he would agree that, as the petitioners put it, "freedmen has a Dogs Life." They therefore were "all in you for our salvason as a poor healpes freed Race." This mix of aggrandizement and outrage met with the most discouraging response. To investigate the complaints against George Hawley, the bureau sent none other than George Hawley himself. Not surprisingly, Hawley blamed the freedpeople for their "confusion + uncertainty," especially their slowness in making contracts. Although Hawley dismissed their personalized view of power as "confusion" and ignorance, Hawley's own unchecked authority confirmed their judgment.[32]

Freedmen in the James City settlement experienced hopes for and disappointment in the Freedmen's Bureau in the most profound way. At the end of the war, as Superintendent Horace James's dreams of a freedpeople's colony faded, the camp became a bleak and terrible place. Determined to reduce the camp's size and cost, James expelled thousands of its residents, sending many of them into unfair and exploitative labor contracts. His successor, a former army chaplain and assistant bureau superintendent named Edward Fitz, was charged with stealing from and torturing black residents of the settlement, although he was only convicted of mistreatment. A politically motivated report to the secretary of war claimed Fitz "has exercised the most arbitrary and despotic power, and practiced revolting and unheard-of cruelties on the helpless freedmen under his charge." In 1867, the government restored the land, which had once been a Confederate camp, to the white family that had owned it prior to the war. Although bureau officials tried to convince the family to sell the land to the freedpeople, they refused, and many of the few hundred remaining freedpeople suffered under intense famine in 1867.[33]

In 1868, a group of 501 freedpeople from James City banded together to call upon Freedmen's Bureau commissioner Oliver Otis Howard in Washington, D.C., for help. As they suffered under an "arbitrary and despotic" agent, it is not surprising that they turned to Howard in intensely personal ways, asking him and the federal government for "tenderness." First, they blamed their helplessness for their request: "We thought we never should be oblige to call upon the US Gov but poverty has driven us to this." Calling themselves "poor creatures left out door exposed to the cold," they nevertheless expressed "great confidence in our United Government therefore we love the Gov for it will do just to all mankind." In return they promised the common pledge of the weak, God's favor: "God will bless the United States fore her aid and support to the poor and will enable her to conquor all Governments upon the surface of the earth by showing love and charity to the poor." Along with these oaths of loyalty and love, the freedmen also proffered other models of mutual obligation. They promised to treat any gifts as a loan and "try to make return at the latter end of the year" if requested. They also offered a covenant of "the performance of every honorable duty characteristic of good citizenship." But this pledge depended upon mutuality; in terms that were daring, even dangerous, the freedpeople said that the government "should not expect our support in any form until the guarantees to use every right privilege secured to other citizen." Upon the delivery of those rights, they continued, "we are willing to die in her deffence." This complex letter shows how many theories of government could operate within one single body of people. At once, the freedmen of James City put themselves forward as loyal and weak subjects, as trustworthy loan recipients, as alienated victims, and as proud citizens who would defend their rights with their lives. If the letter reads as a potluck of aspirations, it reflects African Americans' complex interactions with the Freedmen's Bureau and the contradictory anxieties these encounters with the government fostered.

The response to their letter would only confirm this judgment. The investigating subassistant commissioner was incensed that the freedmen had undercut him, and declared that there was no destitution in the settlement at all. Absent any other way to gain anyone's attention, the freedpeople in desperation apologized to the agent, but to no avail. Over the next three decades, the James City settlers would engage in a long legal struggle that ended in 1893 with the intervention of the state militia and the governor, who convinced residents to give up their claim of ownership and to sign three-year leases.[34]

Not despite but because of its limitations, the bureau served as a potent reminder that power was not stable or reliable. In 1867 and 1868, Congress debated yet again whether to reauthorize the Freedmen's Bureau. In the winter of 1867, General Howard launched a campaign to save it. As he began to discharge officers, "a reaction against the interests of the freedpeople immediately followed." Therefore, Howard asked Congress to extend the bureau for one more year. As Congress considered his request, Jacob Grimes, a North Carolina freedman, petitioned Howard and Congress on behalf of the "Destitue people," asking them to "please [let] the Freedmen Bureau Remain. . . . The Bureau Has ben Great Help to our poor old people. We not see how we can get a long well with out it." Rather than an agency, however, Grimes transformed the bureau into an individual patron. "We Has to Call up on Col. Moore to Enterceed for us," he pleaded, unsuccessfully.[35]

This time, there would be no last-minute salvation for the bureau. In July 1868, Congress authorized the bureau for a final six months, ordering General Howard to dismantle all of the bureau's programs except its schools by the end of the year. Quickly, the national bureau dismissed 141 commissioned officers, 412 civilian agents, and 348 clerks, leaving a skeleton crew to wrap up the paperwork and manage the schools. A year earlier the bureau spent almost $100,000 across the South on rations; by 1869, the amount it spent on rations had dwindled to nothing. After running twenty-one hospitals, the bureau now managed two. Over the course of its existence, the bureau had distributed twenty-one million rations (although none to "able-bodied beggars," as the bureau "has not been a pauperizing agency.") The bureau supported missionary schools attended by more than two hundred thousand black students. Across the South the bureau heard perhaps one hundred thousand complaints a year, ranging from reports of murder and assault to accusations of fraud. "But for the presence of Bureau officers, sustained by military force, there would have been no one to whom these victims of cruelty and wrong could have appealed for defense," General Howard claimed. "No one can tell what scenes of violence and strife and insurrection the whole South might have presented, without the presence of this agency of the government to preserve order and to enforce justice."[36]

If Howard took understandable solace in the fate that would have befallen a South without the bureau, his agents in the field had to continue to face the chaotic world in front of them. Even when they succeeded, the personal nature of their success undermined confidence in the larger project. By promising programs, and then delivering spotty protection and rations, army and Freedmen's Bureau officials reinforced the incorporation of power in individuals. By August 1868, Hugo Hillebrandt had learned this, too. From his post at Greensboro, Hillebrandt heard the story of a freedman who had married a white widow with three children, "which aggravated the citizenry of the neighborhood very much, and they swore vengeance against the couple." In July 1868, the family intended to move to a rental house, but before they settled in, the "house was burned down." Unable to rent from anyone, they then moved into an empty school. Four days later, two men "dressed in the most horrible manner" chased the man into the woods. Then they set fire to the "furniture, bedding everything she had + burned it up." The family fled to Greensboro "without anything and do not dare go back, fearing their lives may be endangered," Hillebrandt wrote. By summer 1868, Hillebrandt had no more faith in the bureau's power. After fighting against chaos with hardly any staff, Hillebrandt now presided over an office in the process of being dismantled. By November, he would be out of the bureau and of North Carolina, and soon he would be in Crete. "I am unable to act," he wrote. "Military Authority having ceased, the perpetrators can only be brought to justice by civil process." He hoped the commissioner would refer the family's case to the governor.[37]

4

The Great Day of Acounter

*Democracy and the Problem of
Power in Republican Reconstruction*

THE GOVERNOR Hugo Hillebrandt and many freedpeople looked to in 1868 was the same William Holden who had been turned out of office only three years earlier. Starting in 1866, Holden adeptly read the transformations in Washington, ingratiated himself with Radical Republicans, and positioned himself atop the expanded democracy envisioned in congressional Reconstruction. By 1868, Holden rode back into the governor's office on heavy turnout by freedmen newly enfranchised by the state constitution and the insistence of Washington Radicals. Now incorporated into formal politics, these freedpeople pleaded to keep Holden's attention on the dire problems of security and survival. Building upon the petitions to the Freedmen's Bureau and to Lincoln, freedpeople and loyal whites created a fused language of individual dependence and group political power, tying their right to be heard to their votes, and fashioning a politics of dependence inside an expanding democracy. Patronal politics, born from the calls of formally excluded white Confederate women and Unionist freedpeople, had always leapt over those divides and served purposes for white enfranchised men. Now, as freedpeople found themselves within the margins of democracy and in the crosshairs of a broad campaign of terror, they pushed dependence into the center of state politics. Increasingly, whites responded in kind, turning Reconstruction elections into a war over which patrons would heed the cry of which subjects. Instead of undermining patronalism, the expansion of democracy strengthened and expanded it.

Across the South, the transition from military to democratic government presented a crisis of legitimacy for Radical Reconstruction. The former Confederate states posed key problems for republican theory. On the one hand, the numerical and political supremacy of white ex-Confederates in many (although not all) of the states made the restoration of self-rule an invitation for Confederate reassertion. On the other hand, many Northerners — including many Radicals — counted self-government among their central principles. Directly administering the defeated states from Washington, as a kind of reterrorialized region, was never widely popular. Without significant Southern representation, asked Senator John Sherman, "What becomes of the republican doctrine that all governments must be founded on the consent of the governed?" Returning the states to the Union without simply handing them over to unapologetic Confederates posed a quandary for a divided Congress. Eventually, resolution to the congressional impasse came in the form of democracy. By requiring states to enfranchise freedpeople and by disenfranchising some ex-Confederates, at least temporarily, Congress could create a democratic counterweight in the South. "The ballot will finish the negro question," one Radical proclaimed. "We will need no vast expenditures, we need no standing army." Instead of resolving these problems, however, the transition from military to democratic Reconstruction posed them in new form. In state after state, governments popularly elected, in part, by the extraordinary organizational efforts of freedpeople, struggled to maintain their hold on authority in the face of intensely violent opposition. As some white Southerners mobilized against these new governments, their actions raised key questions about the relationship between democracy and legitimacy, and about the ultimate source of authority in a society riven by dozens of small-scale wars and hundreds of local power grabs. These struggles tested whether Reconstruction could make itself felt in any kind of systematic way, as a question not of intention but of efficacy. North Carolina's story was one among many where alliances of white and African American Republicans looked vainly for ways to assert their legitimacy in the face of violent, well-organized opposition. Resistance illuminated the weaknesses within Reconstruction governments, exposed the limitations of rhetoric in the face of countervailing realities, and encouraged a panicked effort to claim state resources and protection before they evaporated.[1]

This democracy of dependency grew from the actions of Holden and other state leaders who promised to intervene in new ways to protect the bodies and souls of their constituents. As is often true, patronalism grew not from the retreat of government but from its advance into new fields of endeavor, an advance that could not help but exceed in promises what it delivered in services. As he entered office, Holden pledged the power of the state to safeguard the lives of citizens and to deliver equal justice to a state that not only enshrined inequality but rooted rights deeply in the individual person of local magistrates. As Holden raised hopes, conditions on the ground proved his inability to meet his goals. Conservatives in North Carolina and across the South launched a massive, violent campaign to destroy the state's authority, eviscerate the Republican Party, and drive Holden from office.[2]

From this combination of personal dependence and state weakness, Carolinians fashioned a politics of territorialism, an understudied but significant aspect of popular political thought in the nineteenth-century United States. If patronalism emphasized the personal (and therefore idiosyncratic) nature of government, then territorialism described its scope. As pleas turned from the Civil War cries for food to Reconstruction claims for protection, they increasingly spoke to needs that could not be bound by a single human body. Instead, fear and terror exposed the interdependence of their victims. The appeals therefore celebrated the government's capacity to intervene in narrow geographic terms. Instead of asking for peace in the state or even the county, many pleaders called for intervention solely in the world they could see, an imprecise but common range that urbanites and rural people both called a neighborhood. They not only asked the government to help them where they were, as almost all people do, but stated that the government was only capable of acting in these small circumferences of power and therefore should only be judged upon those terms. This parochialism was no eccentricity of the political system but a key feature, a social basis for producing ideas about power and access during what some call the Gilded Age. In North Carolina and in Jersey City and in many places in between, people entered into their imaginings of a democratized, fragmented politics by looking at its impact upon the world they could see, whether that world was a few square blocks of an Eastern city or the five-mile radius of many rural people's lives. This was not quite the same thing as the more commonly discussed American phenomenon of localism, a normative preference for rule by proximate people. Instead, in claims of territorialism, nineteenth-century Americans did not ask for the right to make their own decisions; they asked for a distant government to rectify problems in their narrow geographical area. It was not an argument against central state intrusion, but an argument that the state could intrude idiosyncratically, the way a man might, helping people in particular neighborhoods without helping everyone. To some degree these tensions are always present within democratic politics and are magnified in the United States by the force of a federalism that encourages people to vote for representatives who favor a neighborhood or county. During the thirty-year period of Reconstruction, the view of a postwar state large enough to do almost anything but not large enough to do everything gave this natural tendency additional force, making it not a stumbling block toward developing a proper political ideology, but a constitutive part of the era's political ideology.[3]

Along with basic problems of building a new state that could enforce its laws, Holden and other elected Southern Republicans faced a massive problem of legitimacy. Although fairly elected, Holden and other Southern Republican governors during this period were hamstrung in their ability to govern by the refusal of a large, militant portion of the population to accept their rule as rightful. Using his elective office as a bully pulpit for the resumption of civil society, Holden attempted to tame this rebelliousness inside the tent of democracy. Now that Carolinians could struggle at the ballot box and the courtroom bar, Holden argued that they no longer needed to resolve their arguments with bloodshed. But in the American South as in other parts of the world, democracy itself did not resolve the problem; instead, elections and electoral outcomes became processes to be manipulated, not conveyors of righteous authority. Desperate to maintain both their local power and the exploitative labor system that relied upon it, Holden's Conservative antagonists launched paramilitary attacks upon the state, most famously through the Ku Klux Klans. In the end, Holden's effort to build a democratic state atop warring constituencies ran into the same problem that troubled military Reconstruction, a lack of force. Unable to create peace in the countryside, Holden had to turn to Washington for additional help to maintain his authority. Holden hoped that democracy would provide the stability and legitimacy he needed; in the end, events taught him the opposite lesson was true. Democracy alone could not pacify society; instead, democracy depended upon a stability it could not by itself create.

Holden's goal of an abstracted, just, and impersonal government collapsed under the weight of his supporters' hopes, his opponents' sabotage, and the flimsy basis for democratic government in the South. Holden could not build a depersonalized state because neither his opponents nor his supporters accepted it, at least upon the limited terms he could offer. His opponents denounced him in the most vicious and intimate words as a black man in white face, a military tyrant, a traitor, and a bad king whose ear they could not reach because it belonged to the freedpeople. At the same time, Holden's supporters—especially freedpeople and needy whites—also engaged in deeply personalistic politics. They made the Holden they wanted, fashioning his image as a shadowed, reduced version of Lincoln. Presuming that power was scarce and could only be spent where most needed, they argued strenuously and heartbreakingly for the intensity of their personal needs. Describing him, they also described themselves: "your humble servant" who "never saw your face," or one of the "thousands . . . who have never seen you, who yet know you and esteem you." A Wilmington man hoped his letter would "open [Holden's] heart" and make him a "companen" to them, motivated to "do every thing in your power" for them. In claiming this new patron, Republicans were not merely exercising their imaginations; they also exercised their power. Over his term, Holden moved first slowly and then sharply to fulfill their fantastic expectations of him as a champion and defender, nudged by conditions on the ground and by the letters that flooded his office. State Reconstruction in Carolina would prove that fantasies could indeed reshape reality, but only within limits. As Reconstruction devolved into a set of guerrilla wars, Holden was able to move the rhetoric of the state, but only at the margins. Although he changed the way his supporters appealed to him, he himself was also forced to become the patron his supporters wanted.[4]

Probably no one was more disappointed by this transformation than William Holden himself. The state he made was not the state he intended to build. Like the rest of his life, his governorship was full of reversals and unexpected outcomes. Born to unmarried parents and practically uneducated, Holden turned his newspaper holdings into a position atop the state Democratic Party in the 1850s. Disgruntled by the party's refusal to nominate him for high office, Holden left the Democrats, and in 1862 helped manage ex-Whig Zebulon Vance's campaign for governor. This alliance did not last long. In 1863, disgusted with the Confederate government's brutal crackdown on deserters, Holden tried to create a peace movement within the state, aimed at forcing negotiations with the Union. This stance broke his relationship with Vance and his standing in the Confederacy. In September 1863, a Georgia regiment passing through Raleigh attacked his newspaper office, crushing the doors and destroying almost everything inside. Increasingly ostracized, Holden in 1864 challenged Vance's reelection and lost handily. In 1865, Holden found himself briefly the provisional governor but could not earn election, so in 1866 and 1867 he remade himself yet again. In the kaleidoscopic politics of the postbellum South, Holden transformed himself — like Georgia's Joseph Brown — from the state's leading Democrat to its most prominent Republican.[5]

Just as he was an unlikely Republican and an improbable governor, so too was Holden an unexpected champion of African Americans' rights. At the end of the Civil War, Holden had displayed no particular interest in equality and had petitioned President Andrew Johnson to remove African American troops from the state. In his first proclamation as provisional governor in 1865, he urged freedpeople to be ruled by the "superior intelligence of the white race" and lectured them on the evils of idleness, which would make them "vicious and worthless" and eventually extinct. After Holden's dispiriting loss in 1865, and with the growth of Radical power in Congress, his stance softened. When Congress revolted against President Johnson's conciliatory efforts, rejected the 1865–66 state constitutions, divvied the Confederacy into military districts, and demanded another round of conventions with freedman suffrage, Holden saw the direction in which Reconstruction was moving and ran to catch up. After plotting the state's progress with Radical leader Thaddeus Stevens in 1866, Holden on New Year's Day, 1867, declared himself openly for enfranchisement. Holden's stance won him enemies among Conservatives but the friendship of many freedpeople. By 1868, when the new state constitution gave the vote to African American men, Holden emerged through the Republican Party as their standard-bearer. Elected in 1868 largely with their support, Holden appointed large numbers of African American magistrates and local officials, and eventually created a special force of state troops to defend against vigilante violence.[6]

As an architect and beneficiary of federal support, Holden found himself immediately challenged by his predecessor, Jonathan Worth. Dismissing the legitimacy of Holden's election, Worth declined to give up the office to him on the grounds that Holden was not actually the elected governor but merely an appointee "of the Military power of the United States." For a moment, it appeared federal troops might evict Worth forcibly from the office. Eventually, however, Worth vacated the governor's chair under "military duress" to, as he described it, a "Military force which I could not resist."[7]

At his inauguration on July 4, 1868, Holden launched a homegrown campaign for systematic, impersonal governance. In front of five thousand people in Capitol Square, Holden articulated a coherent, progressive view of the new state that defeat had created. "The unity of government, which constitutes us one people, has been restored," he said. "Its foundations are now broad enough for the whole people of whatsoever origins, color or former condition. . . . In fine, those [who] conduct the government are not the enemies of any portion of the people of the State. They desire to do justice to all, and as far as may be, to be the friends of all. If the administration of public affairs shall bring peace, prosperity and happiness, all will share in these blessings; if on the contrary, it shall produce disorder, and further suffering and misery, none will be exempt from these calamities." Instead of the traditional metaphor of the government as a body, as a fleshed figurehead, Holden transformed the state into a star. With the triumph of the North, the "full sun" of the national government evaporated the remnants of localism, the parochial hubs that had permitted patronly power to flourish. At least on the level of language, this speech dramatically altered the relationship of state and subject. A government incorporated into a human body possessed not light but eyes, a vision that could be turned intensely upon an individual but could not take in the entirety of the world. If the sun did not see people as individuals, it still cast its heat upon them. In emancipating the slaves, the government had emancipated itself from all particularistic interests; instead of serving slave owners, it now served everyone. "The law," Holden said, is "over all," the rich and powerful and the "poor and the humble." To buttress his position, Holden pointed to North Carolina's new constitution, which "very tenderly provides" for the rights of married women, and for the better treatment of the poor, the orphans, the deaf, and the blind, not as special beneficiaries, but as entitled citizens. Partly influenced by the mania for administration in postwar Washington, Holden's universal language also had a political calculation; it transformed Holden's support for and from freedpeople into a broader campaign to rationalize and equalize government.[8]

As Whittlesey and the other Freedmen's Bureau commissioners had already discovered, translating abstract language into actual conditions was enormously difficult, especially in a violent state. As a governor with few legal powers, Holden was handcuffed from the beginning. Holden understood that fairness could not exist solely as a word in a speech; it had to be enforced on the ground. "It is the duty of the Executive to see that the laws are faithfully executed and to preserve peace among the people," he said in his inaugural. "This duty will be performed promptly, fearless, and firmly. . . . There can be no peace without law, and there can be no efficacy in law without obedience." Holden anticipated disobedience: "Differences in political sentiment are to be expected, and are not calculated in themselves to endanger the State; but a purpose to subvert the Government, on the assumption that it is not properly derived, has not been constitutional[ly] adopted, and is illegitimate and not binding, should be narrowly watched and promptly checked." Immediately he attempted to replace many local officials with sympathetic men, trying to make secessionists "feel that loyal men *will* be the masters of the state." When several officers refused to surrender, what followed his inauguration was not a new set of authority upon the land but a series of local crises. In Randolph County and Charlotte and even in the state capital of Raleigh, Holden was unable to force local officials, much less regular citizens, to obey, and depended upon the military commander's assistance in "putting in operation the new government of this State." In Raleigh, he reported, "police officers" allied to the former mayor "surrounded the City Hall in a defiant and threatening manner, and . . . a colored man was fired upon by a Police officer without provocation and one of my appointees as commissioner was assailed and beaten with a bludgeon by the Chief of Police." Holden blamed the military commander for not sustaining him when he asked for help. With assistance, Holden asserted, "I am sure no riot or commotion of any kind would have taken place." Chastened, the commander sent troops to support Holden's new appointees, and shortly thereafter the legislature authorized Holden to fill some town offices.[9]

Depending upon the army, Holden seemed, as Worth argued, not an elected official but a military appointee. Even worse, if Holden's authority depended on federal troops, he did not have much authority at all. By October 1868, three months after Holden's inauguration, there were only 939 soldiers in the state's three garrisons. By October 1869, there were only 366; across the South, federal troops dropped from 17,657 to 11,237 in the same period, with by far the largest concentration in Texas. By October 1870, there were only 277 troops in North Carolina, and 4,310 total among the ten ex-Confederate states outside of Texas. Throughout his nearly three years in office, Holden again and again articulated a single solution to his problem: the creation of a state militia strong enough to be an "adequate police force in each of the counties of the State." But defining the solution was much simpler than implementing it. Forming a militia required wrestling with the question of who should be included, and the two most prominent groups of Carolina men were also politically the two most troubling. Many of the men in the antebellum militia had been absorbed with their units into the Confederate army in 1861, and their loyalty and eligibility was therefore in doubt. The other large and problematic group of potential militia members were freedmen, a group whose loyalty Holden could count on but whose enlistment might outrage wavering whites. To Holden, these questions were secondary to the governor's power. Against enemies pledged to "disregard the authority of these governments," he asserted, the governor should be "clothed by law with the necessary powers to maintain the authority of the state government against all assaults." Although Holden organized a militia in September 1868 (with the help of arms donated by Northern Republican governors), whites in three-quarters of the counties refused to accept commissions as enrolling captains, and it was largely a failure. Equally troubling, the legislature's militia law required local officials to request help before Holden could dispatch what little force he commanded. This made the militia an instrument not of the governor but of county commissioners.[10]

The politics of friendship troubled Holden's requests for a strong militia. On the one hand, he argued that the militia would allow "the known friends of the government" to defend themselves against "unfriendly hands." On the other, he sought to dissolve the notion of friendship in the solution of abstract "rights of life, liberty and property." Holden tried to resolve this problem through the language of the Bible. In a phrase often quoted by his followers, Holden declared the new government would be a "terror to evil doers and a praise to them that do well." Here, Holden cited Romans 13, which made God's power a form of abstract justice, not the merciful father's love of some of the Psalms. By emphasizing God the Fair Judge over God the Master, Holden attempted to ground his view of government in the language of the people.[11]

The light that shined from the government was dim indeed in the towns and crossroads villages far from Raleigh. Weeks after Holden's inauguration, a merchant named John Conklin wrote from Sladesville in coastal Hyde County to "give you some idea of the condition of the colored people down here, and indeed some of the poor white people." From his storefront Conklin had watched the "suffering poor" and had seen that the "getting of bread has been attended with the greatest difficulty hitherto." Although this dependence presented a humanitarian problem, Conklin argued that, with democratic expansion, it also created an opening for the governor. The key to political power, Conklin argued, was "to intercede for them" and "gain their eternal gratitude." Since desperation made men want friends, the hunger and fear in the countryside gave Holden the opportunity to build gratitude, an emotion and affiliation that bridged the gap between the personal and the political.[12]

Pleas for friendship continued to pour in because Reconstruction confirmed the intensely personalized nature of the law in North Carolina. For most Carolinians, the court system functioned through local magistrates. These magistrates, many untrained and some practically illiterate, played a far larger role in shaping people's experiences with the law than distant state supreme court justices in Raleigh. Individual magistrates not only favored their race, party, kinship group, neighbors, or co-religionists; they often refused to listen to their enemies at all, confirming the notion that rights inhered in individual protectors. In this world, a failure to have one's rights taken into account was not an exceptional flaw in the system; it was the way the system worked. From Caswell County, resident David Richmond wrote of a magistrate who was an "original Secessionist of the deepest dye . . . loves the power thus placed in his hands over the people." As the only magistrate in the area, he handed out appearance tickets and collected debts in nearly despotic fashion, whereby "even honest men are forced to go into bankruptcy." Richmond asked Holden whether this could be done legally. "The people are generally disposed to submit to law, if they know what it is," he wrote; "but in the present confused state of things it is impossible that they know it, and if they ask for knowledge, from the leaders about here, they are often advised to their own hurt." Richmond wished to remain "loyal," but only if "loyal men govern me." In a postscript, Richmond asked the cost of a "cheap grade" of a book of statutes. Richmond's faith in the letter of the law showed not only the potential to create Holden's world of justice but also Richmond's bitter judgment of the world as it was.[13]

Instead of opportunities to enforce justice, however, these local conditions often presented Holden with a morass of competing stories, each deployed to gain his support. An armed battle in coastal Carteret County was as complex as *Rashomon*. At first Holden learned to his horror that a Northern "Worthy lady" had been attacked by a local white man, "thrown upon the ground, and jumped upon and stomped and thereby one or two of her ribs were broken." In a furious letter to the county sheriff, Holden tried to use his moral authority as leverage against what he suspected was a local conspiracy. Instead of arresting the white man, however, local magistrates charged the woman herself and refused to hear her witnesses. To gain the attention of a "higher power" who might "defend her," she claimed the attack was politically motivated. Against this political outrage, the local sheriff presented the case not as a test of justice but a personal feud. The wildly conflicting accounts in these depositions proved not the facts of the case but the importance of patrons in legal proceedings. During their physical struggle, the white man promised to "get a warrant" from a friendly magistrate, while the Northern woman threatened to turn to a higher power in Holden to get "soldiers to protect her" and a pardon if she killed him. Frustrated and angry, Holden acted, but in the only way he could. He forwarded the information on to the local commanding general. When that general pleaded that the "military power is second to the civil in the state," the Northern woman pointed out the emptiness of his words, since the civil authority was helpless. The best way to create order was "the sight of U.S. Muskets or *Straps*," she wrote. Completing the circle, however, the general referred her back to Holden. The search for justice in Carteret County had become a search for a patron, conducted with equal fervor on both sides of the dispute.[14]

Holden remained dependent upon federal troops to enforce his orders, but the military's authority was limited in a state that had been readmitted to the Union. Although the Raleigh post commander offered to "send a force" to execute Holden's orders, the district's presiding general had grave doubts about the military's authority. In one of Reconstruction's nasty ironies, Holden's own inauguration made it impossible for the military to exercise power, for the elimination of the provisional government, according to the general, had taken "with it the power to exercise by the District Commander, any judicial functions." Across the South, governors and generals struggled with this question in 1868. In August, during outright street battles in Augusta, Georgia, General George Meade ruled — with War Department backing — that military officers could only intervene upon authorization from Washington, not upon the application of a governor or mayor. Although the War Department maintained the right, based upon a 1795 domestic insurrection law, to provide assistance, from then on the discretion would lie not with generals or governors on the ground but with the White House.[15]

Instead of an arm of the governor, the army became a sheathed sword. Increasingly, Holden found himself wielding a power that was merely titular. If he relied upon language, it was because he had few other weapons at his disposal. Holden's necessary dependence upon local power created pockets of justice and pockets of institutionalized violence and pockets of something like statelessness. In early September, Holden asked Meade to send troops to Halifax County, where a "small number of troops" in three townships would create a "salutary terror" in the "disaffected and disloyal." Instead of a salutary terror, however, Holden received silence. In a telegram, one of Meade's staffers said that "he will not change the disposition of troops" except in cases of "overt" or "actual" resistance that constituted "emergencies." The powerlessness of local officials was not the military's concern. The "civil authorities must attempt at least to preserve the peace."[16]

To create that civil authority, build a functioning legal system, associate his government with the power of the Union soldiers, and stabilize violent local communities, Holden tied his efforts to the Freedmen's Bureau when he could. Holden made his connections to the bureau clear by drawing ex-agents like William A. Cutter into his administration. At first Cutter wondered whether an active military officer like himself should be allowed to serve as a civil justice of the peace, but he did understand why Holden wanted him. As a bureau agent, he would be immediately visible to the freedpeople, a breathing sign of government. Even for less-sympathetic whites, Cutter's administrative experience and central office would make him a starkly professional contrast to magistrates who heard cases on their farms or in their kitchens, at irregular hours and with even more irregular results. "Should I accept I know that nearly all the business of the county would be put upon me, for it is well known that I have an office here where I may always be found," Cutter wrote in a letter asking his commanding officer if he could accept the position.[17]

In Williamson Buck's town of Company Shops, Alamance County, soon to be the center of violent struggle between Republicans and Conservatives, Frederick W. Liedtke possessed Cutter's insight but not his hesitancy. Liedtke jumped at Holden's offer to augment his bureau title of assistant subassistant commissioner with the civil role of justice of the peace. For Liedtke, the move was part of what he would later term his "sacred duty" to use his authority to protect freedpeople. Disloyal whites, he asserted, "fear that, with the authority of a Justice of the Peace vested in me, there will be no chance left them to discharge people unjustly from Employment, because of the exercise of their political rights, and to oppress them otherwise, and . . . it is my intention, if I have the right to do it, to prosecute all such evildoers and bring them to punishment according to Law." Liedtke's work in North Carolina was part of what would be a lifelong involvement in governance. Forty-one years old in 1868, Liedtke had migrated to the United States from Prussia in 1856. After the war, he would leave North Carolina for the West, serving as state auditor of Nebraska and later as a justice of the peace in Cottle County, Texas. Once appointed, Liedtke would prove a tough-minded magistrate, determined to implement the bureau's goals through the mechanisms of state power.[18]

Despite the strong actions of individual magistrates like Liedtke, the state largely appeared ungoverned and perhaps ungovernable in the summer of 1868. In the absence of state authority, freedpeople and white Unionists gathered together to defend themselves, claiming private rights to violence. Over 1867 and 1868, African Americans flooded into Union Leagues, political organizations with roots in wartime Red Strings, and other loyalist vigilance societies that educated, mobilized, and defended Republicans. For African Americans, the Union and Loyal Leagues were important avenues into electoral politics, community formation, and self-defense. As with Holden, freedpeople and loyal whites made the leagues — originally formed by Northern businessmen — into the kind of organization they wanted, drawing upon their political training in slavery and emancipation. Drilling as military units, Southern leagues became locally controlled political operations. They also roused immense and violent counterattacks from local Conservatives fearful of Republican voting power and armed African Americans. Experience with patronalism did not contradict judgments about the importance of organizing; instead, the two worked hand in hand. Grassroots actions did not eliminate the need for help from above; they made it possible to obtain the help people desired.[19]

Amid this struggle, a justice of the peace in Halifax's South Gaston found himself as helpless as Hugo Hillebrandt had been. In August 1868, a "conspiracy" of Conservatives discussed "shooting the Civil Officers + the heads of the League," "made threats open in public," and wounded two African American Republicans. "No Republicans life is safe just in this vicinity," a magistrate wrote. Although he asked Holden for clarification of "what course to pursue," he tipped his hand about the limits of his power when he asked Holden to "please withhold my name in this matter as my life is threatened day by day and am really in danger." At least the people of South Gaston had a magistrate they could go to. Two weeks later, in the nearby town of Summit, a traveling Union League official found that the "loyal people" were "sunct down in despair." There had been "a great deal of shooting by those who are hired by the ku-klan-kluck, and I believe they intend to kill or at least shoot every man that will cast a vote for Colfax or grant." Therefore the Union League official appealed to Holden "for the most inteligent water proof, + fire tried republicans speakers" to come to a speech in September at Littleton depot. "The people of this state must be protected," he wrote. "Please do what you can for us in our distress."[20]

The November 1868 presidential elections heightened tensions. The national campaign assumed immense local importance in part because of the personalities involved, in part because everyone understood its ramifications for Reconstruction in the South. Running on the Republican side, Ulysses Grant literally embodied Union power, while Democratic New York governor Horatio Seymour pledged to dismantle Reconstruction. At stake were the small number of Union troops still in the state and the potential for military intervention on behalf of freedpeople or Republican governments. In October, hearing rumors that Conservatives imported "repeating rifles" into the state to intimidate Republicans and "prevent a free election," Holden ordered magistrates and sheriffs to protect the "weak against the strong." Every "star" on the American flag "shines down with vital fire into every spot, however remote or solitary, to consume those who may resist the authority of the government, or who oppress the defenceless and the innocent." Holden's vision of a government that "shines with vital fire into every spot, however remote or solitary," was a mirage. In Fayetteville, a local judge, one of the "most upright" men of the town, was "grossly assailed for one of his decisions." His wife fled to Raleigh begging "protection," but without an effective militia, Holden could only ask the mayor and sheriff for help.[21]

As Union Leagues and other Republicans fought for local power, they turned to Holden as a patron, a debtor, and a friend. In calling upon him, they pleaded in three distinct but overlapping languages: a universal statement of the governor's duties to all of his citizens, a claim about the governor's personal obligation to the weak, and a political demand for support for fellow Republicans. Combining Holden's broader, abstract language with their own particularistic pleas, these Carolinians fused together views of state power as a form of friendship and as a right. In the intimacy and intensity of Reconstruction, there was an especially thin line between public and private lives; a political opinion might spark not just debate but shunning, boycotting, and murder. Similarly, personal grudges and feuds quickly became political as they drew in partisans among the local magistrates and officers. In October, a month before the presidential election, Conservatives in Granville County's Tally Ho attacked Union Leagues systematically, "not only now and then." Having placed the violence into its political context, Silas Curtis, the Union League leader reporting the incidents to Holden, then showed its human side. A group of marauding whites "went to a Colored mans house and got him out and Beet him cruely beet his wife ann cut her dress open and tied her to a tree." At the next house, they "got hold" of another man's wife and "shot her in the back and by side of the face." By tying together the political with the personal, Curtis was able to fit every past (and future) assault into a partisan narrative. Holden should act not because they were frightened but because their suffering had become a political problem. "In the first place," Curtis asserted, "you are our State Executive and when we are having outrages committed among us you are our only Refuge to which we have to flee for advice and protection." As their "Refuge," Holden was required, at least in their portrayal, to provide "some protection." "God knows we most have something other wise we will have to give up Gen. Grant and take Seymore," Curtis continued, "and if I have to do it I am going to take me a Rope and go to the woods." The Union League officer's way of addressing the letter reinforced his point about the relationship between the personal and the political. To get this message to Holden, he left its address blank and wrote a note on the side asking someone unnamed to "please hand this to Gov W W Holden. I thought if backed it to him these Rebels would destroy it."[22]

The presidential campaign created both problems and opportunities for Republicans in the neighborhoods. Although the campaign brought down an increasing wave of Conservative repression, it also transformed Republicans' personal suffering into proof of their friendship to Holden, a proof they used in hopes of convincing him to repay loyalty with protection. "Those of us who profess to be friends of Republican party wee are looked upon as the filth of creation and are called negroes and friends of that old Villain of a negro spoiler old Bill Holden," wrote John W. Hoflen. By associating themselves with Holden, white men had blackened themselves, lost their racial status, and also risked their own lives. This association flowed in both directions; as they suffered for Holden, so too might Holden, "a Dammd Negrofied Son of a Bitch," have to suffer for them. Hoflen's local enemies promised to "go to Raleigh and take old Holden out and hang him to the first limb as they would another negro." From this "state of confusion," Hoflen made a personal appeal for rescue to "my der friend," whom he does not seem to have met: "I wish I could see you face to face and could tell you wee are in the way of the opposite party and would be by them Exterminated and wish the Rest of us yourself and the Freedmen but thank God they have not Got it in there power."[23]

With federal troops helping keep peace in various parts of the state, the November 1868 election passed relatively peacefully. Grant triumphed, carrying the nation by about 300,000 votes out of 5.7 million, North Carolina by about 12,000 votes out of 180,000, and the electoral college 214 to 80. Immediately people in North Carolina made the connection between Grant's victory and the continuance of federal power on the ground in North Carolina. Most directly, this idea emerged in a letter from Stephen Walker of New Bern, who had "taken it a pound him self to rite" Grant. "We poor colred people here in this distressed place," he wrote the president-elect, believe "the lord hav place you in a place for as a father [over us]."[24]

To the state, Holden praised the election as the triumph of civil society. On November 17, he declared, "We now have, indeed, a free republic in which every man in nearly every state is fully the equal of every man in political and civil rights." Now the government would have "authority" and "stability" enough to ensure the people's "confidence." Again Holden tried to redefine the relationship between friendship and governance. When Holden stated that "this government is in the hands of its friends and will be administered by them," Holden used the term broadly, not to refer to personal intimacies or even to fictive affiliations but to those people who believed in preserving free elections. Therefore, his government by "friends" would aim not for patronage but "for the protection and benefit of all." By cloaking protection in universal rights, Holden hoped to obscure his own actions in abstract claims, presenting himself not as a patron but as an impartial administrator.[25]

Immediately, however, people on the ground doubted the impact of the November election. Instead of a revolution over society, Frederick Liedtke saw the limits of Grant's victory. A former Freedmen's Bureau agent who was a justice of the peace in Alamance County's Company Shops, Liedtke looked bleakly out on an ungoverned and perhaps ungovernable country. The "election went off quietly," he commented, thanks to military protection, but in the two weeks "since the election everything seems to have changed." The "unreconstructed rebels," "neither respecting nor fearing the Laws enacted by the State Legislature . . . are now giving vent to their abominable hatred and desire of revenge." Hundreds of "families of poor colored people, old and young," had been "thrown out of employment and shelter because they have dared to exercise their rights as freemen at the last election." Despite Liedtke's civil power, it was "but little use to go with them before a magistrate." Like Holden, Liedtke was leery of "upholding and protecting the colored man in everything, right or wrong." In November 1868, however, support for the freedpeople looked to Liedtke not like granting special privileges to them but like ensuring their survival. What he saw was not a few bad actors but "a preconcerted plan, acted upon, it seems, by whole communities of persons lately in rebellion." Too "cowardly" to openly oppose the "Laws of the Land," they sought to "incite riots and perhaps an insurrection by starving and driving from their homes, an ignorant race of people easily led astray." For the moment, an abstract, color-blind approach to governance would be a colossal failure. Since landlords controlled the neighborhoods, the only hope for the freedpeople for the next "year or two" was to find a counterweight in Raleigh to make them "independent" of their employers. Once the state equalized power between landowners and laborers, it would create "peace and mutual relations of dependence upon each other." Then, the state could contain conflict within a civil society. For now, it was either intervene on freedpeople's behalf or let them suffer.[26]

Liedtke was an astute observer. Instead of solving the problems in the state, the 1868 presidential election inaugurated a violent campaign for local control in North Carolina with one epicenter at Liedtke's own Company Shops and neighboring Caswell County. For a time Grant's victory protected

Republicans in North Carolina, maintaining at least some federal troop presence, and some hope for help from Washington. But having a friend in Washington was no panacea. For one thing, as Carolinians well knew, friends could get overburdened or distracted. For another, a friend's capacity to help was limited, especially with fewer and fewer federal troops stationed in the state. Although Grant supported Southern Republicans militarily throughout his first term, he ran out of will and congressional support in his second term, and by 1875 famously refused to dispatch troops to defend embattled Mississippi governor Adelbert Ames. Instead of a uniform power over the land, Holden and Republicans and their Union League exerted significant power over narrow localities, while Conservatives working through the Ku Klux Klans controlled other areas, and parts of the state were essentially no-man's-land. Inside these pockets of statelessness, North Carolinians learned that power depended not upon abstract rules but upon enforcement, and enforcement depended upon both self-defense and the attention of patrons.

Political friendships, formed in the heat of campaign arguments, were powerful even if they were fantastic. In December 1868, a "poor" tenant farmer named John F. Davis from nearby Hillsboro turned to Holden to help him find a job because, as he put it, "I know no one in the city of Raleigh but you and your sons." It turned out, however, that Davis used the word "know" in a highly imaginative way. His definition of knowledge, like his definition of friendship, was more aspirational than descriptive. Davis admitted that "I am not aquanted with you" but claimed intimacy because "I like your politics and principles." Davis blamed "Conservitives" for "trying to Starve me and my family for the last two years but if I am poor I expect to stick up to my principles." By attaching his poverty to his loyalty, Davis shifted his burden onto his prospective patron. Davis was as imaginative in his request as he was in his friendship; while he wanted Holden's help finding a job, he did not want something too strenuous since he was "too weak" for hard labor. Optimistically, he thought teaching school sounded easy. As he made his case, he also literally illustrated his feelings for the governor by decorating Holden's name with ink dots.[27]

Although people continued to plea for money, jobs, and pardons, after the November 1868 election, they particularly begged for protection against the Ku Klux Klans that inspired fear and sometimes exercised something like authority over increasingly large portions of the state. Klans challenged the state's legitimacy. In many areas the Klans were a direct adjunct of the Conservative, soon to be Democratic, Party and scourged Republican legislators and magistrates. Klans also attempted to reconstitute imbalanced labor relationships by attacking resistant workers, preventing freedpeople from traveling to new employers, and assaulting local politicians. Klans also functioned as literally neighborhood associations, and the racial dominance they enforced traced a narrow circumference as they ordered opponents to leave "the neighborhood," "the township," "the district," "the county," "the country," or "the community." While Klan power was often immense, its reach was narrow. Klaverns were recruited from kin and proximate neighbors animated by local anxieties or a desire for neighborhood control. This intensely local base helped bind white Klan members together but also undermined efforts to turn the Klans into a more efficient statewide organization. In Alamance County's Albright Township, Klan leader Joseph N. Wood beat freedpeople in his own area but refused to obey orders to help nearby klaverns assault their opponents, arguing that those were local matters he did not understand. When pressed, he disbanded his den altogether. Although some Klan defenders dismissed their attacks as "private malice," "neighborhood transactions," or "purely personal difficulties," they were all the more intensely political because their focus was local. When Alamance County freedman Caswell Holt was attacked by people he "had always been knowing . . . all my life," his landlord's daughter tried to convince him that "maybe they have come a thousand miles," but Holt and his wife dismissed the idea. "No people a thousand miles off would come that far to beat me," Holt said. When Holt moved to safety, he went not a thousand miles but seven, into the town of Graham.[28]

Klans produced pockets of lawlessness and statelessness that Holden could not control. In the "lower portion of Lenoir County and Duplin County" in eastern North Carolina, a "band of white horse thieves and desperadoes" dominated the region and left citizens unable "to obtain assistance from the civil authority." In 1869 this band murdered five freedmen at the bridge over the Neuse River. The narrowness but intensity of the Klans' control became clear to a man named Charles Isler when he traveled from Wayne County to that region in February 1869 in search of a stolen horse. As soon as he crossed the Neuse River, a sympathetic local white man told him that "there was no chance to get" the horse once the thieves reached "that side of Sam Davis' house." The next day, Isler asked a magistrate for assistance, and the magistrate refused, "saying that it was more than he could do for him, that any common man who undertook to go through there, unless he was well armed would be killed." A local general wanted to help but was so weakly manned that he had to turn to Holden. Instead of a regiment, Isler received a single detective, and one with a daunting travel schedule, as Holden also dispatched the detective at the same time to investigate the Northern widow's case in Carteret County, and others in Lenoir, Wayne, and Duplin. Even when Holden did send militia companies to enforce laws, the effect was only temporary. In Jones County, Holden responded to the murders of the local sheriff and a freedman by sending a white company. When the troops left a few weeks later, another white official was killed.[29]

Not even the Klans or Union Leagues claimed space as fiercely during Reconstruction as the mixed-race Lowry band. The state's absolute weakness was never more evident than in the portions of Robeson County where the band largely ruled supreme. Originating among families of Lumbee Indians and gaining followers from freedpeople and white Republicans, the Lowrys, according to one local white man, dominated "a region of about eight or ten miles square, in which this old free colored population lives; it is called Scuffletown." During the war, Lowrys resisted Confederate impressments and helped escaped Union prisoners using their knowledge of the Back Swamp, a ten-mile-long stretch of land filled with islands, caves, and bogs. "There are very few who know where the islands are," the local man pointed out, "or where their caves or dens are." While the Lowry band was not solely political, its most extreme acts followed a white Conservative takeover of county government, and many family members had supported the local Freedmen's Bureau agent against local Conservative opposition.[30]

In appealing to Holden, fearful and desperate people asked him to live up to his pledge to create a universal peace across the state. These pleas tied together their desperation, their hopes for Holden, and their awareness of his platform. On July 4, 1869, A. L. Ramsour and his friends tried to raise a U.S. flag at Newton, the seat of piedmont Catawba County. "Some of those Hot War men tore it down," Ramsour wrote. Although Ramsour tried to report them, a "reb court" put Ramsour himself on trial. Without recourse close to home, Ramsour turned to Raleigh. Ramsour tried to make his suffering Holden's and to cross the line from private into "publick man" by describing the way that locals mocked the governor, showing "all sortes of ugly pictures" and calling him "worse than negroes." Four months later, Ramsour wrote again; this time he was just as helpless and even more desperate: "I take my pen in my fingers to write to you and ask some protection for my Boddy as I have been almost Beaten to death by those Rebles" intending to give "us union league hell." Ramsour found "that there is no protection here. . . . They have killed my stock . . . and now have determined to take my life." As he wrote, Ramsour added one more character to his story, a God who "overruled all." Through this image of a powerful God, Ramsour shifted his appeal. "We all have our dutyes to perform, if we expect his protection," Ramsour wrote. "I do know that you will have to give an Acount at the great day of Acounter if you do not your duty. . . . I wish some protection from you and will expect it." By clothing himself in God, Ramsour transformed himself from beggar to boss. Over the course of his letter, through his "suffering" he acquired a kind of Christlike "martyrdom for Principals of Love more truth and justice." Ramsour rode the Bible in two directions, as a prod and as a weapon. Despite his intensity and his persistence, Ramsour's efforts had no effect. On the letter, Holden wrote, "File this."[31]

From this lawless society, people fashioned a patron who might help them escape their predicaments. In April 1869, David L. May cast Holden not just as an administrator but as a "friend to the poore and a farther to the fatherless." Here, quoting Psalm 68:5, May suggested the difficulty that Holden was having in persuading even his own followers to believe his universal rhetoric. After May's experience with the law, it is hard to blame him. May had been charged with stealing meat. Although witnesses testified that he was innocent, he was sentenced to three years of hard labor. May sought Holden's help on the grounds of "compashion," for "my poore Suffering children." May needed a friend because his conviction made him friendless. He wrote, "I no the poore is loked on by a great many with contempt and scorn. . . . I put my trust in God that you will notice me as i am poore an unnoticed unless it is by poore friends that cant have power to help me mutch."[32]

Most evocatively, Holden was, in Sarah Mabury's words, a "friend unseen." A widow from Caldwell County, Mabury had tried hard to achieve independence. By 1869, as locals tried to force her from her farm, Mabury hoped to make her individual tragedy the governor's responsibility. "If there is not some provision made for the poor folks they will be oblige to suffur," she wrote. Her choice therefore was not between independence and dependence but between dependence on Holden and dependence on Conservatives, or between acceptable dependence and abject suffering. The gift she wanted from him was "a little understanding." This was a twofold understanding, both actual knowledge of the law's provisions for widows and the compassion Holden might show to her once he recognized her plight. "I know you have the power to befriend me," she wrote, so she seated herself "to write a friend unseen" for help.[33]

In this striking phrase "friend unseen," Mabury illustrated the central role of Christianity in the politics of dependence. Much of the language and many of the images of power that Carolinians pressed on Holden were drawn

Democracy and the Problem of Power

directly from the Bible and from Christian hymns. In making governors little gods, people like Mabury hoped to access divine promises of mercy and grace. Her phrase drew upon the double meaning of the language of dependence, rooted at once in everyday practice of friendship and in the ethereal world of faith and fantasy. Mabury's language probably was drawn from a hymn written earlier in the century by Charlotte Elliott, "O Holy Saviour, Friend Unseen," that defined God through "Thine arm," upon which "Thou bid'st us lean." In the hymn God was the exile's "place of rest," "our strength, our rock, our all." Elliott, the hymn writer, knew her own version of dependence. After a devastating illness at about age thirty-two, she became "weak and feeble in body" and turned toward hymn writing as a way of maintaining her "strong imagination." Most famously, Elliott wrote "Just as I Am," frequently described as the most successful conversion hymn ever published in the English language. In that hymn, she proclaims that though "poor, wretched, blind . . . Yea, all I need in Thee to find, O Lamb of God, I come, I come." In singing about God, her own voice was both erased and visible. Simultaneously, she both disappeared into God and appeared as his worthy offspring, a kind of personal transubstantiation through song. In her hymn to Holden, Mabury performed the same double act, placing words written by others onto her own lips in a song of dependence and need that also became a song of celebration and glorification, a song of a self that disappeared and yet also was at last made present.[34]

Gendered languages of chivalry and honor provided another powerful rhetorical tool for Carolinians who pleaded to Holden. In the piedmont town of Taylorsville, a widow named Sally McDowell in November 1869 "set myself this beautifull eavning to rite you a few lines." "Left a lone in this wide and Sinfull world" after the death of her husband and her oldest son in the war, she had "no friends to look too to help mee." So, she wrote, "i want you to Bee a friend to mee if you pleas for if you don't do something fur me i will haft to sufer. . . . How can I Bair to hear my Dear little son crying for bread." As a "gentleman and all the one that is in this world and a Honerfull man that Bairs a good name," Holden was obliged, she hoped, to silence her children's cries and "have mercy on the poore widowed and fartherless children . . . for god sake please send it as soon as you get this." Yanceyville's Jane McAlpin remade her personal need into a broad effort to "beseech [Holden] to hear the cries of a widow + fatherless child." McAlpin was trapped under debt. Frantic and desperate, feeble and "very destitute," McAlpin asked Holden "as a friend to the poor + needy, not to have my house + lot taken from me." As she called upon Holden's help, she classed herself a worthy dependent, claiming she was willing to work, "taking in sewing if I could get the work to do, but I can get but very little + am often deprived of the common comforts of life." If she were forced to leave her house, she dreaded "the consequences, as all of my relations are dead that are able to help me." With no other person to claim her as a dependent, she wrote, "I beg you to see into the matter + have it stopped if you possibly can + I have no doubt but you can as there is no justice in it." McAlpin was certain that if Holden "could conceive of the unhappiness cased by the thought of being left without a home," he would help. In this, however, she was wrong. On his note to his secretary Holden wrote: "Write her that I regret the trouble in which she is involved, but that I have no power to help her."[35]

Over 1869 Holden did what he could to suppress the Klans and restore the force of the state. In March 1869, he dispatched a militia company to increasingly troubled Alamance County, and in October he declared four counties to be in a state of "insurrection and insubordination," but he still relied upon local officials — many of whom were themselves Klan members — for enforcement. Finally, in January 1870, the legislature authorized the governor to dispatch the militia against a state of insurrection, whether or not county officials requested help.[36]

Holden did not have to wait long to use this new power. In February 1870, the violence in Alamance County created a problem that Holden would never resolve. Company Shops, the Alamance County town where Williamson Buck worked as a carpenter, had long been one of the most lawless localities in the state. In 1868 and 1869, a white teacher named Alonzo B. Corliss described violence as simply another part of the repertoire of politics there, as normal and expected as an overly long speech, a deal-cutting party leader, or a bribe. By threat and assault, Conservatives intimidated local magistrates and Corliss himself into leaving the county. In December 1869, Corliss was "seized and dragged from his home" by a band of disguised men and "cruelly beaten and scourged." Klansmen whipped Corliss thirty times, shaved half his head, and painted half of his face black. While Holden tried to resolve the crisis with federal troops, his efforts were unavailing. On February 26, 1870, a group of disguised men murdered Wyatt Outlaw, a black Union League leader and "industrious mechanic, well to do and prospering" who served as town commissioner and magistrate. To demonstrate their power, they not only killed him but hung his body "to the limb of a tree" near the courthouse with a note pinned to his body reading: "Beware you guilty both white and black." "No crime can be alleged against him except that he is a colored man, a Republican," a witness wrote. Brutal outrages "become common almost nightly, and people have become so terrified that they dare not report the outrages committed on them," another witness wrote. "The civil authorities are powerless to bring these offenders against law and humanities to justice." Shortly after Outlaw's murder, the postmaster at Company Shops "was compelled to flee the county, and while absent a band of men armed and disguised visited his house with the purpose, doubtless, of taking his life, and this within a short distance of federal troops stationed in the county." On March 7 Holden finally gave up on public opinion and declared Alamance County in a "state of insurrection." Still reluctant to use the militia, Holden relied upon forty federal troops to prove the power of the governments and the authority of the law. Holden knew he needed more; he asked Grant to suspend the right of habeas corpus in the county, bring criminals before military tribunals, and have them "shot" in order to create peace and order. "The remedy would be a sharp and a bloody one," he added, "but it is as indispensable as was the suppression of the rebellion."[37]

During this period, Holden experimented with other forms of restoring order that revealed the enduringly personal and localized nature of power. Holden succeeded in pacifying neighboring Orange County largely through the help of an influential Conservative, Dr. Pride Jones. Although no ally of Holden, Jones tried to "embody and direct this public opinion" against vigilantism and restore the "laws to their supremacy" by serving as captain of the county militia. But in relying upon a man who could literally "embody" authority, Holden succeeded not in imposing any kind of universal law but in finding useful patrons. As nearby Alamance County worsened, Jones wanted to use his personal influence there, too, asking Holden to make him captain of the Alamance militia. But Holden had lost his patience. "The civil law is silent and powerless" there, he wrote.[38]

In the spring of 1870, spurred perhaps by the upcoming August state election, whites initiated a reign of terror in the neighboring county of Caswell. Four magistrates reported that they had no power to protect themselves and that unless they could "get protection from the national government," they could not remain in the county. In April, the Conservative insurgency escalated across the state, as twenty-one people were "scourged" by a band of disguised men, and then on May 13 an African American named Robin Jacobs was murdered near Leasburg. On May 14 an African American man in Lincoln was tied to a tree while a band of fifteen Klansmen "in succession committed a rape on his wife." Around the same time, a band of white men raped an African American woman at dusk "and afterwards stuck their knives in various parts of her body." Finally, on May 21, one of those helpless Caswell County magistrates, state senator John W. Stephens, was murdered. As a Freedmen's Bureau agent, a magistrate, a state detective, and a state legislator, Stephens had provoked the enmity of many local whites as he fought to defend African Americans. In August 1868, after a Conservative "riot" during which a black Republican was beaten "very severely," Stephens had begged unsuccessfully for troops. Despite the lack of protection, Stephens continued to behave courageously and provocatively. At a May 1870 meeting of the Conservative-Democrats, Stephens infuriated them by sitting in the front row and taking notes. As the meeting progressed, local Conservatives lured Stephens into an empty office, hung him, cut his throat, stabbed him in the chest, and threw his body into a woodpile in the basement, while speeches continued outside the door. Even one of Stephens's bitterest opponents called the murder "barbarous" and "unparalleled in a civilized country." Stephens was "a bad man," one local Conservative wrote, "but he was a better man than his assassins." Soon after, a black legislator fled the county in fear.[39]

In response, Holden at last acted, dismissing local whites who wanted him to appoint "some liberal, intelligent, moderate *gentleman*" over the region like the hated former Freedmen's Bureau agent William B. Bowe. (Bowe himself was arrested soon after as a Klan member.) Instead Holden declared Caswell to be in a state of insurrection, suspended habeas corpus, and dispatched a special militia of about 350 "native white loyalists" under a former Union commander. The militia Holden sent was not at all like the militia he had been saddled with through most of his tenure; several hundred members had been recruited from heavily white and anti-Klan areas in western North Carolina and eastern Tennessee. Another branch had been completely reorganized by prominent Unionists in June 1870 to "restore order," although this militia lacked even money for uniforms. With the support of Grant, Holden ordered the militia to take control of Caswell and Alamance Counties and arrest about one hundred men. Another detachment settled in Cleveland County, home of statewide Klan leader Plato Durham. In July, Grant accepted Holden's request for federal troops and dispatched forces into three counties. Together, the intensity of the violence and the efficacy of Grant's response helped inspire Congress to act; its 1871 Civil Rights, or Ku Klux Klan, Act offered federal protection to freedpeople, made some violence a federal crime, and authorized the president to suspend habeas corpus.[40]

As Holden declared war in Caswell County, he credited the many letters he received from victims for inspiring him to adopt "some means of protection to society." If any single letter was easy to file away, in the aggregate they had become a demand he could no longer ignore. Later, Holden claimed his actions answered those pleas and proved that the "Power of the State government to protect, maintain and perpetuate itself has been tested and demonstrated." Offenders had "been made to tremble before the avenging hand of power. The majesty of the law has been vindicated."[41]

But Holden's actions would be his undoing. The men his militia arrested were held under indefinite confinement without being charged, and soon state supreme court justice Richmond M. Pearson ordered Holden to bring the prisoners into civil court. Holden refused. "No one goes before me in respect for the civil law," Holden wrote, but "civil government was crumbling around me." In his legal opinion, Pearson agreed that civil authorities were "unable to protect its citizens" but said that this did not empower the governor to suspend habeas corpus. The two of them therefore debated key questions about legitimacy and authority. Holden claimed that a state could be held to the forms of the law only when its survival was not threatened; under pressure, North Carolina — like the wartime Union and Confederacy — might take extraordinary measures to protect itself. That this was not an open war but an undeclared one did not change the issue. To Pearson, a state's legitimacy depended upon its adherence to the form of the law, whether or not its commitment threatened its survival. Even as Pearson issued his opinion, he demonstrated his understanding of the severity of the crisis by sending a writ to Holden but not ordering its enforcement. By August 1870, Holden, believing he had restored order and feeling pressure from the federal courts, accepted Pearson's order and charged or released the remaining prisoners, but it was too late. Along with legal jeopardy, Holden had also risked political fallout. Despite military protection at polling places, his Republicans lost the August election and control of the legislature to the Conservatives.[42]

When the new Conservative-controlled legislature convened, a former Klan member introduced articles of impeachment on the grounds that Holden had unlawfully declared a state of insurrection, ordered arrests, and violated rights of habeas corpus, as well as misappropriated funds from the treasury to pay the troops. By refusing to seat Republican legislators from militarily occupied counties, Conservatives increased their numerical supremacy to more than the two-to-one margin necessary for impeachment. Shortly afterward, Holden turned over his powers to his lieutenant governor. In March 1871, the Senate convicted him of violating prisoners' rights to habeas corpus and other charges, removed him from the governor's chair, and barred him from holding office in the state again. Holden's struggle for distinction led him to one he had not anticipated; he was the first governor in American history to be successfully impeached. For most of the next twenty-one years, Holden lived on in Raleigh, serving as postmaster, editing newspapers, and tending his garden. Although several politicians made efforts to restore his political rights, none of them was successful, and he died a pariah.[43]

The man who replaced Holden, and the man whom Williamson Buck would call "your magisty," was Tod Caldwell. The first lieutenant governor in state history, Caldwell had been a Whig and secession opponent before the war. After surrender, he helped Holden found the state's Republican Party. Although he was not an especially well-known figure, he immediately inherited both Holden's problems and his supporters. Upon his ascension first as acting governor in December 1870 then as permanent governor in March 1871, Caldwell received the same types of begging letters that flooded Holden. At the same time, Caldwell faced Klan uprisings in Rowan County and could only respond with "regret," since the legislature had revoked his power over the militia. In the absence of any constraint, the Klan continued its assaults. While a congressional committee in Washington, D.C., took testimony from abused Carolinians, Klan members back in North Carolina destroyed the newspaper press of one of the testifiers, attacked a state legislator, and drove a judge from town. Caldwell asked President Grant for assistance, saying that the "desperadoes" were "known to their victims, but those who have been punished fear to expose those whom they know, lest they may be more severely visited in the future." Caldwell therefore requested a company of cavalry to preserve the peace.[44]

Again, Grant responded with troops and put down the uprising. Altogether, federal responses to the Klans, although sometimes slow, were one of the most effective government acts of the nineteenth century. Through a combination of military responses and congressional legislation, the federal government largely succeeding in quashing a regionwide insurgency. Grant's interventions into North Carolina had the effect of building faith in Grant as a savior not in the institution of government. Soon, the "donetroten Colord Men" of Sampson County begged Grant to "Pray Your Hon to give us some protaction." In March 1873, a group of "colord poor laboring class of workingmen" in Wadesboro called on Grant to "friend us if you please. . . . We dont Stand back when we go to vote. . . . We beg for this as Sistans as you our Strong. . . . Please to healp us in the Sight of gord." In a quick succession of sentences, they claimed Grant's attention both from their abject need ("we beg") and from their commitment to democratic organizing ("we don't Stand back when we go to vote"). When a band of men in 1873 murdered a "collered boy" in Red Bank, his landlord asked for help first from Governor Caldwell, who was sympathetic, calling it a "crying shame that an *atrocity* such as you represent this to be, should go unpunished." But Caldwell referred him to the "Courts" as "I am powerless." Johnson next turned to Grant, "your Excelency," in a futile request for "justice."[45]

Back in North Carolina, weeks after his inauguration, Caldwell received a plea from a very different Caldwell, one who shared his last name but not his power. Franklin Caldwell lived in Catawba County and had been "called upon by many good citizens" to inform the governor of what was going on between Sherills Ford and Newton. "Thear is at least one Hundred lawless Persons in gaged in making rades at night in disguise whipping poor Whites + Blacks + Ravising women + threting the lives + Property of good union men," he wrote. Franklin Caldwell's letter illustrated both the intensity and specificity of violence. Despite the anarchy in other parts of the state, his own township of Mountain Creek was quiet because the "Union Element is too strong for them." Franklin Caldwell wanted a "company of U.S. Troops sent to Catawba County + arrest some of them + that I think will do a great deal of good if not we must fight or Run." Governor Caldwell disappointed him, calling it "impossible to send troops" and urging him to be a "good citizen" and go through the courts. While Caldwell continued Holden's abstract celebrations of "the civil law" that would be made to "reign supreme in the State" and bring "peace, prosperity or real happiness," he was powerless to enforce it.[46]

By 1871, Republicans had created a creative version of the personality of power, a crown that could be fitted to any available head. An inmate named N. B. Palmer of Guilford County asked Caldwell to "look on us your humble petitionor of human man kind to look on me as such." Another inmate's sister begged Caldwell to pity "a humble female borne down by the weight of sorrow and grief and a subject at your power" and praised him as "our greatest benefactor." This woman also reminded Caldwell that she was not the only one judging him; his failure to behave as a good patron had electoral consequences in a democratic state. People in Anson County, the sister wrote, "hourly denounce[d] [Caldwell] and supporters as thieves" and mocked him for deserting his followers. If Caldwell allowed them to suffer, she said, he would "lose a great amt of voters who polled heavily for [him] through Anson last election." A displaced freedman named Edward Ancrum wrote, "[I was] a frade to approach you sir as I am a black man + a stranger to you." Immediately upon proclaiming his weakness, however, Ancrum also showed his strength: "If you dont protect us we will protect our selves or we mus die in our blood as dogs + hogs that cant speak." Shortly after the presidential election of 1872, J. M. Hinsley challenged Caldwell to give him a present, telling him that people doubted whether the governor would really "give anything" to a "poor man . . . lame and crippled" who asked for a "small present" of "5 10 or 15 dollars." After decorating Caldwell's name, Hinsley wrote: "[I] ask you in the name of the Divine Master to contribute something to me if it is not an insult to you and I pray god that it may not be."[47]

After winning a full term in 1872 by a little more than a thousand votes, Caldwell served an additional year and a half before dying at a meeting of the North Carolina Railroad Company. Quickly Carolinians shifted their attention, their praise, and their talents for exaggeration onto his successor, Curtis H. Brogden. R. A. Cobb of Morganton was not personally acquainted with Brogden but hoped that he would be considered his "friend." After Caldwell's death, Cobb wrote to the new governor, "We now look to you as our future Leader and we hope by your actions that you will merit the same high esteem for you that we did for him which was to stand by him through thick and thin." Brogden's patronage would pay off politically, Cobb promised, with "at least 300 votes for the Republicans." In March 1875, eighty-eight female "citizens" appealed to Brogden as a defender of "widows and persons in indigent circumstances." Their village of eight hundred people had been poisoned by an upstream mill, and their "once, blooming girls, and rosy cheeked children" were sick with "chills and fevers." Turning to Brogden "not only as our Governor but as a man to your better nature," they begged him not to pardon the mill owners.[48]

Although some of his constituents wished it otherwise, when it helped them, the governor they addressed was even weaker than his predecessors. In November 1874, Conservatives won a sweeping victory in the legislative elections. In the face of their control and of a federal troop presence now down to only 142 soldiers, Brogden surrendered. Instead of scolding the Conservatives for failing to give him necessary authority, Brogden congratulated them upon the bountiful fall harvests and "the favorable and auspicious circumstances under which you have assembled." Rather than justice, the goodness of the state was to be measured in prosperity.[49]

This was the world that Williamson Buck lived in and wrote from in December 1872 as he called upon Caldwell to deliver him from the "harde Place" of his marriage. Presumably Buck learned his judgments of power from the violence around him in Frederick Liedtke's and Alonzo Corliss's Company Shops, a place of intense but highly localized political warfare, fights within the neighborhood and fights often but not exclusively waged upon racial grounds. Buck observed that help might not be forthcoming, as it had not been quickly forthcoming to Alonzo Corliss and other Republicans attacked by the Klans in and around Company Shops. Buck also came to understand that if help arrived it might arrive in the form of a gift from above and in the shape of a friendship that was simultaneously political and personal. Therefore, Buck was no eccentric, no individual madman or artist, when he used his loyalty and his promise of a new house to seek Caldwell's support. The school of politics, a school almost everyone attended in the chaos of Reconstruction, taught Buck the virtue and sometimes necessity of begging. Nothing was too intimate to be beyond the government's grasp and yet nothing was so important as to oblige Caldwell to respond. "I am in so much trubbel I doant no what to do," Buck wrote. "I wright you my case and I want you to get me out of this harde Place it is in your Power to do it as you are the Ruler of the state." Even if Buck's language was unusual, he was drawing upon widespread, cross-racial, cross-gender, cross-partisan languages when he made himself "your umble sirvent" and by so doing transformed this distant man, an accidental governor he had never met, into "your magisty."[50]

5

The Persistence of Prayer

Dependency after Redemption

IN 1876, Zebulon Baird Vance rose again. Running to "redeem" the state from Radical Reconstruction, Vance led one branch of a regionwide assault against Republican rule. Between 1874 and 1876, Democrats drove Republicans from state houses, took control of Congress, and nearly expelled Republicans from the White House. By 1877, propelled by the Hayes-Tilden electoral crisis, the demands of federal bondholders, and the perceived need for troops against natives out West and against strikers in the East, one phase of national Reconstruction ended with the withdrawal of the last permanent federal troops from the South. Soon, Democrats in North Carolina and other Southern states sharply curtailed African Americans' political power, and many Northern Republicans lost hope for and interest in civil rights.

Although Vance and other Southern Democrats—like many historians—claimed the 1876 election as a historic break with Reconstruction, a redemption of the state from Radicalism, the election was less an end than a pivot in a thirty-year political system. If much was taken, much still abided. Although new state laws stripped control of some local offices from voters and placed power in the hands of planter-friendly state legislators, African Americans continued to vote for—and elect—state and federal candidates in the 1880s, including congressmen from the famous "Black Second," a majority-black district in eastern North Carolina. Additionally, Republicans in Congress investigated intimidation and fraud, slowing the process of disenfranchisement. Not until the early 1890s—with the failure of the Lodge Federal Elections Bill, the evaporation of Supreme Court protection for freedpeople's rights, and a tidal wave of disenfranchisement laws in the South—would most freedpeople be expelled from formal politics. Even if African Americans were second-class citizens after Redemption, they were still part of the political system, unequal but not yet excluded. This inclusion—however limited—had practical consequences for Vance and other Democratic politicians.

If the events of 1876 suggested the end of sectional cleavage and the diminishment of freedpeople's political power, they did not directly affect other, central aspects of Reconstruction, especially the slow re-creation of government authority in the postwar states. The political styles and state actions of Reconstruction endured well after Redemption. If Carolinians looked to different patrons during Democratic Reconstruction, they often continued to seek the same types of help and to ask in the same languages of appeal. This was not because life stood still in North Carolina. Instead, sweeping economic changes launched many small farmers into national, even global, markets. New state interventions in what people drank and how they ate had the potential to transform the role of the state. A new generation of reformers led a concerted campaign against the eccentricities and corruption of government through friendship, aiming most centrally to transform patronage into a merit-based civil service. Instead of collapsing in the face of these transformations, patronal politics expanded in the era framed by Vance's 1876 Redemption campaign and his death in 1894. Under pressure from the shifting world, patronalism showed itself to be a vibrant, creative way of seeing the world, one capable of reshaping to fit new realities, not an antiquary system that faded with the first contact with modern governance. Patronalism survived because it helped politicians manage a racial system that was hierarchical but not yet exclusionary, defend themselves against reformers, and explain interventionist but geographically narrow state actions in prohibition, fence laws, and railroad subsidies. Even though Republican rule ended in 1876, the politics of Reconstruction—the politics of patronalism—endured in North Carolina through the white supremacy campaign of 1898. Because Democrats lacked both the power and the will to impose a new view of governance on the state, they largely worked within the frameworks established by their Republican predecessors, although they directed their favors at different classes of followers. Only in the last years of the century did the close of Reconstruction take away African American voting rights and the language and system of politics constructed during and after the Civil War.

North Carolina's 1876 campaign was part of the tail end of a regional effort to depose Republican governors and reassert the power of the land-owning class. Like Mississippi's 1875 Redeemers, and simultaneous movements in South Carolina and Louisiana, North Carolina's Democratic Party triumphed through a combination of race-baiting, violent intimidation, fraud, and sectional grievance. To give power to their cries of white supremacy, Democratic orators invented wild stories that African American local officeholders in eastern counties auctioned off white paupers. Democrats also launched a campaign of manipulation and fraud to reduce African American voting power. But the path to white supremacy was not as simple as it looked in retrospect. In North Carolina, the campaign for Redemption pitted Vance against Republican Thomas Settle Jr., a prominent ex-legislator and state supreme court justice from Rockingham County. It was a campaign like North Carolina had never seen. Together, Vance and Settle canvassed the state, delivering scores of long, punchy speeches on the future of Reconstruction, freedpeople, and the economy. In this so-called Battle of the Giants, Vance and Settle's disagreements quickly became wars not only over policy but also over fictive patronage.

Put forward as their parties' biggest men in a campaign about the future of Reconstruction, Vance and Settle found themselves constrained not only by their opponents' arguments but also by the demands of crowds who greeted them "such as a Bolivar or a Napoleon might envy" with "the simple expression of that great yearning for better things." Thomas Dixon Jr., the progressive Baptist preacher and white supremacist novelist, wrote that people turned Vance into "this king among men! . . . Women pressed close and kissed [Vance's] hands, and old men reached forward their hands to touch his garments." In his entrance into the town of Jonesboro, Settle — "a man of masterful personality, eloquent, and in dead earnest" — was accompanied by "a parade of mounted white men . . . while a multitude of darkies, of both sexes, and of all sizes and degrees of blackness, trotted along behind." By cheering, the women and men not only bestowed honor upon their favorite but actually shaped what the candidates could say. Vance's supporters frequently drowned out his words, "not heeding or caring what was said." When Settle rose, African Americans near the back or off to the side responded with their own set of cheers meant to claim their role in the political process through the person of the candidate. Faced with a crowd responding to their personae, not their platforms, the candidates unsurprisingly turned their canvass into sparring sessions about their own honor. In a September speech in Charlotte, after Vance bragged about taking care of "my soldiers" and having "fed the women and children" during the war, he ostentatiously quieted the crowd so Settle could respond. This was a standard Vance tactic for aggrandizing his manly power and making his opponents look weak and feminine. Settle snapped back at him, "You will never find me a suppliant at your feet for your protection." In reply, Vance snarled, "If that is the way my efforts to have him courteously treated are to be received, he may take care of himself." The two descended into a bitter discussion of their responsibility for the behavior of their friends, Settle pledging to arrest any friend who "refused to be restrained," while Vance claimed his friends would never "submit to be knocked down and tied out." In a tense moment when the two stepped toward each other and seemed to be on the verge of blows, Settle demanded that Vance pledge to "preserve order" during the canvass, and Vance answered only that he would be "governed by your behavior." This debate about personal honor and the nature of political friendship was not a distraction from real politics; those terms of honor and friendship framed the way many people talked about what politics was.[1]

One revealing story from the 1876 campaign suggests Vance's appeal. According to the report, a maimed Confederate soldier approached the candidate in despair. Vance took him "in his house, fed [him] a week or more, he and his family treating [the veteran] in my ragged clothes as well as if I had been the richest man in the state." At the end of the week, Vance gave him twenty dollars and a new pair of shoes, reportedly telling him, "Though I am poor myself, I have two good arms and hands and can work. Whenever you are in distress again, come to me and I will divide with you." Allegedly the veteran then "walked thirty miles . . . [to] say to every poor man in North Carolina to vote for Vance; he is their friend; he is the best man in the world; God bless him forever." The story of Vance and the one-armed soldier, although perhaps apocryphal, was popular because it tied Vance's 1876 campaign to his Civil War role and played upon the complex, reciprocal relationship between subject and ruler, client and patron, poor boy and great man.[2]

Making politics a story of personal honor and power helped Vance surmount the peculiar challenges of governing North Carolina, a state where secession critics, including Vance, were locked in a voluntary but uncomfortable embrace with old fire-eaters inside the Democratic Party. After Vance's victory, he famously proclaimed that "there is retribution in history," enfolding his own rise from prison to governor's mansion with the state's redemption. At the same time, Vance used his victory to appear magnanimous to vanquished white Unionists and freedpeople. This stance allowed him to play the benevolent patron, capable of listening to defeated but not yet completely forgotten African Americans. In his inaugural address, Vance pledged to "reconcile the antagonism of the white and the black races" by being the "best friends" of the former slaves. Calling upon the "kindly friendships" that slaves as "humble friends and dependents" showed their masters during the war, Vance sought an imbalanced but accessible friendship between the races, neither equality nor complete "oppression."[3]

Having performed the role of the patron, Vance also began in his inaugural address to shift toward the more prosaic figure of manager. Intelligent and well-read, if sometimes brusque or even crude, Vance, like many ex-Whigs, did not see himself as a man of the past but as a force for progress through his commitment to education, the sciences, and the law, "the parent of liberty, justice and national life." Vance fused his commitments to education and political friendship, defending his support for the state university because it prevented children from falling into the "unfriendly" hands of Northern-trained teachers, who would always be "strangers." Additionally, Vance couched his support for "the education of black people" in an effort to make them useful workers and loyal friends. In the closing lines of his first speech to the legislature, Vance sounded Holden's old metaphor of light, calling the new government "sunlight breaking through the darkness," although in Vance's portrayal the sun was notable less for the fact that it fell upon everyone alike than for the fact that it created "a good crop to be produced" and therefore "prosperity."[4]

Freedpeople immediately understood the deeply imbalanced terms of Vance's friendship. Despite's Vance's victory and his overtures, many continued to turn to the Republican Party — and to the defeated Settle — for a patron. Writing to a "great man like you" and "our refuge," Republicans, particularly African Americans, begged Settle for jobs, gifts, and other favors. "If you knew how I am suffering, I know you would help me," Walter Williams pleaded. Recognizing the way defeat limited Settle's power, however, others despaired of becoming politically friendless. "I have no more confidence in democracy today than I had twenty years ago," an African American noted.[5]

If some freedpeople found hope in Republican patrons, others feared living under a government ruled by their enemies. In the months after Vance's victory, hundreds of female and male African Americans from eastern and central counties petitioned the legislature to help them leave the state. Even though they had "equal rights," they understood their rights not as abstract concepts but as strands within thick webs of power. What mattered was not just the rights themselves but the presence of a patron who might defend them. Since Redemption meant rule not by friends but by "unfriendly" whites, the only solution they saw was departure to a land—perhaps out West—where they might find allies. Shortly after the election, two families in Burke County wrote Vance that they had no "confidence" in Democrats' willingness "to relieve us from any of our present difficulties or oppression." Against this, Vance advised them not to emigrate but to "make friends with your old masters and white neighbors." In Vance's terms, race could be subordinated to patronage; the secret to defending rights lay in having the right friends and in knowing one's place. In Vance's judgment, legislative appropriations for asylums and for freedpeople's teachers "don't look much like taking your rights away from you." During the campaign Vance explained that a politics of friendship could easily encompass inequality. "I have defended you in court without any pay . . . I have helped you out of troubles, and that I never owed one of you a cent that I did not pay," he asserted. If they trusted him with "every cent of money you have with me," they should also trust him "when I come to talk to you of politics." While the vast majority were skeptical of Vance and his followers, some African Americans built patrons among white leaders, whether eagerly or out of a desperate sense of survival. Most colorfully, this took the shape of the wild turkey D. M. Lee sent to Vance to encourage him to feel "kindly toward my race." Vance accepted the gift "as a testimonial of your good will and earnestly" hoped "it betokens an era of good feelings." On the whole, however, the same election that crowned Vance cut deeply into freedpeople's political power. New constitutional amendments gave the state legislature control over county and township positions like magistrates and county commissioners. In eastern Black Belt counties, offices that might have gone to freedpeople or to friendly whites instead went to the appointees of the state legislature in Raleigh.[6]

On the other side of the partisan divide, white Democrats saw in Vance's victory the chance to turn imagined political friendships into tangible favors. Women pressed their claims for the "God of the widow and fatherless" to feel "sufficiently interested in individuals" and free them "from anxiety" by banning saloons, sending money, or procuring jobs. "Of course I know you could not for one minute imagine yourself in our place," Mrs. L. S. Aldrich wrote. "But I feel assured if you could you would feel ever so sorry for us + use your influence. . . . God will bless you." Another writer, left with "not a friend in the world on whom I have a claim," asked Vance for a spot in a post office. "Forgive me if I've offended good taste . . . but I simply could not help it," she wrote. "I am too wretched to live." Miega Long called Vance a merciful ruler based on a campaign speech where he "talked so kind to the poor," and she tried to "beg you're a little please" to send ten dollars "for the sake of one who will depend upon you."[7]

These brief, allusive fantasies were part of a broader cultural imagination that Vance accessed but did not create. Two elaborate dreams pressed in early 1877 not upon the victorious Vance but upon "the men of the state" in the General Assembly show the intensity with which people fantasized about their relationship with the government. One woman, "feeling it divinely impressed upon me, to write those who are *so* much my superior," complained to legislators about the fears of liquor that "day and night . . . haunt me." She worried that "I may expose my ignorance and *fear*, all I may say may be passed unnoticed by you, and be looked upon as 'dream of fancy.'" This "dream of fancy," however, "seems to me a matter of *so* much importance in these 'dark days' and *perilous* times." She admitted that "females have no business in the management of 'great men's' affairs either in church or state" but "we may, now and then, speak a word, urged by the 'holy spirit' to try to *touch* the *hearts* of our more sensible rulers, but *not to manage*, or use authority, but plead humbly, and suggest what we think best while *we* can do nothing for want of wisdom but pray for you all." Despite her many evasions and proclamations of unworthiness, she ended with a straightforward request that sounded more like a demand. "The *cause* of all this sorrow, is plain to every thinking mind . . . overindulgence in spirituous liquors." Therefore, to brighten the "sad faces of these dear mothers, wives, and sisters," the "Great men" should "lend a helping hand." In this remarkable series of assertions, the anonymous writer proclaimed her unfitness to speak before speaking, noted her inability to judge the world before judging the world, and suggested her unworthiness to approach these august leaders before approaching them. To transform her dream into state action, she worked it through a process of deference and subjection, both hers to the "Great Men" and the leaders' to God. In the alchemy of the era, prohibition became not a policy but a favor. In the interdependence of state and subject, her letter was a process of creating power that she could use, but only if she could arrange for it to be granted to her by someone else.[8]

Just as remarkable was a letter sent in early 1877 by Pattie Arrington, a troubled and controversial woman who for decades pressed several bitter legal claims against prominent men in the state. After burning her bridges with the state bar, Arrington later took up her own case, proving her ability to give a "scorching cross-examination." Part of "one of the oldest and best families in the State," Arrington would eventually make legal history, becoming the first woman in the state known to have defended herself in court and the first woman to be convicted of libel. In early 1877, Arrington hoped the Democratic triumph would open avenues of access for her through old patterns of gentlemanly deference to a lady's pleas. She "turned to the men of the state, believing there was surely honor enough in the *entire* state to give a woman her rights. . . . Is this the southern chivalry we read about?" Arrington fantasized that the legislature would convene one evening for a special session where she could address for an hour "the entire body both Senate + House" with "closed doors on all others." Promising to hold herself to an hour, she said she would then ask the legislature whether "after hearing part of my story," they wanted to hear more. If not, she would leave. "Can you deny me this request?" Arrington dared the legislature to ignore her, presuming that her appeal to honor would work without further elaboration or justification. Despite her confidence, however, Arrington proved again the notion that rights — whether vested in statute or in feminine claims in an honor-based society — mattered if recognized by a powerful patron. Both her angry letter and the anonymous writer's deferential one achieved the same outcome: silence.[9]

Over the 1870s and 1880s, North Carolinians continued to plead for help from patrons even as their world shifted underneath them. As the South emerged from the economic upheavals of the war and the panic of 1873, North Carolinians' lives changed dramatically. No longer reliant primarily upon local markets and self-sufficient farming, more and more Carolinians found themselves swept — sometimes eagerly and sometimes unwillingly — into regional and national commercial networks. These networks grew from the wartime development of the piedmont rail line that at last connected central North Carolina to Richmond, and the postwar creation of region-wide transport companies like the Seaboard Inland Air Line, the Southern Railway, and the Atlantic Coast Line that bound together new and previously existing railroads. After the western North Carolina road finally reached Asheville in 1880, the mountain town's population almost quadrupled in ten years, from 2,600 in 1880 to more than 10,000 by 1890. As new markets for cash crops expanded, and as a lien system and declining prices created debts that could not be paid without ready money, self-sufficient yeoman farming fell into eclipse. More farmers turned to cotton and tobacco, which tripled in production between 1860 and 1900. Railroads also spurred a new world of manufacturing; between 1870 and 1890 the number of manufacturing employees nearly tripled, to 36,214, while capital investment more than quadrupled, to $32.75 million. Cotton mills — which by the turn of the century employed nearly 30,000 Carolinians — transformed the region around Charlotte, which expanded spectacularly from 2,200 people in 1860 to 11,500 in

1890 and more than 18,000 by 1900. The development of bright leaf tobacco cigarette manufacturing also transformed the previously sleepy piedmont, as large factories sprung up around Durham (which catapulted from 250 people in 1870 to almost 5,500 in 1890) and Winston-Salem (which more than doubled from 4,100 to 10,700 between 1880 and 1890). Although still rural compared to many other states, North Carolina became increasingly more urban. The number of places with a population exceeding 500 more than quintupled between 1860 and 1900.[10]

Despite these social transformations, patronalism continued to thrive because of both its malleability and its resonance with emerging evangelical ideas. In an important postwar revival, many Christians reasserted the idea that power, when it came, would be wielded by a distant but merciful ruler. To make sense of a postbellum world in which God's favor was sometimes hard to see, many white ministers and laypeople emphasized the otherworldly nature of Christianity, one centered less upon personal virtue than upon the intense relationship between unworthy sinners and a distant, mysterious, but gracious God. In the words of their preachers in the pulpits, and in the songs they sang in the pews, and in the prayers they recited at their bedposts, North Carolinians practiced a language of supplication and subjecthood. Although preachers disagreed fervently on questions of doctrine and dogma, sermons across denominational bounds celebrated God's kingly power, man's abject condition, and the role of grace in connecting sinner with savior. By broadcasting this language of God and man into the state, preachers provided a cultural language that Carolinians, including skeptics and nonbelievers, used to describe the world and their place in it. Like sugar in water, religion both disappeared into and invisibly flavored every aspect of nineteenth-century political discussion. When they turned to Raleigh or Washington, North Carolinians looked perhaps with the same combination of fear and need, of desire and skepticism, of hope and dread, with which they gazed at heaven.[11]

When their petitions to governors made them think of prayer, pleaders drew upon a complex, culturally based understanding of what prayer was and how it should be used. Across sectarian lines Carolina preachers emphasized that prayer could not be merely "asking God for favors" that "we need + [that] He has to bestow" but was "direct, personal intercourse between man + Maker," the "human soul going out in quest of God; it is human weakness casting itself upon Divine strength; it is human need appealing for help from Divine ability." The intimacy of prayerful interaction with God did not suggest equality. Instead, an Episcopal minister in Wilmington preached, efficacious prayer emphasized human failings, "the prostration" of "the creature before his creator." Prayer proved that "we are simply grown-up children. . . . We ask God for it; but our Father knows best, and very often he will not give us the things we ask."[12]

If prayer provided the cultural form for requests, the Bible provided the language. When they used religious words to define righteous earthly power, Carolinians followed the lead not just of their pastors but also of their politicians. Carolina leaders peppered their speeches with biblical phrases, parables, and symbols, and no one did so more than Zebulon Vance. In his inaugural address in 1877, he called North Carolina "our political Zion" and compared the Constitution to the "ark of the covenant" and federal Reconstruction to the ark's captivity in "strange lands." Vance's reference was no rhetorical twitch but the start of an elaborate 350-word analogy in which Vance described the work of the priests of Dagon to expel the ark, the way yoked animals walked as they dragged the cart, the looks on the faces of the harvesters in the valley of Judah as they watched it pass, the upheaval the ark created in the "strange lands of false gods," and, with Vance's election, the return of the ark with "triumph and rejoicings." Less elaborately, religious language seeped into nearly every crevice of his inaugural, giving him his words for the damned and the saved, his imagery of his followers as a "mighty host," his description of carpetbaggers as men who bowed "the knee to Baal," his Revelations-based celebration of his supporters as the "few names left in Sardis who did not defile their garments," and his frequent reference to the state and nation as "sacred." There was a reason why Vance and his peers across the South called their work "Redemption," themselves "Redeemers." While Christianity may not have always guided their decisions, it gave them a connective language with the less educated, less wealthy, less sophisticated men and women in the crowds. Privately Vance was sometimes profane and occasionally skeptical; later in life he scandalized his friends by marrying a Catholic. In public, however, he understood the utility of the Bible as a language for communication.[13]

The connection between church and state was particularly obvious at Thanksgiving, when preachers answered gubernatorial directives to "return heart-felt thanks to Almighty God for . . . His infinite mercy and goodness" by sanctifying the state. Joseph Blount Cheshire, Episcopal bishop and a trained attorney, called — in language reminiscent of John Locke — the government an extension of the divine "*Social Compact*," which grew from the "mutual duties and responsibilities of parent and child." The "powers that be are ordained of God." Drawing upon the famous injunction to render unto

Caesar, many ministers made obedience a sacred value. "God's government is the same today as it always was and will in its principles forever remain unchanged," a Methodist minister preached. "The fundamental idea of all government is found in the right of some to rule, and the duty of others to obey." The lesson of the Bible, this minister claimed, is that "men are subjects of a king." For many white Southerners, especially ex-Confederates, that relationship between God and state was fraught during Reconstruction. In the aftermath of Appomattox, some white Carolinians asked whether God was punishing them like the Israelites for their sins. In Cheshire's first year as minister, not long before the 1880 elections, he noted pointedly that Jews had the love of freedom, "which political subjection is sure to breed in the mind of an intelligent and high-spirited people." That Thanksgiving, Cheshire looked back fondly upon secession, "when every aspiration of our hearts was toward a destiny far other than the one which we now see before us." Later in the 1880s, he replaced the lament for the Confederacy with a paean to the national response to the 1881 assassination of President James Garfield. For Aristides Spyker Smith, who preached to both Presbyterians and Episcopalians, the relationship between God's will and Northern victory was more ambiguous. Despite Confederate defeat, Smith proclaimed Southerners were still "His chosen people." In 1882, Smith wondered how to obey biblical law when the "Caesar of today" (presumably President Chester Arthur) was "highly objectionable to us," as "odious as Caesar to the Jews." However, obvious distaste for federal power, he added, "does not justify us in resisting its authority, or fraudulently endeavoring to avoid meeting our obligations to it. So long as we circulate its coins — even if it consists of but pennies — we shd obey its laws."[14]

To resolve the problem of celebrating a God who ruled over a puzzling, demoralized world, white Protestant ministers turned their eyes heavenward. To convey the power of this God, they called upon him in many ways, but especially as Creator and as King. In one sermon at Centenary Methodist Episcopal Church in Winston, evangelist R. G. Pearson piled his metaphors in stacks like pancakes, naming God or Christ "a ruler and a king," a banker who held a "mortgage on your soul," "Advocate," "Commander," "Elder Brother," and "Judge." In others, God was a personal father: "No abstract being! Not the far-off Sovereign of the Universe" and not an "unfeeling" Providence but a "God whose glory shone forth." Cheshire frequently referred to God as "master" or "owner" but toyed with a number of different metaphors for the human role, especially "servant," "son," "dumb beast," and "slave." Cheshire aimed to show the "mutuality of the benefit" of unequal relationships between a mighty master and a craven human. Instead of behaving like a "vile cur" who shuns his master, man should pattern himself upon the "dumb beast looking up into the face of his master," who "sees and recognizes a superior being, and he fawns at his feet, and thanks him for his kindness." But many ministers returned to the metaphor of kingship. From pulpits across the state, Carolinians heard over and over again, a century after independence, the celebration of monarchy through invocations of God as, in the words of one hymn, "King supreme, to thee I bow, / A willing subject at thy feet; / All other lords I disavow, / And to thy government submit." As a divine king, God resolved the problem of attention that bedeviled so many petitioners. Unlike an earthly king, God "does condescend to notice + take care of the most insignificant of his creatures," including the famous sparrow. "The effort to attend to too great a multitude of affairs wd indeed distract" an "earthly ruler + many of them wd be overlooked," one minister preached, "but such a difficulty cannot exist in the case of an Infinite Mind. To him all things are naked + open. His eye can take in the whole universe at a single glance + His mind can comprehend, in a single moment, all the affairs of all He creates, even down to the minute details." Although ministers debated whether the Kingdom of God might be located in an earthly community of saints, or in a perfected social world, or in an unimaginably ethereal plane, they injected the notion of kingship deep into the popular vocabulary.[15]

Patronal ideas about the role of government also flourished because they continued to fit the politics of the state. In part this was because Zebulon Vance endured as the literal face of power for many North Carolinians, not only during his terms as governor, but also in his subsequent fifteen years in the U.S. Senate. Most strikingly, in his campaign against civil service reform, Vance used his platform in the Senate to play the spokesman for claims of dependence. Vance himself was sometimes more at ease performing the role of patron in public than actually acting upon it in private. A widely read and reasonably intelligent man, Vance preferred to speak not on the glories of the Old South but on "The Scattered Nation," a history of the Jews that embraced close readings of the Bible, some familiarity with modern ethnology, and a personal commitment to tolerance. During Reconstruction Vance worked not as a planter but as chief state counsel of the Southern Railway. If in the mirror Vance likely saw a figure of enlightenment and reform (with a sharp sense of humor), much of the state approached him differently, as a merciful patron. Women and men who claimed to worship "at Gov. Vance's shrine" or to "look to [him] 'as the children of Israel looked to the east'" or to have named their children for Vance[16] pleaded with Vance not to "forget your Best friend when I am Dead you will loose one of your best friends." T. B. Roberts hung Vance's photograph at the foot of his bed to be "the first thing I see in the morning." Another worried that Vance had "forgotten me" but pledged to be "your mule" if Vance would "in plain turms . . . send me some money. . . . If I could meet you on the streets of Charlott + you could recognize mee you wood give me some money + a overcoat." Others dishonored themselves as "a Lilliputian" or "a poor mortal" addressing a "gentleman" in order to ask for "a small mite" or "a favor," or to "come to my rescue. . . . God will bless you for the deed." Vance's success at conveying broad, fictive friendships through his public performances shaped the belief that he "would always listen to the wants of the poorest, blackest and most humble," and that his "big true heart . . . always beats in sympathy with his people, feels for them in their trials and adversity."[17]

In the 1880s, patronalism was tested and proven in public fights over two basic rights of subjects, the power to plead for a pardon and for a job. In these areas, rationalizing reformers sought to excise the corrupting human element from the body politic but ran into a groundswell of opposition. Again, Zebulon Vance stood near the center of both fights. In his brief second tenure as governor, Vance had dispensed pardons at an unusually brisk rate, acting as a benevolent and distant master, a man who offered less justice than mercy. While pardons might seem irrelevant to most law-abiding citizens, they historically have been a key ritual for defining power relations, the "embodiments" and "visible signs" of government's authority. In monarchies, the right to beg a pardon was a subject's final and most sacred possession, and the American pardoning power, more explicitly than virtually any other form of state authority, was a direct holdover from kingly rule. Both in rituals and in a language of "prayer," supplicants affirmed the governor's general authority in begging for a particular exception. Rather than emphasizing their alleged innocence, many portrayed themselves as entirely helpless and begged Vance to allow, as one supplicant put it, "the dictates of your heart to guide you." One condemned man asked Vance for "a self consideration. . . . If you have ever pitied any one poor boy please to look down on me one that is bourn out of due season." Another wrote, "The lord said do unto you fellowmen as you would have them to do to you and I believe you will pardon me. . . . For gods sake please sir. . . . God will reward you for it." Loveday A. Tucker defended her husband's pardon as an act of "compassion on me and my four little children. . . . Think how it would be with you if you was condemned and sent to prison. . . . I pray for you each night and day."[18]

As they embodied the state's new powers in their personal performances, politicians like Zebulon Vance, shown here, became celebrities. A living manifestation of patronly power (despite his back-ground as a middling mountaineer), Vance represented both accessibility and authority to his supporters. For that reason, he and other politicians frequently received requests to endorse tobacco and other products; a local bank asked Vance's permission to use his image on their checks. Thousands of North Carolinians wrote him, seeking help. Hundreds named their children for him. Library of Congress, American Memory, LC-DIG-cwpbh-04049.

Vance, in turn, performed the honor-based roles his subjects constructed for him. Vance issued pardons for prisoners who were the "the only support" for "a large family" so that they could "make a crop." When Ronbury Floyd applied for a petition, Vance "turned him out to take care of his child," and he was glad he did it. Vance emphasized the mercy that his constituents begged from him. Although his rules for pardons asked that every request include "*grounds* and *reasons*," those grounds did not necessarily have to include innocence. Instead, Vance's manner suggested that supplicants could impress him with a sentimental story meant to sway his emotions. "Errors on the side of mercy are scarcely followed by regret and never by remorse," he wrote to a neighboring governor. "[In] some cases I have yielded to the importunity of friends — human nature could scarcely be avoided in a government like ours." Although some newspapers criticized Vance for being overly generous with pardons, his quality of mercy made "the people love [him] the more."[19]

Vance's practices continued through his lieutenant governor and successor, Thomas J. Jarvis, who, like Vance, was trained as an attorney but governed through public performances of honor, mercy, and patronage. From Vance's inauguration in 1877 through the end of Jarvis's full term in 1885, the two men gave 337 pardons and 46 commutations. In the reasons they gave to the General Assembly, they cited doubts over the prisoners' guilt in only 21 cases. Almost always their pardons were motivated either by pity for the inmate's family or by deference to the neighbors and officials who asked his return. After Vance resigned the governorship to take his seat in the U.S. Senate, Jarvis "cheerfully" pardoned people Vance recommended and offered his own mercy to applicants because they had "suffered much" or "as a reward" or "in the hope that it will make him a better man" or "in deference" to the "good citizens" who requested leniency. Jarvis admitted that supplicants' "zeal and persistency" made their petitions "hard to resist." "I think probably I have granted mercy where it was not deserved," he explained. "No one man ought to be required or permitted to discharge alone so delicate and often so painful a duty. If he be a good man the responsibility is too great to trust in his hands."[20]

During the 1880s, North Carolina governors moved slowly and subtly toward a merit-based system. In the eight years after Jarvis's term, the next three governors issued only 204 pardons, even though the number of incarcerated prisoners grew substantially. Part of the reason was a shifting view of the law. Jarvis's successor, Alfred M. Scales, advised the legislature in his inaugural address to strip the governor of his pardon power. In its place, Scales urged the state to follow the nationwide trend toward pardon boards, which would forward only approved cases to the governor for consideration. The personal nature of the pardon power was a "nullification of Justice as meted out by our courts" and an assault upon "respect for the law," Scales said. Those pardons that Scales and his two predecessors granted were "a chance to reform," a recognition that punishment had been "sufficient," a reflection of new information about innocence brought "to the notice" of the governor, an acknowledgment that there was no "counter-petition" against the pardon, or a reward for "reformation." While some pardons continued to be dispensed from mercy, the tone and pace of the act had changed.[21]

This conflict between legal and personal approaches to pardons came to the surface with the election of planter Elias Carr in 1892. As the first non-lawyer to be governor in a generation, Carr served as a living embodiment of the tension between patronal mercy and legal expertise. Some editors and reformers ridiculed the idea of a layman overturning the judgment of the state's leading lawyers. "Think of the absurdity, the inexcusable unreason-ableness of the finding of courts, under charges of qualified Judges, being set aside by a man who is not a lawyer, can know nothing of law, and is disqualified, therefore to deliver a sound judgment in a matter of life and death," one newspaper editorialized. Calling it "unwise" and "ridiculous" to entrust a non-lawyer with this power, the editor called again for the creation of a pardon board. This critique arose from the slowly evolving professional-ism of the state's bar, as legal training shifted from a series of haphazard apprenticeships and brief summer courses toward more rigorous and stan-dardized preparation. The petitions that lawyers presented in the 1880s and 1890s tended to be far more technical and far less sentimental than the petitions of prisoners' families. Instead of a story, the lawyers' appeals offered an explanation.[22]

While Carr claimed that he "in no case" granted a pardon "without a full and careful investigation," he defended, even celebrated, his acts of mercy. In four years, he pardoned 213 prisoners, a faster rate than either Vance or Jarvis and more than double the performance of his three most immediate predecessors. Even when some former inmates committed additional crimes, Carr had "no cause for regret." For Carr, pardons were in the end personal acts. One December, in a show of idiosyncratic mercy, he pardoned a peti-tioner because it was the holiday season, "when all the world should feel kindly toward his unfortunate fellow being." Against lawyerly claims that the state's legal system functioned equitably, Carr used the pardon system to mitigate what he called the "barbarism" of fixed sentences and the unfairness of harsh penalties for people with poor representation. As proof of his commitment, Carr refused even "to give to the public the records of the pardons issued in this office, believing that with the pardon punishment should cease to be inflicted." Carr's constituents, in turn, pleaded in intensely sentimental language for him to help "an Afflicted man" and his "5 little children" or to "pray your merces on me" or to "releas me off so mutch troble" on behalf of a "sad hart looking mother and sister oh my triales is soy grat." After Carr pardoned an Asheville man, the mayor called it a "righteous, Christian act, and you may depend upon the Christian people of Asheville remembering it." By the mid-1890s, however, Carr represented the last gasp of a fading system; later governors would modernize pardons, steer applicants to lawyers, and create forms and procedures to govern mercy.[23]

Although the struggle over pardons was relatively quiet, the fight over the government's right to give jobs was one of the most prominent public issues of the 1880s, a direct challenge to the politics of dependence. Not surprisingly, Vance placed himself in the center of it. In 1879, having done little in his term in Raleigh except pardon inmates, Vance left for the U.S. Senate, a seat he would hold until his death in 1894. In Washington, he was mostly safe from pardon pleas, but he found himself even more deluged than ever by requests for patronage. Jobs were the most obvious and important gifts a politician could distribute, but they were also among the scarcest. A congressman of the president's party might control at most a few hundred positions to distribute among tens of thousands of supporters. Because leaders did not have enough jobs to satisfy their constituents, rational actors should have given up on patronage. To be convinced of the power of patronage, however, a pleader did not necessarily need to receive a job; he or she needed to believe in the power of access. Patronage promised not jobs but the enduring right to beg.[24]

Patronage requests overwhelmed politicians (and, not infrequently, the scholars who now peruse their papers.) Thousands of pleas fill hundreds of boxes of governors' correspondence and personal papers. Petitions came fastest and most furiously right after elections; Vance received about four hundred requests in the first few months after Democrats elected Grover Cleveland president in 1884, and another several hundred following Cleveland's 1892 victory. North Carolina's other U.S. senator received twenty-nine job requests that were mailed on a single day in November 1892. One applicant joked that there were "not less than 40,000,000 applicants for office"; another referred to the "thousand + one offices to be bestowed upon the millions of office seekers." These "numberless" crows "crying for corn" created what one state legislator called "a continual swarm. I never saw such a scramble, even now while I try to write they are pulling at me." These "hundreds of beggars" were driven not only by need but also by the implicit (and sometimes explicit) pledge that a candidate would "with his promises of Government patronage" deliver a "time of milk and honey" for his supporters. Sometimes these oaths were ludicrously unreliable; one sheriff allegedly offered sixty men a job as his deputy. "The man was elected, but fifty-nine men were disappointed," a newspaper reported. Politicians near the Hatteras lighthouse kept voters in line by promising "every young man" the "first vacancy" if he voted for the incumbent party. Although these examples were probably exaggerated, dozens of individuals claimed after elections that governors, congressmen, or other politicians had pledged to, as one person put it, "put a ring on his finger."[25]

Dishonoring themselves as "beneath you" and "mean + shaim-faced," beggars for jobs linguistically groveled to their "only friend" as they asked for a "listening ear" or a "little sympathy." These were often appeals based on pity, not merit. Leaders' success in passing "from unrequited struggle to the zenith of deserved and ambitious power" should obligate them to listen to those who "call to you to-day from the depths of black and awful ruin." These calls to the "Poor Man's friend" for "charity" toward "men on the down grade" or "humble ones" or a "broken-hearted wife" or "a poor fellow struggling to make a living" painted leaders as men with "noble and generous principles" who should "live for ever." One woman "put forward the only claim [she had] any right to press on [Vance's] consideration; viz, the deference of a true gentleman for helpless women, and his christian recognition of the claims of widows and orphans." A Carolina man promised his senator, "A just God will reward you, and the yeomanry of this county . . . will with one accord send special petitions to Heaven in yr behalf." These "special petitions" would deliver, he went on, "a double reward when you meet St. Peter at the gate, for he will surely beg you within the gate and to the best seat in the Shade of the great throne. He will say walk in senator and make yourself at home; everything here is yours, call for what you want."[26]

North Carolinians advanced the idea that patronage was a form of government-sponsored relief for people like Jane Backus, who signed her letters, "Yours in Need." The "poor" required help from distant patrons, Cornelia Henderson wrote, because they "have few friends." Asking Vance not to "cast [her letter] aside without reading it," she admitted, "I have no claim upon you whatever, but my helplessness and need." In many pleas, desperation was the most important argument applicants raised, even more than partisan advantage or merit. Need did not just excuse writers for applying; it advanced their claims. Sometimes, personal wealth seemingly disqualified candidates from consideration for a job. "Several of our good citizens have applied for the position," Emma Bennett wrote, "but they are abundantly able to live without it while I have nothing for a support but my hands." Another writer acknowledged other applicants' qualifications but asked for the position because "the needs of my family are more stringent." A county party chairman dismissed one candidate even though "I have nothing against" him and "know him to be a good clever fellow" because he "is well able to live without the place." It is simple, even reassuring, to contrast these idiosyncratic forms of government work for the needy to New Deal–era systematic programs like the Works Progress Administration. In fact, the reformers who opposed nineteenth-century patron-politicians were in many ways the forerunners of the New Dealers. Nevertheless, the reinforcement of the idea that government work was a form of aid to the needy likely laid the groundwork for the popularity of later New Deal–style programs by making them seem less novel, an expansion of familiar efforts.[27]

The rituals of these fictive friendships grew alongside and drew sustenance from actual relationships between elected officials and their allies. Primarily, political friendship grew from the promise that active party members would benefit from the party's success, or, as one applicant put it, "the ox that does the plowing ought to eat the fodder." Claiming that parties represented not temporary alliances but a "family (politically speaking)" whose membership was largely "inherited," lower-level workers asked to share in their leaders' rewards. "I told you I would do what I could to send you to Washington," one man wrote Vance, "now I shall only expect the same towards me whenever I need your help." Political friendships, like familial relationships, were simultaneously affectionate and hierarchical. Although a relationship offered the opportunity for a politician to "use or worry" his friends, it also invited patrons' criticism and discipline. Senator Matt Ransom refused to appoint a friend's son to office because of "his talk on the streets about" the senator. After the boy apologized by calling himself "unmanly," and the father expressed regret that his son "had so little self respect or respect for you," Ransom forgave and assisted the son. "I hope and believe that it will be a good lesson for him and that he will be benefited by it," the father wrote.[28]

The circles of friendship had defined limits; everyone understood that the government's largesse was too small to be equally distributed. Drawing lines against political enemies was also an important part of the vernacular vocabulary of politics. In the world of patronage, race served as a key way to define who was and who was not included in a political family. White Democrats, in particular, reacted angrily to Republican officeholders, especially African Americans. On a rational level, the force of this response makes little sense; only a single white Democrat, after all, stood to gain by expelling an African American Republican from office. But on the level of fantasy, many white Democrats saw African American officeholders as a denial of their general right to access jobs. Invoking race was good strategy; white Democrats were confident they could succeed in pressing their claims against "a d—— nigger." A deeper imaginative competition was also at work, one that operated on a scarcity-driven approach in which whites could gain only if African Americans lost. W. W. Latham made this clear when he wrote that African American workers were "an imposition on the many poor young men of our own race + color who are needy and would grace instead of *disgrace* these places." In these fantasized rivalries, the politics of Reconstruction intertwined race and friendship. Some of the most intense racial jockeying was around post offices, a "congregating point for the village and the neighborhood," a place where "everybody felt free to drop in . . . just to say 'howdy.'" When Charles Clark wrote that "no more acceptable service could be rendered the people of this community" than the removal of an African American postmaster, it was clear how he defined "people" and "community." Others complained that African American postmasters gained power over white female customers, an "outrage" upon the "people."[29]

For North Carolina Democrats, Grover Cleveland's 1884 election turned their eyes and their hopes to Washington. Breaking a twenty-four-year Republican hold on the presidency, Cleveland's rise seemed to open doors to new bounty in the federal government. Like other forms of the politics of dependence, the emphasis upon patronage grew not from archaic beliefs but from new government acts as the expanding national state hired increasing numbers of men and women. In 1884, the United States employed more than 50,000 postmasters nationwide, and North Carolina by the 1890s had a total of 1,000 post offices, 600 staffed by salaried postmasters. Additionally, executive departments of the federal government (which did not include the postal service or the military) grew from 1,268 employees in 1859 to 7,688 by 1880 and 17,304 by 1893, and large numbers of them (5,637 by 1893) were women. The economic power of the federal government helped create a politics of fantasy and dependence that was hardly unique to North Carolina. Charles Francis Adams Jr. grumpily called presidential campaigns a "popular hallucination" that made each new presidency a "new millennium." At each change in administration, Adams wrote, "the same expectation is seen of a new and brighter epoch." From "talk heard on the streets" a foreigner might suppose the new leader "a species of arbitrary monarch." After Cleveland's victory, Democrats across the country sang songs about climbing the "golden stairs" with him, while some white farmers joked that "you don't have to work any more[;] Cleveland . . . has promised to give every white man a Negro, a mule, and forty acres of land." The complex nature of these "hallucinations" was perhaps on display in an 1884 election-day celebration in Lenoir County. Democrats proclaimed their victory through floats and slogans and wild stories of Cleveland's promises. They also celebrated by listening to a man who "could imitate the crowing of a rooster to perfection." Like the imitated crowing, the popular vocabulary of politics was simultaneously a con man's mimicry and a people's hope for the coming of a new day.[30]

Those same Lenoir Democrats sang exultantly that Cleveland's election meant that white men could now "put down your shovel and hoe." Even if most did not actually believe that the first Democratic president since the Civil War would really free "every white man" from working again, many did expect the election to provide them with something nearly as appealing: a government job, or at least the right to ask for one. These deferred dreams of the "riff raff" came due in the winter of 1884–85 as Democrats crowed about the opportunities that awaited them. After "the victory," one Democrat with "hungry eyes" wrote, "then the vision of the spoils." Hundreds of "Umble" North Carolinians begged U.S. senator Zebulon Vance to remember his promise that "we wood take the next Presidend and we wood get a good chance" for an office. J. B. Jones saw in Cleveland's victory the opportunity for "a higher calling than following a horse up and down corn rows. . . . The cross has been bourn and the Democratic party has risen up again in glory and I wish to be with it in paradise as I was when it descended into hell."[31]

Instead of the bonanza of government jobs, however, Cleveland's election delivered a great deal of disappointment to Democrats. Cleveland proved to be far more receptive to antipatronage arguments than his supporters in North Carolina hoped. For more than a decade, civil service reformers — like Charles Francis Adams Jr. — had worried over exactly this set of vernacular beliefs. Certain that patronage corrupted not just the individual job-seekers but politics more broadly, businessmen, journalists, and social scientists lobbied through new organizations like the American Social Science Association and the National Civil Service Reform League. During the Grant and Hayes administrations, leaders worked fruitlessly to place federal offices outside of politics, and to require new applicants to advance through tests. When the first serious civil service reform, the Pendleton Act, passed in

1883, it was due in large part to practical considerations. Spurred by President Garfield's assassination by a disappointed office-seeker and by fears that Democrats would win the 1884 presidential election, congressional Republicans tried to protect the federal employees they had earlier appointed. Despite the Pendleton Act's limitations (it protected only about 10 percent of federal jobs), the debate largely focused on the transition from a government of presumed "friends" to a government of strangers. In 1884 Vance and other Southern Democrats hoped to use opposition to reform as a campaign issue, but, to their dismay, Democrat Grover Cleveland courted the same liberal reformers responsible for civil service. Recognizing that these men disliked the Republican nominee, James Blaine, Cleveland presented himself as a reformer, and garnered much support. Despite Cleveland's own rhetoric, Southern Democrats made the Cleveland they wanted, transforming the election into a national Redemption campaign to "turn the rascals out." In November 1884, Southern Democrats celebrated "with more than political joy" the bonanza of patronage jobs Cleveland's victory would deliver, and Northern reformers cheered for precisely the opposite reason.[32]

Once inaugurated, Cleveland cautiously but steadily backed civil service, eventually doubling the number of classified employees. While some Democrats kept quiet for fear the president would cut off their patronage, Vance broke dramatically with his party's president to lead a broad-based, quixotic fight. Vance advanced a wide-ranging critique of civil service on the Senate floor and in a speaking tour of Northern cities. Vance's argument drew upon a mix of partisan expediency, everyday forms of racism, sectional resentment, honor-based definitions of friendship, skepticism about modern testing, and a citizen's right to appeal for help. Vance's speeches against civil service, "broad cast" across the state by mail and newspaper reports, both created and reflected popular opinion. In about 150 letters sent to Vance after his Senate speech, women and men claimed that "*God speaks to you*," and "You just live in the hearts of the people." The "common people" of Edgecombe County, Henry C. Bourne claimed, "believe as strong as holy writ" in the evils of civil service. The "sentiments of my surroundings," another correspondent wrote, were an "echo" of Vance's attack on "this illegitimate offspring of shame and disgrace *civil service*." When a Concord resident received the speech in the mail, he "could not help saying d — -n the Civil Service law." Copies of Vance's speech were passed around towns and rural neighborhoods and "it has taken like fire," another writer claimed. "Everybody in this town is talking about it and wants a copy," a Laurinburg attorney suggested. In the most personal and religious terms, some North Carolinians described their faith in Vance and their opposition to what one called that "Satan or Civil Service Reform (both mean about the same.)" In exchange for speaking on behalf of "the people who have been looking on from a distance," "our Zeb" received "in exchange" words of adulation, "love," and "honour." "You are a true man," one wrote. "I am a Zeb Vance man."[33]

The intensity of public reaction prompted the reform-minded Raleigh *State Chronicle* to initiate a crude survey of public opinion. These questionnaires, sent to county officials, Democratic Party leaders, and well-known attorneys, reported the sentiments of the people they talked to. Placed awkwardly between their party's president and its most popular state politician, many struggled to answer. Several echoed one county chairman's claim that the president was correct but the "majority of our people, I fear, do not concur with me." Although a few reported that "the people are with Cleveland and put their trust in him," most respondents acknowledged that "nine-tenths of the people" were opposed to reform and "have on these subjects the same opinions held by Zeb Vance — a man whom they regard as a safe and wise leader — one whom they delight to follow." The *Wilmington Morning Star* questioned whether even the few pro-Cleveland sentiments accurately reflected the public mood. "It would not be difficult . . . to obtain five thousand letters from sound, intelligent voters in opposition" to reform, the editor wrote.[34]

In response, reformers in North Carolina, like those nationally, defined their opponents as ignorant, ill-intentioned, or irrational. In the state, the primary supporters emerged from a small group of young men in the Raleigh-based Watauga Club, one of whose members promised that the people "can be taught to be for" reform. Josephus Daniels, editor of the *State Chronicle*, framed the argument as influence versus "merit," describing poor, educated boys who lost positions to less-qualified politically connected rich men. Thomas Dixon, whose racist novels and films would obscure his role as a progressive politician and preacher, declared that if people were educated properly, they would enter the "door" to "conversion." Dixon's use of religious metaphors to describe his path toward political enlightenment was no accident; like many other young reformers, Dixon saw his progressive views as religious in nature, a wholesale cleansing of the sins of the old politics. Both in North Carolina and nationally, reformers described public opinion as faulty, expertise as objective, and education as the method for helping to convert the ignorant.[35]

Patronage supporters celebrated the value of friendship over reformers' cold, impersonal, and fraudulent claims of merit-based expertise. While civil service defenders claimed the tests were "as practical as may be," opponents asserted that they measured not education or fitness but "book learning." The "honesty and capacity demanded to fill office does not require simple ability to answer the routine questions of the schools," one county chairman claimed. A New York woman wrote Vance that she deserved a job, as her "claim upon the attention of the August body is not based upon mathematical or grammatical qualifications." Older letter writers complained that the tests denigrated their practical knowledge in favor of abstract learning. "Any boy just from school could stand better than myself," one applicant complained. Privately, Vance subscribed to this view, dismissing his step-son's poor grades on the grounds that his college "examinations too much resemble those of the Civil Service humbug for me to attach any importance to them as tests of capacity." Publicly, Vance mocked the exams as the effort of "strong, influential men" to avoid "their legal, but not their social equals as they fancy." Instead of relying upon "personal knowledge of a lifetime," they constructed a system dependent on "college training" to answer questions about the causes of the War of 1812 or "the Kinetic theory of the constitution of gases," which would give educated applicants "every time the advantage over a better and much more practical man who had never been to college." Many North Carolinians suspected that the tests were flawed not only because they denigrated practical knowledge but also because they were essentially fraudulent, a mere excuse for elites who wanted to deny them jobs. To complainants, testing seemed the "flimsiest pretence" to eliminate favors to "the friendless." "I really do not think these examinations amount to anything unless you have influential friends to attend to it for you," one woman wrote. These ideas challenged the civil service system at its core. Instead of creating a meritorious class, reform created a new way to say no.[36]

The debate over civil service reform also was a debate about political parties. Democrats were naturally suspicious that the new law was a devious effort to protect Republican officeholders, as indeed it partly was. This suspicion exacerbated popular belief that reformist language was simply a veneer. Some opponents drew heavily upon racial competition. An outraged Washington, D.C., resident asked Cleveland if his election meant "to keep the twelve hundred big burly negros here in Washington with their snowey white shirts and pickadilly collars lounging on government stools . . . when we have so many soldiers and sailors more worthy and more competent." A county Democratic leader called it "an infamous outrage to make a campaign with the battle cry of 'Turn the Rascals out' and after we have won the fight say to our party there is no rascals to turn out." Opponents of reform argued that parties, not bureaucrats, defined American democracy. A Democratic newspaper asked, "Why should any man worry himself about elections . . . if Republicans are as good and as acceptable for office as Democrats are?" Another claimed, "It takes democrats to make a democratic administration. . . . You cannot build an iron house out of wood paint." While this argument relied upon a crass view of office, there was logic in suggestions that civil service reform was "essentially" and intentionally "undemocratic." In his speeches, Vance defended parties as features, not flaws, in American democracy. "A government by party is the only way in which there can be government by the people," he said, while civil service reformers hoped to remove politics "as far as possible away from the control of the people."[37]

Broadly, the debate over civil service was an argument about the nature of friendship. Reform led E. B. Roberts to believe he "had no Democratic friend in Washington (no room for them — all the places filled by Rads)." In his Senate speech, Vance argued that "the mass of the people on both sides" believe "in the common virtues of humanity, among the most noble of which is reckoned gratitude." Instead of complaining about favors, politicians should celebrate them. "If a man's friends take him up and enable him after a great struggle to arrive at the point coveted by his ambition he owes something to them," Vance said. "They believe that . . . in the bestowal of favors that man should give preference to his friends over his enemies; and so do I. They believe that the man who is lacking in the ordinary sentiment of gratitude may be likewise wanting in other kindred and cardinal virtues; and so do I."[38]

Throughout the debate, Vance defended the subjects' imagined right of access to government. In his speech to the Senate, Vance claimed one of the four cornerstones of American democracy was that "every citizen of the United States" had the "right to seek office." Every job in the government had "one million American citizens competent to fill it. Each has a right to apply for it equal in law to the right of any other man. Each has the right to go directly." By whittling the eligible list down to the top scorers on an examination, the law "disfranchised" the vast majority of American citizens. Vance acknowledged that the right to apply was no guarantee of actual benefit. "Only one man out of the million can get the vacant office," but "the million have the right to seek for it and take their chances." In place of this "birthright," reform created a "monarchical and aristocratical" class of bureaucrats. Vance embodied this conflict in an Old Democrat who in 1884 traveled to Washington after "the feasting had ended . . . [and] in the simplicity of his heart . . . modestly ask[ed] for a position, naturally supposing that the king in making up his jewels would remember his faithful servants."

Instead of a king, however, the Old Democrat encountered a "government representative" who proclaimed both him and his son ineligible for office. "You are behind the times," the bureaucrat said. "Away with you!" According to Vance, "There are thousands of just such men, and we meet them or hear from them every day."[39]

Vance lost the debate in Congress, but he won respect in North Carolina and across the country. In an argument about reform, he had tapped a language of politics that celebrated intimacy over merit. By imagining a fantastic but meaningful attachment of an individual subject to a particular patron, people in the 1870s through the 1890s tried to make politics work for them.

Not all politicians possessed the charisma to perform Vance's role in public, but needy North Carolinians, especially whites, constructed a portable Democratic version of rulership in the years after Redemption. In the 1890s Mrs. George N. Banks begged a new governor in almost exactly the same way an earlier generation of Civil War wives turned to Vance. Calling the new governor "a gentleman of such a big heart . . . in sympathy with a poor widow like me," Banks claimed a right to apply to "the head of the state" for "some consolment" since no male relatives were able to help her. A Monroe woman named Mary C. Krauss, who had "not enough education to write as it ought to be written," seized the right to address "such a great man" as then-governor Alfred Scales based in part on sheer will as "no one can hinder me." Krauss's confidence rose from her certainty that her appeal "makes me think of prayer, we can pray to our great heavenly father when we please and no one can hinder. He has promised to hear, even if it be imperfect language, if our hearts are right in his sight. He will answer in the way that is best for us." Against this confidence, her husband warned her, "Don't tell anybody or they will make fun of you." Up to this point, Mary Krauss sounded a great deal like other people who wrote in the language of subjecthood. Then, Krauss asked for help in retaining land that was hers not merely by virtue of begging but also by proper title. Along with the governor's listening ear, she wanted his legal advice. In the messy mixture of popular politics, Krauss did not separate her appeals but instead asked as a subject to a king, as a plaintiff to a judge, and as a wronged woman to a wise man.[40]

New modes of communication, especially improved newspaper and advertising networks, did not displace but often augmented the notions of patronal power. In an era before celebrities became politicians, politicians became celebrities. Imbued with a power that seemed personal not programmatic, they fashioned images that were widely known even in rural, hard-to-reach places. Drawing their public notoriety from the gossip and chatter of politics, many of these men became endorsers. Tobacco magnates R. J. Reynolds and B. F. Hanes competed for the right to sell "Zeb Vance Tobacco." The Bank of Laurinburg asked to emboss Vance's face on their checks, and the American Medicine Company requested that he join William Gladstone's endorsement of its sarsaparilla. Julian S. Carr, the force behind the Bull Durham tobacco brand, attempted to use Governor Elias Carr's photograph to advertise smoking tobacco; even scholarly state supreme court justice Walter Clark endorsed the Electropoise, a metal cylinder that allegedly helped people absorb oxygen. These advertisements not only reflected but augmented the iconic power of these individuals.[41]

Innovative new government programs often reinforced — or were interpreted as if they reinforced — the essential subject-patron relationship. Just as the Civil War itself created an immediate expansion of social welfare provisions, the problem of veterans' suffering prompted new postwar entitlements. Over time, the federal government established massive programs for disabled Union veterans and their widows, and in turn the state government created its own services for Confederates. Even when North Carolinians asked for help from these government relief and pension programs, they blended those rights-based appeals with pleas of dire dependence. In this way, a politics of personality could be grafted onto seemingly merit-based programs without doing violence to either. Union veterans, filling out extremely legalistic applications, were encouraged to indicate not just their eligibility but the depth of their need. Neighbors therefore described applicants as "total disable" and "fully depending on the hands of charity for his support. If it were not for the neighbors he would suffer be there without any thing to eat." North Carolina Confederate pensions, established in 1879, also seemed to establish objective criteria for inclusion, with four designated classes of need, each with different levels of payment. Nevertheless, veterans begged the governor to "see for me . . . i will thank you kindly for it i am sore in need." Veterans understood that they still required friends in Raleigh; for one thing, the legislature never anticipated the number of applicants and so never fully funded the program. Over the 1880s and 1890s, pensions grew to about 12 percent of state expenditures; to control costs, legislators underfunded the program, leading to reduced payments and grave fears. Additionally, the program left a great deal of leeway with local examining boards who could certify the class of need. Therefore, veterans quickly asked for help upon extreme desperation, because, as one put it, "my life is at stake." An anonymous writer speaking for a "poverty stricken maiden sister" of a Confederate begged for a widow's pension on the grounds that she was "dependent on her fellow beings for food. . . . You have wisdom, and she is weak." One ex-Confederate called himself "one of the most pitiful objects living on this Earth . . . compelled to Beg." Describing his "shrunken limbs and blinded Eyes," he wrote, "If you could see me yourself . . . you would not hesitate a moment."[42]

Federal seed programs, established to promote scientific agriculture, quickly became ways to distribute gifts to favored subjects. Devised originally to encourage more varied harvests, seed distribution turned into proof of "the benefits of 'Uncle Sam's' *liberality*." The thousands of packets of seeds mailed out by individual congressmen created a multilayered system of favors as local distributors passed them to "the poor" who traveled "10 miles" to get what "not 10 in a hundred" were "able to buy." Senators and congressmen also distributed government publications, valued not just for their practical uses but also for the way they embodied the promise of a personal connection. "We would never know we had any Congress excepting for the seeds + books," one farmer wrote. "We want to be reminded now + then that we are represented."[43]

Despite the pull of new transportation and communication networks that directed attention to the wider world, North Carolinians continued to assert the importance of the immediate, proximate world because the weak government they saw seemed incapable of addressing problems everywhere at all times. Therefore, they called for geographically narrow interventions not because of a disdain for broad programs but because of a skepticism in the state's power to implement them. Although all people judge politics by the world in front of them, many Americans during Reconstruction did not make leaps from the particular to the national in ways that would be commonplace by the twentieth century. In 1880, an African American man told a congressional committee that the law meant solely what his local magistrate said it meant. To that magistrate, he said, "a nigger is no more a human being than a horse is a mule. . . . The colored people when that man administered the law . . . of course can have no confidence in him." The problem of arbitrary justice was not limited to freedpeople. In 1889, Delk Finches of Union Grove complained that "there rulers the Justics that was appointed by the Legislator is oppressive." The local justice of the peace "is never sober if he can git Liquor if you want any business done by a Justice you neede not go to his house to find him go to some still house or some hore shop." The people of the area "will not sumit to be ruled by a drunkin Leeder that is not governed by Law but punishes whoever he will and release whoever he will." Instead of an anomalous flaw in the legal system, such deeply personalized power was a formative element of the law. In judging rules to be not abstract or rights-based but narrow and personally enforced, Carolinians were not making mistakes; they were in many respects accurately reading the world around them.[44]

Voting rituals also confirmed the centrality of local struggles for power to democratic practice. These horizontal forms of organization did not counteract but often coincided with patronal power. On a tally sheet, votes could look like nothing more than recorded preferences for officeholders in distant capitals, but on the ground the practice of voting suggested that its primary meaning lay in its impact upon the local precinct. In the 1876 election between Settle and Vance, African Americans and whites at one township lined up separately to enter the voting area, and election judges let them in "five whites and then five blacks . . . in turn." By forcing residents to vote racially in a predominantly African American precinct, white election supervisors made it more difficult for freedpeople to cast their ballots; 135 freedpeople in one precinct were unable to do so. At the same time, these electoral practices, based upon the whimsical decisions of individual election judges, localized the struggle for political supremacy. In precincts without such segregation, African Americans and whites sometimes grouped themselves into flying wedges, trying to block the other side from getting to the ballot box. When one white man arrived at the courthouse, he found "the colored people . . . crowded around the Polls, so that it was with great difficulty that outsiders could get to the Polls to vote. Seeing this I told some of my friends to tell the white people if they did not crowd around in they would not be allowed to vote." In the chaos, some people "would not press through the crowd" and left without voting; others fought closer to "see my friends vote and to see others vote." This competition for proximate power helped to reinforce the imaginative ways that people appealed to distant authority; unsurprisingly, they constructed governors and congressmen who would act with great vigor for their friends and complete disdain toward their enemies.[45]

New state programs in the 1880s reinforced the centrality of localism. In the 1880s, the state government intervened broadly in economic and personal lives through laws encouraging railroad construction, regulating fencing, and prohibiting alcohol. In each case, after failures to pass broad-based legislation, the state then acted in extremely narrow ways, defining tightly circumscribed boundaries of power and encouraging competitive petition drives among antagonists within those narrow confines. In liquor, after one unsuccessful attempt at statewide prohibition in 1881, later laws allowed churches and schools to request two- to five-mile dry territories around their buildings. People's petitions creatively combined religious opposition to liquor and territorial views of power. Petitioners "earnestly beseech[ed] and pray[ed]" to the General Assembly to rescue "localities," "the neighborhood," "said vicinity," "the community," and "the village." Local applications of power were necessary because the evils were also local in their effect; members of the Bills Creek Baptist Church complained that the "moral standard" of a previously "sober and orderly" community had been "greatly lowered" by the opening of a distillery and barroom a mile away. In these competitions for the application of geographically narrow power, an important question was who comprised the community. One pro-liquor petition from Union County defined the "sentiments of the people" by noting signers' precise distance from the incorporated church, claiming authority based upon proximity. Everyday forms of race making mattered; some local prohibitionists encouraged African American signatures and speakers at integrated rallies, others included them on segregated lists, and some whites opposed themselves to "vicious negroes" and stated explicitly that the community opinion was determined by "the white voters." The narrow focus and moral emphasis of these claims helped create space for women, who circulated many petitions against liquor (and a few for it), signed in both segregated and intermixed lists, and claimed a right to speak "earnestly desirous of promoting the good" or "in interest of our husbands + brothers + sons + homes and our continued happiness."[46]

Stock or fence law debates also combined vernacular notions of territoriality and state action. At stake in these struggles was whether small-scale farmers and landless tenants could graze their animals upon open range; many large landowners wanted to limit grazing to an owner's fenced land. The fight over fence laws therefore cut directly to the way people in an agrarian society farmed and found food; without fence laws, poor, landless people could run small herds of cattle or goats on open land but landowners had to build strong, expensive fences to defend crops. With the fence law, many poor people had to give up their livestock altogether while landowners could increase crop yields. The struggles were fights not only between rich and poor but also over representation between African Americans and white landowners. Because counties frequently included patchworks of fence and no-fence townships, the power of the state seemed immense but of limited circumference. Again, a key question was who defined the community. The "majority proper" should be determined not by headcount, one proponent argued, but by the "majority of the landlords. . . . because they pay the tax . . . not the Negro at our expense." Other supporters characterized backers as "every intelligent man" or "all the reading and thinking people" and opponents as "every Negro + every white renter + every man who . . . wish to make his living by grasing his stock on other peoples land" or "a few broken down dead beats." Opponents — who believed they had the majority on their side — frequently argued that the issue should be settled not by the legislature but "at the Ballot Box." Even though the laws were motivated by a "greedy desire" and would consign the "poor" and the "laborers of the country" to "Purdition," as one opponent put it, a "great many are willing to submit to the law cheerfully if left to a Popular vote."[47]

The Ocracoke oyster controversy illustrated the spectacular thinness of the state and the territorialism this weakness engendered. Seeking to profit from the declining oyster population in Maryland's Chesapeake Bay, the state government between 1885 and 1887 commissioned a naval lieutenant named Francis Winslow to begin cultivating oysters in the large sounds between coastal Carolina and the Outer Banks. From afar, this looked of a piece with the state's railroad subsidies and its other steps toward scientific planning and economic development. Up close, however, it prompted a massive backlash. When Winslow — now at the head of a private company — sought to cultivate areas he had leased from the state, "bands of lawless men" chased him from Pamlico Sound in what Winslow called "revolt and defiance." Oystermen on Ocracoke Island defended spots they considered "their own peculiar property," "which our fathers and grand fathers and our selves have always looked to for food and cloths . . . to obtain support for our wives and children." Islanders viewed "people from different parts of the county or state" to be "foreigners." This territorial claim was reinforced by racial solidarity; hundreds of islanders petitioned the governor to favor them since "we are all white men" while Winslow's company hired "imported negroes." When Winslow asked the county sheriff for help, the sheriff refused. Even if he crossed the sound with a "posse comitatus," the sheriff insisted, the result would be not an imposition of law but the inauguration of a "feud of an angry and lasting character." Eventually the governor finessed the problem by offering general support for the islanders, demanding future obedience to the law, and encouraging the formation of a newly empowered commission. This support for the forms of law masked the fact that those who "defied the Sheriff and judicial authorities" had won, Winslow complained, especially when the governor promised to protect all customary grounds. The state's lease to Winslow meant nothing without the power to enforce it.[48]

Nothing proved the weakness of the state and the assertions of territorial power more gruesomely than the growing number of lynchings in the state. Across the South between 1880 and 1930, about 2,500 African Americans were lynched, about seventy-five of them in North Carolina. Lynchings demonstrated the power of local communities and the limits of the law. Often lynchings were not efforts to punish an offender who would otherwise go free but attempts by local people to exert control. Some white Carolinians treated lynching as a right granted to the locals, a claim based upon proximity, not legal jurisdiction. This idea of communal vigilantism was contagious, not a consistent or inherent view of rural people, but something they learned by observing the weakness of the state. In June 1881, a crowd lynched an African American man in Rockingham County on charges of sexual assault. Immediately, whites and African Americans across the state began to speculate about the potential for more lynchings. Within days, 150 people in the isolated town of Danbury, "50 miles from the nearest telegraph station," stormed the jail and attacked two men charged with "outraging" a twelve-year-old girl and a "white married woman." Beyond the edge of town, the group halted, "formed into a square, and gave the prisoners a few moments in which to prepare for the death that awaited them." After hanging them from a tree, the crowd dispersed, and "the names of those who participated in the lynching" were "not known." Nevertheless, a *New York Times* report claimed, "the punishment meted out . . . is generally approved" of by "the community." In 1891, a future U.S. senator celebrated the murder of Mose Best, who was charged with assaulting a married white woman. "Though a dangerous precedent," the lynching was "justified by public sentiment, if not by law" because white citizens' "pitch of rage" impelled them to take the "law into their own hands" and hasten "the coming of justice." While some well-to-do white Carolinians expressed dismay over lynchings, there was no coordinated effort to suppress them until the twentieth century.[49]

From experiences with lynching, eccentric local magistrates, narrowly defined prohibition and fence laws, and other forms of territorialism, North Carolinians learned to be skeptical of the idea that rights applied everywhere, to everyone. Against new conditions and against the efforts of reformers, North Carolinians did not discard but reshaped this politics of territorialism and dependence. Patronalism was not a fragile pillar of dust to crumble with the touch of modernity; instead it was a creative language formed within encounters with the state, capable of withstanding attacks from reformers and new social conditions. As the economy and the law changed around them, North Carolinians remade patronalism for their new era, finding proof of the power of patrons and the narrow range of legal authority. Rather than relics to be discarded, these arguments were present in and central to the creation of modern political styles.

6

Crazes, Fetishes, and Enthusiasms

The Silver Mania and the Making
of a New Politics

IN 1896, two years after Zebulon Vance died, the son of his old rival Tom Settle paged through a series of distressing field reports about the "silver craze" sweeping through his congressional district. In a campaign about the gold standard, a fantastic, incorrect rumor about a government-sponsored gift of money disrupted the younger Settle's already tenuous reelection prospects in piedmont North Caro-

lina. As a solid supporter of his Republican Party's gold position,[1] Settle increasingly found himself trapped by an upsurge of popular sentiment that combined Reconstruction's patronal hopes with a newly broad view of government's reach and scope. Rather than being a gift from one patron to a loyal supporter, the silver standard seemed to make a present of policy itself—a promise of a "pocket full of money whether worked for or not," one organizer complained. Another was mystified by "Negroes" who "tell me, 'they's gwine to give me 16 dollars for every dollar I has at election time in my pocket.'" For Settle and other gold standard supporters, these rumors sounded "like folly" but were a "hard thing to fight." On the stump, Settle tried to convince audiences that their hopes were rooted in misunderstanding. The Populists' and Democrats' call for the free, immediate, and un-limited coinage of silver was no gift of cash but a plan to expand the money supply by including silver at the widely understood ratio of sixteen ounces to one of gold. As Settle's aides watched the intense swell of popular support, however, some of them urged Settle to give up on persuasion. "The politicians float with the tide because they are powerless to stop it," one warned the young congressman.[2]

Inspired by organizational, economic, and governmental upheavals, some Carolinians — like those rumormongers who perplexed Settle — grafted the politics of dependence onto the webs of a more systematic state in the 1890s. In the process, they edged toward seemingly modern views of policy not by discarding patronalism but by remaking it. The 1890s political upheavals dramatically but not completely transformed politics. In the face of agricultural, economic, and social crises, various groups of reformers — including agrarian Populists, urban Progressives, and Christian prohibitionists — tried to replace the old language of ruler and subject with a new, compressed, impersonal vision; instead of governing persons, reformers increasingly spoke of governing the people. None of these innovators could afford to detach themselves from popular currents, at least not until the success of disfranchisement in the early 1900s. In the alchemy of U.S. democratic politics, 1890s candidates still had to appeal to people who spoke in Reconstruction's vocabulary of patrons and persons, translating novel programs into familiar terms. Populists and other agrarians faced this dilemma first, and in the process inadvertently created a vision that grafted the new, expansive state onto the old patronal politics, making government currency policies into a broad-based gift of money. From the friction between new technocratic ideas and intimate appeals, a new, modern politics emerged over the last decade of the nineteenth century and the first decade of the twentieth, one that on its surface appeared to be a self-conscious rejection of patronalism. Underneath the surface, in the crossroads speeches and dinner-table gossip where politics was also made, there still remained sedimentary layers of the old political style that resurfaced, like the gossip about the magic of silver, at unexpected moments.

Although it is impossible to say for certain how many people heard, much less believed, these particular rumors about the gift of silver, there was little question that a wave of support for silver reshaped American politics in the 1890s. This enthusiasm played a key role in the formation of a new politics. The Populist Party, the most significant third-party challenge in American history, scrambled elections and seemed for a moment to be on the verge of displacing Democrats in the South. African American Republicans used this political upheaval to claim local, state, and federal offices in the South in the mid-1890s. In turn, panicked Democrats broke with gold standard New York financiers, sending the party to the left. Gold-supporting Republicans, led by coal magnate Mark Hanna, generated their own passion for gold among sound-money men in the Northeast and Midwest, creating a success-ful national coalition that shaped national campaigns until the Great Depres-sion. Over the last years of the nineteenth century and first years of the twentieth, intense competition nudged the two main parties toward the stat-ist interventions that would become Progressivism.

Although much of silver's support was rooted in a calm appraisal of the way looser money would benefit the South and the Great Plains, many observers also pointed to a field of politics beyond the bounds of the rational to de-scribe the intensity of the backing for silver. To explain this upheaval, one observer described the nearly religious fervor of silver support through the evangelical term "enthusiasm." Although Populists professed support for broad programs of government warehousing, direct democracy, and state control of the railroads, a former U.S. senator warned party leaders that "no enthusiasm" could be raised for those issues because the "masses" did "not so readily understand" them. But "more money, more circulation, more life-blood" was visceral. The people "feel it daily." By connecting this excitement about silver to what people felt, both tactilely and emotionally, the senator tied it to the evangelical concept of enthusiasm, a belief in a world "visibly penetrated with supernatural influences" and replete with the "evident re-sults of the grace of God." This enthusiasm grew in part from the popular fusion of currency debates and patronalism.[3]

By the 1890s, both silver and gold backers sparked intense enthusiasm through their use of religious imagery. In the North and Midwest, gold backers attributed gold's power to its associations with masculinity, Anglo-Saxon superiority, racial fixity, and divine power. In the South and Great Plains, speakers celebrated the intense power of the white metal, even as they also made elaborate rational arguments. In campaign events where "Silver was Crowned King!" Populists and pro-silver Democrats in North Carolina held up silver dollars that were circulated during the 1790s, calling the coin-age "the money of our fathers, and our father's fathers," accepted "as coin since the dawn of history." "Silver money has stood by them and the fathers, and they and their children will stand by it," one silverite wrote. In cam-paign talks, silver was imbued with divine qualities. A Whiteville man claimed that as "Abraham incarnates for us faith; Solomon, wisdom; and Samson, strength; so a true Populist incarnates for us faith in silver." These "con-verts" to the "old-time religion" described a fervor rooted not in intellectual thought but in emotion. "I would not mind giving my life" for silver, a Michigan man wrote. For North Carolina's white population, Zebulon Vance came to stand for silver as he had stood previously for patronage. In the

1880s, Vance broke with goldbug Democratic president Grover Cleveland and became one of the party's most committed silver spokesmen. Although Vance justified his position on bimetallism through statistics, he also celebrated silver's timeless, mystical value, and in so doing, attached it to his own personality of power. In Vance's flowery speeches, silver was holy. It was Abraham's medium, a glimpse of the divinity of the "glittering hosts of heaven," and an "indispensable necessity" from "the very earliest records of humanity."[4]

From some vantage points, the turbulent politics of the 1890s seemed to be a fight not over issues but over icons. "While our far away neighbors in Africa worship stones or animals, some of our people worship gold," a pro-silver newspaper editor complained. Silver-supporting writers described gold defenders as heathens for their "humble devotion" and their "blind faith" in "idols." Goldbugs made gold a "king" before whom people were "made to sacrifice at their altars." A Carolina congressman compared gold supporters to "modern Nebuchadnezzars. . . . You may set up your images and heat your furnaces seven times hotter . . . but there are three times three millions who will not bow down nor worship them." At the same time, gold writers mocked the notion that the "ignorant have been led to believe that the government will distribute as a charity sixteen dollars to every man, woman and child." Wedded not to reason but to "idols," people "not intelligent enough to understand this difficult matter" were misled by "impossible promises," including the thought "that [they] would get a bag full" of silver. To them, "silver worship" was a "quasi-superstition," a "craze or a fetich."[5]

By attributing silver's success not to momentary hysteria but to an unnatural, even supernatural, dependence upon government, well-educated gold supporters thought they isolated a deeper-rooted and more ominous flaw in American popular politics. At the root of these fantasies about politics lay a troubling reliance upon a "government [that] is all-powerful and ought to be all-willing," one critic wrote. "The saving grace of Government is a personal influence to him, a thing of life." In ascribing fetishistic powers to silver, gold supporters compared American citizens to subjects, peasants, and savages in other parts of the world. "Receptive and credulous farmers" who believed silver "shall be *free* to all—will be distributed to all the people without charge of any kind," were, the *Wilmington Messenger* editorialized, akin to "befooled and beguiled Negroes" with their fantastic expectation of " 'forty acres and a mule' that never cometh." Critiquing the fetishistic political beliefs of white Americans turned the world full circle and revealed enduring doubts about the rationality or disenchantment of modern politics.[6]

Of course historians should not mistake overheated partisan denunciations for truth. At the same time, we must be equally careful not to dismiss judgments simply because they do not conform to the way we now understand politics. As Tom Settle knew, gauging public opinion meant looking beyond campaign speeches or platform pronouncements and into the strange play of thought and emotion, of preaching and passion, of fact and fantasy, that was visible — if sometimes just barely — in the reports of the practical political scientists who marched through the countryside recording what they heard. Politicians did this work not just so that the people could be fitted to the candidates, but so that the candidates could be fitted to the people. Although it may seem safer to ignore the messy corners of politics, bypassing them raises problems even beyond foolishness; it guarantees that our understanding of politics will be unnecessarily impoverished and incomplete.

Silver's support is an especially useful realm because its popularity has flummoxed many scholars, especially those drawn to the Populists' broad program. Some historians see silver's appeal as obvious. By expanding the money supply, a bimetallic standard would help circulate money and capital through cash-poor regions like the South and West and drive up crop prices; for these reasons, many Southern Democrats and Western Republicans had supported silver for decades by the 1890s. Other scholars remain confused by the intensity of the attachment to silver, especially compared to broader platforms aimed at the heart of the nation's political economy. These historians often run into rhetorical dead ends, blaming the passion solely on the manipulation of mine owners, or the chaos of an economic panic. Or they mystify it as "a single-cure-all of the popular thought," a "will-o'-the wisp," or an example of "ominous credulity." In a more recent, sympathetic account of Southern Populists, a leading historian's powers of analysis failed him when he reached the topic of silver, finally calling it a "heavily symbolic burden." But this popular politics was not inscrutable. By moving beyond the simple binary between rationalism and pathology, scholars can ask much richer questions about the way popular fantasies and rumors entered (as they enter now) into political life, leaving political organizers and party leaders almost helpless against them.[7]

This budding, incomplete state patronalism emerged because of economic and political transformations in the twenty years since Vance defeated Tom

Settle's father. The world had been upended by two economic crises, one happening in double time, one in slow motion. In the 1880s, the agrarian economies of the West and South collapsed in the face of new global competition from India, Egypt, and Latin America that halved the value of some crops, especially cotton. At the same time, the government's tight money policy starved the South and West of cash and capital. Driven by Civil War bondholders' desire to be repaid in money backed directly by gold, not inflated greenbacks, the U.S. government contracted the currency dramatically. The nation moved to the gold standard in the 1870s, withdrew some greenbacks from circulation, and stopped coining silver. In this the United States followed a global trend, as nations around the world trailed England into the gold standard in the late nineteenth century. Only in the United States did the money fight become a defining political issue. There, the fluidity and relative openness of American democracy and the regional power of silver supporters thrust the issue into the center of politics. As both Democrats and Republicans failed to respond to discontent with tight money policies, several new parties formed to represent loose-money supporters, including the Greenbackers. By the 1890s, a new People's Party arose from a massive grassroots agrarian organization, the Farmers' Alliance, with a wide reform platform that included the coining of silver, as well as government warehousing, state control of railroads, and an expanded democracy. The global depression of the early 1890s that froze credit and shuttered businesses across the country accelerated the political upheaval. By 1893, a dollar in North Carolina was "a very great thing," one canvasser wrote. Political organizers confronted the continual "cry of 'hard times'" and "What are we to do?" Petitioners begging for help claimed this "great money famine" among the "voting and suffering class of people" tore "from their grasp the only means by which they could earn." In the aftermath of the Panic, Populists made significant gains in 1894, including capturing North Carolina, and panicked Democrats by 1896 abandoned the gold standard for the young silver icon William Jennings Bryan.[8]

In a grand irony, the expansion of fantastic ideas about government had its roots in a slow, methodical effort to rationalize the state. The Farmers' Alliance, the agrarian movement at the center of the political upheaval, was part of the age's mania for organization. Born in Texas, the Alliance spread to North Carolina in part through the work of a former Vance protégé named Leonidas L. Polk. Raised in a family of Whigs and slave owners, Polk was a planter with a passion for statistics. Appointed by Vance as the state's first agricultural commissioner in 1877, Polk constructed perhaps the most comprehensive system of communication of any agricultural board in the nation, corresponding with almost two thousand farmers in virtually every township. What Polk wanted was "facts and figures," "a proper and intelligent comprehension of our wants and necessities." Therefore, Polk mailed out 100,000 requests for data on market conditions in 1877–78. By the spring of 1879, he had developed an extensive plan to talk back to those farmers through 240,000 reports mailed across the state per year. Polk used that information to produce dense evaluations of the condition of the state's agriculture, fishing, and manufacturing. Organized, empirical, and analytic, Polk saw the agricultural crisis as a series of problems for "the farmer" in need of a scientific solution. Instead of relying upon Vance's sympathy, Polk depended upon organization, at times losing sight of the individual persons in his quest to define policies that would be good for the "the people" or, frequently, "the farmer." One of his earliest campaigns was to require livestock owners to graze their cattle inside fenced pastures, since the time and money invested in damaged fences was a "prodigious waste of labor and energy." Instead of a benefit to a certain class, Polk portrayed this law as a simple matter of efficiency, and conflict between farmers seemed to disappear behind scenes of progress for the abstract, disembodied farmer. Polk's notion of the farmer who deserved consideration was circumscribed by his vision of a virtuous community, one that in his own petitioning against alcohol included solely the worthwhile people of the town. "The other five sixths [of the people] were ignored," Polk wrote, as men "without families, without local interest, without morals," and "vicious negroes + whites + mere stragglers + 'birds of passage' having no 'abiding place.'" After Vance left Raleigh for the U.S. Senate, Polk followed other reformers of his generation in turning away from political office and toward journalism. His *Progressive Farmer* became a leading agrarian paper and propelled him into the leadership of first the state grange and then the Farmers' Alliance, a cooperative organization that spread quickly throughout the South and West in the 1880s. Once in the Alliance, Polk carried with him his systematic approach to communication and the era's mania for the "wonderful power" of "organization."[9]

Alliance leaders labored to "unlearn the false education taught to us" and to teach farmers to view the government in a new way. Through discussions at regular meetings, traveling lecturers, and publications like the *Progressive Farmer*, Alliancemen created a new method for forming rural public opinion. Because information was "the secret of success," leaders funded local newspapers to break down farmers' "isolated lives" and promote the "association of ideas." Although the Alliance was "political in the higher sense," it was not originally "formed as a political body," North Carolina governor and state Alliance leader Elias Carr wrote. "The object of the Alliance is to educate the farmer to know the effect of laws and proposed laws, to learn him political economy." The lesson was that "the government is under the control of Plutocracy—money-kings, who are driving the producer to starvation in the midst of plenty." Even if many held that the "ideal government" still "governed least," the "farmers assert—and assert truly—that other classes have appealed to the government for protection and aid, and it has been granted at the expense of the farmers." Alliance sublecturers trained people to look not to their local or state politicians but to Washington both for help and for blame.[10]

Alliances' efforts to remake the countryside were hamstrung by the tools at their disposal. As Alliances conveyed new information and ideas, they worked through intensely local networks, reinforcing deeply held notions of territoriality. Additionally, by celebrating self-sufficiency, proximity, and segregation, the Alliances not only accepted but also sacralized a narrow vision of a community of "brethren" working for their own benefit, not the good of neighboring Alliances. Women—who in some neighborhoods outnumbered male members by five to one—played central roles in creating and policing this rural community through the Alliance's system of blackballing. As Alliances excluded would-be members, disgruntled members complained that the meetings had fallen under the sway of particular individuals who excluded someone for a "pirsonal matter" or because of opposition by one family. Therefore, the narrow circumference of Alliance life—many were formed about five miles from the next most proximate meeting—reinforced the intense nature of personal power, leading the Soldier Bay Alliance to call on state leader Elias Carr in an intimate way to "Bee a father to Soldier Bay alliance. . . . We pray for the to help us in the hour of need."[11]

Intense local organization gave the nonpartisan Alliance significant political capital, and by 1890 Polk was ready to spend it. That fall, Senator Zebulon Vance was up for reelection to the U.S. Senate by the state legislature, and Polk decided to use that vote as leverage to get a subtreasury bill introduced in Congress. This bill, a central part of the Alliance and Populist platforms, would issue bonds backed by warehoused crops, inflating the currency and allowing farmers to sell their goods at advantageous times and prices. Aware that Vance opposed the subtreasury, Polk threatened to run for his seat. Over the spring of 1890, "the agitation caused by this Alliance" turned "men who have heretofore been enthusiastic" for Vance against him, a supporter wrote. "The Sub Treasury is above everything and everybody."

One man who had named his son for Vance promised not to support Vance anymore because Vance was "insincere." Another writer blamed "anxiety," "impatience," "anger," and the power of the Alliance-backed *Progressive Farmer* newspaper for the "flagrant" opposition to Vance in the summer. "They want relief, and they want it as the texas man wanted his pistol." In pathetic letters, people begged Vance to "come to our relief" or "avenge your own people. . . . You have never turned a deaf ear to your own, so hear us this one time again." After surveying the landscape, and recognizing the threat to his power, Vance backed down, a little, constructing a compromise in which he introduced — but did not endorse — the Alliance's bill.[12]

The anguish of those letters to Vance suggests the limitations of Alliance education; many were convinced of the subtreasury's benefit but continued to practice a politics of personality, approaching Vance as a necessary patron. Even though the subtreasury was a program, it was something that they asked for as a gift. Once Vance proved his accessibility by introducing the subtreasury bill, he stymied much of the opposition to his Senate race. In caucuses during the summer of 1890, Vance's supporters defended him in intensely personal terms of affection and obligation. In Iredell County, a soldier who served under Vance blocked any legislative candidates who would not support Vance's reelection. In the Union County canvass, "every candidate that in any way objected to Vance was defeated," and the winners promised to "Stand on the Zeb Vance Platform." In the Anson County campaign, one candidate for state legislature said he endorsed Vance but held open his options. "Suppose he were to steal a sheep . . . I should not vote for him," he told his audience. The other candidate attracted applause when he responded, "He would vote for Vance against the world if he should steal two sheep." This support propelled Vance back for one more round in the Senate, where he died in 1894.[13]

By the 1890s, Vance was an almost anomalous figure in public life. Younger generations of politicians in all three parties practiced their art upon different terms, rooted in languages of expertise, statistics, and social evolution. But the politics of pleading endured in a new class of would-be patrons in the wealthy businessmen who came to prominence in the era. Nationally, people turned to Andrew Carnegie and John D. Rockefeller to supply help that government would not provide. In North Carolina, much of this attention settled upon the Duke family of Durham. Newspaper coverage of the family's generosity in the 1890s encouraged North Carolinians to appeal to the Dukes as "the poor man's friend" or "a fellow helper 'In His Name'" or "one willing to help the distressed, and needy" or more generous than "John

D. Rockefeller." Faced with starvation because neighbors and family were "not able to do much" or were "poor and can't help," beggars pleaded necessity. "I did not know who else to apply to," one wrote. To make connections, strangers called the Dukes "Brother," "for such I certainly regard you to be," or explained they had "no mother no brother no uncle to care for me," or created categories of fictive connection with the Dukes like being a "good Methodist." If they "succeeded in touching [the Dukes'] heart" or found a "tender spot," they hoped this connection would encourage the Dukes to, as one writer put it, "send me what you can." Susie H. Watkins, "a little hare lipped girl from birth," wrote, "It gives me so much trouble I thought I would write to some philanthropist. . . . If you have any little children I hope they are not deformed like I." Many writers, like Watkins, used religion to explain the Dukes' obligations; they asked favors not of the Dukes as individuals but from "God through you." They also promised the customary reciprocity; in return for generosity, one wrote, "I will pay you in prayer."[14]

This widespread cultural patronalism shaped Alliance plans despite Alliancemen's best efforts. In April 1890, Polk carried a cry for "relief" from "fifteen hundred thousand farmers" to the doors of the U.S. Senate Committee on Agriculture and Forestry. There, Polk and Texas Alliance leader Charles Macune dispensed not tales of woe but "facts as substantiated by statistics." The numbers were indeed grim; prices for key crops like wheat, corn, and cotton had fallen by 50 percent over the previous twenty-three years, and farmers' share of the nation's wealth had dropped from 70 percent to less than 25 percent in four decades. In a cold, analytic presentation, Polk argued that "the American farmer"—nameless, faceless, and known only through data—suffered under the "legalized tyranny" of "centralized capital" and "corporate power," which reduced the money supply, drove down crop prices, and made the "dollar" the "sovereign in this country." For relief, Polk asked the Senate to expand the currency by issuing money based upon silver holdings and enacting the subtreasury plan, which he called no "paternalism" or "charity" or "special legislation" but a simple application of political and agricultural "science" to create an "open field and an equal chance." Polk's appeal to rationality fell on deaf ears, however, and their disappointment with Congress convinced many Alliancemen that in the future they needed power to make their organization felt and their argument heard.[15]

Enthusiasm for silver provided the opening Alliancemen needed to move into popular politics. In 1892, both the Democrats and the Republicans nominated gold standard supporters, and many Alliancemen formed the new People's Party. Polk seemed likely to be their first presidential candidate. A former Confederate, he promised to draw white Southern farmers away from the Democratic Party in a way a Northern candidate could not. These plans collapsed in June 1892, when Polk died of a hemorrhaging bladder. Although the eventual nominee, former Union general James B. Weaver, struggled in the South, the new People's Party fared credibly, receiving more than a million votes and carrying four states. Still, not all Alliancemen were eager to jump into the new party. In North Carolina, state Alliance president Elias Carr took over the state Democratic Party, winning the governor's chair over more conservative candidates and working with many Alliance Democrats in the legislature. Although it is easy for scholars to draw sharp lines between Alliance Democrats and Populists, Carr's decision to remain in the Democratic Party did not indicate a lack of commitment to the Alliance. A participant in both the 1886 Farmers' National Congress and the crucial 1890 Farmers' Alliance Convention in Ocala, Florida, Carr truly believed in the importance of building a counterweight against capitalists' influence over government. He reacted with fury and disbelief when the Democrats nominated goldbug Grover Cleveland in 1892. Like many white Southern Democrats, Carr could critique the party; he just could not leave it. Even as he worked within the Democratic Party, Carr expanded its message. In his inaugural address in 1892, Carr was the first governor to address himself primarily to international economics, rather than state issues or the legacy of the Civil War. "I am sorry to say that the majority of the people of North Carolina are not prosperous," he said, not because they lacked virtue but because they lacked access to currency and capital.[16]

After the disappointment of 1892, Populists moved more emphatically into the electoral arena, a decision that led many to emphasize silver as the most marketable and easily understood piece of their platform. New state leader Marion Butler, an ambitious newspaper editor, strengthened its infrastructure, communicated actively with hundreds of local observers, and explored the possibility of building a pro-silver alliance with some state Democrats. In 1894, when it became clear that Democrats would not deal, Butler turned instead to the Republicans, who shared Populist commitments to democratic reform though not to bimetallism. In 1894, Populists and Republicans took control of the legislature, elected Butler and a Republican to the state's U.S. Senate seats, and passed a series of bills granting local control over county and town offices and creating more transparent systems of registration. With this expansion of democracy, still-vigorous African American networks moved aggressively into politics, electing a new generation of county, state, and federal officeholders between 1894 and 1898.[17]

Although the Farmers' Alliance could depend upon a small movement culture, Populist leaders confronted a much more complex problem: how to motivate "tired" voters. To appeal to the "hundreds" of "doubtful voters" who "change their minds immediately before and upon the day of election," the Populists stirred up the masses with an evocative language of silver's gifts and the cruelty of tyrannical enemies. This was necessary because observers on the ground described a "floating element" of undecided voters. Of seventy-seven residents polled in Buncombe County, thirty-five expressed no opinion at all, although only four indicated they would not vote. One man said he did "not care anything about the election any way," while two others were "tired and undecided." To inspire their enthusiasm, silver supporters distributed cartoons depicting cotton's relation to money, and one admirer of the famous, widely distributed (and silver mine interest–funded) pamphlet *Coin's Financial School* urged people to look first at two sketches: "Study the picture there, and you need not read the book if you do not want to, for those two whittle wood-cut pictures tell the whole story and tell it well." By the 1896 campaign, North Carolina politicians systemized printing processes so newspapers across the state could make simultaneous use of cartoons like the *Caucasian's* portrayal of the "demon of contraction" and the "goldbug devil." In turn, gold speakers did the same, running their own propaganda campaign that sacralized gold as a timeless, absolute, mystical signifier of value. In print, silver and gold were literally transformed into totemic figures like the wrecked boat that sent Jonah into the belly of the whale, the scissors that Delilah used to cut the hair of a sleeping Samson, the stone that covered the grave of Christ, a crown of thorns, and especially — following Bryan — the crucifixion cross. By equating money with divine power, cartoonists helped to reinforce gossip about its potential for causing magical transformation on earth. Other speakers relied upon earnestness or slow talking so that "the people will catch [their] enthusiasm as well as [their] facts."[18]

In North Carolina, silver backers also stoked enthusiasm through portrayals of tyrannical enemies defined by their unwillingness to listen to their constituents. The shape of the inaccessible tyrant changed from Southern townsmen to distant oligarchs to Jewish bankers in London to lawyers to political bosses, but all shared the common trait that, in Populist terminology, they were kings who no longer needed to pay attention. Defining enemies, like friends, started close to home, as Alliancemen and Populists condemned towns and cities as "aristocratic" and run by a "money caste" of "railroad attorneys" and "misled graduates of these money controlled college." As Populists entered into alliances with some of these very groups, they emphasized farther-flung enemies. Thus, they blamed "the monopo-lized lords of the nation," the "bankers, shylocks and money kings, the "Plu-tocracy," an "aristocracy . . . born to rule," "Shylock's greedy grasp," the "money-changers . . . polluting the temple of our liberties," "office-holding aristocracys," and the "czar of the White House." In some speeches, par-ticularly by Populist gubernatorial candidate William A. Guthrie, the dis-tant, unapproachable enemies were "those rich Jews." Jews and Northern industrialists were useful targets because they represented the impossibility of access, a "new era of slavery." While this language of tyranny grotesquely simplified political economy, it did combine a comprehensible — if nasty — logic of power with a widening sense of power's scope. It also reinforced the notion that politics functioned through gift-giving; the problem of the gold standard was that bankers had severed those intimate ties. Gold backers therefore were not merely applying bad theories; they were bad kings.[19]

Although the Populist critique of the Democratic Party was broad in scope, the struggle between the parties was a series of local wars. As Populists recruited white Democrats into their party, many found it excruciating to abandon neighborhood coalitions. One Democrat had been "taught from my very earliest recollection to respect" the Democratic nominee but now believed the party "offers nothing to the poor man that I can see." To main-tain their newly formed political communities, Populists relied upon tradi-tional systems of patronage. Neighborhood leaders invoked their identity as a "true and tried Populist" or as a "poor man" to buttress their appeals for jobs. Populist communities were incorporated most powerfully in election-day rituals of inclusion and exclusion at precincts filled with "crowding" and "drinking." In this context, parties were defined around local organizers, rather than just platforms. When voters in an 1894 legislative election were asked who they voted for, they answered by naming the men who gave them their tickets. One voter could not remember "all the names" on the ticket but knew that "if there was any Republican nominee for Governor I voted for him." Another neatly summarized the importance of ticket distribution in political decision-making: "The ticket I voted voted for me." When one silver supporter was asked why he voted for a goldbug Republican candidate, he simply refused to believe the man a gold supporter because he had faith in the men who had given him his ticket. The personal nature of these struggles often provoked physical confrontations. As Populist and Republican orga-nizing disrupted local power networks, the response could be vicious and even deadly. When Arthur Abernethy defected from the Democrats in the 1896 election, his "life was threatened," and, his brother wrote, "it has driven his mind from its balance, and for some time we have been forced to keep him under constant guard." Justly paranoid, Abernethy shot a Democrat who had threatened him, and was left a "physical wreck" and a "political martyr." Abernethy and his brother turned to their new political community's leaders for the "personal favor" of state protection.[20]

Befuddling levels of fusion among the three political parties reinforced the notion that Populism should be interpreted within local arrangements of power, not solely upon abstract political claims articulated in its platforms. Some voters encountered Populist parties that combined with Democrats locally, Republicans in state elections, and Democrats in the presidential campaign, and also ran independent Populist candidates. "Like a kaleidoscope every turn brings new and unexpected combinations," one Populist wrote. While fusion offered African American Republicans and white Populists the chance to win legislative and county seats, it also strained the political communities they had constructed. To some African Americans, Populists were not natural allies but "Klu Klux" who aimed to restore slavery. In fact, Populist leader (and *Caucasian* editor) Marion Butler had long advocated "Anglo-Saxon rule," and other Populists demanded a "white man's government for a white man's country." Given a choice between white ex-Democratic Populists and white Democrats, African American voters might either "vote for the Rebs" or "not vote at all." Many Populists resisted allying with African Americans, like the Columbia organizer who grumbled that he did not mean to be "governed" by "resolutions set forth and passed in Negro school houses in the dead hours of night." If fusion meant "to bring the negro into the front in political prominence, the Alamance Pops don't want it," a politician claimed.[21]

The neighborhood enthusiasms for silver took on a national scope in the popular campaign of William Jennings Bryan. Like Lincoln among the freed slaves, or Franklin Roosevelt among the Depression-era poor, Bryan drew disparate local myths to him like a magnet and bound them into a national language. Bryan's nomination for the White House was the culmination of a complex combination of silver mania, personal performance, and luck. His victory had roots in the transformations on the ground in places like North Carolina. After the Populist victories of 1894, panicked North Carolina Democrats led a grassroots effort to disrupt the party's long-held alliance between silverite agrarians and goldbug New York City merchants. Democrats overthrew local and state parties to guarantee a silverite presidential nominee in Chicago. They were motivated by the force of the enthusiasm they witnessed close to home. "More than 90 percent of the vote" in one rural North Carolina region "is unchangeably for the free coinage of silver," one Democratic canvasser warned in 1894. If the party nominated a gold-bug in 1896, "a large number will not vote." At the 1896 Chicago convention, North Carolina and other states conspired on Bryan's behalf, allegedly pledging support to him before he entered the race, and leading marches at opportune moments during his speech. In a talk that in many ways resembled unsuccessful attempts by other silver orators at the same convention, Bryan succeeded in part because of dramatic pauses, which gave time for his supporters — especially North Carolinians whom Bryan credited for his victory — to perform the passionate chants and parades that helped convince silver-leaning-but-undecided delegates of the power of the "mighty silver tide" sweeping aside "tricksters, demagogues and traitors." Bryan elicited that enthusiasm in part by his mastery of evangelical language, which sacralized their campaign, a "cause as holy as the cause of liberty." Comparing his supporters to the "crusaders who followed Peter the Hermit," Bryan celebrated their transformative "zeal" that shattered old identities, pitting brother "against brother, and father against son." Famously, Bryan ended his speech with the promise: "You shall not press down upon the brow of labor this crown of thorns. You shall not crucify mankind upon a cross of gold."[22]

In Bryan's innovative national speaking tour, he balanced his economic appeals with sacralizations of silver's timeless value. "Our opponents say that the advocates of free coinage do not think; that is too bad," Bryan told a crowd in Louisville, Kentucky. "I affirm that the advocates of free coinage are the only people who, in this campaign, apply natural laws to the money question and carry into discussion of finance the same intelligence which is used in ordinary business. Our opponents refuse to apply the law of supply and demand to money." In Asheville, North Carolina, he quoted former governor Vance's biblical defense of silver: "The money changers are polluting the temple of our liberties. To your tents, O Israel!" In a speech in Minneapolis, Bryan compared "converts" to free silver to Saul of Tarsus, who "gloried in relating his experience" of the "scales" falling "from his eyes." Converts, he continued, "do not come mourning; they come rejoicing. . . . They come with the enthusiasm of missionaries who go forth to preach the gospel to others." Speaking in Fredericksburg, site of a monument to George Washington's mother, Bryan associated silver with national iconography: "They say that here George Washington once threw a silver dollar across the river; but remember, my friends, that when he threw that silver dollar across the river it fell on American soil. . . . Would you believe, my friends, that a silver dollar which was good enough to be handled by the father of his country is so mean a thing as to excite the contempt of many of our so-called financiers?" As Bryan spoke, a man in the crowd shouted, "Bryan, I am not a Christian, but I am praying for you." Later, in Missouri, Bryan proclaimed that every suffering person throws "up a silent prayer that we may win."[23]

On his speaking tour, there were signs, some serious, some silly, that the crowd responded as much to enthusiasm as to reason. Both sympathetic and unsympathetic newspaper reporters often described the passion of his crowds in terms that made his speeches a kind of secular (or, at times, not-so-secular) sermon. At his events, people who saw "in him the embodiment of all their hope of better things" lined the roadsides, "their fingers on their lips . . . prayers in their hearts." Like any politician, Bryan could be interpreted in a vast, disconcerting number of ways, but his papers prove that at least some of the audience responded to him as a heaven-sent patron. Between Bryan's unsuccessful 1896 and 1900 presidential campaigns, thousands of "unknown friends" across the country, "converts" to the "Free silver faith" from places like Apple Grove, Ohio, and Walnut Cove, North Carolina, and Mediapolis, Iowa, wrote pleading letters that addressed the Nebraska orator not as their candidate but as their savior, begging gifts because they were "very poor" and "left alone in the world." "Help me a little," one woman pleaded. In peculiarly personal ways, these strangers named their children for Bryan, asked his "counsel upon their most intimate concerns," described a "surprising and bewildering number of prophetic dreams," and offered him bizarre presents, including a "tremendous alligator," rabbits' feet, a cane made from the vertebrae of a fish, and potatoes with "sixteen sprouts" to represent the sixteen to one ratio of silver to gold. This presumed intimacy had its roots not in any actual connection with Bryan but in the transformative power of silver.[24]

The Democratic Party's nomination of Bryan created "chaos" in local political communities in North Carolina. Although Bryan ignored many Populist reforms, his advocacy of silver "cut the foundation from under" the People's Party, one leader wrote. Although some state and national leaders struggled to maintain a Populist identity, the association of the party with silver made this work nearly impossible. Desperately, U.S. senator and national party chairman Marion Butler attempted to negotiate a Populist/Democratic fusion on the national and state levels. When Bryan refused, Populists endorsed Bryan while maintaining a shadow campaign for their own vice presidential nominee, Tom Watson of Georgia. Despite criticisms of this surrender, many local Populists had no heart to fight against Bryan.

If "the leaders do not arrange for [Democrats and Populists] to vote to-gether . . . the people will as a body rebel against parties and leaders," one Populist wrote. In state politics, Butler attempted to unite with Democratic silver supporters as well, but Democratic bosses rejected him. Just before the election, Populists and Republicans fused again in state campaigns, support-ing a partially combined legislative ticket and Republican Daniel Russell's bid for governor. Despite the turmoil at the top of the ticket, the Republican/ Populist alliance continued to deliver at the state and local levels, as Russell became the first Republican governor in twenty years, and Populists and Republicans controlled the state legislature.[25]

Among the most interested and conflicted observers of this wave of enthu-siasm was the young Republican congressman Tom Settle III. A strong sup-porter of the gold standard, the thirty-one-year-old Settle began his 1896 reelection campaign as one of the bright stars in a Republican Party eager to build up its strength in the South. Already people speculated that he might end up on a national ticket. An adept political operator, Settle had delivered impressive Republican wins by fusing together his African American base with white Populists who disagreed with his monetary policy but admired his support of electoral reform and his fighting spirit. Settle, a "true patrician" and "elegant idler" educated at Georgetown, had first ridden his father's name, his political savvy, and his dashing looks into Congress four years earlier at the age of twenty-seven. A "young Adonis" and "paragon" of "mas-culine loveliness" with "a certain poetry of motion about him" and "a slov-enly curl of his mustache," Settle attracted the attention and financial back-ing of the goldbug and protectionist Duke family, who had a "personal and intense interest" in his election and helped him become the "conservator and controlling factor in the politics of the district." In 1896, however, Settle's alliance fractured under the pressure of silver's growing popularity, as first Populists and then African Americans began to abandon Settle over his support of the gold standard. Desperate to maintain his office, Settle com-missioned a series of local field reports from his canvassers. In their precise replies, his precinct-level organizers described an impossible political situa-tion created not by any change in Settle's position but by a series of myths and rumors.[26]

In 1892 and 1894, Settle also faced complaints about his support for the gold standard. Through a debate notebook preserved by his 1894 opponent, Augustus W. Graham, it is possible to chart not only Settle's words but also some degree of crowd response. The book records Settle's inability to explain the gold standard to his audiences during their tour of the district. Many of the jottings demonstrate the honor-based roles Settle and Graham performed for the crowd; each mocked the other's manhood and used audience laughter to construct a powerful public persona. In early speeches, Settle addressed his arguments to "intellect not to passion" and asked silver backers to abjure "sentiment" for "principle." However, Graham's notebook suggests that during the canvass, Settle's approach changed. While Settle continued to use some of his successful laugh lines and mockery, he discussed silver less thoroughly and then hardly at all. Instead, as their speaking tour continued, he turned to issues like voting rights as a way of maintaining his base of African American support. Over time, Settle perhaps despaired of convincing his audience to oppose the silver standard. Faced with the necessity of gaining audience applause, Settle may have shifted to safer ground. Even if the audience's cheers and jeers did not force Settle to change his positions, they nudged him to change what he said in public. By 1896, the compromise of silence he had reached in 1894 would no longer suffice.[27]

Among Settle's local African American informants and allies, the most important was Maurice N. Corbett, a Shaw University–educated schoolteacher. Over the 1890s, Corbett held various local and state political offices in Caswell County, where freedpeople a generation earlier had organized unusually effective Union Leagues. Corbett was a year-round political organizer, a member of a local "combine" that triumphed in Caswell County's "fearfully and wonderfully made" political wars. Even a skeptical white newspaper editor respected Corbett. "White people think well of him," he wrote. "He is said to have good grit, as an evidence of which is the fight against great ends he is making for Settle." Along with his political work, Corbett was a prodigious letter writer who would eventually compose a book of poems, *The Harp of Ethiopia*, meant to "awaken the slumbering spirit of race pride" by telling the story of the Middle Passage, slavery, emancipation, political organization, and, eventually, disenfranchisement. Fiercely ambitious, Corbett would describe the frustrations of Jim Crow: "There could not be a greater sin / Than thus to teach a set of men / To highest places to aspire / And then attempt to check the fire." When Settle began to maneuver for the congressional nomination in 1892, Corbett frankly outlined his reasons for his skepticism. Corbett and other African American Republican leaders were holding out on Settle, he wrote, because of "the set belief of the colored voters of the district that you are opposed to their appointment to federal or local offices and that they would receive no recognition from you." They feared that Settle would not be accessible to them and that African Americans "would not be consulted at all" on patronage. In a series of remarkable letters over the summer, Corbett claimed it a "duty to our race to defeat any man who . . . believes us his inferior politically." However, Corbett also noted Settle's "glorious and honorable" family history, and promised, "I have no personal or political reasons to oppose you if you can assure my people of your friendliness toward them." If Settle could pledge friendship to Corbett's "people," the local organizer could deliver "1400 votes in Caswell which will be cast as" he and his associate Albert Bigelow "dictate."[28]

Settle won over Corbett with a series of promises, and the Caswell County man became a broker between the white Republican and a network of neighborhood organizers. Although African Americans continued to vote Republican in overwhelming numbers, the "desperate fight" of Populists in some counties and the growing enthusiasm for silver raised the prospect that African Americans might abandon their traditional tie to the Republican Party. A group of "colored voters" in a section of Craven County advised African Americans across the state to dismiss the old plea to "stick to the party," which has "brought us to the point where we can hardly get bread for ourselves and wives and children." A Populist organizer wrote that "the colored people are split all to pieces and 4 to 1 say they will vote for silver." In Caswell County, only the work of "a few leading Negroes" prevented "a large portion" from voting for "free silver," according to a Populist informant. An organizer pleaded for literature on "the gold side of the question in such shape that our people can understand it. . . . Some of the Negroes have got the silver craze too." Corbett treated this challenge as a series of distinct local problems, dispatching speakers and fixers into neighborhoods where they had particularly close connections. Corbett's goal was to attack the rumors and myths in those hamlets before they gained acceptance as fact. Settle's top deputy, after inspecting Caswell County, reported that Corbett "is one of the most intelligent and systematic workers that I ever saw." Corbett and Settle's practical political science required deep local knowledge and a sharp appreciation of the personal nature of politics. One neighborhood was in no danger, Corbett reported, because the African American Populists were led by a man who "can influence no one and control his own vote only. He is a stranger here and is unpopular with all the members of his church." In another neighborhood, however, a "colored preacher" with "several brothers + cousins in Fishing Creek + Brassfields" was "making some impression on the colored voters." At Mangum's Store, the Populist candidate attracted twenty-five or thirty followers who had not heard or seen Settle. "It would be well to have a colored speaker go there," one of Settle's advisers wrote. In Granville County, Populists recruited a blacksmith, a mill

The Silver Mania [181]

operator "and his half dozen followers[,] and a few choice grumblers in Tally Ho + Dutchville." African American political communities, like other political communities, had geographical boundaries. Race, like rumor, was made and remade within the circumference of people's lives, and a politician who sought African American votes could not count on distant endorsements but had to convey his message believably into many dense neighborhoods and kinship groups.[29]

Despite this pressure, Settle could not alter his position on silver; his ties were too close to goldbugs in the Duke family and in the party hierarchy. Therefore, he responded by dispensing favors. Because of his rumored personal aversion to African Americans, Settle had to prove himself to African American organizers who complained he failed to "advise with them or to grant them any material or needed assistance." Another politico groused that he wanted a congressman "whose garments we can touch, if we can't speak to him." Corbett consistently pressed for more and better patronage assignments for himself and his allies. "I will say frankly that there is no man in the district who has built higher hopes of a position than I or who would feel worse disappointed," Corbett warned Settle. "I am paying for my home and have a payment to make in the early spring and times are hard and money so close." Settle eventually hired Corbett to be his private secretary, a posting that inspired outrage across the congressional district.[30]

After Settle tapped Corbett, the political magic of silver worked in concert with another popular fetish that dramatically influenced turn-of-the-century politics, a belief in the power of white skin to deliver access to government. As Settle began to assign patronage positions to African American Republicans, he encountered a deep-rooted fantasy among some whites that skin color promised every white man access to a job. If none believed that their skin color guaranteed them a position, many presumed, in the logic of patronalism, that it guaranteed them the right to beg. Hiring Corbett in a position previously held by a white man "alienated many strong influences" and "invited their open, avowed, and intense hostility," Settle's advisers warned. Settle's opponents played upon the fantasy that this single job could have belonged to the "20,000 [white] people in his District" who wanted it. The portrayals of Corbett emphasized his aggression: he "kicked again, and this time with a big K." "We were aware of the fact that [Settle] did not draw the color line at the polls but we did think whenever the matter of selecting a private secretary came up he would consider the question of 'race, color or previous condition of servitude,'" one editor complained. Some Republicans simply refused to believe the news.[31]

In 1896, after narrow victories in his two previous congressional races, Settle faced William W. Kitchin, a silverite Democrat whose father for a time had been a prominent Populist. In Kitchin's "white metal, white skin" campaign, fantasies of silver intertwined with gossip about the fantastic promise of jobs. Kitchin's appeals suggested that the talismans of "white metal" and "white skin" delivered gifts to favored subjects. An informant from High Point defined Settle's dilemma. "There is considerable leaning in this Congressional District toward the free coinage of silver," he wrote. "What policy is best on financial questions right now, I am unable to advise, for it is hardly probable that the National Republican Convention will declair for free coinage of silver." Trapped between popular enthusiasm and his party's stance, Settle's only hope was that Populists and Democrats would continue to squabble, leaving Populists to again vote for him. A Durham County Republican worried that "some good men who were for you before are getting off every day. They say they want free coinage unlimited silver." During the campaign, Kitchin emphasized silver relentlessly and declared Settle a tool of "Wall Street." Settle attempted without much success to explain that "16 to 1 did not mean [people] would have more money but was simply a term used to represent the coinage ratio."[32]

As the silver craze spread, Settle's support from Populists evaporated. A Caswell County Populist dismissed efforts to work with Settle, "a gold bug of the deepest dye." "If you call that Populism," he continued, "I want none of it. . . . If the Gold Standard is fastened upon our people this time our liberty are gone and nothing but revolution will satisfy our people." The "idolatry" that some Populists had for Settle—based on his support for election reform—turned during 1895 and 1896 into "iconoclasm." Populists "are done with him," one editor claimed. Although Settle convinced Populist leaders to nominate a candidate to draw votes from his opponent, the tactic failed. After Kitchin defeated Settle, the Democrat attributed his success to the "3000 populist votes" he received. In a postelection story, Settle's hometown paper attributed his loss to "a district where the free and unlimited coinage of silver is held in high favor." Instead of bending to popular will, Settle relied futilely "upon bringing a majority of the voters to his way of thinking." Corbett also blamed silver. "You were the only consistent republican candidate in the state who had previously advocated the policy of the party," he wrote.[33]

Settle's loss suggested the political system that was being born. Through his "white metal, white skin" campaign, Kitchin learned to transfer the enthusiasm over silver into enthusiasm over white skin, a lesson the Democrats would implement with great skill in the next campaigns. In 1898 and 1900, a fetishistic, popular style drove the white supremacy movement that toppled African Americans, Republicans, and Populists from power and helped establish a Jim Crow regime. Horribly, Settle's defeat embittered him against the African Americans who made up the bulk of his supporters but whom he blamed for his loss. After a break with Corbett in 1898, Settle became a leader of the lily-white faction of the state Republican Party and a supporter of disenfranchisement. Although his stance on racial politics changed, his attitude about silver did not, and he never again won an election in the state of North Carolina.

As fresh ideas about governance and immense financial crises trained Americans in the 1890s to look beyond their individual relationship to a personalized state, the claims of dependence did not disappear but expanded. Exposure to the rumors about silver was, in part, exposure to the programmatic nature of modern governance. Unlike the thousands of people who begged for individual favors from politicians, supporters of silver asked for their gift in the form of a policy from Washington, one that would be universal and all-encompassing. These fantasies helped bind together a tangle of patronalism and rationalization, the admixture of Civil War–era hopes and a Progressive view of a systematic government. The education of Americans toward a modern state that would prove so powerful in the Progressive Era, when rural congressmen passed regulatory and public health reform, may have been a product not just of enlightenment but of enthusiasm.

A Compressive Age

White Supremacy and the Growth
of the Modern State

TWO YEARS AFTER Tom Settle's defeat, young Democrats toppled Republicans and Populists in an infamous white supremacy campaign. As they captured the state legislature in 1898, then confirmed disenfranchisement in a 1900 referendum, they created not just Jim Crow but a new image of the relationship between state and subject in North Carolina. Leaving behind postwar patronalism, they reached both forward and backward to replace the government of needy persons with the management of an undifferentiated, abstracted people. Their leader, and the state's new governor, Charles B. Aycock, recast the now-familiar inauguration-day comparison of statecraft and sunshine. Instead of Holden's justice shining down into every crevice, or Vance's crop-luring prosperity, Aycock's sun blurred the boundaries between individuals. In his new regime, "ten thousand lights" would meld into a single ray, "shining together to brighten life and make the state more glorious." The disappearance of the individual self and its pesky bodily needs made people's actual wishes irrelevant. In his inaugural address, Aycock dismissed the will of the people expressed in universal suffrage as a "theory" that had "outrun practice" because democracy proved "incapable of enforcing and preserving order," especially over allegedly bestial African Americans. In its place an intelligent class would manage the "safety of the state" by building a powerful government. Privately, Aycock and his collaborators compressed the citizens even further into what they called the social organism. Drawing upon broad, transatlantic currents, they managed the proper evolution of the state through education, public health, segregation, and, eventually, alcohol prohibition. In the process they answered a conun-drum of democratic liberalism: How can the state restrain people's extrava-gant expectations for government? By defining happiness upon evolutionary terms, they made personal needs irrelevant.[1]

The balance of power between politicians and the people shifted at the turn of the century. Fueled by national, even global, disenfranchisement and new technologies of governance, people's individual pleas played a much smaller, although not negligible, role in shaping the political system than they had in the previous three decades. In the long Reconstruction that lasted from the 1860s through the mid-1890s, the particular configurations and vulnerabilities of state power extended the boundaries of politics. When those boundaries contracted in the 1890s, so too did the way politics was made. Understanding this shift from governing persons to the people re-quires looking beyond petitions and pleas to the intellectual, social, and po-litical world that made this transformation possible. This view recasts schol-arly assumptions about the intellectual roots of modern white supremacy, the appeal of political racism to rural audiences, and the relationship between democracy and state-building reform. Although historians frequently por-tray the well-known North Carolina white supremacy movement as a prod-uct of thwarted ambition and personal neuroses, it emerged as part of a global selectionist moment. Driven by the notion that society left to its own devices would degenerate, a eugenic movement used newly expanded states to guide society's evolutionary progress. Often, although not always, utiliz-ing ethnological racial theories of Teutonic superiority, these leaders made white supremacy an evolutionary necessity. In North Carolina this thinking class included several classmates from the University of North Carolina who allied with conservative leaders in 1898 and turned North Carolina into the "Wisconsin of the South," a model of Southern progressivism known for its scientific, or, later, businesslike, management of the state through education, public health, segregation, disenfranchisement, and alcohol prohibition.[2]

The transformation of the state-subject relationship was never as com-plete as Aycock's collaborators hoped. Like Populists who dreamt of broad reforms but learned to appeal to the enthusiasm of the crowd, these new governors had to fit their message to their constituents. Along with well-studied appeals to white men's power over white women, they also relied upon a less understood way of accessing the fantastic notion of government gifts. Instead of a present of money made through silver, white supremacy Democrats invoked the benefits of membership in an imagined white family. Additionally, they called upon the state as punisher on behalf of aggrieved whites, capable of scourging its enemies like sunlight vanquishing germs. And at times, they ended up relying upon the very patronalism they aimed to displace.

Progressive statism was therefore born within white supremacy. Through the invocation of white familialism, the white supremacy campaign created the language for discussing universal, or at least statewide, policies necessary for the formulation of an abstracted government. The rhetoric of white supremacy, rather than a reactionary throwback, trained Carolinians to the radical idea that people should judge politics not upon the world in front of them but on its effect upon a distant, imagined community. By associating the state with the happiness of all white people, and then defining that happiness upon whites' continued reproductive success, the movement created the logic for public health and education movements. This new state therefore possessed the potential to provide unprecedented assistance and to do unparalleled harm. The complex embrace between intellectual and popular forms of racism built the bridge toward a modern state in North Carolina, another example of the way racial ideologies were central to the construction of twentieth-century governance.

Rather than an outcry of neurosis or traditionalism, North Carolina's white supremacy was a mandarin moment led by a newly self-conscious group of public intellectuals. These men were participants, if not leading or systematic ones, in a still-misunderstood global project, one in which social scientific theories of progress, race, reproduction, and degeneration inspired new waves of statist reform programs across Europe and the United States. Instead of a paradox to be explained, their intertwined commitments to racial dominance and social reform emerged from an internally consistent but oft-ignored set of ideas sometimes termed soft eugenics or, by prominent contemporary sociologist Edward A. Ross, "selectionism." Although we most often associate eugenics with forced sterilization, a broader politics of heredity made the state into a physician and used evolutionary theory not to support laissez-faire but to promote government intervention to stave off degeneration. In German *Rassenhygiene* movements devised by Alfred Ploetz and Wilhelm Schallmayer, in weaker but still important British social hygiene efforts that tied older sanitary reform to reproduction, and especially in a French "hygienic idealism" based upon "homeopathic doses of welfare" delivered by hundreds of "medico-politicians" of the Third Republic, European intellectuals backed biologically based reforms of child labor, wages, parks, drinking water, food safety, working conditions, taxation, pensions, alcohol, insurance reform, and segregation of the feebleminded and immi-

grants on the grounds that these measures would improve society's reproductive health. North Carolinians' simultaneous commitment to segregation
and public health, disenfranchisement and education grew not from a peculiar paradox of Southern racism but from a transatlantic set of ideas about the
state's role in promoting the progress of the social organism.[3]

These ideas entered North Carolina through a newly self-conscious class
of thinkers, many of whom studied together at the University of North
Carolina in the 1870s and 1880s. In a state without a large metropolitan area
or "intelligent or cultivated society," late-nineteenth-century North Carolinians created a metropolis of the mind in its university. Its clubs, publications, and reunions brought together "the rich and the fashionable" to make
what the leading scholar of the contemporaneous New York bourgeois called
a "common cultural vocabulary" deployed to "transcend" localism and "their
particularistic economic interests." With their frequent trips to campus for
the university's new alumni banquets, Chapel Hill became physical grounds
for intellectual and political class formation among key lawyers, educators,
and publishers dispersed across the state. Although some alumni led the
People's and Republican Parties, and several key Democrats were affiliated
with Trinity, Wake Forest, and Davidson Colleges, the connection between
the university, white supremacy, and Progressivism was obvious to its participants. Among the key beneficiaries of the overthrow of the Populists
and Republicans were three men who had been close friends at the university in the late 1870s: the movement's leading orator (and future governor),
Charles B. Aycock; the leader of the key western campaign (and also future
governor), Locke Craig, and the organizer of the white supremacy clubs (and
also future lieutenant governor), Francis D. Winston. Other important figures included Henry G. Connor, the legislative leader, disenfranchisement
author, and father of several university students, and the alumni association leader and newspaper editor Josephus Daniels. In the aftermath of the
1898 election, the *University Magazine* published an article celebrating the
evolutionary-based triumph in the Philippines, Cuba, and North Carolina of
Anglo-Saxons, "the predominant race wherever they have gone." The university yearbook staff (which included a writer who would become a leading
historian of the movement) dedicated its volume to Francis Winston, an
alumnus and trustee who proved his "loyal service to his State and University" by organizing violent white supremacy clubs and helping author the
disenfranchisement amendment. Aycock, Craig, and Winston's former college classmate, university president Edwin Alderman, praised Connor for his
stewardship of disenfranchisement, "an act of citizenship not less heroic than

going to war," and offered the uneducated attorney a new professorship of law and government. A recent alumnus summed up his position in support of both disenfranchisement and education on the grounds that "I owe all that I have in this world to the University and to the Democratic Party."[4]

The university emerged as a central place for the dissemination of new ideas about state and society in part because of one of its long-forgotten professors. When the university reopened in 1875, the trustees hired George T. Winston, Francis Winston's elder brother, from ultramodern Cornell. In his first years, George Winston taught social evolution and racial science to a veritable who's who of the white supremacy movement: Aycock, Craig, and Frank Winston, as well as their close friends, future university presidents Alderman and Charles D. McIver, and state education superintendent James Joyner. Now almost completely forgotten, the elder Winston was, Alderman wrote, a "source of real inspiration to men of my generation, who saw in him a man of real genius." No one in North Carolina "left a deeper impression upon the intellectual and social life of his time." Another of the group called Winston "the most powerful vitalizing intellectual force this generation of North Carolina has furnished." Winston seemed "modern" to his students because he followed the national trend from classics into the emerging fields of sociology, ethnology, and natural history, tracing for his classes "the upward movement of the race, interpreting dead civilizations and explaining their collapse." Inspired by evolutionism's teleologies and by the analogy of species to human societies, Winston lectured his students about change versus fossilization and extinction, and helped them move away from individual to social notions of progress. Like many nineteenth-century social scientists, Winston used theories of "child races" to revitalize staid theories of Anglo-Saxon predominance and to make a new, seemingly objective correlation between progress, so-called inborn Teutonic qualities, and the proper management of competition. For Winston these ideas were clarified by a summer spent at German and British colleges, where a bleak Atlantic crossing of advanced racial science inspired his pamphlet "The Greek, the Roman, and the Teuton," a work the university distributed across the state. "Among the races of men, there is endless conflict for dominion," Winston wrote. "The victory is ever to the strong. There is no almshouse for decrepit and pauper races." Irish and African Americans lost this race because of inherited weakness, while Teutons thrived because of their "inborn qualities of courage and liberty, fidelity and reverence."[5]

In the close quarters of the university, Winston's young pupils quickly began to imitate and creatively reinterpret his ideas about the organic nature of society. In a sign of the complexity of the discourses, many moved from Winston's laissez-faire toward scientifically managed interventions for social progress. In this, they followed Washington School anthropologists John Wesley Powell and Lester Frank Ward in celebrating "artificial selection" through bureaucratic management. This reform Darwinism helped inspire the first cohesive American statism, determined to forestall degeneration caused by unnecessary "antagonistic competition." By making sure that the most civilized — meaning Teutonic — elements guided society, the government protected itself from democracy but also committed itself to interventions in new realms of private life. In their speeches and essays, these students quickly quoted Winston's words on Teutonic superiority to justify social reforms like railroad regulation, antimonopoly legislation, progressive taxation, and land conservation to foster "that essential Teutonic principle, equality." Their primary progressive commitment was to universal, segregated public education. Education inspired progress by fostering broad views of society and higher intellectual life, and it also prevented racial decay by training the masses to keep "free from contact with degenerate races" and telling students about what Alderman called "the political genius of the Teutonic mind." Education was "an absolute condition for progress" because it worked against reversion, what Alderman called "the weary path from barbarism back to barbarism." Alderman, who would go on to become president of the University of North Carolina and the University of Virginia as well as Tulane, feared degeneration because he saw worrisome signs of it in his tour of country schools, where he witnessed "the direst ignorance" among white Carolinians, who were "isolated, ignorant, illiterate as a rule."[6]

Over the 1880s and 1890s, university men, particularly Winston and his protégés, spread these ideas across the state by building a self-conscious alumni base. Winston himself gave thirty-three different lectures — including "The Greek, the Roman, and the Teuton" — to seventy-five alumni and community groups in one school year. University men also transformed the campus, creating the first annual alumni banquet and inviting hordes of supporters to commencements, where they heard speeches on "Evolution in Politics," "Manifest Destiny and Manifest Duty," "The Conquering Race," and "The Color Line." This alumni consciousness helped Winston and his protégés take control of the college, appoint more openly progressive evolutionists to the faculty, and elect Winston as the new president of the university. When the University of Texas doubled George Winston's salary and made him its first president, alumni rallied in support of Alderman as his replacement. This alumni cohesion also helped Winston and Alderman stave off

Francis Winston, pictured third from the left in the first row, was a member of one of the first classes of the reopened University of North Carolina, where young men learned the language of selectionism that helped spur the white supremacy Progressive movements they led in the 1890s. Although the photograph was not labeled, among those with Frank Winston appear to be future governors Charles Aycock and Locke Craig and future university president Edwin Alderman. Francis Donnell Winston Papers, 2810, Southern Historical Collection, The University of North Carolina at Chapel Hill.

Baptist and Methodist efforts to slash the university's state funding. By beating back this campaign, Winston believed he had saved the state from the degeneration he witnessed across the border in South Carolina, where demagogic anti-university governor Benjamin Tillman handed over control to "pigs + pigmies." Among these university men, selectionism was not a psychological aberration but a sophisticated set of intellectual ideas conveyed through respect, admiration, and love. Within this world of intense affection, George Winston's passion for evolutionary progressivism and white supremacy passed not as wound but as gift.[7]

In public, at the kinds of crossroads canvasses that flummoxed Tom Settle, white supremacy leaders bent their appeals to match popular sentiment. To reach the crowds, white supremacy leaders copied the organizational innovations of the Populists. Constructing a statewide network of speakers and newspaper editorials and cartoons, they broadcast a message that promised benefits to white Carolinians who stayed true to their race and their skin color. By harping upon the alleged advantages of African American job applicants under Republican-Populist rule, they invoked what one leading editor called the key basis of "race antipathy," an illusory but powerful notion of "self interest." The central role of access in shaping the political imagination helped explain the tangible benefits of white supremacy to men in the crowds. Under the terms that white supremacy speakers laid out, the imagined right to plea — a birthright they could claim by their white skin — was threatened by the ascension of African Americans into political office. Rather than simply denying a patronage post to a single white man, African American political power eliminated whites' right to make requests. Every single black employee seemed to strike all white men from consideration. A description of "Where the Negro Rules" was punctuated by the claim that for public offices, "no white man need apply for places" because all the clerks and deputies were African Americans. Instead of real or imagined friendship, the proxy of race determined access. Therefore, eliminating African Americans not simply from the franchise but, more crucially, from the pool of favored dependents seemed to give white North Carolinians benefits that were not elusive to their audience, even if they seem illusory to distant observers.[8]

White supremacy orators connected the statewide struggles to everyday race-making in the countryside. While leading Democrats made abstract arguments about white supremacy, popular interpretations were rooted in what women's club leader Sallie Cotten called "our local conditions" and "our peculiar environment." For Cotten, African American and white Republican success in local offices altered rural social relations immediately. Her husband's "authoritative 'halloo'" to the ferryman, once answered with deference, was ignored after Republicans hired "a common white man" and a "negro" to run the ferry. When "pronounced negro office-holding" produced "insolence," "race assertiveness," and a tendency to act "biggity toward white labor," this threatened not merely customs but the access that many whites believed was a mark of their pigmentation. Competition over county and state offices quickly translated an individual loss into a defeat for the race. In one instance, white Populists complained that "an old confederate soldier" was turned out for a "big Black Negro weighing over 200 lbs," and another "negro [was chosen] . . . in preference to a one-legged third party confederate soldier." In 1900, some whites feared that African American census enumerators would be "traveling object lessons" of white men's loss of access to power and favor. At the key rural sites of post offices, well-publicized campaigns against black postmasters simultaneously played upon envy of their salaries and unease with their proximate power over white female customers. Proclaiming that African American gains penalized all whites, local Democrats offered explicit financial incentives — including jobs and bribes — as a reward to white backers.[9]

Orators extended the family metaphor to make the entire state — not just a bounded locality — the property of its white people. White supremacy campaign mythology drew upon racial competition and fears that were much more tangible in eastern and piedmont North Carolina than in the overwhelmingly white western portion of the state. Through the analogies of racial familialism, Democrats sought to create among western audiences a shared politics of pain. By arguing that government was broad enough to encompass an entire state, Democrats fashioned an image of a punitive state delivering protection and access to white members, exclusion and punishment to all others. Democrats claimed an attachment to "our country, our State . . . not the Negro's." Their love was "consecrated in blood," one future governor proclaimed, and another speaker described a type of ancestor worship for "the home of my mother" that "contains the ashes of my dead father . . . the home of my wife and children . . . the home of my ancestors for 200 years." To promote this imagined kinship, Democrats fashioned a politics of desperation and need. "I come to you to-day in behalf of the east. Will you come to the rescue?" Aycock asked. Another future governor turned his speeches into an appeal from the "women of the east" to "come to our rescue with the men of the west." Rather than sharing in the glory of a politician's power, audiences could participate in what a leading figure termed his "humiliations and horrors." To cement the analogy between west and east, Democrats made extensive use of personal testimonies from western white men who described horrifying trips to the east to discover "what negroizing means."[10]

Democratic speakers needed to transcend localism and create a portable statewide version of white supremacy. Therefore, Democrats celebrated an abstract state ruling over an extended white family. The central plank of this argument was a shared whiteness built upon family metaphors. They turned a political gathering into a "Democratic family reunion" meant to create "sympathy of blood" for those who were "bone of my bone and flesh of my flesh, my kinfolks and your kinfolks." Drawing upon traditions of clannish rivalry, white supremacists argued that an inequity for any white man was an insult to every white man. If a single white man in Robeson County paid a larger fine than an African American, then it was treated as proof that "a negro was a more important personage than one of your own race." By making the Democratic Party the natural home of white men, orators also created a mutually constructing relationship between whiteness and party membership. At the center of white supremacy rhetoric was the principle of exclusion, which could be applied not only to African Americans but to "tainted" white people, too. One Democrat suggested that any white man who voted against the party should "have a BLACK MARK made across his forehead to show the negro he has in him." "Whenever white skins begin to hobnob with negroes and to be tooth and nail with them in elections and office-seeking and the after grabbing they easily reach the level of the lower animal and take on hue fellowship and principles much of the same sort," one editor proclaimed. A "robust, rosy-cheeked, auburn-haired country girl of about 16 summers" argued that any white man who voted against the Democrats "may have white skin over black hearts."[11]

To construct an imaginative empathy among white North Carolinians, Democrats mounted a media campaign based upon invented stories of rape and pillage. As leading newspaperman Josephus Daniels acknowledged, these accounts created more than reflected popular agitation and fear, exaggerating tales to convince readers that "Fusionists had some part in the increase of attacks." Correspondents tried to sway readers with imaginative statements about "turbulent and dangerous classes of negroes" who have "gotten on top" and insulted whites with impunity. Violence "reported with lurid details" brought forward a "manufactured" "hidden fury" even among whites who knew the stories to be a "horrid lie." "[It made] our blood boil to read the accounts of niggerism in the good old state," one expatriate North Carolinian noted. In the 1898 campaign, the Democratic Party chairman Furnifold Simmons sent approximately forty thousand weekly newspapers to doubtful voters and more than two million documents through county chairmen. In 1900, Simmons orchestrated the mailing of approximately five million more documents, including seventy-five thousand personal letters. Although Populists ran their own media campaign, in some rural areas Democrats established a literal monopoly on information.[12]

Along with stories, this campaign worked through mass-produced images. During the 1898 campaign, Josephus Daniels brought noted cartoonist Norman E. Jennett back to North Carolina from New York to draw nearly an image a day on behalf of the campaign. Jennett's images, published on the cover of most *Raleigh News and Observer* issues and distributed in mailings, had a dramatic impact upon readers. Cartoons depicting African American politician James Young inside a white girl's apartment at an institute for the blind advanced sexualized arguments for supporting Democrats. "There is a sentiment in it, that overshadows reason and even facts, especially when published under cartoons," one Populist editor complained. Although Josephus

Daniels claimed the cartoons were "for all," they were clearly directed at the many thousands of white voters who could not read, "good men who are uneducated who take the paper for their wives and children to read." Furnifold Simmons recounted, in a story perhaps too neat to be entirely true, that during a speech about "the humiliations and horrors suffered in the black counties of the east," the whites in the audience "seemed unconvinced. They shook their heads and showed clearly that they did not believe what I was saying; whereupon I said in substance: 'I see you people think I am lying. You are far removed from these disgraceful occurrences.'" Simmons promised to print photographs of "these Negro officials and candidates." Certified by a judge "whom you know," the photographs would assure them of his veracity. " 'Do that,' they said, 'and we shall be convinced and take action.'" Thus inspired, Simmons commenced a "pictorial campaign." "I observed that many could not be convinced by words," he commented. "It was necessary for them to view the situation with their own eyes." The photographs created imaginative space in which mountain whites might fantasize that they too suffered under the alleged "negro domination" of the east. At their most effective, cartoons allowed readers to dream their way into the portrayal, to absorb these experiences into their own.[13]

Although gender was an important language for transmitting white supremacy, it was not the only one. More frequently and tellingly, cartoons stirred their audiences by portraying racial competition as a fight over government access. Of seventy cartoons featured prominently in the *Raleigh News and Observer* during the 1898 campaign, at most eleven utilized images of female sexuality or vulnerability. Although a few were highly charged — like the one that showed a black vampire reaching out for a white women — some of these eleven included only a general figure of a woman identified as "the Goddess of Democracy" or "North Carolina." Even among those cartoons that portrayed white women in proximity to African American men, only two are actually suggestive of sexual violence. More common and more intense were cartoons connecting African American success to white impoverishment. These sketches suggested that whites were friendless and abandoned, while African Americans profited from their relationship with, and access to, white Republican politicians. One image shows a Fusionist embracing a black applicant while a white Confederate hobbles down a staircase. In "Scene at the Jenkins Jubilee," African Americans eat heartily while a staggering white man picks at bones. In "The Source of the Governor's Inspiration" African American Jim Young literally occupies the ear of white politicians. In "I Make Them Dance or I Crush Them," white politicians dance in the hairy palm of a black hand. On one level this was an effort to humiliate white politicians. Beyond that, however, the cartoons sent the message that only blacks could have access to — or whisper in the ears of — Republicans or Populists. Even as they mocked white Republicans, these cartoons reinforced the notion that Republicans had abandoned the white people of the state.[14]

Against allegedly heartless Republicans, Democrats promised to take care of whites in a new way, not just by distributing favors but by punishing their African American rivals. As they utilized categories of favored and unfavored, included and excluded, their rhetoric shed appeals based upon mercy and instead turned to force. A punitive state arose to restore the alleged white man's prerogative to live without fear, and it assumed abstract, statewide meaning by making every act a racial one. The less sensitive or the more ambitious politicians simply abandoned their high-minded beliefs on the stump and appealed to the crowd crudely. Charles Aycock, a lifelong opponent of lynching, a committed supporter of education, and a thoughtful commentator on the limits of Social Darwinism, was a good politician, which is to say he was both ambitious and adept at cultural translation. On the stump, Aycock proclaimed that true white men punished opponents, including by lynching. "You white men of Cabarrus don't even wait for the law when the negroes have dishonored your helpless, innocent women," Aycock told a cheering crowd. "It was like a thunderbolt," a reporter wrote. "The room went wild. Men sitting rose unconsciously to their feet! The thunder of the cheering rose and fell and rose again." Although Aycock claimed that he was "tired of strife and bloodshed," his words "made the faces of women whiten with fear while the cheeks of men burned red with anger and indignation." Through historical allusions, other Democratic orators defined whiteness around the race's bloody past. "This great race has carried the Bible in one hand and the sword in the other," a Democrat told a white supremacy convention in Goldsboro. Similarly, a prominent white woman said "amen" to a "bloodletting" for the "health of the commonwealth . . . as did our great grandmothers in 76 and our mothers in 61."[15]

Democrats claimed that violence was necessary to defend key privileges conveyed through the magic of white skin: impunity, invulnerability, and a portable protection. The perquisites of white people, especially women, were portrayed spatially, as the entitlement to move unimpeded and unafraid through rural territories. White women's rights depended upon white men's willingness to indulge in violence. More common than stories about jostling upon the sidewalks of Wilmington were those set in rural spaces, where white power was felt not through immediate enforcement but through a diffused climate of fear. By undermining African Americans' fear of white men, Republican political strength challenged the ability of a "country girl" to trip "lightly along our roads with gladness in her heart," one speaker claimed. "She goes, if she must go alone, with fear upon her heart, with blackened face and trembling form, lest a fate befall her worse than death." Women "cannot attend church or Sunday School" or a "neighbor's house" or the post office "without having a body-guard to protect them from the lustful black brutes who roam through your country." Egged on by numerous, false rape stories in statewide newspapers, "farmers who had been accustomed to go to town and come back in the night ceased doing so." Democratic media operatives transformed rural spaces from the playground of protected whites into a world of terror. The resolution of this terror lay not primarily in individual force but in politics. According to their rhetoric, white women were never assaulted "in any county" controlled by Democrats, and white power pulsed unseen but irrepressible throughout the land the party controlled.[16]

As Democratic orators toured the state in the spring and summer of 1898, they connected their language of white familialism to the reinforcing rituals of the Spanish-American War. In the story North Carolina orators told about the war, American and British (as well as Northern and Southern) branches of the "great conquering, civilizing, dominating, colonizing, educating, humanizing White Race" had been "reunited" by a war against a "race of blood-thirsty savages." A much-quoted editorial by the state's leading Presbyterian minister aligned white supremacy at home and abroad as a simple product of the "Anglo-Saxon race instinct." Performances of white unity in wartime augmented these arguments. At the state fair in Raleigh, white supremacy orations, "highly imperialistic" parades, and martial celebrations reinforced each other. The conflict also revived a proudly exclusionary strand of American political philosophy, one that celebrated disenfranchisement and domination of Puerto Ricans and Filipinos abroad and African Americans at home as a "necessary abandonment of our French revolution philosophy that all men are fitted for self-government." Josephus Daniels's newspaper proclaimed that "no man has a right to vote." If voting were anything but a special privilege, then "all could take part — women, children, idiots, lunatics, foreigners, the immoral and the vicious." Defining exclusion as "the very central idea upon which the Republic is founded," Democrats naturalized their assumptions, turning them from partisan arguments into reflections of a broad global consensus.[17]

The Source of the Governor's Inspiration.

FUSION OFFICE SEEKER

The New Slavery.

THE NEGRO GETS HIS SHARE OF BARBECUE.

Scene at the Jenkins Jubilee at Marshbourn's Mill, Wake County.

"THE CONFEDERATE SOLDIER HAS PLAYED OUT."

The Wake Commissioners Kick Out a Wounded Confederate Soldier to Make a Place for a Negro Politician.

Along with the enduring idea of black male power over white women, white supremacy political cartoons in the fraught 1898 and 1900 elections emphasized the economic competition between black and white men for the spoils of political office. In images like these, cartoonists showed black politicos literally monopolizing the ear of Governor Daniel Russell, or requiring white office-seekers to bend down in "The New Slavery," or making off with the scarce food at a jubilee, or turning out white men from office. These images sold white supremacy not just for its psychological or sexual relief but for its seemingly fantastic economic benefits. Access to the government meant access to jobs, and, in the logic of these images, this access was a zero-sum competition between white and black men. Raleigh News and Observer, *September 30, October 6, 15, 25, 1898, p. 1. North Carolina Collection, The University of North Carolina at Chapel Hill.*

Soldiers' segregated performances of white familialism in camps near Raleigh and Jacksonville, Florida, helped ground the abstract language of white supremacy in everyday practices. Even though eastern and western companies competed for favor and recognition, they also developed a broader sense of solidarity. In rather quick fashion, many soldiers shifted from writing about differences among the companies to talk of "our men," a "we" who together suffered, received kindnesses, and imagined a common future. In the Jacksonville camp, the companies were "carrying on" like a "crowd of school boys at play, wrestling, joking, singing, dancing and listening to the camp story tellers" and also participating in "a big Democratic rally and barbecue" for "white supremacy." This nascent group identification was expressed negatively, too, in shared complaints about conditions, grumbling about "North Carolina's present disgrace (the Governor)," and mean-spirited jokes about leading Republicans and Populists. White soldiers in segregated camps redefined public opinion so that it was bounded not by geography but by race. An "ambitious young lawyer" from Winston who hoped to be "actively identified with the army" noted, "One of the results of the war, I think, will be new political issues, a new shuffle + deal, 'old rings' broken and new combinations formed." Edwin MacKethan, a recent University of North Carolina graduate, accurately predicted the time in camp "may be the making of a number of us" in politics. After his discharge, MacKethan was elected captain of his town's Light Infantry, presided over a White Man's Convention that reserved "special seats" for "all veterans," and then won election to the state legislature. There was good reason, therefore, to believe one corporal's claim that "the enlisted men of the 1st NC Vols and its friends can control public opinion."[18]

By defining public opinion through whites-only military camps, soldiers and their families naturalized the exclusion of African Americans and of women. Rural Carolinians, of course, had much experience with other forms of racial domination, but, for many of them, army camps and train rides were their first experiences with rigid exclusion and spatial segregation. Although North Carolina — unlike many states — did enlist an African American regiment with African American officers, their Third Regiment never shared camps or accolades with the white regiments. As white soldiers constructed a statewide identity, African Americans did not count, except as competitors for scarce state resources. From the beginning, some white guardsmen took the enlistment of African Americans as an "insult" on the grounds that they filled the state quota and took places from "much distressed" whites. Even Republican governor Daniel Russell, who appointed an African American regiment, called it "monstrous and illegal" to "turn down a white Regiment" and "State guard companies" for a "colored Regiment." Once in service, white regiments scrambled against the African American Third Regiment for postings and favors. The adept hand of Third Regiment colonel and Republican powerbroker James Young in providing for his regiment of African American soldiers fostered bitterness among whites who believed that "no white Republican politician" countered Young's efforts "to get all these good things for them." In parades and other rituals, whites enacted the exclusion of African Americans from public space. White regiments returning home marched through the streets to cheering crowds and patriotic songs, but African American regiments were not allowed to participate in such public rituals. When the Third Regiment crossed the state en route to a posting in Tennessee, hundreds of African Americans gathered around the Raleigh depot hoping for a glimpse of the soldiers as they passed by. Fearing political fallout, however, Russell arranged for the railroad to "put them right on through" without stopping.[19]

Days later, when the all-white Second Regiment arrived in Raleigh, local whites cheered them enthusiastically. Then, the soldiers characteristically began to assault African Americans. Soldiers' violent cross-racial confrontations were common during the summer and fall of 1898 and helped indoctrinate far-western white soldiers into the eastern culture of domination. On their first night back, an "invading army of soldiers" descended "upon the [East Raleigh] tenderloin district," fired pistol shots, knocked down an African American man, and beat an African American woman in what the white police chief called "one of the most lawless nights he had ever known in Raleigh." On September 18, a white corporal struck an African American during an argument, then fled in the face of a gathering crowd. The next day, a Sunday, one or two "extremely low white" civilians fought African Americans near a "blind tiger" and called for help from fifteen to twenty soldiers. When the African Americans did not disperse, three soldiers fired shots, and African Americans responded with gunshots and rock-throwing. A crowd of African Americans, "angry and threatening," held the street while white people gathered at the provost guard's office to plan an attack. By the evening, as wild rumors swirled, commanders placed East Raleigh under martial law and confined the soldiers to camp. Although one white lieutenant called "this nigger business" just "a mountain made of a mole hill," the incident had lasting consequences. In October, when the Second Regiment was slated to return to Raleigh, Governor Russell prevented it, fearing the political fallout of further clashes with East Raleigh African Americans. When the Second

Regiment was mustered out elsewhere, they turned "riotous," shooting at African Americans on trains and in towns. Although the largely western Second Regiment had been known as a Republican regiment, many people believed that these encounters with African Americans and the experience of segregation in army camps turned many soldiers toward the Democrats in the autumn of 1898.[20]

Although military events confirmed the importance of statewide familial-ism, the Democrats still had to translate these feelings into politics. In cam-paign rituals at rallies and at the ballot box, Democrats attempted to fuse their abstract rhetoric with everyday practices of race-making. Taking a cue from wartime parades, white supremacy rallies excluded African Americans, creating a whites-only public space in rural and small-town areas. By elimi-nating African Americans from the group white politicians had to appeal to, Democrats signaled the race's irrelevance long before election day. Gen-der roles were particularly useful ways to make racist arguments hit home; both sexualized and chivalric notions of women's weakness tied arguments about state power to male authority over wives and daughters. Learning once again from the Populists, Democrats made politics women's business in the 1898 and 1900 campaigns. In huge picnics meant to create an illusion of familial ties, women cooked bushels of meal, dozens of pigs, and barrels of cabbage. In Concord, twenty-five "young ladies in purest white" paraded behind red-shirted men while bearing a sign that read, "Protect Us." In the fall, women participated in organizational meetings for precinct- and town-level white supremacy clubs, and on election day, in "scores of places the mothers and daughters were assembled near the voting places and between patriotic songs, worked for the success" of white supremacy. For women, the white supremacy movement threatened to silence their voices even as it made them newly visible. As their wants disappeared into the need of the abstracted state, women would find it more difficult to reach a listening ear in Raleigh. Even as the new government empowered female teachers and social workers, it also shut off the complaints of the weak, what had previously been women's final means to access people in authority.[21]

In scripted performances during the campaign, terroristic Red Shirts took ownership of public space for Democrats and wrote Republicans and African Americans out of political life. By creating a politics of fear, white suprema-cists silenced many Populists and Republicans. At most, these acts scared people from politics; at the least, they convinced voters that Populists and Republicans were too weak to be effective patrons. Therefore, at meetings across the state, Red Shirts chased Populists away from parades amid "rioting and bloodshed," egged Populist speakers, and dragged them from their stands. In Pender County, Red Shirts "marauded the county at least three times a week at the dead hours of midnight, with Winchesters and pistols" and told whites to "fall in ranks with them if they wanted to be respected any more by decent white people and that it was no use to vote against them." Because of the "system of intimidation, Red Shirtism, ostracism, +c," it took a "degree of courage" to speak for Populists or Republicans in some areas. This silence was a key to Democratic efforts to achieve hegemony. A climate of fear shaped registration, where Red Shirts worked to ensure not only that no African Americans voted but that "no negro" would "be seen." Along with control of public space, Democrats used law to establish a seemingly impregnable hegemony. Through gender-based definitions of domicile, Democrats excluded many divorced or separated African Americans and white men upon the grounds that they did not possess an adequate home to claim membership in the governing class.[22]

On election day, Democrats resorted to bloodshed or fraud. In one contest, Red Shirts stationed "men and boys" at "street crossings" to "turn off or run off every colored man." In Lexington, "they had 47 armed officers—armed with clubs on election day." A Robeson County man wrote that the Democrats "were coming in on wheels, in hacks and in buggies" wielding "Winchester rifles." Democrats also took control of the election returns, hiding unfavorable ballots and manufacturing useful ones. "The truth is we had no election in this county," a Hertford County Populist wrote. "The Democrats voted their own way but refused to let the other side vote." This hegemony depended upon the promise that no greater power would resist Democratic efforts. Not only did the state guard fail to defend African Americans, it attacked them on the streets of Wilmington in 1898 and again in 1900 in Bertie County and Clinton. In Tarboro, militia men cheered on Democratic violence by playing music during a Red Shirt white supremacy meeting.[23]

The infamous postelection Wilmington massacre exemplified white supremacy, although not always for the reasons scholars cite. After preventing African Americans from voting on election day, a "Wilmington Army" of prominent white men, laborers, and naval reservists staged an attack on African Americans and a coup of elected officials that toppled the city government and killed perhaps hundreds of African Americans. On the Thursday after the election, white men led by Colonel Alfred M. Waddell marched from the armory on the city's Market Street to "Love + Charity Hall (which was owned by a society of negroes)" and set it on fire. Shooting with artillery and rapid-fire guns, according to one witness, they "went over in Brooklyn, another negro settlement mostly, and began searching every one and if you did not submit, you would be shot down" on the spot. Even though many African Americans cooperated, coup leaders "to satisfy their Blood thirsty appetites would kill unoffending negro men to or on their way home from dinner." A white man involved in the massacre bragged, "We are just shooting to see the niggers run." The massacre unfolded because leaders were confident they could "keep back federal interference" or even recruit federal troops to help them, and members of the First North Carolina Infantry home on furlough "took a high hand in this nefarious work." After the massacre, the "state troops" paraded through "the streets singing hang Gov. Russell on a sour apple tree." This "object lesson" or "day to be remembered" was an effort to make hegemony through fear. The most striking thing about the Wilmington assault was not its cause but its size and the resulting media coverage. Although historians frequently cite Wilmington-specific explanations for the so-called riot, these arguments privilege anomalously urban experiences on sidewalks. But Wilmington was no anomaly. It was instead the largest but by no means sole flowering of a statewide explosion of punitive white familialism, and it had its roots not just in sidewalks but in the promise of access. Wilmington whites complained about African American officeholding, and massacre leaders promised preferential hiring for white men. Given the deeply rural nature of the state, and the broad overlap between events in Wilmington and other election assaults, the Wilmington attacks may be more useful as an archive than as a historical explanation for white supremacy.[24]

The Wilmington outrages, and similar, smaller uprisings across the state, led many African Americans to lose hope in a government that would not listen to them. For solace, some rural Carolinians turned to agencies like the American Colonization Society for help for "us as a people" in "forming a colony to settle in Liberia" because "the race problem has been put in politics." Others asked politicians to lobby the "Nation to giv or sell us a plas" outside of the state. Faced with a weak government in Raleigh and vicious Democrats in county offices, some African Americans sought assistance from Washington. There they made William McKinley, "Your Excellency," their "great American leader, defender of human rights and privileges and Christian advocate." In letters that combined liberal legalism and patronalism, they bemoaned the assaults upon "poor, defenceless Americans" as a violation both of their constitutional rights and of divine justice. One writer pleaded with McKinley to "help these humble subjects" for the sake of their patriotism, "Humanity," and "Christ." "Are we to die like rats in a trap?" he asked. "With no place to seek redress or go with our Grivances?" Without friends at home, "the negro can do nothing but pray. . . . To day we are mourners in a strange land with no protections near. God help us." One writer asked for aid "not in my name But the name of the almighty God knowing that He is a just God and knowing that you are a just man who has all the power of this land in thy hands. . . . The almighty will bless you in the day of resurrecton add a star to your crown + bless you thro out eternity. . . . Will you hear my plea? Or will you turn a deaf ear, in the name of God don't say no. But let me hear thy voice say yes." At the close of her letter, the writer emphasized the importance of requests in shaping government's response. "Many say the reason the President don't protect us because we don't ask," she wrote. "Now no one cant say we did not ask for I had asked and in the name of *God*." Despite her pleas, the federal government did little to protect African Americans in North Carolina, either in 1898 or through much of the first half of the twentieth century.[25]

After their success on election day, the triumphant university men disenfranchised African Americans and many whites. Through constitutional amendments and new laws, they required poll taxes, re-registration, and literacy tests, although whites received a short-term exemption under the grandfather clause. Segregation of steamboats, railroads, schools, streetcars, and textbooks soon followed. Between 1896 and 1904, 130,000 fewer voters cast ballots in the presidential election, a decline of nearly 40 percent. State elections shrank even more precipitously, excluding many whites and almost all African Americans. Many North Carolinians and other Southerners in the age of Jim Crow saw themselves not as part of a regional anomaly but as part of a broad movement, "not the slightest different" from efforts to regulate immigrant rights in Massachusetts. There, the Immigration Restriction League and former Harvard professor and U.S. Senator Henry Cabot Lodge lobbied to curtail immigration on the grounds that only native-born Americans possessed the "indestructible stock of ideas, traditions, sentiments, modes of thought, an unconscious inheritance from their ancestors, upon which argument has no effect." Together with Western acts to bar Chinese, these efforts against "a large number of stupid negroes" and "ignorant foreigners" aimed to protect society from the regression that would follow from their taking control of the government. Although Southern politicians were by far the most successful at disenfranchisement, their efforts paralleled what the leading historian of American voting called the "Redemption of the North," a national retraction of suffrage through laws barring resident aliens and paupers from voting, requiring Australian or secret ballots, and implementing de facto literacy tests.[26]

Over the next decades, these men and their successors transformed North Carolina into a model of Southern progressivism. Primarily, they relied upon education to manage the social organism. In office, they expanded schools within locally funded districts and then established the first state-funded education system. Education served pedagogical, economic, and reproductive ends. The state university, by combining "sons of poor men" and "old family stocks," promoted "good ancestor material" by teaching "some pride of race" to "ungainly" boys and fitting them to "beget children," Alderman wrote. Along with maintaining racial hygiene, education also encouraged social efficiency by lifting more people into competition. These progressive statists defended funding for segregated African American schools as the best way to save black people, and the state, from degeneration. They made this argument at some political risk. In the aftermath of the vicious 1898 campaign, many white legislators saw no reason to contribute anything to African American schools. Treating governance as race war, these radicals tried in 1899 and again in 1901 to slash African American school spending. Although university men fought hard to preserve funding, their support for education had its limits; many of them assumed inferior African American schools would guide pupils into industrial work. Calling upon a vision of parenthood rooted not in mercy but in control, they made "childlike and helpless" African Americans into infants who deserved neither respect nor input in their lives. "The Negro is yet a child, grown up in body and physical passions yet weak in judgment, foresight, self-control, and character," George Winston told the Fourth Conference for Education in the South. "It will take several centuries yet to make him a man. . . . The white race . . . must be his teacher and guardian." The work of university men in public health was a natural extension of their efforts for segregation and disenfranchisement. There, the state established hygiene laboratories, a tuberculosis sanitarium, a major campaign against hookworm, and, after World War I, the nation's longest-lasting eugenics program, which eventually sterilized 6,700 women.[27]

White supremacy leaders worked to rationalize other areas of the state, including pardons and divorces. Although Aycock issued pardons upon his "genuine love of humanity," his successor Robert Glenn essentially eliminated the old form of pardons. Instead Glenn developed a new conditional pardon, a parole based upon "good behavior" and a pledge to remain "sober and industrious." Although an occasional letter persisted in asking him for "mercy" from "the deep of my heart," Glenn's stance reshaped the ways people approached him. Many learned to solicit not Glenn's mercy but his willingness to "act as a moral lever in making" an inmate "a better man." At the same time, Aycock and Glenn critiqued legislators for being too responsive to the pleas of the people in the state's divorce laws. Whenever a person described a "terrible calamity existing in individual cases of married life," Aycock complained, the legislature responded with pity by passing general acts broadening the divorce statutes. To him and to Glenn, this reversed the importance of uniformity and mercy. "It is better that a few individuals should suffer from being unhappily married than that the public view with reference to the solemnity and permanence of the marriage relations should be in the slightest degree weakened," Aycock said. Both lobbied to make divorces harder to obtain.[28]

White supremacy governors' efforts against lynching raise questions about alleged paradoxes within Southern progressivism. Why did a notorious race-baiter like Aycock expend significant political capital to protect accused African American criminals? Aycock and Glenn's efforts to exert control over lynchers, however, make sense once viewed not through the lens of race or ethics but through that of state power. Offended by the way the "mob spirit" and "lawlessness" in the state undermined government authority, Aycock declared that the "the law must have full sway. The mob has no place in our civilization." Embarrassed by governors who refused to extradite prisoners back to North Carolina, Aycock called out the state militia, chastised local sheriffs, and encouraged judges to schedule swifter executions in order to maintain the state's performance of power over its jurisdiction. "The highest test of a great people is obedience to the law," Aycock said in his inaugural address. Defining "universal justice" as the "perpetual decree of Almighty God," Aycock simultaneously increased and narrowed the state's claim of authority and its vision of God. To a God who promised not mercy but a distant and abstract fairness, lynching was an abomination precisely because it was so personal. Instead Aycock urged the "best people" to demonstrate to the "lawless" their "ready submission to the law." "We cannot stop crime by committing it," he said. "We cannot teach obedience to law by disobeying it; we cannot preserve order by means of a mob." Dismissing localist claims of authority over criminals, progressive governors extended government power over the entirety of the state.[29]

In 1908, social management and popular politics fused in an important prohibition campaign that helped catapult liquor back onto the national stage. Alcohol had been a prominent issue in state politics at least since 1881, when religious leaders launched an unsuccessful prohibition referendum. In the intervening decades, and especially after disenfranchisement, prohibitionists fought for liquor bans at the county and township level. A strange series of events helped press prohibition onto the statewide ballot in 1908. Governor Glenn called the legislature into a special session in order to rewrite a railroad rate law that was believed to be damaging commerce in the state. As they contemplated the special session, leaders of the powerful Woman's Christian Temperance Union and the Anti-Saloon League decided that "now is the time to strike" and commenced an enormous petition campaign to add prohibition to the session, submitting thousands of names on preprinted forms to the legislature. Fearful of a public backlash, legislators put the question to the state's voters. There, prohibition found support upon many different grounds. Selectionists pushed for it because they, along with many WCTU members, believed that alcohol abuse caused deviations among offspring, making liquor "race suicide." Prohibition speakers carved out special roles for women in society as reproducers and transmitters and demanded that the state protect pure women from the evils of liquor, because "the future of the country" depends "upon the girls." Others turned to statistics, especially data about the staggering level of drinking and its effect upon economic and physical well-being. Many Anti-Saloon League members acted upon an early form of the Social Gospel, moving toward a kingdom theology that made improvement of this world central to salvation in the next. Some drew upon multiple strands, including the Anti-Saloon League leader and prominent Baptist layman who defended prohibition not just as good theology but as good science because it would eliminate the "bacillus" of crime and spur the "evolution from brute to brother."[30]

On the stump, the Bible provided a much more effective language for celebrating prohibition than selectionism or science. God, however, was no longer the merciful father but often the stern judge, concerned not with the ails of the body but with the righteousness of the soul. Giving in to liquor was "surrender" to "evil," a prominent layman claimed. Only by voting dry could Christian voters prove they were really "identified with Christ and His Kingdom, which is one of purity and holiness. . . . To vote for moral wrong against moral right, is to antagonize Christ and trample under-foot the principles for which He suffered and died on a malefactor's cross." To reinforce the connection between religion and politics, the Anti-Saloon League printed electoral tickets with scripture verses on the back. During campaign events women sang, "We'll take the world for Christ's own kingdom." Placing the fight on a heavenly plane made it, in Glenn's words, "a great conflict" between "God and the devil, light against darkness, righteousness against wrong, the school house and the church against the saloon, distillery, brothel and gambling hall. Christianity and the bar room cannot continue to exist side by side and the saloon must go." The right of the state to outlaw liquor was self-evident to one Burke County man, who called liquor unconstitutional because "God outlaws it." "If our country has any constitution," he added, "God is the author of it."[31]

Prohibition drew heavily upon white supremacy vocabularies because its leading orators were prominent white supremacy politicians. Dry leaders tried to create an obligation to save the souls of distant white people by using white supremacy's claims of white familialism. Claiming that white supremacy had eliminated local government as a way of stanching "Negro domination" in the east, Aycock articulated a broad identity rooted in state and racial pride. "I am a North Carolinian," Aycock said. "I am not for Wayne [County] or for Goldsboro but for North Carolina." Comparing liquor to a natural disaster, a Republican prohibitionist described the mutual obligation family members had to each other. If men saw fires burning ten miles away, they would rush to put them out, and "the fire is burning in Salisbury. It is burning in Wilmington, and in other places in North Carolina. If it sweeps west of Charlotte, it will destroy not only our properties, but the bodies and souls of our people. And by the Eternal God, we're going to put it out." Other speakers advanced a time-tested language of tyranny and oppression. Now, alcohol, "the mightiest single enemy of civilized man," stood in the place of African Americans as "the common enemy." Describing liquor in the same way white supremacy orators had defined African Americans, prohibitionists proclaimed that the true opponent lay within the hearts of white men. The "triumphant hordes of whiskey and corruption" were not strangers but men showing their "beastly sensual" nature under the influence of alcohol. In a shorthand that they did not need to explain, prohibitionists essentially argued that only the power of the state could prevent liquor from turning white men black. Although they continued to call upon the state to save them in their moment of weakness, people now frequently defined weakness not as bad luck but as personal failing. Instead of solace against a cruel world, they needed the state to protect them from themselves.[32]

Fired by confidence in their cause, and skeptical of arguments about individual rights, prohibitionists launched a redefinition of classic American political language. Mocking notions of "freedom" and "liberty," they defined the punitive state around divine revelation and the protection of "society, the home, and the family." The liberty to drink "was a freedom which made long hours of court and full jails . . . empty larders, bare floors, cheer-less homes, ragged children, and mother's tears," white supremacy orga-nizer and U.S. senator Furnifold Simmons proclaimed. "In God's name we have had enough, and too much, of that sort of freedom in North Carolina." Liberty, Aycock declared, was the "liberty to do right. . . . I will thank any man to take away the liberty to do wrong." "Liberty to do what?" Glenn mocked. "Liberty to get drunk, to neglect, to desert your families, to take provisions away from those dependent upon you? . . . The true rule for lib-erty is that nothing shall be taken away from an individual that is help-ful," but "it becomes the duty of the State to take away from him that which is a curse to himself and to others." During white supremacy, speakers had argued that African Americans needed external control to avoid self-destruction; in the prohibition campaign, this view applied not only to black men but to white ones, too. The relationship between African Americans and the state under white supremacy became the model for the state's interaction with all its subjects.[33]

To a greater extent than in white supremacy, women participated in the construction of this gendered language of guardianship. The particularly domestic impact of alcohol and the powerful role of the WCTU helped push women into new positions of authority. In one prominent advertisement, dozens of named women termed the saloon the "Destroyer of all that wom-anhood holds dear" and called themselves "the victims of the SALOON." "You are SOUTHERN MEN," they exhorted; "and helpless womanhood has never appealed to SOUTHERN MEN in vain. . . . The law of God and man makes you our protectors and we look to you to stand between us and our foe." Women personalized prohibition through family metaphors, describing the "curse" of liquor upon "your boy, flesh of their flesh and bone of their bone." Some woman would "let her indifference and carelessness ruin her own boy. . . . Will this woman be you?" Women also played prominent roles in reaching out to voters, in "organizing a Committee of Ladies" to "get up Prohibition Rallies, scatter literature, songs +c, influence voters and in every possible way advance the cause." In the campaign, female speakers drew large crowds, and local prohibitionists fought to get the best female lecturers to their towns. After the campaign, WCTU leaders lobbied for enforcement. "We cannot vote (and more's the pity)," the *White Ribbon* temperance newspaper editorialized, "but we can influence the voters of our families and social circles, and *women, do it!*"[34]

When North Carolina voters approved the liquor ban by a 62–38 margin in May 1908, the victory signaled the groundswell of Southern support for prohibition. Following closely behind wins in Georgia and Mississippi, the North Carolina result inspired promises from other Southern politicians that their state "would be next." Over the next decade, Carolinians played important roles in writing congressional acts limiting the transportation and sale of liquor and eventually in crafting the ill-fated Eighteenth Amendment for national prohibition. Along with other Southern states, North Carolina helped established the idea that prohibition was a "Wave that is sweeping in South," in Trinity president John C. Kilgo's words, not the creation of organized forces but a "sentiment that seemed to rise out of the earth, a revolution that came upon the people." North Carolina's use of the Progressive referendum reinforced claims that the liquor ban reflected the will of the people, even though Progressive majoritarianism depended, in North Carolina as elsewhere, upon ballot restriction. Although some political historians dismiss prohibition as a short-term aberration, the liquor struggle is one of the key issues of American history, central to what one political scientist called "American governments' overlooked growth spurt" that empowered the state to "change the way people lived." Like many Progressive efforts, prohibition had its roots in the South and the West, and particularly within the punitive and democratic rhetoric of modern white supremacy.[35]

During the 1900s, as people refashioned the language of white supremacy to advance prohibition and other statist reforms, they both broadened and narrowed its vocabulary. What emerged in the 1908 prohibition campaign was a refurbished white supremacy tailored to the momentary needs of politicians and audiences. The prohibition movement, for all its linguistic similarities to white supremacy, was notably different in one respect. While white supremacy promised white men a fantastic gift based upon their skin, prohibition's promises were mostly negative: access that could lead to deliverance or purification but not a job or a present. In its place was a new form of dependence, one rooted not in circumstance or bad luck but in sinfulness or weak character. The access that white supremacy promised turned out to be a right to ask for protection from one's own weaknesses, not for favors.

Even as state leaders spoke in increasingly moralistic and punitive ways about the relationship between state and subject, claims of dependence persisted. Because Governor Robert Glenn disdained mercy in his approach to pardons and prohibition, he received very few appeals upon those grounds. Despite his powerful performance, and the creation of new preprinted pardon forms that steered requests to lawyers and bureaucrats, declarations of dependence did not disappear but were pressed hopefully again upon Glenn's successors. For the next decades pardons continued to be a prime place where people sought an intimate relationship with a merciful ruler. Carolinians called upon later governors based upon their "big-hearted" nature and begged them to "help struggling humanity . . . to treat others with kindness." One writer invented a tradition that the governor "could not refuse the first" to "ask a favor," and a Brownsville woman claimed that she had "prayed very serious over this matter." Finding her support for patronalism not from the state's actions but from above, she wrote that the "Lord had directed me to correspond with you" to "Favor me with your kindness."[36]

Coda

Desperate Times Call for Distant Friends

Franklin Roosevelt as the Last Good King?

ALMOST FOUR DECADES after the white supremacy campaign, a federal interviewer called
on an aged ex-slave from Jones County, North
Carolina, at her residence in Saint Louis, Missouri. Despite the oddity of a government listening to people it had long excluded, Susan
Davis Rhodes was not surprised by the visit.
Rhodes's own experiences with the burgeoning
New Deal state taught her a great deal about
the reach of the new government. She and her daughter were on relief, and a
nephew worked for the Works Progress Administration. But there was another reason she expected the encounter, one that had roots in what she
called her "common sense education" in slavery, emancipation, Reconstruction, and Jim Crow. Her life taught her the usefulness of patrons, real or
fantastic, for defense against the vicissitudes of the world, whether those
guardians be kinsmen, friendly whites, or a God before whom she could
"Spread [her] wants before his face, and pour [her] woes abroad. My God will
pity my complaints, and heal my broken bones. . . . He calls thee to his throne
of grace, / To spread thy sorrows there." As she welcomed the Federal
Writers' Project agent into her rooms, Rhodes advanced her own interpretation of the strange circumstances that led a federal employee to knock on the
door of a former slave. "I see'd in a dream a long time ago, honey, dat one of
dese United States presidents was going to send folks around to get some of
us slaves living to tell about our lives way back yonder, 'cause dey wants to
know 'bout it from us ourselves and not what someone else wants to say,"
Rhodes told the interviewer. "And course de President was not old 'nough

hisself to know, and he wants to learn de truth 'bout it all for hisself and he's right, honey. Yes, he is."[1]

Rhodes's dream and the pleas of the many thousands of people who wrote directly to Franklin D. Roosevelt suggest the strange embrace between novelty and familiarity in the New Deal, and the peculiarly intimate roots of modern American liberalism. While scholars often cite vivid letters of Depression-era poor people to Roosevelt and his government, they usually treat them as unmediated statements of need, rather than political claims. Taking these pleas seriously may suggest new ways of thinking about the enthusiasm for Roosevelt and the New Deal. Rather than just a response to new, useful government interventions, the political passion of the 1930s may be read also as the momentary, problematic revitalization of Reconstruction patronalism to explain (and perhaps spur on) an expanding state. Roosevelt's popularity grew not just from his mastery of radio but also from his capacity to play upon well-established patterns of interaction between the governors and the governed. None of this was straightforward or simple. Even as the New Deal encouraged a revitalization of (or at least a resurfacing of a perhaps submerged) patronalism, these programs also undercut patronalism through their sheer magnitude and duration. While Civil War states failed to deliver upon many of their promises, the New Deal was much more effective, systematic, and enduring. Between 1932 and 1936, federal expenditures more than doubled, with part of the increase going to soften the Depression for people like Rhodes and her family. Over time, the New Deal established the framework for the federal government at least through the Great Society and the 1970s, if not beyond. This expansive — and increasingly bureaucratized — state answered some of the pleas of patronalism, inspired legalistic rather than personalistic methods of appeal, and, through standardization, redrew the lines of politics to make intimate appeals seem once again out of bounds. What endured was the way the New Deal and World War II taught Americans to look toward Washington. For the first time in history, huge numbers of letters flooded Washington, not state capitals, a pattern that holds to this day. Roosevelt elicited these responses by seeking them, asking for "your counsel and your help" from radio listeners and from clergymen. When people answered with glowing praise and sometimes groveling requests, they applied ideas about figures like Lincoln and William Jennings Bryan and even Grover Cleveland to the novel situation of the 1930s.[2]

A thorough study of popular responses to the new state would undoubtedly fill multiple volumes. Even a cursory glance at the way people called upon Roosevelt, however, suggests the utility of thinking through 1930s visions of the government in light of a long-standing history of American patronalism and dependence. Although Roosevelt relied on modern media — particularly radio addresses — and new methods of governance, his admirers made of him something that was also familiar: a "Modern Moses" who had "come to lead us." Calling Roosevelt "our Earthly Father" crowned by God to be the "Loving Provider of the Poor," letter writers from North Carolina and across the country turned Roosevelt into a distant and powerful friend. Men and women who were "your Loyal Subject" begged for help since "they are not to blame," for their "strength + nearve + blood + constitution + mental life are blowed a way in the wind." White and African American Carolinians called him "king" and the "Great White Father," and pledged tokens of "love and faith." "I love to look at his picture," Hannah Plummer said. "I love him because he has done so much for humanity. I pray to the Lord to let him serve his country, and help his people." People from across the country called upon Roosevelt, as they did Bryan, in fervent evangelical language. Rather than a North Carolina or Southern peculiarity, this was a broad-based way of making sense of a period of great promise and peril, a product not of Southern backwardness but of the creative confusion unleashed in moments of state intervention and economic need. The friendship Roosevelt created was not caused solely by his newly intimate presence in radio addresses; it also grew from deeply held ways of thinking through power. Along with Roosevelt's image as the first great liberal, it is worth thinking through the ways people also called upon him as the last good king. These two seemingly contradictory images — the governing liberal and the good king — may have blended together in unexpected but coherent ways for people seeking to understand what the new government could do for them.[3]

New Deal liberalism was constructed in part within a seemingly antique, but actually updated, patronalism. Instead of arising from timeless cries of the poor, these claims used older languages to navigate, and perhaps even bend, new realities. People did this by trying to combine the promise of New Deal interventions with a personalistic view of power. One Carolinian mailed Roosevelt a "fine stick" for having "done so much good for the people." "I am not looking for anything for my stick but . . . a letter from you," he claimed. But he added, "Sometime you may have a second-hand car you might give me. My wife and I are too old and can do but little." In other correspondence, many Carolinians claimed they named their children for Roosevelt in order to show that he could "depend on" them. In return, Mrs. Joe Osborne begged the president for "any little thing you would love to send" little Franklin Delano Osborne. "We are very poor and times are so hard we can bearly live," she wrote. "We wont be able to have anything for thanksgiving or xmas." The children themselves — or, more likely, parents writing under their names — pleaded with Roosevelt for a "Christmas present" to prove that Roosevelt loved "little boyes my age" since "Mama has so many Christmas presents to buy." Others begged for a "light job" or the "means" to get "medicine and food." "To my mind you are one of the best rulers our nation has ever had," another wrote. "Could you help me in a financial way? If so I will pay you back as soon as I can. . . . I am very needy." North Carolinians were not alone in these requests; writers from other parts of the nation asked Franklin or Eleanor Roosevelt for "under cloths" or a "few old discarded dresses" or an "old bunch of stockings" or any "old things." Laid low by the death of her husband, a Georgia woman claimed, "My Last Chance now is to beg. . . . I haven't any one to help me make my way. . . . I am almost a cripple at times. . . . I know the Lord will repay you for any thing you Can do."[4]

These vernacular vocabularies of politics were not just Roosevelt's creation but had been disseminated among people far from power during the long, punitive dry spell of the early twentieth century. Relayed through stories, gossip, and myth, these ideas survived out of the sight and minds of most political leaders. In conversations at firesides, market days, and picnics, women and men told each other how politics worked, what power meant, and why fairness might be a chimera, among other things. On their own, these attitudes about politics could not force political change, but, combined with Roosevelt's unusual skill and the exigencies of the Depression, they helped fashion a peculiar, new style that intertwined these aspirations with the national and bureaucratic vision of Roosevelt's brain trust. At the same moment, the flood of responses to Roosevelt could seem both anachronistically naive and deeply modern, a product both of experience with a new state and of long-held personalistic fantasies. Their impact was also surely complex, as patronalism could suggest both the righteousness of the New Deal and the sense that the state could not help everyone. A persistent cynicism that the government could deliver fairly and equally upon its promises plagued both the New Deal and more-recent efforts. This was not pure conjecture. In battles over Social Security and agricultural programs, policies designed to provide broad-based assistance became mechanisms for favoring large landowners at the expense of laborers, especially black women who worked as maids. The peculiar nature of interest-group politics in America reinforced the anxiety that state expansion was in fact a cover to deliver favors to a privileged few, a fear that has never been expunged from American public opinion because it draws not just from traditional views of scarcity but also from experience with the government itself.

Critics deployed other facets of classical liberalism against the New Deal, arguing that it encouraged a pathetic and enfeebling dependence. Using a punitive language familiar from the prohibition campaigns and from Union fears of rationing, these writers begged Roosevelt not to let people revert to a natural "spirit of laziness and dependence." Infuriated by the "army of professional beggars" and the "simple-minded," these writers argued that the government ought to declare its independence from the needs of its individual subjects, no matter how desperate. Previewing the backlash conservatism that would dominate late-twentieth-century American politics, these writers called not for a return to an imagined past but instead for the creation of something to some degree quite new, a purely individualistic and moralistic government unburdened by the detritus of sentiment or reliquary attachments. These writers complained about the old practice of "indiscriminate giving" that "will weaken instead of strengthen the moral fiber of our people" and prevent them from trying "to help themselves." Reduced to "indolence and insolince by what is known as The Relief," these "lower classes" had the "audacity to depend upon government aid" or held to the foolish notion that the "President is going to keep on giving." Although scholars often portray the New Deal as innovative and its critics reactionary, from the viewpoint of its recipients the New Deal may well have seemed familiar in its intentions, if not its scope, and what may be the most forward-looking product of the period may be the invigorated moralism that grew in opposition to Roosevelt's policies. Instead of being surprised to find that leaders could play a role in saving them from starvation, it is possible that many Americans were surprised at the idea that they could not.[5]

In the seventy-five years after the Civil War's close, a patronal approach to politics lived a cat's nine lives. Pressed under water by reformers, scholars, and other seeming rationalists, these ideas resurfaced in unexpected ways. The very success of the New Deal and World War II, however, may have silenced or at least altered these approaches. As the web of the war caught an increasingly large number of people in daily interaction with government through rationing, advertising campaigns, and service, more people became accustomed to bureaucratic relations with their government. Although dependence remains an important concept, and imaginative connections between people and their leaders continue to play a role in politics, patronal appeals were in part replaced by an important metaphor of the populace as consumers of (or, eventually, plaintiffs against) government. Through the expansion of federal income tax rates and the proliferation of bonds-buying programs, people were tied economically to the federal government in a new way. Government efforts to monitor and boost public morale through advertising campaigns taught new forms of connection between people and the state, particularly through the resonant comparison of citizen-workers to soldiers. More importantly, the contact that people had with the government occurred not through individual patrons but through a massively expanding bureaucracy.[6]

Since Roosevelt, popular portrayals of politicians have shifted from a hierarchical to something more like an affectionate model of friendship. In an increasingly bureaucratized state, presidents still mediate between the people and their government but in a different way. Instead of an escape valve for needy people or a distributor of favors to friends, a president frequently appears to be the human face upon a bewilderingly vast government. Rather than a patron who might deliver a favor, the president is often put in the role of a slightly dimwitted, mostly ineffectual but well-meaning pal; thus the incessant, inane polling about which candidate the populace would like to drink a beer with or hire as a babysitter. Despite the enduring influence of evangelical religion upon politics, our presidents may well be viewed in a more secular light than their nineteenth-century predecessors. While it was not then unusual for people to call on a politician as a savior, this is now a discredited, ridiculous notion, advanced as an insult against alleged (but never revealed) Obama admirers who consider him a Messiah or Bush supporters who purportedly (although rarely in practice) believed in him as fervently as they do in Jesus.[7]

Although not a relic during the New Deal era, patronalism may well be a relic in ours. If so, few will mourn its passing. At best it may mediate unfair practices for one individual; it can never be the basis of a broad-based reform, much less revolutionary change in government. At worst it reinforces a devil-take-the-hindmost view of politics, a zero-sum certainty that only a sucker believes government can help all the people even some of the time. Although bureaucrats and political aides still receive pleas rooted in alleged personal connection, these appeals now seem bizarre, thoroughly anathematized by new technologies of governance that have placed them beyond the boundaries of politics. In many respects the narrowing politics of the Progressive Era are still with us, for better and for worse. Politicians are supposed to outline programs that will help everyone; in the process they are obligated to help no one in particular. Even the ubiquitous, boring personal anecdotes candidates since Bill Clinton use in their speeches illustrate general conditions, not the kind of intimate attachment that Vance or Bryan or others invoked.

At the same time, one wonders whether the struggles of liberalism since the Great Society stem from a willful amnesia about the patronalism that once helped inspire new forms of state intervention during the Civil War and the New Deal. If older liberalisms were built in conversation with popular dependence, can a new liberalism be built in its absence? Without the capacity to make people believe — even wrongly — that government is helping them individually, how can liberals inspire enthusiasm? The abstractions taught at universities and practiced in campaigns too often make liberalism dry and expert-driven. Without a way of arousing popular passions, overconfidence in the righteousness of broad solutions leaves an emotional hole in politics, one that can too often be filled by the kind of moralistic anger that drove prohibitionists (of different stripes) in the early and the late twentieth century. This gap has been caused not just by increasing specialization and stratification but by 1970s wars over the alleged dependence created by Great Society welfare programs. Since then, leftists have too frequently joined in an amen chorus proclaiming the untruth that people can live without government. This acquiescence has left many liberals without an ability to articulate what government can do, except serve as an educated, distant manager. It can seem as if politics begins with the false assumption that the veneer of independence we construct is real.

If respectable politics no longer normally takes notice of intimate needs, there are still moments when these desires enter back in to the conversation. Patronalism, for all its failures, arises from a simple, if sometimes ugly or even unbearable truth, one illustrated in the destruction of a Southern seaport one hundred and seven years after the massacre at Wilmington. On August 29, 2005, Hurricane Katrina struck the Gulf coast, killing more than 1,500 people and destroying large swathes of New Orleans and other coastal towns and cities. Immediately this natural disaster revealed two enduring patterns in American life, patterns that would not have surprised anyone on Ocracoke Island or in New Bern, North Carolina, one hundred and forty years earlier. The garments of autonomy and independence can be blown away; many people are one disaster away from a necessary reliance upon forces greater than themselves, and others are even closer than that. Basic human need continues to drive many people's relationship with the state. Although often stifled or diverted or judged beyond politics, these wants and necessities reemerge at moments of crisis. And in the face of that need, just as many people of both liberal and conservative persuasions are still ready to anathematize any reliance upon government as pathology. One hundred and fifty years after the Civil War revolutionized governance, creating new subjects and new citizens, the needy and the people anxious to deny them remain locked in an intimate, if sometimes obscure, embrace that makes dependence an enduring American condition, a formative part of the intimate and fantastic history of the relationship between Americans and their state.

Acknowledgments

In writing this book, and in the long and slow intellectual path that led me through teaching and journalism and fiction to American political history, I have had good cause to recognize the enduring power of dependence. For graduate students and beginning historians, reliance upon others is not merely a virtue; it is often a necessity. Although the name on the manuscript (and the responsibility for any errors) is mine, this is a product of many hands and many minds.

For their support, I am grateful to the Josephine de Karman Foundation, which funded a much-needed year of writing; the Mellon Foundation and the Center for Humanities at the Graduate Center of the City University of New York, which funded a much-needed year of revisions; the PSC-CUNY Research Awards; the CUNY Faculty Fellowship Publication Program; the Research Foundation–CUNY Equipment Grant that helped purchase a microfilm reader; the University of Pennsylvania, whose Benjamin Franklin Fellowship and Faye Rattner Grant funded research; Northwestern University, which funded my early years of graduate education and several important research trips; the North Caroliniana Society for its Archie K. Davis Fellowship; the Southern Historical Collection at the University of North Carolina for the J. Carlyle Sitterson Stipend; Duke University for the John Hope Franklin Research Grant; and the Memphis African American History Conference for the Memphis State Eight Best Paper Prize.

Like every historian, I am dependent upon archivists past and present for their daily assistance and for their great work of preserving the past. Particularly, I relied upon Laura Clark Brown and the staff of the Southern Historical Collection at the University of North Carolina, who went beyond the call of duty in pulling hundreds of boxes and in preparing unprocessed collections for my viewing; the North Carolina Collection staff at the University of North Carolina; the excellent archivists at the Special Collections Library at Duke University; and the well-utilized employees of the North

Carolina State Archives, as well as many, many others. At the Freedmen and Southern Society Project at College Park, Maryland, Steven F. Miller and Leslie Rowland generously opened their vast collection of documents copied from the National Archives. All historians of the period benefit immensely from their efforts, particularly in the exemplary edited volumes they have produced for both scholars and teachers. The staffs at the University of Pennsylvania, Northwestern, and City College of New York libraries, particularly in the Interlibrary Loan departments, indulged far too many requests with good cheer and encouragement. At City College, administrators went out of their way to provide me with support, encouragement, and time, particularly Dean Fred Reynolds, interim dean Geraldine Murphy, and history department chairs Darren Staloff, Clifford Rosenberg, and Nicholas Pappas.

At conferences and seminars, I was fortunate to field serious and tough questions from Winthrop Jordan, Stephanie M. H. Camp, Beverly Bond, Scott R. Nelson, Elizabeth Sanders, Sven Beckert, Robert Gough, Elizabeth Varon, Peter Logan, Bryant Simon, the members of the Temple University Center for the Humanities Nineteenth Century Forum, the members of the CUNY Center for the Humanities Sacred and the Secular Seminar, the CUNY Faculty Fellowship Publication Program, Michael Johnson, the members of the Graduate Student Seminar at Northwestern University's history department, William Thomas Allison, Nancy Bercaw, Roy Rosenzweig, and C. Wyatt Evans, among others. Ira Berlin, Julie Saville, Dylan Penningroth, Emily West, Adam Rothman, Melissa Macauley, René Hayden, and Tessie Liu read an early excerpt of the manuscript. In North Carolina, David Perry, William Powell, John Sanders, Barbara Hahn, Kerry Taylor, and Yonni Chapman guided me through thickets of Tar Heel lore.

Many other people read and critiqued parts of the manuscript, including Steven Hahn, Stephanie McCurry, Sheldon Hackney, Barbara Savage, Bruce Kuklick, John Dittmer, Leon Fink, Stephen Steinberg, Tom Sugrue, Jim Goodman, Martha Hodes, Jane Dailey, Glenda Gilmore, Cliff Rosenberg, Andreas Killen, Adrienne Petty, Anne Kornhauser, Judith Stein, Danian Hu, Beth Baron, Craig Daigle, David Jaffee, Edward J. Blum, Anthony R. DeStefanis, David Nord, Elizabeth Wissinger, Grace Davie, Andrae Brown, Michele Gregory, Anne Rice, Gail Garfield, Aoibheann Sweeney, Michael Washburn, Tony Alessandrini, Tom Head, Alyshia Gálvez, Sara Pursley, Raja Abillama, Rafael de la Dehesa, Marlene Hennessy, Ana Mercedes Acosta, John Torpey, David Hoffman, Jill Stauffer, Nivedita Majumdar, Eric Taylor, Erik Mathisen, Joanna Cohen, Sarah Manekin, Justin Behrend, Erik

Gellman, Jonathan Blum, and Daniel Amsterdam. At the *Journal of Southern History*, I had the great good fortune of excellent anonymous reviews, clear guidance from John Boles and Randal Hall, and expert fact-checking and copyediting by their staff. I am proud that a portion of Chapter 7 appeared in the seventy-fifth volume of the *Journal of Southern History* (May 2009): 267–304.

Every writer has an ideal reader. I am fortunate to have several. Steven Hahn, Jim Oakes, Darren Staloff, Kate Masur, Laura Edwards, Scott R. Nelson, Diane Downs, Monty Downs, and David Sellers Smith read every word of the manuscript, many of those words several times, without complaint (although not without criticism). David Sellers Smith, in particular, offered so many helpful critiques that I would be tempted to include his name on the title page. Kate Masur's expertise on Reconstruction helped me connect the argument more carefully to political and economic transformations in the nation and region. At University of North Carolina Press, David Perry discussed this with me over every conceivable meal from dawn breakfast oatmeal to postdusk lamb stew, over coffee, beer, and red wine. He believed in the project long before there was a project to believe in, a faith in me (and in his own judgment) that I hope I have met in these pages. He had the good sense to send the manuscript to two extraordinarily broad-minded and careful readers, Laura Edwards and Scott R. Nelson. In extensive, sympathetic, critical, and precise reports, Laura and Scott pushed this book from the shell of my own fears and assumptions and toward the needs and desires of readers. They wanted the book to be better than it was, to be the book I imagined it could be, and their encouragement and their occasional skepticism helped make it so. Mary Caviness tightened the prose and saved me from errors with her fine copyediting.

Guy Ortolano, Jenny Mann, Tim Buckner, Ben Irvin, Gayle Rogers, Abram Van Engen, Jim Downs, and many, many others read not a word of the manuscript but gave me plenty of good advice about the process, read over précis and job letters, and cheered me on without letting me get sloppy.

As an undergraduate at Yale University, I had the good fortune to stumble into Melvin Patrick Ely's popular and exciting courses on the Civil War, African American history, and Southern history. From Mel, I learned not only what it means to be a historian, with the daily joys and irritations of archival research, but also what it means to be a Southerner and a teacher and an ethical human being.

When I first entered the Iowa Writers' Workshop, I kept my enduring love of history quiet, for fear I would be branded a thief in the temple of fiction, but James A. McPherson and Barry Unsworth and Marilynne Robinson through their words and their deeds reminded us all that history matters, not just in academic debates but in the meaning people try to make of their lives.

I had the good fortune to start my Ph.D. program at Northwestern University, where Melissa Macauley, Jock McLane, T. H. Breen, Adam Green, Nancy MacLean, Dylan Penningroth, and many others asked a great deal of us students and even more of themselves. I also entered a lively graduate student community, which included Justin Behrend, Erik Gellman, David Sellers Smith, Aaron Astor, Carole Emberton, Guy Ortolano, Gayle Rogers, Deborah I. Cane, and many others.

In the middle of my graduate studies, I left Northwestern for the University of Pennsylvania, where I learned about Populism from Sheldon Hackney, twentieth-century politics from Barbara Savage and Tom Sugrue, intellectual history from Bruce Kuklick, and narrative and history from Michael Zuckerman and Tom Childers, and also joined another vibrant mix of graduate students, including Daniel Amsterdam, Eric Taylor, Erik Mathisen, Jo Cohen, Sarah Manekin, René Alvarez, Michael Clapper, Clem Harris, and many others. Sarah Igo and Kathleen Brown helped broaden my reading lists.

Sheldon Hackney taught me more than Populism; his grace and good cheer fail to mask a mind eternally on the move in search of the big questions. Barbara Savage possesses an enviable mind and an even more enviable character. Frank and reliable, demanding and humane, she is a model teacher as well as an exceptional scholar.

Throughout my graduate career, I had the good fortune to be able to work with Stephanie McCurry. In my first semester of graduate school, her seminar on American slavery scrambled my brain, and I am not sure that it yet has settled back into place, or if I want it to. Early on, she gave me governor's papers to read, and shared with me the joy of encountering the strange letters from distant villages that make up a portion of this book. As the project moved farther conceptually and chronologically from her period, she remained a prod and a guide.

Steve Hahn is the adviser students hope for. He reads everything, remembers most of it, and still becomes excited with the half-baked ideas advanced by second-year graduate students. When I blundered into a project that seemed formless and idiosyncratic, he encouraged me to explore my interests by reading broadly, working through the archives, and writing and writing and writing. Committed to archival research and yet fascinated by comparative and conceptual questions, he represents what is most interesting about the discipline of history, the constant and sometimes contradictory engagement with both the stubbornly mundane and the airily theoretical. His struggle to find words to describe the way everyday people made their politics became, for many of us, an inspiration to our own separate, but related, struggles to do the same thing.

If it is a great boon to work under the inspiration of certain ways of pursuing history, it is also a special privilege to have to work out, defend, rethink, and modify those ideas in engagement with smart, sympathetic colleagues with quite different premises and inspirations. No one pushed me harder to explain myself and sharpen my ideas than Jim Oakes. After graduate school, I was lucky to land among a supportive group of historians, colleagues, and friends at The City College of New York. Darren Staloff not only helped integrate me into the department but took time from his own schedule to read the manuscript with extraordinary care, to nudge me gently to broaden my views and also to shy away from overstatement and sloppy binaries, and to talk me through revisions deep into the evening. Dear friends like Cliff Rosenberg, Andreas Killen, Adrienne Petty, and, especially, the unsinkable Judith Stein, welcomed me into the department and served as both models and guides for the life of the scholar, teacher, and department member. Beyond the boundaries of City College, Jim Oakes, Jim Goodman, Martha Hodes, and Stephen Steinberg read my work with enthusiasm (and, sometimes, skepticism) and engaged with me as peers and friends. In the final days of revision, friends like Anthony Guinyard and Michael Washburn and Glenn Hendler helped me disappear from the worries of rewriting.

I cannot remember a time when I did not love history, and for that I must thank my mother, Ann Patterson Howard, and her parents, Dorothy Elizabeth Patterson Howard and David Russell Howard. My earliest and strongest memories are of their stories about the past they lived through in their world around Elizabethtown, Kentucky. From an unseemly age and at indecent hours, I begged my mother to read biographies to me, particularly one of John F. Kennedy, whose venerated visage hung on my grandfather's wall, the only person pictured there, other than family members and Jesus. My brother, Wil, made his own history as a two-time Mr. Basketball–award winner in Tennessee. My father, William Montague Downs, and his family, particularly my grandfather Wilbur George Downs and my grandmother Dorothy G. Downs, always encouraged the life of the mind, through their support and through the examples of their own lives.

Fifteen years ago, in a crisis in both of our lives, I asked Diane Michelle Cardona to believe in me, and she has never stopped. Nine years ago, as I struggled my way back into history, Diane cheerfully shouldered the psychological, practical, and financial burdens of being a graduate student's spouse, reading endless drafts, falling asleep alone while I read heavy monographs, waiting for phone calls while I slogged through archives far away. Near the end, as this project swelled, her belly grew with it. By a whisker, the first draft of the manuscript won the race with our future, in the form of our first child, Sophia Marie, born into her own histories, personal and political. A year later, our second, Gabriella Francesca, arrived. Now, as I complete the manuscript, the girls yank at the keyboard, pull on my fingers, grab my glasses, and do whatever else they can to sabotage "Daddy's work." For many of the people I studied, people who exulted and suffered and died, their greatest fear was in being abandoned, left alone. I take great comfort in the knowledge that in the embrace of Diane's love, our children, like me, will never feel alone.

Notes

Abbreviations

DUA	Duke University Archives, Durham, N.C.
ECU	East Carolina Manuscript Collection, Joyner Library, East Carolina University, Greenville, N.C.
FDRL	Franklin D. Roosevelt Library, Hyde Park, N.Y.
FSSP	Freedmen and Southern Society Project Files, College Park, Md.
GLB	Governors' Letter Books
GP	Governors' Papers
HU	Houghton Library, Harvard University, Cambridge, Mass.
LOC	Library of Congress, Washington, D.C.
NA	National Archives, College Park, Md., and Washington, D.C.
NCDAH	State Archives, North Carolina Division of Archives and History, Raleigh, N.C.
OR	*The War of the Rebellion: A Compilation of the Official Records of the Union and Confederate Armies*, 128 vols. (Washington, D.C.: Government Printing Office, 1880–1901)
RG 60	General Records of the Department of Justice
RG 94	Records of the Adjutant General's Office
RG 105	Records of the Bureau of Refugees, Freedmen, and Abandoned Lands
RG 107	Records of the Office of the Secretary of War
RG 109	War Department Collection of Confederate Records
SCL	Rare Book, Manuscripts, and Special Collections Library, Duke University, Durham, N.C.
SHC	Southern Historical Collection, University of North Carolina, Chapel Hill, N.C.
UA	University Archives, Wilson Library, University of North Carolina, Chapel Hill, N.C.
UNCG	University Archives and Manuscripts, Walter C. Jackson Library, University of North Carolina, Greensboro, N.C.

UVA   Albert and Shirley Small Special Collections Library, University of
             Virginia, Charlottesville, Va.
WFU   Z. Smith Reynolds Library, Wake Forest University, Winston-Salem,
             N.C.

Introduction

1. Ramsay, *Dissertation*, 3; Wood, *Empire of Liberty*, 7.

2. Spurred by feminist critiques, historians have recognized the deep patterns of dependence within American culture — especially in treatment of slaves, women, children, Native Americans, and apprentices. In this book I examine dependence not just as a structural condition but as a tool that people used to mediate politics for their own benefit. For examples of scholars' critical but confident presumption that autonomy and individualism define much of American politics, see Foner, *Story of American Freedom*, 10; Bellah, *Broken Covenant*, xix; Myrdal, *American Dilemma*, 4; Patterson, *Freedom*; and Kaye, *Joining Places*, 9.

Kate Masur uses the term "upstart claims" for those appeals that "were not claims to existing rights, nor were they supported by existing policies." Instead "upstart claims" draw upon appeals rooted in status and individual privileges to try to expand the boundaries of legal rights. Along related lines, Laura Edwards describes the phenomenon of a person "talking for her rights" as an interpretive window into the way people "stretched the rubric of rights to accomplish their own goals within the legal system." See Masur, *Example for All the Land*, 7–8; and Edwards, *People and Their Peace*, 291.

3. Arden A. Nelson to Vance, Dec. 6, 1877, GP 248, Vance Papers, NCDAH; H. M. Guiney to Marion Butler, Dec. 4, 1897, ser. 1.2, folder 78, Marion Butler Papers, #114, SHC; David L. May to William W. Holden, Apr. 22, 1869, GP 222, Holden Papers, NCDAH; Sarah Mabury to Holden, July 15, 1869, GP 222, Holden Papers, NCDAH; W. W. Scott Jr. to Vance, Mar. 16, 1893, reel 36, *Papers of Zebulon Vance*; E. A. Poteat to Mrs. Graham, Dec. 15, 1896, box 4, folder 47, Graham Papers #955, SHC; W. C. Rencher to Vance, July 12, 1885, reel 5, *Papers of Zebulon Vance*; Mrs. Jane L. Backus to Vance, Apr. 12, 1885, reel 32, *Papers of Zebulon Vance*; Mrs. Cornelia Henderson to Vance, Feb. 25, 1885, reel 31, *Papers of Zebulon Vance*; Dollie J. Hill to Vance, Jan. 8, 1888, reel 33, *Papers of Zebulon Vance*; Adams, "Mr. Cleveland's Tasks," 298–99.

4. Vance to Weldon N. Edwards, Sept. 18, 1862, GLB 50.1, Vance Papers, NCDAH; McCurry, *Confederate Reckoning*; McCurry, "Women Numerous and Armed"; McKinney, *Zeb Vance*; Escott, *Many Excellent People*, 53–58; R. D. W. Connor, *North Carolina*, 223; Mobley, *Papers of Zebulon Vance*, 28; Dowd, *Life of Zebulon Vance*, 70; *Wilmington Morning Star*, Nov. 1, 1876, p. 2; *Congressional Record*, 49th Cong., 1st sess., 2948–52; H. C. Turner to Vance, July 27, 1886, reel 9, *Papers of Zebulon Vance*.

5. Recently, scholars pursuing transnational history (and building upon earlier work of comparative and Marxist historians) have tried to undermine narratives of American exceptionalism by tracing intersections and interactions between the developing American state and other nations. See, especially, Bender, *Rethinking American History*; Bender, *Nation among Nations*; Tyrrell, *Transnational Nation*; and Rauchway, *Blessed among Nations*.

6. Because scholars use the more common term "clientelism" to describe an underlying social reality, I call the imaginative understanding of politics "patronalism." This book asks not whether the world of the nineteenth-century United States was fundamentally clientelist but whether people spoke as if it was, and what effect this had upon democratic practice. In clientelism, patrons might be politicians, family leaders, businessmen, or, especially, large landowners. Clientelism produced relationships that were voluntary, vertical, reciprocal, not contractual, rooted in skepticism of universalism, and reproduced through symbolic rituals. Once considered a relic found in landowner-dominated Latin American states, clientelism is now studied in modern American urban political machines, eighteenth-century British patronage networks, and the bureaucracies of newly democratized Eastern European nations. Some scholars of clientelism have themselves begun to question the virtue of segregating truly clientelist societies from societies where clientelism is an "addendum." Instead, Simona Piattoni argues that "*politics is inherently particularistic.*" The distinction between clientelist and nonclientelist societies is therefore a difference in "how particular interests are presented, promoted and aggregated." See Eisenstadt and Roniger, "Patron-Client Relations," esp. 48–50, 57–59, 68, 69, 74; Roniger, "Citizenship"; Roniger, "Political Clientelism"; Terry Nichols Clark, "Clientelism, U.S.A."; Martz, *Politics of Clientelism*, 8; Markoff, "Where and When"; Markoff, *Waves of Democracy*, 107; Kitschelt and Wilkinson, *Patrons, Clients, and Policies*; and Piattoni, *Clientelism, Interests*, 3.

7. Over the past fifteen years, a rush of feminist scholarship in Southern history has dramatically altered the field, casting new light upon how power worked in the American South, and exploring the interrelationship between cultural construction and social experience to flesh out the particular ways that people worked within and at times against worlds not of their own making. See, among others, McCurry, *Masters of Small Worlds*; Gilmore, *Gender and Jim Crow*; Dailey, *Before Jim Crow*; Laura Edwards, *People and Their Peace*; Laura Edwards, *Gendered Strife and Confusion*; Kathleen Brown, *Good Wives*; Bryant Simon, *Fabric of Defeat*; and Bercaw, *Gendered Freedoms*.

For political historians, religion is best understood not as ironclad, unthinking belief, nor as a type of ethnocultural division but instead as, in Harry Stout's words, a set of "rhetorical worlds" that provide the symbol systems that help shape public speech. These worlds, as Stout reminds us, are remarkably persistent, and listeners and speakers often draw upon multiple, contradictory rhetorical fields without a sense of contradiction. See Stout, "Rhetoric and Reality"; Creech, *Righteous Indignation*, xix–xxix; Mathews, " 'Christianizing the South'"; Blum, *Reforging the White Republic*; Chappell, *Stone of Hope*; Paul Harvey, *Freedom's Coming*; Foster, *Moral Reconstruction*; and Schweiger, *Gospel Working Up*.

Recent work in legal history has aimed to reconstruct the social experience of the law in the aftermath of the radical decentralization of the Revolutionary era. Rather than rely upon narratives constructed by and about legal modernizers on state supreme courts, scholars have explored the day-to-day use of law to understand the most common encounters of early national Americans and their state. See, especially, Kramer, *People Themselves*; Laura Edwards, "Status without Rights"; Laura Edwards, *People and Their Peace*; Tomlins, *Law, Labor, and Ideology*; Penningroth, *Claims of Kinfolk*; Gross, "Beyond Black and White"; and Gross, *Double Character*.

8. Even Eric Foner, probably the greatest nineteenth-century historian of our era, twice describes freedpeople's pleas for "protection" and "care" from Southern governors as examples of "political inexperience." In fact, experienced women and men used precisely the same language. Instead of a trajectory of naive people learning modern practices, the political culture was much more fluid, creative, and complex. No one has more persuasively balanced the interactions between high politics, social organization, and cultural change than Foner; nevertheless, even he finds himself flummoxed by the intervention of the intimate into the political realm in the post–Civil War era. See Eric Foner, *Forever Free*, 170; Eric Foner, *Reconstruction*, 194; and Escott, *Many Excellent People*, 55.

Edmund S. Morgan and Anthony E. Kaye both take the personalism of power seriously, but both end up reinforcing the centrality of the consensus story of American citizenship by putting an unnatural expiration date upon imaginative subjecthood. Morgan, far more than any other historian of the early national period, describes the transition from subjecthood to citizenship as complex and agonizing. Kaye's fine study of slave political beliefs argues convincingly that slaves utilized notions of "personality of power" to understand their relationship to their masters and the American state. By failing to address political beliefs among their white neighbors, however, Kaye presumes a segregation of ideas that did not exist on the ground. Despite their creative interventions in American political history, these scholars end up handling subjecthood not as a live aspect of American political culture but as an anomaly. The study of the "personality of power" grows from scholarship on the imagined relationship between European monarchs and subjects, particularly in Bendix, *Kings or People*; Kantorowicz, *King's Two Bodies*; Taussig, *Magic of the State*; Morgan, *Inventing the People*; and Kaye, *Joining Places*.

On scholarly treatment of, and discomfort with, dependence, and the related problem of giving agency to our subjects, see Walter Johnson, "Nettlesome Classic"; Walter Johnson, "On Agency"; Reed, *Class Notes*; Sandage, *Born Losers*; Steinberg, *Turning Back*, esp. 137–55; Fineman, *Autonomy Myth*; Fraser and Gordon, "Genealogy of Dependence," 309–10, 330–31; Zundel, *Declarations of Dependency*; and Chad Alan Goldberg, *Citizens and Paupers*.

The most-powerful claims of Southern distinctiveness have emerged from the work of scholars inspired by Eugene D. Genovese's study of slavery, paternalism, and the development of an indigenous conservative tradition in the South. For the most-stimulating examples of this, see Genovese, *Roll, Jordan, Roll*; Genovese, *Political Economy of Slavery*; Genovese, *World the Slaveholders Made*; Genovese, *Southern Tradition*; Fox-Genovese and Genovese, *Mind of the Master Class*; Wyatt-Brown, *Southern Honor*; and Wyatt-Brown, *Shaping of Southern Culture*.

For a strong critique of the tendency to read Southern history as distinct from American history, see Laura Edwards, "Southern History as U.S. History."

9. Williamson Buck to Tod R. Caldwell, Dec. 28, 1872, GP 233, Caldwell Papers, NCDAH; Marriage License, Williamson Buck and Harriet Weeden, Nov. 27, 1872, Alamance County, Certificates of Marriages, 1868–83, vol. 1, C.001.62002, NCDAH. On the redefinition of Southern marriage, see McCurry, *Masters of Small Worlds*; Laura Edwards, *Gendered Strife and Confusion*; Bardaglio, *Reconstructing the Household*; Bynum, *Unruly Women*; and Hodes, *White Women, Black Men*.

10. Escott, *Many Excellent People*, 3–19; Guion Griffis Johnson, *Ante-Bellum North Carolina*, 52–63; Bolton, *Poor Whites of the Antebellum South*, 11–41; Kennedy, *Population of the United States*, 358–59. Eugene Genovese most famously advanced the notion of slave owners' paternalism in Genovese, *Roll, Jordan, Roll*. With further study of industrial paternalism, it is unclear how specific this concept was to slavery, or to the American South. Although many scholars doubt the extent to which paternalism defined the practice of Southern slave owners, its ubiquity as a language of power was meaningful even if it was often observed in the breach. See, especially, Oakes, *Ruling Race*.

11. Wood, *Creation of the American Republic*, 179; Keyssar, *Right to Vote*, 29, 35, 61; Wilentz, *Chants Democratic*, 66–68, 102, 152, 393; Eric Foner, *Free Soil*, xx, xxv, 23, 299; Oakes, "Radical Liberals," 503–11; Stanton, Anthony, and Gage, *History of Woman Suffrage*, 6:808–9; McMillen, *Seneca Falls*, 80–89; Isenberg, *Sex and Citizenship*, 131; Ginzberg, *Untidy Origins*; Ellen Carol DuBois, *Woman Suffrage*, 83–87; Douglass, *My Bondage*, 45, 247. For feminist scholarship on the construction of independence within dependence, see, especially, Pateman, *Sexual Contract*; Kerber, *No Constitutional Right*; and Gordon, *Pitied but Not Entitled*.

12. Sheldon Wolin's disconcerting reinterpretation of Tocqueville suggests that the French aristocrat's admiration for American politics grew not from its dissociation from feudalism — as Louis Hartz famously argued — but rather from the "feudal present" he found in "decentered corporativism," an "aristocracy of the bench and bar," and "local distinctions of rank, achievement and value." De Tocqueville, *Democracy in America*, 1:295–306, 2:786; Wolin, *Tocqueville between Two Worlds*, 231–34; Wolin,

Presence of the Past, 79–80; Wendy Brown, *States of Injury*; Cruikshank, *Will to Empower*; Holland, *Body Politic*; and Orren, *Belated Feudalism*.

While Adams's proclamations remain controversial, scholars of all persuasions have ruefully come to recognize the truth of one of Adams's other comments to Taylor: "Mankind do not love to read any thing upon any theory of government," he wrote. "Very few read any thing but libels. Theoretical books upon government will not sell." See Diggins, *Portable John Adams*, 41, 415–20, 427, 436, 447; and Taylor, *Inquiry into the Principles*, 31, 37–38.

Darren Staloff reminded me of the importance of the Adams-Taylor correspondence, for which I am grateful. See Staloff, *Hamilton, Adams*, 132–233; Adam L. Tate, *Conservatism and Southern Intellectuals*; and Hutson, "John Adams' Title Campaign."

13. Abstract arguments about whether individual acts of defiance, like spitting in the French fries at a McDonald's, count as political have obscured the way the boundaries of politics are made and remade in each context. Without careful attention to the particular formulation of the private/public divide, it is far too easy for some to romantically expand politics to include everything, thus making politics meaningless, or other skeptics to exclude almost everything from politics, reducing it to narrowness and near-irrelevance.

For the purposes of this book, however, the question is much simpler, and its simplicity exposes the rigidity and complacence of defining politics so narrowly as to exclude these pleas. These are, after all, appeals to the state for action on behalf of one of its citizens. To define politics so narrowly as to exclude direct pleas to the government is to make politics either a debating society or a knife fight, a place for arguing about abstractions or a war zone for the winning of elections. For a nuanced account of the difficulty of separating the political from the personal during this era, see Hahn, *Nation under Our Feet*, 3–4. Also see James C. Scott, *Domination and the Arts of Resistance*. Works that have helped expand politics beyond campaigns and legislative acts include Guha, *Elementary Aspects*; Kelley, *Race Rebels*; Portelli, "History-Telling and Time"; Berlant, *Anatomy of National Fantasy*; Berlant, *Queen of America*; Amin, *Event, Metaphor, Memory*; and Hahn, "Extravagant Expectations."

The line between the political and personal was transformed by the revolutionary nature of the Civil War. On the revolutionary aspects of the Confederate experience, see, especially, McCurry, *Confederate Reckoning*; Faust, *Creation of Confederate Nationalism*; Faust, *Mothers of Invention*; Rable, *Civil Wars*; Thomas, *Confederacy as Revolutionary Experience*; Emory M. Thomas, *Confederate Nation*; and Bensel, *Yankee Leviathan*. For efforts to conceptualize Reconstruction as an occupation, see Ayers, *What Caused the Civil War?*, 145–66; Bradley, *Bluecoats and Tarheels*; and Sefton, *United States Army and Reconstruction*.

14. For a national view of Reconstruction, see, especially, Eric Foner, *Reconstruction*; and Heather Cox Richardson, *West from Appomattox*.

15. Scholars have long argued about the functional nature of urban bossism and

about the degree to which city machines distributed goods to their constituents. Despite disagreements over the relationship between bossism and urban liberalism, and Peter McCaffery's broad critique of the functional argument, most scholars seem to agree that, to some extent, city bosses distributed needed services and participated, sometimes reluctantly, in the development of an urban liberal pluralism. See Riordan, *Plunkitt of Tammany Hall*, 7, 17, 18, 19; Merton, *Social Theory and Social Structure*, 71–81; McCaffery, *When Bosses Ruled Philadelphia*; Zane L. Miller, *Boss Cox's Cincinnati*; Buenker, *Urban Liberalism*; Bridges, *City in the Republic*; Shefter, *Political Parties and the State*; Shefter, "Emergence of the Political Machine"; Katznelson, *City Trenches*; Ethington, *Public City*; Beckert, *Monied Metropolis*; Oestreicher, "Urban Working-Class Political Behavior"; Wade, *Urban Frontier*; Boyer, *Urban Masses*; Mushkat, *Tammany*; Allswang, *House for All*; Erie, *Rainbow's End*; Schneirov, *Labor and Urban Politics*; and Teaford, *Unheralded Triumph*.

16. For a long time, scholars emphasized the weakness of the nineteenth-century American state. Recently, however, historians and political scientists have argued that the nineteenth-century government was robust, even if on different terms than European states. With its large ownership of land, its considerable intervention into economic development, and its involvement in the resettlement of one race and the enslavement and then emancipation of another, the nineteenth-century state was not nearly as feeble as it seemed to be, or as notions of a Gilded Age laissez-faire suggested. By emphasizing the role of the nineteenth-century state, scholars suggest the possibility of considering Reconstruction as state-building, not solely sectional reconciliation or emancipation, while also serving as a reminder that the state could not make the world it wanted. Although this book approaches the state from a different angle, the popular vision of a powerful, if also eccentric, state suggests that people at the time thought of their government in more interesting, if not systematic, ways than scholars have generally supposed. See, especially, Novak, "Myth of the 'Weak' American State"; Novak, *People's Welfare*; Balogh, *Government out of Sight*; Einhorn, *Property Rules*; John, "Ruling Passions"; and John, *Spreading the News*. On different grounds, Edward Ayers suggests rethinking Reconstruction in light of other global state-building projects in his *What Caused the Civil War?*, 145–66.

In many respects, the persistence of the Gilded Age trope suggests the way Reconstruction is classed as regional, not national, history. For more than a century, Southern historians of various stripes have argued for the continuity between Reconstruction and the so-called Gilded Age. Long ago, William A. Dunning called Reconstruction "a huge social and political revolution" that lasted until the 1890s. Arguing from a radically different view of that revolution, most modern scholars do treat Reconstruction as, in the words of Heather Cox Richardson, "a process, not a time period. . . . When—or if—the nation was reconstructed into a unified nation on principles of freedom and equality remains an open question." Especially after the emergence of gender-inspired studies of postbellum politics, "redemption as an end-point seems less natural," Michael W. Fitzgerald wrote. More and more historians have extended the life of Reconstruction—or of the problems it posed—to the 1880s defeat of the Knights of Labor (like Laura Edwards), 1890s disfranchisement (like Steven Hahn), the 1898 Spanish-American War (like Edward J. Blum), or the 1910s half-centennial of the Civil War and the beginning of World War I (like David W. Blight.) For a few of the many efforts to redefine the duration of Reconstruction, see Dunning, *Essays on the Civil War*, 250, 353; Heather Cox Richardson, "North and West," 90; Fitzgerald, "Reconstruction Politics," 104; Laura Edwards, *Gendered Strife and Confusion*; Hahn, *Political Worlds*; Foster, *Moral Reconstruction*; Rauchway, *Blessed among Nations*; Dailey, *Before Jim Crow*; Blum, *Reforging the White Republic*; and Blight, *Race and Reunion*.

17. Keyssar, *Right to Vote*, 117–71.

Chapter One

1. Watford, *Civil War*, 10–11; Potter, *Impending Crisis*, 490; Sitterson, *Secession Movement*, 218.

2. Freehling, *Road to Disunion: Southerners at Bay*; Freehling, *Road to Disunion: Secessionists Triumphant*; McPherson, *Battle Cry of Freedom*; Ashworth, *Slavery, Capitalism, and Politics*.

3. Depending on how one dates secession, some scholars cite Tennessee as the last state to secede.

4. By contrast Paul Escott treats these appeals as simple "grievances" about "suffering" and "injustices," in which "always their needs were the same" (Escott, *Many Excellent People*, 55).

5. Walter Clark, *Histories of the Several Regiments*, 417–18.

6. Berlin et al., *Destruction of Slavery*, 59–68.

7. Ibid., 59–60, 64, 65, 68, 81, 89; Singleton, *Recollections*, 8; Parker, *Recollections*, 85–89.

8. Memory Mitchell, *Legal Aspects*, 16; Hilderman, *They Went into the Fight*, 19–62, 77–132; Albert Burton Moore, *Conscription and Conflict*, 12–82.

9. Memory Mitchell, *Legal Aspects*, 16; Hilderman, *They Went into the Fight*, 19–62, 77–132.

10. Prewar slave control taught Southern whites the necessity of depending upon others for help in controlling "everyone else's" slaves, as historian Stephen Ash suggests, and reinforced what William Freehling refers to as the "effective deterrence *between* as well as inside masters' private realms." See Rawick, *American Slave*, 10 (A) 149; 14 (A) 25–26, 171; 15 (A) 53; 17 (A) 101; Parker, *Recollections*, 85–89; Berlin et al., *Destruction of Slavery*, 89; Finkelman, *Dred Scott*, 216; Ash, *When the Yankees Came*, 166–67; and Freehling, *South vs. the South*, 28.

11. N. P. Pope to Vance, Nov. 29, 1864, GP 182, Vance Papers, NCDAH; Berlin et

al., *Destruction of Slavery*, 94–95, 720–21, 806–7; Celia A. Taylor to Vance, Nov. 10, 1863, GP 171, Vance Papers, NCDAH.

12. Poteat, " 'Modest Estimate.' "

13. Jas. W. Wilson to Kemp Battle, Dec. 8, 1896, box 7, folder 107, Battle Family Papers #3223, SHC; John K. Ruffin to Battle, Dec. 7, 1896, box 7, folder 107, Battle Family Papers, SHC; McKinney, *Zeb Vance*, 5–30, 110–230; Yates, "Zebulon B. Vance," 46–48; William C. Harris, *William Woods Holden*, 116–20; Dowd, *Life of Zebulon Vance*, 22.

14. Vance to Brig. Gen. G. J. Rains, Mar. 31, 1863, GLB 50.1, Vance Papers, NCDAH; Vance to Jefferson Davis, Mar. 31, 1863, GLB 50.1, Vance Papers, NCDAH; Mobley, *Papers of Zebulon Vance*, 34, 40, 41, 56–57, 91; Escott, *Many Excellent People*, 39.

15. Mobley, *Papers of Zebulon Vance*, 34, 40, 41, 56–57, 91; Hodges to Vance, Sept. 29, 1863, GP 169, Vance Papers, NCDAH; O. McMath to Vance, n.d. [1864], reel 4, *Papers of Zebulon Vance*; Dowd, *Life of Zebulon Vance*, 70; Vance to Weldon N. Edwards, Sept. 18, 1862, GLB 50.1, Vance Papers, NCDAH; Mrs. A. M. A. Gay et al. to Vance, Aug. 8, 1863, GP 168, Vance Papers, NCDAH; Elizabeth Y. Garrison et al. to Vance, May 20, 1863, GP 167, Vance Papers, NCDAH.

16. Nathan Bagley et al. to Vance, Nov. 19, 1863, GP 171, Vance Papers, NCDAH.

17. Escott, *Many Excellent People*, 54.

18. Sarah L. Johnston to Vance, Oct. 11, 1864, GP 181, Vance Papers, NCDAH; Vance to Weldon N. Edwards, Sept. 18, 1862, GLB 50.1, Vance Papers, NCDAH; McCurry, "Women Numerous and Armed"; Escott, *Many Excellent People*, 53–58; R. D. W. Connor, *North Carolina*, 223.

19. Mary F. Andrews to Vance, n.d., GP 184, Vance Papers, NCDAH; Mobley, *Papers of Zebulon Vance*, 28.

20. Mary F. Andrews to Vance, n.d., GP 184, Vance Papers, NCDAH.

21. Sallie C. Crandell to Vance, Nov. 28, 1864, GP 182, Vance Papers, NCDAH; Anabella Davis to Vance, Jan. 11, 1864, GP 173, Vance Papers, NCDAH. See also Martha A. Allen to Vance, May 6, 1863, GP 165, Vance Papers, NCDAH.

22. Michael Brown to Vance, Mar. 18, 1863, GP 163, Vance Papers, NCDAH; Soldiers Wives [Mary C. Moore] to Vance, Mar. 21, 1863, GP 163, NCDAH; J. W. Ellis et al. to Vance, Apr. 13, 1864, GP 176, Vance Papers, NCDAH; J. A. Richardson to Vance, Apr. 8, 1864, GP 176, Vance Papers, NCDAH; Pardon, Apr. 13, 1863, GLB 50.1, Vance Papers, NCDAH; Barrett, *Civil War*, 188; McCurry, "Women Numerous and Armed."

23. Ann E. Hodges to Vance, Sept. 29, 1863, GP 169, Vance Papers, NCDAH; Hebrews 1:8, 1:14, 4:13, 4:16, 6:18, 11:1, 13:24. All biblical quotes are from the King James Version.

24. Frontis W. Johnson, *Papers of Zebulon Vance*, 312–13, 368–71; John L. Johnson and John S. Fullam to Vance, Mar. 16, 1863, GP 163, Vance Papers, NCDAH.

25. *OR*, 1:6:2: 709–10, 4:2: 783–86; Lonn, *Desertion*; Gallagher, *Confederate War*; Rable, *Confederate Republic*, 153–65.

26. Escott, *Many Excellent People*, 44; James W. Stricklen to Vance, Mar. 10, 1863, GP 163, Vance Papers, NCDAH; J. E. Robertson to Vance, Jan. 13, 1864, GP 173, Vance Papers, NCDAH.

27. Mobley, *Papers of Zebulon Vance*, 250–51.

28. Otis Porter to Vance, Mar. 9, 1863, GP 163, Vance Papers, NCDAH; William L. McDonald to Vance, Mar. 6, 1863, GP 163, Vance Papers, NCDAH; 26th Regt. Band to Vance, Sept. 5, 1863, GP 169, Vance Papers, NCDAH.

29. Michael Bollinger to Vance, Mar. 3, 1863, GP 163, Vance Papers, NCDAH; Proclamation, Jan. 26, 1863, GLB 50.1, Vance Papers, NCDAH.

30. John D. Hudson to Vance, Aug. 5, 1863, GP 168, Vance Papers, NCDAH; T. C. Parks to Vance, Jan. 8, 1864, GP 173, Vance Papers, NCDAH; Thomas A. Nicholson to Vance, Jan. 23, 1864, GP 173, Vance Papers, NCDAH; Mary E. Shearin to Vance, Apr. 24, 1864, GP 176, Vance Papers, NCDAH. See also P. J. Sinclair to Vance, Aug. 17, 1864, GP 179, Vance Papers, NCDAH.

31. Daniel Locklar to Vance, July 28, 1863, GP 167, Vance Papers, NCDAH.

32. Romans 12:15–16.

33. Eliza A. Thomas to Vance, Oct. 25, 1864, GP 181, Vance Papers, NCDAH; P. J. Sinclair to Vance, Aug. 17, 1864, GP 179, Vance Papers, NCDAH. See also Anabella Davis to Vance, Jan. 11, 1864, GP 173, Vance Papers, NCDAH.

34. Mobley, *Papers of Zebulon Vance*, 3.

35. Petition, Nancy Daken, Nov. 28, 1862, D-649 (1862), reel 44, Letters Received, Records of the Office of the Secretary of War, M437, RG 109, NA; Kathy Doughtry to the Secretary of War, Sept. 15, 1862, D-502 (1862), reel 44, Letters Received, Records of the Office of the Secretary of War, M437, RG 109, NA; Petition, E. R. Duncan et al., Nov. 8, 1862, D-656 (1862), reel 44, Letters Received, Records of the Office of the Secretary of War, M437, RG 109, NA; R. F. Simonton et al. to James Seddon, July 9, 1863, D-627 (1863), reel 63, Letters Received, Records of the Adjutant and Inspector General's Department, M474, RG 109, NA; Petition, Joel James et al., July 17, 1863, B-537 (1863), reel 83, Letters Received, Records of the Office of the Secretary of War, M437, RG 109, NA.

36. Vance to Jefferson Davis, Feb. 9, 1864, GLB 50.1, Vance Papers, NCDAH; Davis to Vance, Feb. 29, 1864, GLB 50.1, Vance Papers, NCDAH; Vance to Davis, Mar. 9, 1864, GLB 50.1, Vance Papers, NCDAH; Davis to Vance, Mar. 31, 1864, GLB 50.1, Vance Papers, NCDAH.

37. Johnson Boner to Vance, Mar. 2, 1864, GP 175, Vance Papers, NCDAH; Mrs. Sarah A. Barden to Vance, Mar. 15, 1864, GP 175, Vance Papers, NCDAH; L. N. Durham to Vance, Mar. 7, 1864, GP 175, Vance Papers, NCDAH; Durham to Vance, Mar. 25, 1864, GP 175, Vance Papers, NCDAH; Joseph Cline to Vance, Sept. 8,

1864, GP 180, Vance Papers, NCDAH; S. R. Hanly to Vance, Sept. 8, 1864, GP 180, Vance Papers, NCDAH; Evey S. Jackson to Vance, June 5, 1864, GP 178, Vance Papers, NCDAH.

38. James Carroway et al. to W. F. Martin, June 12, 1863, B-1350 (1863), reel 58, Letters Received, Records of the Adjutant and Inspector General's Department, M474, RG 109, NA; Allsmand A. McKey et al. to Jefferson Davis, Jan. 14, 1864, T-73 (1864), reel 146, Letters Received, Records of the Adjutant and Inspector General's Department, M474, RG 109, NA; Mrs. Charles H. Howcott to Davis, Oct. 6, 1863, H-1821 (1863), box 45, Letters Received, Records of the Adjutant and Inspector General's Department, RG 109, NA [FSSP F-295]; J. J. Bowman to Davis, Sept. 17, 1863, B-686 (1863), reel 83, Letters Received, Records of the Office of the Secretary of War, M437, RG 109, NA; Hayden Alexander to the Secretary of War, July 7, 1863, B-1665 (1863), reel 58, Letters Received, Records of the Adjutant and Inspector General's Department, M474, RG 109, NA.

39. M. S. Wiggins to Vance, Jan. 4, 1864, GP 173, Vance Papers, NCDAH; Wiggins to Vance, Jan. 1, 1865, GP 183, Vance Papers, NCDAH; N.C. Soldiers of Lee's Army to Vance, Jan. 24, 1865, GP 183, Vance Papers, NCDAH.

40. J. Felton to Vance, Feb. 10, 1865, GP 183, Vance Papers, NCDAH; Mary A. Windsor to Vance, Feb. 1, 1865, GP 183, Vance Papers, NCDAH; Psalms 25:6, 16–17, 22; 40:11, 13, 17; 69:16.

41. Anonymous to Vance, Jan. 10, 1865, GP 183, Vance Papers, NCDAH.

42. C. D. Smith to Vance, Jan. 20, 1865, reel 4, *Papers of Zebulon Vance*.

43. Cornelia Spencer to Andrew Johnson, Nov. 9, 1865, reel 4, *Papers of Zebulon Vance*.

Chapter Two

1. "From Miss Ella Roper," *American Missionary* 9 (July 1865): 157–58, available at <www.roanokefreedmenscolony.com/let13.pdf>; Rawick, *American Slave*, 15 (A) 60; Click, *Time Full of Trial*; Horace James, *Annual Report*, 59.

2. Horace James, *Annual Report*, 44–45.

3. Along with the exemplary volumes produced by the Freedmen and Southern Society Project at the University of Maryland, the most formidable works that explore emancipation as a collision of labor ideologies include Foner, *Reconstruction*; Hahn, *Nation under Our Feet*; Montgomery, *Citizen Worker*; Lawrence Powell, *New Masters*; Willie Lee Rose, *Rehearsal for Reconstruction*; Saville, *Work of Reconstruction*; O'Donovan, *Becoming Free*; Glymph, *Out of the House of Bondage*; Heather Cox Richardson, *Death of Reconstruction*; Fields, *Slavery and Freedom*; Magdol, *Right to the Land*; Penningroth, *Claims of Kinfolk*; and Kaye, *Joining Places*.

4. Stansell, *City of Women*, 35; Keyssar, *Right to Vote*, 61–63; Stanley, *From Bondage to Contract*, 101, 104, 108, 113–14; Isenberg, *Sex and Citizenship*; Ginzberg, *Women*

and the Work; Kerber, *No Constitutional Right*; Fraser and Gordon, "Genealogy of Dependence".

5. Fox-Genovese, *Within the Plantation Household*; McCurry, *Masters of Small Worlds*; Shammas, *History of Household Government*; Bardaglio, *Reconstructing the Household*; Laura Edwards, *Gendered Strife and Confusion*; Mary P. Ryan, *Cradle of the Middle Class*.

6. Pierce, "Contrabands of Fortress Monroe," 627; *Correspondence of Gen. Benjamin F. Butler*, 105–19, 165, 183–87, 215–16.

7. Pierce, "Contrabands of Fortress Monroe," 628, 635–37; *Correspondence of Gen. Benjamin F. Butler*, 105–19, 165, 183–87, 215–6.

8. *Correspondence of Gen. Benjamin F. Butler*, 105–19, 165, 183–87, 215–6.

9. Pierce, "Contrabands of Fortress Monroe," 628–29, 635–37; Quarles, *Lincoln and the Negro*, 77; Randall, *Confiscation of Property*, 11–12.

10. Pierce, "Contrabands of Fortress Monroe," 632–35, 640; *Correspondence of Gen. Benjamin F. Butler*, 105–19, 165, 183–87, 215–16; Willie Lee Rose, *Rehearsal for Reconstruction*, 21–48, 152–54.

11. *Correspondence of Gen. Benjamin F. Butler*, 105–19, 165, 183–87, 215–16; Engs, *Freedom's First Generation*, 16–20; Pierce, "Contrabands of Fortress Monroe," 632–35, 640.

12. Berlin et al., *Destruction of Slavery*, 89–90.

13. Singleton, *Recollections*, 1, 2, 5; Ferebee, *Brief History*, 8.

14. Singleton, *Recollections*, 1–8.

15. Parker, *Recollections*, 78–90.

16. Rawick, *American Slave*, 14 (A) 80–81, 268; 15 (A) 347, 428.

17. Colyer, *Report*, 34.

18. Rawick, *American Slave*, 15 (A) 201, 311; 9 (A), 362–63.

19. Ibid., 14 (A) 25–26, 171; 17 (A) 101; Ash, *When the Yankees Came*.

20. Click, *Time Full of Trial*, 10–11, 20–21, 25, 32–33, 35, 37; Colyer, *Report*; "Letter from Chaplain James," *The Congregationalist* 15 (Sept. 18, 1863): 149, available at <http://www.freedmenscolony.com/james5.pdf>; "Letter, Horace James to the Public," June 27, 1863, Letters Received, Department of North Carolina, RG 393, pt. 1, ser. 3238, box 2, NA, available at <http://www.roanokefreedmenscolony.com/james27.pdf>.

21. Berlin et al., *Destruction of Slavery*, 80–81, 86, 88; Berlin et al., *Wartime Genesis of Free Labor: The Upper South*, 122–26, 183–85; Colyer, *Report*, 31, 44–52; Mobley, *James City*, 9–16, 23–31, 39–40, 56–58.

22. Colyer, *Report*, 3, 9–10, 31, 34, 35, 63; Colyer, "Notes"; Click, *Time Full of Trial*, 35–41, 45, 52–55.

23. Berlin et al., *Destruction of Slavery*, 80–81, 83–86, 88; Berlin et al., *Wartime Genesis of Free Labor: The Upper South*, 122–26, 183–85; Colyer, *Report*, 31, 44–53; Mobley, *James City*, 9–16, 23–31, 39–40, 56–58.

24. Singleton, *Recollections*, 1–8; Berlin, Reidy, and Rowland, *Black Military Experience*, 12, 113–15, 127, 128, 134.

25. Berlin, Reidy, and Rowland, *Black Military Experience*, 12, 113–15, 127–28, 132–34; Berlin et al., *Wartime Genesis of Free Labor: The Upper South*, 170; Reid, *Freedom for Themselves*, 11–13, 52; William C. Harris, *"In the Country,"* 174.

26. Berlin et al., *Wartime Genesis of Free Labor: The Upper South*, 20, 135–37.

27. Ibid., 347–48, 493–94, 670–71; Elijah W. Ives to Col. McChesney, Aug. 21, 1863, 1st N.C. Infantry, box 3451, Regimental Books and Papers, RG 94, NA [FSSP OO-9]; J. H. Murphy and James Hardy to Edwin Stanton, Aug. 21, 1865, box 136, M-569, ser. 360, Colored Troops Division, RG 94, NA [FSSP B-270]; John Cook to Secretary of War, Aug. 14, 1866, box 136, C-613 1865, Letters Received, ser. 360, Colored Troops Division, RG 94, NA [FSSP B-223].

28. Berlin et al., *Destruction of Slavery*, 92, 97–98.

29. Berlin et al., *Wartime Genesis of Free Labor: The Upper South*, 104, 198–200; Horace James, *Annual Report*, 3–5, 7, 39–43; David Heaton to Hon. S. P. Chase, May 31, 1864, H-64 (1864), Letters Received by the Division, ser. 315, Division of Captured Property, Claims, and Land, RG 56, NA [FSSP X-74]; Heaton to Chase, Apr. 19, 1864, H-35 (1864), Letters Received by the Division, ser. 315, Division of Captured Property, Claims, and Land, RG 56, NA [FSSP X-52]; Colyer, *Report*, 44–52; Alexander, *North Carolina Faces the Freedmen*, 161; "Letter, Horace James to the Public," June 27, 1863, Letters Received, Department of North Carolina, RG 393, pt. 1, ser. 3238, box 2, NA, available at <http://www.roanokefreedmenscolony.com/james27.pdf>; "Letter from Miss E. James," *American Missionary* 8 (Feb. 1864): 39–40, available at <http://www.roanokefreedmenscolony.com/let1.pdf>.

30. Click, *Time Full of Trial*, 65, 91–92, 94–95; Berlin et al., *Wartime Genesis of Free Labor: The Upper South*, 200; Reid, *Freedom for Themselves*, 155; "Letter from Miss E. James," *American Missionary* 8 (Feb. 1864): 39–40, available at <http://www.roanokefreedmenscolony.com/let1.pdf>; "From E. James," *American Missionary* 8 (June 1864): 140–41, available at <http://www.roanokefreedmenscolony.com/let2.pdf>; "Letter from Mrs. S. P. Freeman," *The Freedmen's Advocate* 1 (Oct. 1864): 34, available at <http://www.roanokefreedmenscolony.com/let4.pdf>.

31. Horace James, *Our Duties to the Slave*, 1; Horace James, *Annual Report*, 9, 33; "Letter from Chaplain James," *The Congregationalist* 15 (Sept. 18, 1863): 149, available at <http://www.roanokefreedmenscolony.com/james5.pdf>; Click, *Time Full of Trial*, 61, 95, 99, 101, 125, 127, 130–31, 134, 148; Reid, *Freedom for Themselves*, 243–44; Horace James, *Annual Report*, 32.

32. Click, *Time Full of Trial*, 61, 95, 99, 101, 125, 127, 130–31, 134, 148; Horace James, *Annual Report*, 32; "Letter from Miss E. James," *American Missionary* 8 (Feb. 1864): 39–40, available at <http://www.roanokefreedmenscolony.com/let1.pdf>; "From E. James," *American Missionary* 8 (June 1864): 140–41, available at

<http://www.roanokefreedmenscolony.com/let2.pdf>; "A Letter to be Read and Circulated, in Public and Private Meeting, in aid of the Freedmen," *The Freedmen's Advocate* 1 (Nov. 1864): 38, available at <http://www.roanokefreedmenscolony.com/let5.pdf>; "Letter from Mrs. S. P. Freeman," *The Freedmen's Advocate* 1 (Oct. 1864): 34, available at <http://www.roanokefreedmenscolony.com/let4.pdf>.

33. Berlin et al., *Wartime Genesis of Free Labor: The Upper South*, 104, 198–200; Horace James, *Annual Report*, 3–5, 7, 39–43; Report, Edward A. Wild, Dec. 28, 1863, enclosed in Benjamin F. Butler to E. M. Stanton, Dec. 31, 1863, B-06 (1864), Letters Received, box 299 (123), RG 107, NA [FSSP L-39]; David Heaton to Hon. S. P. Chase, May 31, 1864, H-64 (1864), Letters Received by the Division, ser. 315, Division of Captured Property, Claims, and Land, RG 56, NA [FSSP X-74]; Heaton to Chase, Apr. 19, 1864, H-35 (1864), Letters Received by the Division, ser. 315, Division of Captured Property, Claims, and Land, RG 56, NA [FSSP X-52]; Colyer, *Report*, 44–52; Alexander, *North Carolina Faces the Freedmen*, 161.

34. Berlin et al., *Wartime Genesis of Free Labor: The Upper South*, 104, 198–200; Horace James, *Annual Report*, 3–5, 7; David Heaton to Hon. S. P. Chase, May 31, 1864, H-64 (1864), Letters Received by the Division, ser. 315, Division of Captured Property, Claims, and Land, RG 56, NA [FSSP X-74]; Heaton to Chase, Apr. 19, 1864, H-35 (1864), Letters Received by the Division, ser. 315, Division of Captured Property, Claims, and Land, RG 56, NA [FSSP X-52]; Horace James, *Annual Report*, 39–43.

35. Berlin et al., *Wartime Genesis of Free Labor: The Upper South*, 166, 202–3; Horace James to General Butler, July 19, 1864, box 23A, July 1864, Letters and Orders Received, ser. 4108, RG 105, NA [FSSP A-8312].

36. Berlin et al., *Wartime Genesis of Free Labor: The Upper South*, 231–36.

37. Ibid., 231–36.

38. Ibid.

39. Ibid., 76, 231–36; Click, *Time Full of Trial*, 136–49, 184.

40. Berlin et al., *Wartime Genesis of Free Labor: The Upper South*, 183–85; Mobley, *James City*, 9–16, 23–31, 39–40, 56–58; Horace James, *Annual Report*, 57–58; Jacqueline Glass Campbell, *When Sherman Marched North*, 86–92.

41. Berlin et al., *Wartime Genesis of Free Labor: The Upper South*, 727–30; "Industrial School, Roanoke Island," *The National Freedmen* 1 (Dec. 15, 1865): 347–48, available at <http://www.roanokefreedmenscolony.com/let18.pdf>; "Roanoke Island," *The National Freedman* 1 (Jan. 15, 1866): 13–14, available at <http://www.roanokefreedmenscolony.com/let19.pdf>.

42. Rawick, *American Slave*, 15 (A) 121–23, 429. For discussions of the mythic status of Lincoln, see Hahn, "Extravagant Expectations"; Genovese, *Roll, Jordan, Roll*, 115; and Donald, *Lincoln Reconsidered*, 144–66. On naive monarchism, see Field, *Rebels in the Name of the Tsar*.

43. Rawick, *American Slave*, 11 (1) 187–93; 14 (A) 193; Psalms 123:2; Proverbs

27:18; Matthew 6:24, 8:19, 23:8; Colossians 4:1; Berlin et al., *Wartime Genesis of Free Labor: The Upper South*, 798–99; Horace James, *Annual Report*, 45. Anthony Kaye brilliantly analyzes the personality of power among slaves in Mississippi, although he presumes this way of inscribing power onto individuals was peculiar to slaves, rather than part of a broader Southern, or even American, repertoire. See Kaye, *Joining Places*.

44. *Report of the Joint Committee on Reconstruction*, 245; Annie Joyner Gavin, interviewed by Chris Stewart, New Bern, N.C., Aug. 3, 1993, in *From Behind the Veil: Documenting African American Life in the Jim Crow South*, Center for Documentary Studies at Duke University, SCL; Rawick, *American Slave*, 14 (A) 59–60, 415.

45. Rawick, *American Slave*, 15 (A) 160, 427–29; Annie Joyner Gavin, interviewed by Chris Stewart, New Bern, N.C., Aug. 3, 1993, in *From Behind the Veil: Documenting African American Life in the Jim Crow South*, Center for Documentary Studies at Duke University, SCL.

46. Rawick, *American Slave*, 14 (A) 193, 236, 317, 378, 456; 15 (A) 268, 304–5.

Chapter Three

1. Howard, *Report*, 6; *Report of the Joint Committee on Reconstruction*, 187–88; Randall M. Miller, "Introduction," xxix.

2. John Richard Dennett, *South As It Is*, 109–10; Click, *Time Full of Trial*, 164, 184; Alexander, *North Carolina Faces the Freedmen*, 101; McFeely, *Yankee Stepfather*, 81; E. Whittlesey to O. O. Howard, n.d., Quarterly Report Fall 1865, vol. 7, Records of the Assistant Commissioner of the State of North Carolina, ser. 2446, RG 105, NA [FSSP A-747]. George C. Rable, Michael Fellman, and Steven Hahn each define the postwar South in part through the intense nature of everyday violence, especially political violence. Although both Rable and Fellman are highly attuned to the political implications of the violence, they each seek psychological explanations for it. Hahn, building on the antebellum work of John Hope Franklin, finds the South a paramilitary society, and its politics essentially warlike, not because of postwar trauma or affronts to honor, but because of intense and unrestrained competition for power in an overturned world. Recently, Mark W. Summers has recast national Reconstruction as a story of paranoia and fear. Michael W. Fitzgerald captures the problem of military pacification and the role of the bureau in enforcing order. See Rable, *But There Was No Peace*; Fellman, *Inside War*; Summers, *Dangerous Stir*; Hahn, *Nation under Our Feet*; Franklin, *Militant South*; and Fitzgerald, "Emancipation and Military Pacification."

3. James B. Steedman and J. S. Fullerton to E. M. Stanton, May 8, 1866, in *Executive Documents*, 68; Click, *Time Full of Trial*, 144–45; Petition, James Harris et al., Dec. 25, 1867, Letters Received, Records of the Assistant Commissioner of the State of North Carolina, ser. 2452, RG 105, NA [FSSP A-21]; Rable, *But There Was No Peace*.

The finest modern studies of Reconstruction in North Carolina are Laura Edwards, *Gendered Strife and Confusion*; William McKee Evans, *Ballots and Fence Rails*; Raper, *William W. Holden*; Alexander, *North Carolina Faces the Freedmen*; and the relevant sections of Anderson, *Race and Politics*, 3–60; Scott Reynolds Nelson, *Iron Confederacies*, 95–114; Perman, *Reunion without Compromise*; Carter, *When the War Was Over*; and Escott, *Many Excellent People*, 113–70.

4. The history of describing Reconstruction as a revolution dates back to the days of Reconstruction itself, when both supporters and opponents described its transformations in revolutionary terms. In previous generations, William A. Dunning, Charles A. Beard, Barrington Moore, and W. E. B. DuBois each treated the Civil War and Reconstruction as a revolutionary period for different reasons.

Eric Foner's magisterial *Reconstruction* still stands as the most significant and influential version of Reconstruction. Foner, with characteristic care, modifies the notion of a failed revolution by both engaging with its limited but real successes and carefully detailing the forces that prevented it from becoming a complete revolution. More optimistic about the essentially revolutionary nature of Reconstruction, though less complimentary of Radical Republicans, Steven Hahn describes a revolution forced up from below upon a quiescent political establishment. See Eric Foner, *Reconstruction*; Hahn, *Nation under Our Feet*; and Woodward, *Future of the Past*, 183–202.

5. *Report of the Secretary of the Navy*, iii, iv, ix, x, xxxii, xxxiv; Nicolay and Hay, *Abraham Lincoln*, 10:336–7; Melville, *Battle-Pieces*, 88–89.

6. Sefton, *United States Army*, 261; *OR* 3:5:495–520.

7. Skowronek, *Building a New American State*, 50–51; Sharkey, *Money, Class, and Party*; Hormats, *Price of Liberty*, 79–86; Dewey, *Financial History*, 299, 329; Sefton, *United States Army*, 65, 207–8; McKitrick, *Andrew Johnson*, 369–70; Mark R. Wilson, *Business of Civil War*, 202–3. Richard Franklin Bensel credits bonds and the growing power of financial capitalists in New York City for many of the limitations of Reconstruction, arguing that "Union financial policy mortgaged a radical Reconstruction of the South even before the war ended." Bensel's argument is clearer and more fully developed for the 1867–68 heyday of Reconstruction than in its earlier phase. See Bensel, *Yankee Leviathan*, 14, 237.

8. Ferleger, *David A. Wells*, 6; P. S. Evans, *Funeral Elegy*, 5; Dean, *Eulogy*, 9; Brooks D. Simpson, *Ulysses S. Grant*, 391; *Memoirs of General William T. Sherman*, 2:252; Wells, *Theory and Practice of Taxation*, 18–39; Wells, *Our Burden*; *New York Times*, Mar. 19, 1864, p. 6; Dec. 5, 1864, p. 4; Apr. 28, 1865, p. 4; Jan 7, 1865, p. 4.

9. *OR* 1:47:3:243, 302; 3:4:1280; 3:5:1, 65, 509–17; *New York Times*, Apr. 28, 1865, p. 4; Jan. 7, 1865, p. 4; Apr. 30, 1865, p. 4; *Philadelphia Inquirer*, Apr. 14, 1865, p. 4; *Report of the Joint Committee on Reconstruction*, viii.

10. *OR* 1:47:3:206–7, 221, 225, 237, 243–44, 263–64, 301–3, 313; Bradley, *This Astounding Close*, 190–217; Bradley, *Bluecoats and Tar Heels*, 98–99; Brooks D. Simpson, *Let Us Have Peace*, 98–9.

11. Eric Foner, *Reconstruction*, 35–36, 74–76; Beale, *Critical Year*, 57; Welles, *Diary*, 2:279–80; *OR* 1:47:3:461–63; Moores, *Lincoln*, 217–23.

12. Eric Foner, *Reconstruction*, 181–84; James D. Richardson, *Compilation*, 6:310–14; *OR* 1:47:3:529.

13. Brock, *American Crisis*, 42.

14. Richard Dennett, *South As It Is*, 358–60; *Report of the Joint Committee on Reconstruction*, 181, 203, 249, 270.

15. R. A. Jenkins to the President of the United States, May 26, 1865, Items 374–75, vol. 1865, P–Z, Miscellaneous Letters Received: K Series, ser. 103, RG 56, NA [FSSP X-18]; Peter Johnston to Andrew Johnson, Nov. 23, 1865, J-48, box 3, ser. 88, Letters Received, Land Division Headquarters, RG 105, NA [FSSP A-62]; Peter Johnston et al. to Chairman and Members of the U.S. Senate, Dec. 21, 1867, 40A-H21.1, Senate Committee on Public Lands, Petitions, and Memorials, ser. 582, 40th Congress, RG 46, NA [FSSP E-98].

16. Richard Dennett, *South As It Is*, 110–11; Andrews, *South since the War*, 188; *Report of the Joint Committee on Reconstruction*, 175–76, 182, 187–88, 199–202, 270.

17. *Report of the Joint Committee on Reconstruction*, 175–76, 182, 187–88, 270.

18. *Congressional Globe*, Senate, 38th Cong., 2nd sess., 688, 693, 768, 960–61. Over the last decade, scholars have softened earlier critiques of the Freedmen's Bureau. After stinging criticism of bureau tyranny by early pro-Southern scholars and equally stinging denunciation of bureau racism and paternalism by 1960s and 1970s post-revisionists like William McFeely, historians — most prominently Paul A. Cimbala — have recaptured the good intentions and even heroic efforts of some agents and administrators. Although historians continue to be critical of the paternalism of the bureau — especially Carol Faulkner's gendered critique — they seem increasingly sensitive to the limitations imposed upon it. See McFeely, *Yankee Stepfather*; Cimbala, *Under the Guardianship*; Berlin et al., *Wartime Genesis of Free Labor: The Upper South*, 109, 466–67; Eric Foner, *Reconstruction*, 124–75; Bardaglio, *Reconstructing the Household*, 98–104, 124–32, 145–46; Laura Edwards, *Gendered Strife and Confusion*, 1–15, 42–51, 94–104; Faulkner, *Women's Radical Reconstruction*; Crouch, *Freedmen's Bureau*; and Cimbala and Miller, *Freedmen's Bureau*.

19. Gates, *Men of Mark*, 2:394–96; McFeely, *Yankee Stepfather*, 78–83; Howard, *Autobiography*, 298, 353; Alexander, *North Carolina Faces the Freedmen*, 50, 99; Click, *Time Full of Trial*, 148; E. Whittlesey to O. O. Howard, n.d., Quarterly Report Fall 1865, vol. 7, Records of the Assistant Commissioner of the State of North Carolina, ser. 2446, RG 105, NA [FSSP A-747].

20. Click, *Time Full of Trial*, 148, 164, 184, 193–203; Alexander, *North Carolina Faces the Freedmen*, 50, 99, 101; McFeely, *Yankee Stepfather*, 78–83, 250–54; E. Whittlesey to O. O. Howard, n.d., Quarterly Report Fall 1865, vol. 7, Records of the Assistant Commissioner of the State of North Carolina, ser. 2446, RG 105, NA [FSSP A-747]; Howard, *Autobiography*, 298, 353; Gates, *Men of Mark*, 394–96; J. R.

Fleming to Lt. Col. Stephen Moore, Jan. 17, 1868, reel 11, Records of the Assistant Commissioner of the State of North Carolina, RG 105, M843, NA.

21. John C. Barnett to E. Whittlesey, June 29, 1865, box 1, B-3 (1865), Letters Received, Records of the Assistant Commissioner of the State of North Carolina, ser. 2452, RG 105, NA [FSSP A-506]; Barnett to Whittlesey, July 12, 1865, box 1, B-4 (1865), Letters Received, Records of the Assistant Commissioner of the State of North Carolina, ser. 2452, RG 105, NA [FSSP A-507]; Whittlesey to Barnett, July 13, 1865, vol. 1, p. 4, Letters Sent, Records of the Assistant Commissioner of the State of North Carolina, ser. 2446, RG 105, NA [FSSP A-506]; Barnett to Whittlesey, Quarterly Report 1865, box 1, B-6 (1865), Letters Received, Records of the Assistant Commissioner of the State of North Carolina, ser. 2452, RG 105, NA [FSSP A-508].

22. E. Whittlesey to O. O. Howard, n.d., Quarterly Report Fall 1865, vol. 7, Records of the Assistant Commissioner of the State of North Carolina, ser. 2446, RG 105, NA [FSSP A-747]; Whittlesey to Howard, Dec. 8, 1865, N-53 (1865), Letters Received, ser. 15, Washington Headquarters, RG 105, NA [FSSP A-712]; Whittlesey to Howard, Feb. 15, 1866, and n.d., reel 1, Records of the Assistant Commissioner of the State of North Carolina, RG 105, M843, NA; McFeely, *Yankee Stepfather*, 78, 83, 245–53; Howard, *Autobiography*, 279–80; Brooks D. Simpson, "Ulysses S. Grant," 12.

23. Alexander, *North Carolina Faces the Freedmen*, 102–3, 134–35; Berlin et al., *Wartime Genesis of Free Labor: The Upper South*, 801–2.

24. Foner, *Reconstruction* 242–75; McKitrick, *Andrew Johnson*.

25. *New York Times*, Apr. 7, 1896, p. 5.

26. Hugo Hillebrandt to E. Whittlesey, May 13, 1866, reel 7, Records of the Assistant Commissioner of the State of North Carolina, RG 105, M843, NA; Hillebrandt to Clinton A. Cilley, June 29, 1866, Letters Received, reel 7, Records of the Assistant Commissioner of the State of North Carolina, RG 105, M843, NA; Hillebrandt to William H. Wiegel, June 25, 1866, reel 7, Records of the Assistant Commissioner of the State of North Carolina, RG 105, M843, NA.

27. James Thurston to H. Wilson, Jan. 10, 1866, reel 9, Records of the Assistant Commissioner of the State of North Carolina, RG 105, M843, NA.

28. Wm. B. Bowe to E. Whittlesey, Jan. 27, 1866, reel 16, Records of the Assistant Commissioner of the State of North Carolina, RG 105, M843, NA; Allan Rutherford, Report of Cases of Outrages upon Union Men in North Carolina, June 1866, reel 7, Records of the Assistant Commissioner of the State of North Carolina, RG 105, M843, NA.

29. Sefton, *United States Army*, 261.

30. Peter Price to Mr. Freedmans Bureau, Mar. 17, 1868, enclosed in Peter Price to General Nelson A. Miles, Mar. 25, 1868, reel 14, Records of the Assistant Commissioner of the State of North Carolina, RG 105, M843, NA.

31. L. A. Owens et al. to O. O. Howard, Dec. 12, 1867, enclosed in H. Adams to

Howard, Dec. 17, 1867, reel 10, Records of the Assistant Commissioner of the State of North Carolina, RG 105, M843, NA; Simon Handy et al. to Col. Moore, Sept. 6, 1867, Letters Received, Records of the North Carolina Superintendent for the Eastern District, ser. 2755, RG 105, NA [FSSP A-889]; Joe Case et al. to Howard, July 29, 1866, and Samuel Dowdy to S. H. Birdsall, Aug. 1, 1866, enclosed in Birdsall to Howard, Aug. 7, 1866, reel 7, Records of the Assistant Commissioner of the State of North Carolina, RG 105, M843, NA.

32. James Gilom et al. to Freedmen's Bureau, Feb. 10, 1866, enclosed in George Hawley to F. Seeley, Feb. 28, 1866, vol. 162, pp. 41, 52–53, 57–58, 91, Letters Received, Records of the Assistant Commissioner of the State of North Carolina, ser. 2752, RG 105, NA [FSSP A-876]; Nat Parker et al. to the Head Commissioners of the Freedmen's Bureau, Apr. 4, 1866, enclosed in Hawley to Thomas H. Ruger, May 18, 1866, reel 8, Letters Received, Records of the Assistant Commissioner of the State of North Carolina, RG 105, M843, NA; Alexander, *North Carolina Faces the Freedmen*, 114–15.

33. *Executive Documents*, 60, 68, 71; Click, *Time Full of Trial*, 159–60; Mobley, *James City*, 47–61.

34. *Executive Documents*, 60, 68, 71; A. Blunt to O. Howard, Jan. 30, 1868, enclosed in Jas. G. Haniford to Howard, Jan. 31, 1868, reel 13, Records of the Assistant Commissioner of the State of North Carolina, RG 105, M843, NA; Mobley, *James City*, 62–84.

35. Jacob Grimes et al. to O. Howard, Dec. 16, 1868, 40A-F10.5, House Committee on Freedmen's Affairs, Petitions and Memorials, Records of the United States House of Representatives, RG 233, NA [FSSP D-44]; Peirce, *Freedmen's Bureau*, 70–72.

36. Howard, *Report*, 7, 15, 20, 23.

37. Hillebrandt to Jacob Chur, Aug. 8, 1868, enclosed in Chur to William W. Holden, Aug. 1868, GP 219, Holden Papers, NCDAH.

Chapter Four

1. Eric Foner captures the exhilaration and the limitations of the expansion of democratic rights in his monumental survey. As Foner demonstrates, enfranchisement was simultaneously extraordinary and inadequate, a historic transformation and an incomplete method for remaking the South. See Foner, *Reconstruction*, 278.

2. George C. Rable and Michael Fellman give perhaps the best sense of the extraordinary levels of disorder and bloodshed in a world that, even by nineteenth-century standards, appeared to have descended into anarchy. See Rable, *But There Was No Peace*; and Fellman, *Inside War*.

3. On territoriality, see Guha, *Elementary Aspects*, 6–8, 12–13, 170–71, 333–34; and Ludden, *Agrarian History*. Anthony Kaye used the notion of neighborhood to trace

the important imaginative geography of slave politics, but on the whole, American historians have been less adventurous in their handling of territoriality. Many scholars of Progressive North Carolina have described a self-conscious localism, which, while important, is distinct from the territoriality I describe because it is rooted in people's ethical preference for local knowledge. See Kaye, "Neighbourhoods and Solidarity"; William A. Link, *Paradox of Southern Progressivism*; Leloudis, *Schooling the New South*; and Redding, *Making Race*.

4. David Richmond to Holden, Feb. 19, 1869, GP 221, Holden Papers, NCDAH; James Cashwell to Holden, June 24, 1869, GP 222, Holden Papers, NCDAH; Wm. R. Haughton to Holden, Oct. 14, 1868, GP 219, Holden Papers, NCDAH; John A. Williams to Holden, Apr. 26, 1868, P.C. 65.1, Holden Papers (Personal), NCDAH.

5. William C. Harris, *William Woods Holden*, 17, 74–77, 117–20, 138–52, 244; Raper, *William W. Holden*, 3–44, 48–49, 54–56;

6. Holden, *Memoirs*, 49–50; William C. Harris, *William Woods Holden*, 169–75, 211–15; Raper, *William W. Holden*, 90–93.

7. Jonathan Worth to Holden, July 1, 1868, GLB 61, Holden Papers, NCDAH.

8. "Inaugural Address of Gov. W. W. Holden, Delivered July 4th 1868," GLB 61, Holden Papers, NCDAH; Williams C. Harris, *William Woods Holden*, 17, 245.

9. "Inaugural Address of Gov. W. W. Holden, Delivered July 4th 1868," GLB 61, Holden Papers, NCDAH; Holden to Canby, July 4, 16, 1868, GLB 61, Holden Papers; Canby to Holden, July 15, 16, 1868, GLB 61, Holden Papers, NCDAH; E. Fullings to Holden, July 15, 1868, GLB 61, Holden Papers, NCDAH; John Pool to Holden, May 9, 1868, Holden Papers, quoted in William C. Harris, *William Woods Holden*, 248–49.

10. Holden to the General Assembly, July 17, 1868, GLB 61, Holden Papers, NCDAH; William C. Harris, *William Woods Holden*, 248–50; Raper, *William W. Holden*, 107, 162; Sefton, *United States Army*, 262.

11. Holden to the General Assembly, July 17, 1868, GLB 61, Holden Papers, NCDAH; Romans 13:1–3; 1 Peter 2:13–14.

12. John Conklin to Holden, July 20, 1868, GP 218, Holden Papers, NCDAH.

13. David Richmond to Holden, Feb. 19, 1869, GP 221, Holden Papers, NCDAH; John M. Davis to Holden, May 11 1870, GP 224, Holden Papers, NCDAH; Laura Edwards, *People and Their Peace*; Laura Edwards, "Status without Rights"; Laura Edwards, "Enslaved Women and the Law"; Waldrep, *Roots of Disorder*.

14. Holden to Hon. C. R. Thomas, Jan. 4, 1869, GLB 61, Holden Papers, NCDAH; Holden to Mrs. J. H. Moore, Jan. 4, 1869, GLB 61, Holden Papers, NCDAH; Holden to Sheriff of Carteret County, Jan. 4, 1869, GLB 61, Holden Papers, NCDAH; Mrs. H. J. Moore to Holden, Jan. 8, 1869, GLB 61, Holden Papers, NCDAH; O. B. Bidwell to Holden, Jan. 9, 1869, GLB 61, Holden Papers, NCDAH; John Davis to Holden, Jan. 9, 1869, GLB 61, Holden Papers, NCDAH; Thos. Hill to Holden, Jan. 11, 1869,

GLB 61, Holden Papers, NCDAH; Holden to Nelson A. Miles, Jan. 13, 1869, GLB 61, NCDAH; Raper, *William W. Holden*, 441–42.

15. Holden to Col. Geo. A. Williams, July 17, 1868, GLB 61, Holden Papers, NCDAH; Williams to Holden, July 18, 1868, GLB 61, Holden Papers, NCDAH; Edward R. S. Canby to Holden, July 22, 1868, GLB 61, Holden Papers, NCDAH; Holden to the General Assembly, Aug. 4, 1868, GLB 61, Holden Papers, NCDAH; Maj. Genl. George Meade to President Ulysses S. Grant, July 30, 1868, John A. Rawlins to Meade, July 31, 1868, and Rawlins to Maj. Genl. Robert C. Buchanan, Aug. 10, 1868, enclosed in R. C. Drum to Holden, Aug. 21, 1868, GLB 61, Holden Papers, NCDAH.

16. Holden to George Meade, Sept. 14, 1868, GLB 61, Holden Papers, NCDAH; R. C. Drum to Holden, Sept. 15, 1868, GLB 61, Holden Papers, NCDAH; Jacob Chur to Holden, Oct. 5, 1868, GLB 61, Holden Papers, NCDAH.

17. Wm. A. Cutter to Maj. Genl. Nelson A. Miles, Aug. 24, 1868, reel 14, Records of the Assistant Commissioner of the State of North Carolina, RG 105, M843, NA.

18. F. W. Liedtke to Col. Jacob Chur, Sept. 3, 1868, Nov. 15, 1868, reel 14, Records of the Assistant Commissioner of the State of North Carolina, RG 105, M843, NA.

19. Hahn, *Nation under Our Feet*, 176–78; Saville, *Work of Reconstruction*, 162–98; Trelease, *White Terror*; Scott Reynolds Nelson, *Iron Confederacies*; Scott Reynolds Nelson, "Red Strings and Half-Brothers"; Fitzgerald, "Extralegal Violence"; Hayden, "Root of Wrath."

20. Henry W. Paschall to Holden, Aug. 18, 1868, GP 219, Holden Papers, NCDAH; John H. Everitt to Holden, Aug. 5, 1868, GP 219, Holden Papers, NCDAH; Matthew 10:5.

21. "A Proclamation by W. W. Holden," Oct. 12, 1868, GLB 61, Holden Papers, NCDAH; Holden to Miles, Oct. 24, 1868, GLB 61, Holden Papers, NCDAH; Holden to T. A. Byrnes, Oct. 23, 1868, GLB 61, Holden Papers, NCDAH; Holden to the Sheriff of Cumberland County, Oct. 24, 1868, GLB 61, Holden Papers, NCDAH; William C. Harris, *William Woods Holden*, 251; John Y. Simon, *Papers of Ulysses S. Grant*, 19:299.

22. Silas L. Curtis et al. to Holden, Oct. 11, 1868, GP 219, Holden Papers, NCDAH.

23. John W. Hoflen to Holden, Aug. 22, 1868, GP 219, Holden Papers, NCDAH.

24. John Y. Simon, *Papers of Ulysses S. Grant*, 19:62–63, 381.

25. Governor's Message, Nov. 17, 1868, GLB 61, Holden Papers, NCDAH; William C. Harris, *William Woods Holden*, 252.

26. F. W. Liedtke to Col. Jacob F. Chur, Nov. 15, 1868, reel 14, Records of the Assistant Commissioner of the State of North Carolina, RG 105, M843, NA.

27. John F. Davis to Holden, Dec. 20, 1868, GP 220, Holden Papers, NCDAH.

28. U.S. Senate, *Select Committee of the Senate*, lvi–lvii, lxii, 44, 146, 191, 201–2, 259, 342–46; *Testimony Taken by the Joint Committee*, 24, 106–10, 114, 124, 134, 167,

179, 194, 206–11, 308, 367, 470–91, 509–11, 574; D. W. Cummings deposition, Aug. 5, 1870, GP 225, Holden Papers, NCDAH; S. B. Williams to Holden, Sept. 16, 1869, GP 222, Holden Papers, NCDAH; Confession of Joseph N. Wood, n.d. [1870], GP 225, Holden Papers, NCDAH; W. B. Bowe to Holden, Sept. 25, 1870, GP 225, Holden Papers, NCDAH; Statement, Charles Isler, enclosed in Edward W. Hinks to Holden, Feb. 18, 1869, GP 221, Holden Papers, NCDAH; Hahn, *Nation under Our Feet*, 165–68; Trelease, *White Terror*; Scott Reynolds Nelson, *Iron Confederacies*; Fitzgerald, "Extralegal Violence"; Hayden, "Root of Wrath."

29. Ed. W. Hinks to Holden, Feb. 18, 1869, GLB 61, Holden Papers, NCDAH; Charles Isler deposition, enclosed in Hinks to Holden, Feb. 18, 1869, GLB 61, Holden Papers, NCDAH; Holden to Hinks, n.d. [Feb. 1869], GLB 61, Holden Papers, NCDAH; Holden to F. H. Whitney, May 5, 1869, GLB 61, Holden Papers, NCDAH; William C. Harris, *William Woods Holden*, 279–80.

30. William McKee Evans, *To Die Game*, 258–66; Benj. A Howell to Holden, Feb. 11, 1869, GP 221, Holden Papers, NCDAH; Elder George W. Grice et al. to Holden, n.d., GP 225, Holden Papers, NCDAH; Henry H. Sampson et al. to Genl. O. O. Howard, Nov. 27, 1868, reel 15, Records of the Assistant Commissioner of the State of North Carolina, RG 105, M843, NA; Patrick Lawsin et al. to Lt. Genl. Nelson Miles, enclosed in Allan Rutherford to Lt. Col. Jacob Chur, Jan. 13, 1868, reel 11, Records of the Assistant Commissioner of the State of North Carolina, RG 105, M843, NA; U.S. Senate, *Select Committee of the Senate*, 284–86, 295; *Testimony Taken by the Joint Committee*, 253, 305–6.

31. A. L. Ramsour to Holden, July 5, 1869, GP 220, Holden Papers, NCDAH; Ramsour to Holden, Nov. 23, 1869, GP 223, Holden Papers, NCDAH.

32. David L. May to Holden, Apr. 22, 1869, GP 221, Holden Papers, NCDAH; Psalm 68:5.

33. Sarah Mabury to Holden, July 15, 1869, GP 222, Holden Papers, NCDAH.

34. Mabury was hardly unique in using Elliott's phrase for her own purposes; no less a figure than William James praised one of his distant collaborators as a "friend unseen" in *Varieties of Religious Experience*. Billy Graham, among many others, would later write that "Just as I Am" was the song that led him to declare himself a Christian. See Sarah Mabury to Holden, July 15, 1869, GP 222, Holden Papers, NCDAH; Bonar, *Bible Hymn-Book*, 134; William James, *Varieties of Religious Experience*, xvi; Elliott, *Hours of Sorrow*, 176–77; and Graham, *Just as I Am*, 29.

35. Sally McDowell to Holden, Nov. 28, 1869, GP 223, Holden Papers, NCDAH; Mrs. Jane W. Wilkins to Holden, July 8, 1869, GP 222, Holden Papers, NCDAH; Jane McAlpin to Holden, Sept. 21, 1868, GP 219, Holden Papers, NCDAH.

36. To the Honorable The General Assembly, Mar. 4, 1869, GLB 61, Holden Papers, NCDAH; Proclamation, Apr. 16, 1869, GLB 61, Holden Papers, NCDAH; Holden to L. S. Gash, Feb. 9, 1869, GLB 61, Holden Papers, NCDAH; Holden to Sheriff of Robeson County, Nov. 30, 1868, GLB 61, Holden Papers, NCDAH;

Holden to Secretary of War, Apr. 24, 1869, GLB 61, Holden Papers, NCDAH; Holden to Genl. Belknap, Nov. 23, 1869, GLB 61, Holden Papers, NCDAH; Proclamation, Oct. 20, 1869, GLB 61, Holden Papers, NCDAH; Governor's Message, Nov. 16, 1869, GLB 61, Holden Papers, NCDAH; To the Honorable General Assembly, Dec. 16, 1869, GLB 61, Holden Papers, NCDAH; Holden to G. J. Williams, Jan. 31, 1870, GLB 61, Holden Papers, NCDAH; Williams to Holden, Feb. 8, 1870, GLB 61, Holden Papers, NCDAH; Wm. A. Walton to Holden, Feb. 4, 1870, GLB 61, Holden Papers, NCDAH; Holden to Tod Caldwell, Feb. 23, 1870, GLB 61, Holden Papers, NCDAH; Instructions to Detectives, Apr. 3, 1869, GLB 61, Holden Papers, NCDAH; Raper, *William W. Holden*, 159, 163; William C. Harris, *William Woods Holden*, 283.

37. U.S. Senate, *Select Committee of the Senate*, 144–50; Holden to Maj. Genl. A. H. Terry, Dec. 3, 1869, GLB 61, Holden Papers, NCDAH; H. A. Badham et al. to Holden, Feb. 28, 1870, GLB 61, Holden Papers, NCDAH; Proclamation, Mar. 7, 1870, GLB 61, Holden Papers, NCDAH; Holden to the President of the United States, Mar. 10, 1870, GLB 61, Holden Papers, NCDAH; Raper, *William W. Holden*, 161, 174; William C. Harris, *William Woods Holden*, 280–81, 284; Scott Reynolds Nelson, "Red Strings and Half-Brothers."

38. J. W. Norwood et al. to Holden, Mar. 5, 1870, GLB 61, Holden Papers, NCDAH; Pride Jones to Holden, Mar. 4, 9, 1870, GLB 61, Holden Papers, NCDAH; Holden to Jones, Mar. 7, 17, 1870, GLB 61, Holden Papers, NCDAH; Raper, *William W. Holden*, 163.

39. Proclamation, May 25, 1870, GLB 61, Holden Papers, NCDAH; Proclamation, June 6, 1870, GLB 61, Holden Papers, NCDAH; J. W. Stephens et al. to Holden, n.d. [1870], GP 225, Holden Papers, NCDAH; L. A. Donoho to Holden, May 24, 1870, GP 224, Holden Papers, NCDAH; Vanessa Siddle Walker, *Their Highest Potential*, 13–14; Raper, *William W. Holden*, 165–66; Raper and Mitchell, *Papers of William Woods Holden*, 1:314–15, 364–65.

40. T. A. Donoho to Holden, May 16, 1870, GLB 61, Holden Papers, NCDAH; Holden to the President of the United States, July 20, 1870, GLB 61, Holden Papers, NCDAH; Ulysses S. Grant to Holden, July 22, 1870, GLB 61, Holden Papers, NCDAH; Raper, *William W. Holden*, 168–76; John Y. Simon, *Papers of Ulysses S. Grant*, 20:176–77, 210–13.

41. Third Annual Message of Governor W. W. Holden, Nov. 22, 1870, GLB 61, Holden Papers, NCDAH.

42. Holden to Richmond M. Pearson, July 19, Aug. 5, 1870, n.d. [1870], GLB 61, Holden Papers, NCDAH; Opinion of Chief Justice Pearson in ex parti Adolphus G. Moore, GLB 61, Holden Papers, NCDAH; Pearson to Holden, Aug. 18, 1870, Holden Papers, NCDAH; William C. Harris, *William Woods Holden*, 295–6.

43. William C. Harris, *William Woods Holden*, 301–19.

44. Judge G. W. Logan to Caldwell, Dec. 27, 1870, Apr. 9, 1871, GLB 62, Cald-

well Papers, NCDAH; Caldwell to Logan, Jan. 5, 1871, GLB 62, Caldwell Papers, NCDAH; Message to the General Assembly, Jan. 18, 1871, GLB 62, Caldwell Papers, NCDAH; Caldwell to Ulysses S. Grant, Apr. 20, 1871, GLB 62, Caldwell Papers, NCDAH; Caldwell to J. B. Carpenter, May 22, 1871, GLB 62, Caldwell Papers, NCDAH; *Testimony Taken by the Joint Committee*, 157, 308, 474–75; Raper, *William W. Holden*, 204.

45. John Y. Simon, *Papers of Ulysses S. Grant*, 22:361–70; 24:389–90, 476; 25:421–22; 27:213–14; 28:129.

46. Franklin Caldwell to Tod Caldwell, May 20, 1871, GP 227, Caldwell Papers, NCDAH; Tod Caldwell to Franklin Caldwell, June 1, 1871, GLB 62, Caldwell Papers, NCDAH; Annual Message, Nov. 20, 1871, GLB 62, Caldwell Papers, NCDAH.

47. N. B. Palmer to Caldwell, Oct. 22, 1871, GP 229, Caldwell Papers, NCDAH; Mrs. James B. Morris to Caldwell, Dec. 21, 1873, GP 237, Caldwell Papers, NCDAH; Petition, Emory Henry, May 2, 1872, GP 231, Caldwell Papers, NCDAH; Jane Henry to Caldwell, June 11, 1872, GP 231, Caldwell Papers, NCDAH; Edward Ancrum to Caldwell, Sept. 15, 1872, GP 232, Caldwell Papers, NCDAH; J. M. Hinsley to Caldwell, Nov. 28, 1872, GP 232, Caldwell Papers, NCDAH; S. M. Moran to Caldwell, Mar. 18, 1873, GP 234, Caldwell Papers, NCDAH.

48. *New York Times*, Nov. 28, 1874, p. 6; Inaugural Speech, July 14, 1874, GLB 63, Brogden Papers, NCDAH; R. A. Cobb to Brogden, Apr. 26, 1875, GP 240, Brogden Papers, NCDAH; Mrs. M. A. Moseley et al. to Brogden, Mar. 18, 1875, GP 240, Brogden Papers, NCDAH.

49. Governor's Message, Nov. 16, 1874, GLB 63, Brogden Papers, NCDAH; Sefton, *United States Army*, 262.

50. Williamson Buck to Caldwell, Dec. 28, 1872, GP 233, Caldwell Papers.

Chapter Five

1. The best survey of the election, and of Vance's life, is McKinney, *Zeb Vance*, 302–23; Dowd, *Life of Zebulon Vance*, 146, 159; *Wilmington Morning Star*, Aug. 27, 1876, p. 1; Sept. 27, 1876, p. 1; *Raleigh Weekly News*, Aug. 2, 1876, p. 1; Sept. 27, 1876, p. 1; *Raleigh News*, Nov. 7, 1876, p. 1; Testimony of Charles Skinner, Contested Election "Maddry vs. Horton," box 17, General Assembly Session Records, 1876–77, NCDAH; Thomas Dixon, *Leopard's Spots*, 242–43; R. D. W. Connor, *North Carolina*, 351–52; and Crow, "Thomas Settle Jr."

2. *Wilmington Morning Star*, Nov. 1, 1876, p. 2.

3. Vance, *Inaugural Address*, 3, 4–10, 15–30.

4. Ibid.

5. Walter Williams to Settle, Jan. 3, 1876, box 1, folder 15, Settle Papers #3345, SHC; Jno. H. Smyth to Settle, Nov. 12, 1876, box 1, folder 17, Settle Papers, SHC; Thomas Dixon, *Leopard's Spots*, 242–43.

6. Petition, John Jackson et al., Jan. 20, 1877, box 15, General Assembly Session Records, 1876–77, NCDAH; Petition, Andrew Robinson et al., Feb. 12, 1877, box 15, General Assembly Session Records, NCDAH; Hooper Moore et al. to Vance, Mar. 1877, reel 14, *Papers of Zebulon Vance*; Vance to Moore et al., Mar. 9, 1877, reel 14, *Papers of Zebulon Vance*; D. M. Lee to Vance, Jan. 27, 1877, reel 14, *Papers of Zebulon Vance*; Vance to Lee, Jan. 31, 1877, GLB 65, Vance Papers, NCDAH; L. A. T. Wright to William Coppinger, Aug. 2, 1879, ser. 1A, vol. 236, American Colonization Society Papers, LOC; *Report and Testimony of the Select Committee*, 287, 303; *Raleigh Weekly News*, Sept. 27, 1876, p. 1.

7. Arden A. Nelson to Vance, Dec. 6, 1877, GP 248, Vance Papers, NCDAH; Miega Long to Vance, May 4, 1877, GP 247, Vance Papers, NCDAH; Petition, M. M. Chambers et al., n.d., box 15, General Assembly Session Records, 1876–77, NCDAH; Mary Andrews to Vance, May 30, 1879, reel 30, *Papers of Zebulon Vance*; Sue and Bettie Robards to Vance, June 12, 1877, reel 29, *Papers of Zebulon Vance*; Mrs. L. S. Aldrich to Vance, Aug. 24, 1877, reel 29, *Papers of Zebulon Vance*; A. P. Patton to Vance, Oct. 6, 1881, reel 8, *Papers of Zebulon Vance*.

8. Petition, A Friend to Dear and Honored Friends, Jan. 7, 1877, box 15, General Assembly Session Records, 1876–77, NCDAH.

9. Petition, Mrs. Pattie Arrington, n.d., box 15, General Assembly Session Records, 1876–77, NCDAH; *New York Times*, Jan 9, 1896, p. 1. My thanks to Tom Vincent of the North Carolina Division of Archives and History for helping me track down these petitions.

10. Scott Reynolds Nelson, *Iron Confederacies*; Hall et al., *Like a Family*, 6; Historical Census Browser, retrieved July 16, 2009; Carlton, "Revolution from Above," 73–80; Philip J. Wood, *Southern Capitalism*, 28.

11. Marcy C. Krauss to Scales, June 18, 1887, GP 266, Scales Papers, NCDAH; Petition, Wm. Toler et al., n.d., box 19, General Assembly Session Records, 1891, NCDAH; A. P. Patton to Vance, Oct. 6, 1881, reel 8, *Papers of Zebulon Vance*; Sarah M. Blalock to London Green, n.d., box 23, General Assembly Session Records, 1897, NCDAH; Diary entry, Oct. 1, 1863, Flintoff Diary, P.C. 1484, NCDAH.

12. Hebrews 11:1; "Sketches + Sermons," Mar. and Apr. 1877, box 2, folder 29, vol. 6, Hume Papers #3239, SHC; Church Minutes, Jan. 2, 1869, vol. 1, p. 178, box 9, University Baptist Church Papers #4162, SHC; Ephesians 6:18; Nettleton, *Village Hymns*, 190, 226; Matthew 6:9–13; Luke 11:2–4; "The Nature and Duty of Prayer," box 7, folder 61, Harrison and Smith Family Papers #5144, SHC; Clinton, *Christianity under the Spotlight*, 129–30, 132, 136–41; Watson, *Divine Worship*, 4, 8; "Sketches + Sermons," Mar. and Apr. 1877, box 2, folder 29, vol. 6, Hume Papers, SHC; Baird, *Hymns of the Voice of Praise*, 12–13; R. G. Pearson, *Truth Applied*, 67–86; Robert Campbell, *Don't Worry*.

13. Vance, *Inaugural Address*, 8, 15–18.

14. "A Proclamation by the Governor of North Carolina," Oct. 28, 1871, GLB 62,

Caldwell Papers; Sermon 99, "Thanksgiving Day A People Saved of the Lord," box 3, folder 159, Cheshire Papers #146, SHC; Sermon 71, "Thanksgiving Day Man Doth Not Live by Bread Alone," box 3, folder 157, Cheshire Papers, SHC; Sermon 67, "The Kingdom of God," box 3, folder 156, Cheshire Papers, SHC; Sermon, "God the Author of All Good and of Good Only," box 4, folder 33, Harrison and Smith Family Papers, SHC; Sermon, "Our Duty to God and to Government," box 6, folder 52, Harrison and Smith Family Papers, SHC.

15. R. G. Pearson, *Great Evangelist*, 62–63; Untitled Sermon, box 2, folder 29, vol. 6, Hume Papers, SHC; Sermon 134, "The Servants of God or the Servants of Sin," box 3, folder 164, Cheshire Papers, SHC; Sermon 203, "No More a Servant, But a Son," box 4, folder 178, Cheshire Papers, SHC; Untitled Prayers, box 5, folder 226, Cheshire Papers, SHC; Sermon 157, "The Ox Knoweth His Owner," box 4, folder 169, Cheshire Papers, SHC; Sermon, "Safety Within the Ark," box 5, folder 78, Osborne Papers #567, SHC; Manly and Manly, *Baptist Psalmody*, 61, 62, 115, 293; Sermon, "The Lord Reigneth, Let the Earth Rejoice," box 3, folder 30, Harrison and Smith Family Papers, SHC.

16. Vance received many letters from parents who claimed to have named their sons for him and asking in return a "present of something as a matter of encouragement." While each individual letter should be treated with skepticism, it does seem that the name Zebulon increased dramatically in popularity during his time in power. Between 1870 and 1900, the number of Zebulons in the state increased from slightly more than one hundred to well over three hundred, according to a census search. Vance himself complained good-naturedly about the money he lost to namesakes. See J. E Burroughs to Vance, Apr. 8, 1886, reel 9, *Papers of Zebulon Vance*; and *Charlotte Daily Observer*, May 20, 1900, p. 4.

17. Scott Reynolds Nelson, *Iron Confederacies*, 160; R. L. Abernethy to Vance, May 2, 1878, reel 30, *Papers of Zebulon Vance*; A. H. Stokes to Vance, Sept. 4, 1893, reel 36, *Papers of Zebulon Vance*; T. B. Roberts to Vance, Dec. 25, 1889, reel 10, *Papers of Zebulon Vance*; Thompson Robinson to Vance, Feb. 12, 1885, reel 9, *Papers of Zebulon Vance*; W. C. Galloway to Vance, Mar. 31, 1888, reel 33, *Papers of Zebulon Vance*; J. S. Brooks to Vance, Mar. 12, 1888, reel 33, *Papers of Zebulon Vance*; Alpheus McGinfrey to Vance, Jan. 27, 1881, reel 31, *Papers of Zebulon Vance*; A. A. Abernethy to Vance, Feb. 26, 1891, reel 35, *Papers of Zebulon Vance*; H. C. Tyson to Florence S. Vance, Apr. 17, 1894, reel 11, *Papers of Zebulon Vance*; *Wilmington Morning Star*, July 3, 1892, p. 2.

18. Arden A. Nelson to Vance, Dec. 6, 1877, GP 248, Vance Papers, NCDAH; H. M. Guiney to Butler, Dec. 4, 1897, ser. 1.2, folder 78, Marion Butler Papers, #114, SHC; N. B. Palmer to Caldwell, Oct. 22, 1871, GP 229, Caldwell Papers, NCDAH; Loveday A. Tucker to Carr, Mar. 11, 1896, GP 286, Carr Papers, NCDAH; Laura Ann Hairston to Russell, June 14, 1897, GP 293, Russell Papers, NCDAH; Mrs. James B. Morris to Caldwell, Dec. 21, 1873, GP 236, Caldwell Papers, NCDAH;

S. A. Newberry et al. to Jarvis, n.d., GP 262, Jarvis Papers, NCDAH; Digeser, *Political Forgiveness*, 123–35; Fiskejo, *Thanksgiving Turkey Pardon*, 1–2; Kesselring, *Mercy and Authority*, 136; Koziol, *Begging Pardon and Favor*, 7, 8, 24; Kathleen Dean Moore, *Pardons*; Jensen, *Pardoning Power*, 3, 10, 11.

19. Zebulon B. Vance Term, Records and Reasons for Granting Pardons, 1877–1901, Vance to Daniel L. Russell, 1877–1901, #5, 31, 33, NCDAH; Rules for Application for Pardon, Feb. 1877, reel 14, *Papers of Zebulon Vance*; Vance to Jas. L. Kemper, May 1877, reel 14, *Papers of Zebulon Vance*; Vance to F. F. Axley, May 15, 1877, reel 14, *Papers of Zebulon Vance*; C. M. Cooke to Vance, Feb. 14, 1891, reel 35, *Papers of Zebulon Vance*; Cheek, "Pardoning Power," 77.

20. Cheek, "Pardoning Power," 78, 92; Thomas J. Jarvis to Vance, May 9, 1879, reel 30, *Papers of Zebulon Vance*; Thomas J. Jarvis Terms, Records and Reasons for Granting Pardons, 1877–1901, Vance to Daniel L. Russell, 1877–1901, #38, 138, 142, 181, 298, NCDAH; Jarvis to E. Sanderlin, May 13, 1884, GLB 68, Jarvis Papers, NCDAH.

21. Inaugural Address, Jan. 21, 1885, GLB 71, Scales Papers, NCDAH; Alfred Moore Scales Term, Records and Reasons for Granting Pardons, 1877–1901, Vance to Daniel L. Russell, 1877–1901, #327, 335, 336, 347, 371, 409, NCDAH; Daniel G. Fowle Term, Records and Reasons for Granting Pardons, 1877–1901, Vance to Russell, 1877–1901, #60, NCDAH; Thomas M. Holt Term, Records and Reasons for Granting Pardons, 1877–1901, Vance to Russell, 1877–1901, #87, 95, 98, 130, 139, 157, 188, NCDAH; Cheek, "Pardoning Power," 80, 92; Many Citizens to Scales, Sept. 29, 1886, GP 264, Scales Papers, NCDAH.

22. *Raleigh News and Observer*, Oct. 5, 1894, p. 2.

23. Message to the General Assembly, Jan. 9, 1897, GLB 90, Papers, NCDAH; Elias Carr Term, Records and Reasons for Granting Pardons, 1877–1901, Vance to Russell, 1877–1901, #57, 105, 224, NCDAH; John H. Gabriel to Carr, June 9, 1894, GP 282, Carr Papers, NCDAH; Andrew Barden to Carr, Oct. 4, 1896, GP 288, Carr Papers, NCDAH; William Miller to Carr, May 4, 1894, GP 282, Carr Papers, NCDAH; Laura A. Butler to Carr, Nov. 11, 1896, GP 289, Carr Papers, NCDAH; T. W. Patten to Carr, Feb. 5, 1895, box 22, folder b, Carr Papers #160, ECU; Cheek, "Pardoning Power," 80, 92.

24. Patronage has played an important though perhaps too structural a role in studies of American politics. See, particularly, Altschuler and Blumin, *Rude Republic*, 40–46; Bensel, *Yankee Leviathan*, 24, 396; Michael F. Holt, *Political Parties*; McCormick, *From Realignment to Reform*; Teaford, *Unheralded Triumph*, 7, 176, 184–85; and Summers, *Party Games*.

25. Reel 32, *Papers of Zebulon Vance*; box 28, folder 285, Ransom Papers #2615, SHC; H. H. Dukes to Vance, Jan. 30, 1877, reel 29, *Papers of Zebulon Vance*; W. G. Granberry to Vance, Nov. 12, 1885, reel 31, *Papers of Zebulon Vance*; Archibald Brady to Settle, Nov. 21, 1895, box 8, folder 125, Settle Papers, SHC; Mitchell to My Dear

Wife, Jan. 12, 1895, Mitchell Papers, P.C. 1757, NCDAH; D. S. Ellis to Vance, Nov. 13, 1884, reel 31, *Papers of Zebulon Vance*; *Reidsville Times*, Nov. 4, 1880, p. 2; *Caucasian*, Mar. 10, 1892, p. 1; A. W. Simpson to Small, Sept. 16, 1898, box 1, Small Papers, SCL; Mrs. Thomas C. Evans to Vance, Feb. 21, 1877, reel 29, *Papers of Zebulon Vance*.

26. W. W. Scott Jr. to Vance, Mar. 16, 1893, reel 36, *Papers of Zebulon Vance*; E. A. Poteat to Mrs. Graham, Dec. 15, 1896, box 4, folder 47, Graham Papers #955, SHC; W. C. Rencher to Vance, July 12, 1885, reel 5, *Papers of Zebulon Vance*; Mrs. L. S. Aldrich to Vance, Aug. 24, 1877, reel 29, *Papers of Zebulon Vance*; R. C. Duffy to Vance, Dec. 2, 1885, reel 32, *Papers of Zebulon Vance*; Mrs. J. B. Banks to Vance, Feb. 25, 1881, reel 31, *Papers of Zebulon Vance*; S. H. McElanny to Butler, Oct. 7, 1896, folder 35, Marion Butler Papers, SHC; Caroline S. Pool to Ransom, May 12, 1876, box 2, folder 14c, Ransom Papers #2615, SHC; Jno. Norwood Webb to Vance, Jan. 25, 1879, reel 30, *Papers of Zebulon Vance*; R. S. Harris to Vance, Dec. 2, 1884, reel 31, *Papers of Zebulon Vance*; W. T. Dough to Vance, Jan. 29, 1886, reel 5, *Papers of Zebulon Vance*; Mrs. Jane L. Backus to Vance, Apr. 12, 1885, reel 32, *Papers of Zebulon Vance*; Dollie J. Hill to Vance, Jan. 8, 1888, reel 33, *Papers of Zebulon Vance*; Jake H. Hallyburton to Vance, Jan. 22, 1877, reel 29, *Papers of Zebulon Vance*; L. A. Long to Vance, Mar. 28, 1888, reel 33, *Papers of Zebulon Vance*; Thomas H. Sutton to Ransom, Apr. 30, 1892, box 27, folder 272, Ransom Papers, SHC; W. E. Ardrey to Vance, May 26, 1893, reel 10, *Papers of Zebulon Vance*; R. P. Waring to Vance, Oct. 30, 1885, reel 9, *Papers of Zebulon Vance*; W. W. Latham to Vance, Apr. 28, 1879, reel 30, *Papers of Zebulon Vance*; M. V. Ingram to Butler, June 16, 1898, folder 102, Marion Butler Papers, SHC.

27. Mrs. Cornelia Henderson to Vance, Feb. 25, 1885, reel 31, *Papers of Zebulon Vance*; Mrs. Jane L. Backus to Vance, Apr. 12, 1885, reel 32, *Papers of Zebulon Vance*; Mrs. Emma Bennett to Vance, Feb. 25, 1885, reel 38, *Papers of Zebulon Vance*; Fred J. Hill to Vance, Dec. 3, 1884, reel 31, *Papers of Zebulon Vance*; F. F. Glenn to Col. W. H. Yarborough, Nov. 29, 1888, box 6, Hawkins Papers, P.C. 106, NCDAH; Petition, W. L. Holt, K. A. Hamilton, and S. F. Fonville, n.d. box 6, Hawkins Papers, NCDAH; Marmaduke Hawkins to Yarborough, Aug. 20, 1888, box 6, Hawkins Papers, NCDAH; Jas. W. Forbes to Yarborough, July 30, 1888, box 6, Hawkins Papers, NCDAH; W. D. Whitted to Settle, Feb. 3, 1872, box 1, folder 6, Settle Papers, SHC; Jas. W. Albright to Polk, Jan. 11, 1878, box 2, folder 24, Polk Papers #3708, SHC.

28. D. D. Stanford to Vance, Mar. 6, 1893, reel 36, *Papers of Zebulon Vance*; Thos. K. Davis Jr. to Settle, box 7, folder 113, Settle Papers, SHC; H. L. Brower to Vance, Aug. 18, 1893, reel 36, *Papers of Zebulon Vance*; Jonas W. Derr to Vance, May 2, 1881, reel 8, *Papers of Zebulon Vance*; James G. Brown to Vance, Sept. 14, 1877, reel 29, *Papers of Zebulon Vance*; W. L. Harris to Ransom, Apr. 14, 1892, box 27, folder 271, Ransom Papers, SHC; W. L. Harris to Ransom, Apr. 21, 1892, box 27, folder 272,

Ransom Papers, SHC; Z. Vance Harris to Ransom, Apr. 25, 1892, box 27, folder 272, Ransom Papers, SHC.

29. W. J. Barrett to Vance, Mar. 7, 1885, reel 32, *Papers of Zebulon Vance*; W. W. Latham to Vance, Apr. 28, 1879, reel 30, *Papers of Zebulon Vance*; Jas. N. Williams + Sons to Settle, Jan. 22, 1894, box 6, folder 85, Settle Papers, SHC; Crowell, *Personal Recollections*, 444; Mrs. John McDonald to Vance, Mar. 25, 1885, reel 32, *Papers of Zebulon Vance*; Mary N. Benard to Settle, Mar. 6, 1893, box 5, folder 67, Settle Papers, SHC; Walter Brem to Vance, Mar. 9, 1893, reel 36, *Papers of Zebulon Vance*; Chas. C. Clark to Vance, Dec. 17, 1884, reel 31, *Papers of Zebulon Vance*; A. M. Noble to Ransom, May 16, 1887, box 18, folder 183, Ransom Papers, SHC; J. H. Cain to Vance, Sept. 19, 1890, reel 34, *Papers of Zebulon Vance*; J. H. Hermesa to Vance, Mar. 29, 1885, reel 32, *Papers of Zebulon Vance*; H. L. Curie to Ransom, Aug. 6, 1894, box 44, folder 440, Ransom Papers, SHC; Mrs. John McDonald to Vance, Mar. 25, 1885, reel 32, *Papers of Zebulon Vance*.

30. Adams, "Mr. Cleveland's Tasks," 298–99; "Women Have to Keep on Strivin'," p. 3, box 21, folder 640, Federal Writers' Project Papers, #3709, SHC; Anonymous to Cleveland, Nov. 18, 1858, reel 2, *Grover Cleveland Papers*; "Politics of the Eighties in Lenoir County, North Carolina," box 1, Jones Manuscript #473, ECU; John, *Spreading the News*; Skowronek, *Building a New American State*, 72; Carpenter, *Forging of Bureaucratic Autonomy*, 65–143; Redding, *Making Race*, 39; Roller, "Republican Party," 131; Anderson, *Race and Politics*, 243–51; Aron, *Ladies and Gentlemen*, 5.

31. "Politics of the Eighties in Lenoir County, North Carolina," box 1, Jones Manuscript, ECU; Vance to Florence S. Vance, June 4, 1885, reel 9, *Papers of Zebulon Vance*; Patrick Brady to Vance, Apr. 23, 1885, reel 32, *Papers of Zebulon Vance*; Lily V. B. Higgins to Vance, Dec. 26, 1885, reel 32, *Papers of Zebulon Vance*; R. L. Parrott to Vance, Mar. 16, 1885, reel 32, *Papers of Zebulon Vance*; J. B. Jones to Vance, Mar. 8, 1885, reel 32, *Papers of Zebulon Vance*; A. E. Oglesby to Vance, Apr. 11, 1886, reel 32, *Papers of Zebulon Vance*; W. G. Granberry to Vance, Nov. 12, 1885, reel 31, *Papers of Zebulon Vance*.

32. Carpenter, *Forging of Bureaucratic Autonomy*, 25, 45–48; Daniels, *Editor in Politics*, 202; Haskell, *Emergence of Professional Social Science*, 118–21; Hoogenboom, *Outlawing the Spoils*, 242–44, 262–63; Johnson and Libecap, *Federal Civil Service System*, 15, 32–37, 52–56; McKinney, *Zeb Vance*, 372–74; Mosher, *Democracy and the Public Service*, 61–70; Skowronek, *Building a New American State*, 47–84; Summers, *Rum, Romanism, and Rebellion*, 64, 75; Van Riper, *History of the United States Civil Service*, 96–100, 122–31; Aron, *Ladies and Gentlemen*, 97–106.

33. H. C. Turner to Vance, July 27, 1886, reel 9, *Papers of Zebulon Vance*; Henry C. Bourne to Vance, Feb. 10, 1886, reel 5, *Papers of Zebulon Vance*; O. R. Smith to Vance, Mar. 16, 1886, reel 9, *Papers of Zebulon Vance*; J. W. Mehaffy to Vance, May 3, 1886, reel 9, *Papers of Zebulon Vance*; E. T. B. Glenn to Vance, Apr. 5, 1886, reel 32, *Papers of Zebulon Vance*; Walter H. Neal to Vance, Mar. 12, 1886, reel 32, *Papers of Zebulon*

Vance; A. R. Johnston to Vance, Apr. 8, 1886, reel 32, *Papers of Zebulon Vance*; P. M. Pearsall to Vance, Mar. 20, 1893, reel 36, *Papers of Zebulon Vance*; P. F. Duffy to Vance, Apr. 13, 1886, reel 32, *Papers of Zebulon Vance*; W. J. Harris to Vance, Apr. 6, 1886, reel 32, *Papers of Zebulon Vance*; S. S. Satchwell to Vance, Apr. 3, 1886, reel 32, *Papers of Zebulon Vance*; James C. Parsons to Vance, Apr. 1, 1886, reel 32, *Papers of Zebulon Vance*.

34. *State Chronicle*, Mar. 4, 1886, pp. 1–2; Mar. 11, 1886, p. 1; *Wilmington Morning Star*, Mar. 6, 1886, p. 2. For a broad discussion of such early efforts to measure public opinion, see Herbst, *Numbered Voices*, 69–88.

35. Adams, "What Mr. Cleveland Stands For," 665; *State Chronicle*, Feb. 11, 1886, p. 1; Mar. 4, 1886, p. 2; Mar. 11, 1886, p. 1; Apr. 8, 1886, p. 2; Apr. 15, 1886, p. 2; Arthur Link, *Papers of Woodrow Wilson*, 2:233; Leloudis, *Schooling the New South*; Haskell, *Emergence of Professional Social Science*.

36. *State Chronicle*, Feb. 11, 1886, p. 1; Mar. 4, 1886, p. 2; Apr. 8, 1886, p. 2; Mary C. Murray to Vance, Apr. 2, 1886, reel 32, *Papers of Zebulon Vance*; S. S. Satchwell to Vance, Feb. 12, 1886, reel 5, *Papers of Zebulon Vance*; J. W. Happoldt to Vance, Dec. 6, 1889, reel 33, *Papers of Zebulon Vance*; Vance to Florence S. Vance, Oct. 14, 1887, reel 9, *Papers of Zebulon Vance*; *Congressional Record*, 49th Cong., 1st sess., 2948–50; *Raleigh News and Observer*, Apr. 4, 1886, p. 2; *Wilmington Morning Star*, Apr. 6, 1886, p. 2; Hattie Andrews to Vance, Apr. 1, 1886, reel 32, *Papers of Zebulon Vance*; W. M. Hawley to Butler, Apr. 12, 1900, ser. 1.2, folder 149, Marion Butler Papers, SHC; Annie Goodloe Randall to Ransom, Nov. 12, 1892, box 28, folder 285, Ransom Papers, SHC; Sallie Floyd Watson to Webb, Mar. 28, 1908, box 1, folder 4, Webb Papers #3482, SHC.

37. Colonel Sellers to Cleveland, Jan. 1, 1885, reel 4, *Grover Cleveland Papers*; A. M. Noble to Vance, Jan. 11, 1886, reel 9, *Papers of Zebulon Vance*; *Wilmington Morning Star*, Mar. 26, 1888, p. 2; Jas. E. Moore to Vance, Apr. 3, 1886, reel 32, *Papers of Zebulon Vance*; C. T. Wooten to Vance, Apr. 5, 1886, reel 32, *Papers of Zebulon Vance*; O. R. Smith to Vance, Mar. 16, 1886, reel 9, *Papers of Zebulon Vance*; J. W. Harden to Settle, Dec. 27, 1896, box 10, folder 158, Settle Papers, SHC; *State Chronicle*, Mar. 4, 1886, p. 1; J. B. Welch to Vance, Apr. 13, 1886, reel 32, *Papers of Zebulon Vance*; *Congressional Record*, 49th Cong., 1st sess., 2945, 2948, 2952.

38. E. B. Roberts to Vance, Apr. 4, 1886, reel 32, *Papers of Zebulon Vance*; *Congressional Record*, 49th Cong., 1st sess., 2952.

39. *Congressional Record*, 49th Cong., 1st sess., 2948–52.

40. Mrs. Geo. N. Banks to Russell, Aug. 30, 1897, GP 294, Russell Papers, NCDAH; Redick Henry et al. to Fowle, Dec. 10, 1889, GP 271, Fowle Papers, NCDAH; Mary C. Krauss to Scales, June 18, 1887, GP 266, Scales Papers, NCDAH.

41. R. J. Reynolds to Vance, Aug. 17, 1886, reel 9, *Papers of Zebulon Vance*; B. F. Hanes to Vance, Sept. 12, 1886, reel 9, *Papers of Zebulon Vance*; Thos. J. Gill to Vance,

Feb. 24, 1894, reel 37, *Papers of Zebulon Vance*; American Medicine Co. to Vance, Feb. 5, 1894, reel 11, *Papers of Zebulon Vance*; J. S. Carr to Elias Carr, Mar. 20, 1891, box 13, folder b, Carr Papers #160, ECU; *Caucasian*, June 7, 1894, p. 4.

42. Joule Bolton to Scales, Nov. 22, 1886, GP 264, Scales Papers, NCDAH; B. F. Poteat to Scales, Sept. 13, 1887, GP 267, Scales Papers, NCDAH; Petition, "North Carolina," Jan. 29, 1897, box 22, General Assembly Session Records, NCDAH; D. H. West to Kemp Battle, July 31, 1890, box 19, folder 624, University of North Carolina Papers, UA; Testimony, Alexander Henderson, case of Manuel Hall #652283, pp. 98–99, box 1, folder a, Douglass Papers, #323, ECU; Testimony, Nathan Bryant, pp. 67–68, box 2, folder a, Douglass Papers, ECU; Message to the General Assembly, Jan. 17, 1895, GLB 90, Carr Papers, NCDAH; Message to the General Assembly, 1903, GLB 109, Aycock Papers, NCDAH; *Laws and Resolutions* (1889), 159–63; *Laws and Resolutions* (1885), 394–98; *Public Laws and Resolutions*, 484–85.

43. W. Staples to Vance, Feb. 16, 1881, reel 31, *Papers of Zebulon Vance*; *Progressive Farmer*, Feb. 4, 1896, p. 1; Jas. M. Wright to Vance, Feb. 15, 1894, reel 11, *Papers of Zebulon Vance*; Ransom Hinton to Marion Butler, July 30, 1898, ser. 1.2, folder 107, Marion Butler Papers, SHC; Carpenter, *Forging of Bureaucratic Autonomy*, 179–211.

44. *Report and Testimony of the Select Committee*, 286; F. W. Liedtke to Holden, Sept. 22, 1868, GP 219, Holden Papers, NCDAH; James Chavers to Jarvis, Aug. 12, 1882, GP 258, Jarvis Papers, NCDAH; W. G. Templeton to Fowle, Aug. 16, 1889, GP 271, Fowle Papers, NCDAH.

45. Silas N. Stilwell to Holden, July 14, 1868, GP 218, Holden Papers, NCDAH; Testimony, Nelson Plummer, Hinton Jordan, Lewis Hawkins, Rich. W. Kearney Jr., and W. M. Davis, Contested Election "King vs. Carter," box 17, General Assembly Session Records, 1876–77, NCDAH; Testimony, George H. Mitchell, Leander W. Harris, Joseph W. Perry, Joseph J. Jordan, James B Chamblee, James A. Ramsay, and Charles Skinner, Contested Election, "Maddry vs. Horton," box 17, General Assembly Session Records, 1876–77, NCDAH. For a fascinating effort to combine philosophies about everyday life with scholarship on race-making, see Thomas C. Holt, "Marking."

46. Petition, J. W. Harper et al., Jan. 9, 1891, box 19, General Assembly Session Records, 1891, NCDAH; Latta, *History of My Life*, 157–59; Petition, Isham Taller-white et al., Nov. 10, 1876, box 15, General Assembly Session Records, 1876–77, NCDAH; L. L. Polk to E. R. Liles, Jan. 1877, box 15, General Assembly Session Records, 1876–77, NCDAH; J. G. Branch to Col. Liles, Jan. 19, 1877, box 15, General Assembly Session Records, 1876–77, NCDAH; Petition, Callie R. Lamb et al., Nov. 1876, box 15, General Assembly Session Records, 1876–77, NCDAH; Petition, Mrs. Emma F. Bass et al., box 22, General Assembly Session Records, 1893, NCDAH; Petition, E. V. Lackey et al., Feb. 4, 1893, box 21, General Assembly

Session Records, 1893, NCDAH; Petition, Wm. Toler et al., n.d., box 19, General Assembly Session Records, 1891, NCDAH; Petition, Henry T. Bahnson et al., n.d., box 15, General Assembly Session Records, 1876–77, NCDAH; Petition, Wm. Flinn et al., Nov. 15, 1890, box 19, General Assembly Session Records, 1891, NCDAH; Petition, M. P. Baughan et al., n.d., box 19, General Assembly Session Records, 1891, NCDAH; Petition, J. E. Mullis et al., n.d., box 21, General Assembly Session Records, 1893, NCDAH.

47. J. L. Currie to Graham, Jan. 27, 1885, box 2, folder 17, Graham Papers, SHC; Wm. A. Jordan to Graham, Feb. 2, 1885, box 2, folder 18, Graham Papers, SHC; J. V. Roberts to Winston, Feb. 25, 1885, box 1, folder 7, Robert Watson Winston Papers #2369, SHC; D. F. Crawford to Graham, Feb. 20, 1885, box 2, folder 18, Graham Papers, SHC; R. G. Linnin to Graham, Feb. 7, 1885, box 2, folder 18, Graham Papers, SHC; Jno. A. Watkins to Winston, Mar. 6, 1885, box 1, folder 7, Robert Watson Winston Papers, SHC; Thomas M. Cheek to Graham, Feb. 18, 1885, box 2, folder 18, Graham Papers, SHC; G. W. Watkins and Jno. A. Watkins to Graham, Mar. 6, 1885, box 2, folder 19, Graham Papers, SHC; A. Landis Jr. to Winston, Feb. 24, 1885, box 1, folder 7, Robert Watson Winston Papers, SHC; Thurtell, "Fusion Insurgency," 43, 65, 257, 323; Bromberg, "Pure Democracy and White Supremacy," 115–16; Redding, *Making Race*, 80–83; Hahn, *Roots of Southern Populism*.

48. Scales to Hon. Wm. C. Whitney, Oct. 5, 1885, GLB 71, Scales Papers, NCDAH; Governor's Message, Jan. 1, 1887, GLB 71, Scales Papers, NCDAH; Howard Jackson et al. to Fowle, Jan. 31, 1890, GP 272, Fowle Papers, NCDAH; Thomas H. Sims to Fowle, Feb. 1, 1891, GP 272, Fowle Papers, NCDAH; F. Winslow to Fowle, Feb. 4, 1890, GP 272, Fowle Papers, NCDAH; Winslow and Thos. McGuinn to L. D. Bragg, Jan. 30, 1890, and B. B. Bragg et al. to Winslow, Jan. 28, 1890, enclosed in Winslow to Fowle, Feb. 4, 1890, GP 272, Fowle Papers, NCDAH; Wilson T. Farrow to Fowle, Feb. 13, 1890, GP 272, Fowle Papers, NCDAH; B. J. Pollard to Holt, Sept. 9, 1891, GP 275, Thomas M. Holt Papers, NCDAH; Will B. Rodman to Fowle, Feb. 4, 1890, GP 272, Fowle Papers, NCDAH; S. T. Beckwith to Fowle, Feb. 4, 1890, GLB 74, Fowle Papers, NCDAH; Winslow to Fowle, Feb. 4, 1890, GP 272, Fowle Papers, NCDAH.

49. Fowle to B. F. Long, Oct. 18, 1889, GLB 74, Fowle Papers, NCDAH; Fowle to Col. J. T. Anthony, Oct. 25, 1889, GLB 74, Fowle Papers, NCDAH; Fowle to Long, Oct. 26, 1889, GLB 74, Fowle Papers, NCDAH; Fowle to Sheriff Brewer, Jan. 14, 1890, GLB 74, Fowle Papers, NCDAH; Thos. H. Battle to Fowle, Feb. 22, 1890, GLB 74, Fowle Papers, NCDAH; *New York Times*, June 23, 1881, p. 1; Stuart Ellison et al. to Jarvis, Jan. 1, 1885, GP 262, Jarvis Papers, NCDAH; *Caucasian*, Sept. 10, 1891, p. 3; Brundage, *Lynching in the New South*; Tolnay and Beck, *Festival of Violence*, ix; Feimster, *Southern Horrors*; Bruce Baker, *This Mob Will Surely Take My Life*; Brundage, *Under Sentence of Death*.

Chapter Six

1. Like many gold standard supporters, the younger Thomas Settle was not unalterably opposed to silver but echoed the 1896 Republican Party platform that fiercely opposed the unilateral free coinage of silver but pledged (perhaps disingenuously) to lobby for an international agreement on a gold and silver standard.

2. Wm. E. Clark to Settle, June 26, 1896, box 9, folder 149, Settle Papers #3345, SHC; Thomas Watkins to Settle, July 9, 1896, box 9, folder 150, Settle Papers, SHC; J. T. Hairston to Settle, Apr. 25, 1896, box 9, folder 146, Settle Papers, SHC.

3. T. M. Norwood to Polk, Mar. 27, 1892, box 7, folder 100, Polk Papers #3708, SHC; Holmes, "Southern Farmers' Alliance"; Knox, *Enthusiasm*, 1–2.

4. Silver speech, reel 6, *Papers of Zebulon Vance*; *Caucasian*, Aug. 15, 1895, p. 1, Oct. 17, 1895, p. 1; G. R. Ekard et al. to Vance, Matt Ransom, and J. S. Henderson, Aug. 8, 1893, reel 36, *Papers of Zebulon Vance*; National People's Party Platform, July 4, 1894, folder 713, Marion Butler Papers #114, SHC; *State Chronicle*, Jan. 21, 1886, p. 2; J. B. Schulken to Butler, Dec. 2, 1896, folder 42, Marion Butler Papers, SHC; *Reidsville Weekly Review*, Sept. 6, 1895, p. 2; W. Stevens to Vance, Oct. 9, 1893, reel 37, *Papers of Zebulon Vance*.

5. *Progressive Farmer*, June 28, 1892, p. 4; Sept. 13, 1892, p. 2; Aug. 20, 1895, p. 3; *Caucasian*, Oct. 12, 1893, p. 3; Laughlin, "Coin's Food for the Gullible," 573–75; *Wilmington Messenger*, July 14, 1892, p. 2; Dixon, *Open Letter*, 5; J. S. Carr to Page, Apr. 12, 1892, container 208, Page Papers, MS Am 1090 (Personal), HU.

6. Tracy, "Rise and Doom of the Populist Party," 240; *Wilmington Messenger*, Sept. 10, 1892, p. 2. For a provocative argument about the symbolic and symbiotic relationship between the fixity of the gold standard and the hardening of racial ideology, see O'Malley, "Specie and Species"; Painter, "Thinking about the Language of Money and Race"; O'Malley, "Free Silver."

7. The gravest critic of the appeal of silver was Richard Hofstadter, who considered it something close to a psychological disorder. Many of Hofstadter's sharpest critics, especially Lawrence Goodwyn, largely accepted Hofstadter's dismissal of silver in an effort to defend the true, radical Populism beyond it. For accounts that treat silver as a rational response to the economic crisis, see, among others, Walter Nugent, *Tolerant Populists*; Allen Weinstein, *Prelude to Populism*, 8–33, 301–53; and Ritter, *Goldbugs and Greenbacks*, 62–109, 152–207. See also Hofstadter, *Age of Reform*, 244; Goodwyn, *Democratic Promise*; Ayers, *Promise of the New South*, 294–97; Palmer, *Man over Money*, 103, 143–54; Hahn, *Roots of Southern Populism*, 1–6, 270–88; and Unger, *Greenback Era*, 322–73.

8. W. D. McIver to Charles McIver, Jan. 11, 1895, box 4, folder 2, McIver Records, UNCG; N. O. Petree to Settle, Jan. 25, 1894, box 6, folder 86, Settle Papers, SHC; T. J. Sting to Settle, Feb. 21, 1896, box 9, folder 136, Settle Papers, SHC; *Caucasian*, Apr. 30, 1896, p. 1; J. L. Lane et al. to Vance, Sept. 26, 1893, reel 37, *Papers of Zebu-*

lon Vance; T. J. Mitchner to Settle, July 23, 1894, box 7, folder 101, Settle Papers, SHC; Diary entry, Oct. 1, 1893, Flintoff Diary, P.C. 1484, NCDAH; Friedman and Schwartz, *Monetary History*, 15–88; Ritter, *Goldbugs and Greenbacks*, 62–109, 152–207; Unger, *Greenback Era*, 322–73; Allen Weinstein, *Prelude to Populism*, 8–33, 301–53; Steeples and Whitten, *Democracy in Desperation*; Walter Nugent, *Money and American Society*.

9. Noblin, *Leonidas Lafayette Polk*; *Public Documents of the General Assembly*, 1–7, 25, 26, 35; Polk, *Tabulated Statement*; Polk to T. J. Jarvis, Apr. 10, 1879, box 3, folder 33, Polk Papers, SHC; Polk to E. R. Liles, Jan. 1877, General Assembly Session Records, 1876–77, box 15, NCDAH; Daniel McN. McKay to Polk, May 8, 1886, box 6, folder 83, Polk Papers, SHC; Postel, *Populist Vision*; Trachtenberg, *Incorporation of America*; and Chandler, *Visible Hand*. The most interesting discussion of Polk's life is Deborah Beckel's portrayal of his involvement in a Raleigh world of 1870s and 1880s reform. Charles Postel vividly captures the modernizing impulse in Populism in his recent, prize-winning intellectual history. In extremely different ways, the leading business historian Alfred Chandler and the prominent cultural historian Alan Trachtenberg described the role of organization and consolidation near the turn of the century. See Beckel, "Roots of Reform";

10. Carr to E. J. Brooks, May 22, 1891, box 14, folder a, Carr Papers #160, ECU; *Caucasian*, Jan. 16, 1890, p. 1, May 1, 1890, p. 1; *Progressive Farmer*, Apr. 25, 1893, p. 2; Butler and Thompson, *Addresses*, 2–3.

11. *Progressive Farmer*, July 18, 1893, p. 4; W. H. Baker to Carr, Feb. 21, 1890, box 9, folder a, Carr Papers, ECU; S. G. Pomyduval to Carr, Feb. 2, 1891, box 13, folder a, Carr Papers, ECU. For a sense of the preponderance of women in some local Alliances, see Marion Butler's Quarterly Reports, ser. 2.3.1, folders 700–702, Marion Butler Papers, SHC. More generally, on women and Populism, see Rebecca Edwards, *Angels in the Machinery*, 91–110; Buhle, *Women and American Socialism*, 82–90; and Michael L. Goldberg, *Army of Women*.

12. L. L. Polk to Winston, Sept. 11, 1890, box 2, folder 22, Robert Watson Winston Papers #2369, SHC; S. A. Ashe to Vance, June 30 1894, reel 34, *Papers of Zebulon Vance*; Josephus Daniels to Vance, July 19, 1890, reel 34, *Papers of Zebulon Vance*; E. C. Beddingfield to Vance, July 12, 1890, reel 34, *Papers of Zebulon Vance*; Anonymous to Vance, July 15, 1890, reel 34, *Papers of Zebulon Vance*; T. B. Parker to Vance, Aug. 28, 1890, reel 34, *Papers of Zebulon Vance*; J. M. Wright to Vance, July 21, 1890, reel 34, *Papers of Zebulon Vance*; W. A. Norbold to Vance, July 14, 1890, reel 34, *Papers of Zebulon Vance*.

13. J. L. Shepherd to Vance, June 24, 1890, reel 34, *Papers of Zebulon Vance*; S. S. Satchwell to Vance, July 4, 1890, reel 34, *Papers of Zebulon Vance*; F. M. Little to Vance, Aug. 23, 1890, reel 34, *Papers of Zebulon Vance*; W. M. Pickett to Vance, Aug. 25, 1890, reel 34, *Papers of Zebulon Vance*; B. F. Grady to Vance, Sept. 23, 1890, reel 34, *Papers of Zebulon Vance*.

14. Miss Lou Holmes to Washington Duke, Nov. 4, 1901, box 2, Washington Duke Papers, SCL; D. L. Earnhardt to Washington Duke, Sept. 11, 1895, box 1, Washington Duke Papers, SCL; Miss L. E. Amis to Washington Duke, Jan. 26, 1894, box 1, Washington Duke Papers, SCL; Mrs. H. H. Harper to Washington Duke, July 6, 1891, box 1, Washington Duke Papers, SCL; Mrs. W. B. Glenn to Washington Duke, May 15, 1901, box 2, Washington Duke Papers, SCL; Thos. S. Eaton to Benjamin N. Duke, Dec. 3, 1900, Benjamin Newton Duke Papers, SCL; J. H. Shuford to Washington Duke, Feb. 6, 1898, box 1, Washington Duke Papers, SCL; G. E. T. McDaniel to Washington Duke, Oct. 3, 1898, box 2, Washington Duke Papers, SCL; S. H. Helsaback to Washington Duke, n.d., box 1, Washington Duke Papers, SCL; Fannie and Leslie Harper to Washington Duke, Apr. 11, 1891, box 1, Washington Duke Papers, SCL; Susie H. Watkins to Benjamin N. Duke, Oct. 27, 1896, box 5, Benjamin Newton Duke Papers, SCL; Laura Maxwell to Washington Duke, Aug. 9, 1893, box 1, Washington Duke Papers, SCL; Nancy Mangum to Washington Duke, Mar. 15, 1894, box 1, Washington Duke Papers, SCL; W. D. Latta to Benjamin N. Duke, June 16, 1896, box 5, Benjamin Newton Duke Papers, SCL; Rachel Price to Washington Duke, Apr. 7, 1895, box, 1, Washington Duke Papers, SCL; Alice Duke to Washington Duke, Feb. 15, 1894, box 1, Washington Duke Papers, SCL; G. W. Starling to Washington Duke, Feb. 22, 1892, box 1, Washington Duke Papers, SCL; J. D. Cameron to Washington Duke, Mar. 30, 1891, box 1, Washington Duke Papers, SCL; Susan Watson Rhen to Benjamin N. Duke, June 6, 1896, box 5, Benjamin Newton Duke Papers, SCL; Hennie Threatt to Washington Duke, Feb. 19, 1892, box 1, Washington Duke Papers, SCL. Compared to the proudly independent begging letters to Northern philanthropists that Scott Sandage studied, these letters to the Dukes provide a record of the uses of abject dependence. See Sandage, "Gaze of Success."

15. Polk, *Agricultural Depression*, 1–23.

16. Inaugural Address, 1893, GLB 90, Carr Papers, NCDAH; Message to the General Assembly, Jan. 17, 1895, GLB 90, Carr Papers, NCDAH; W. K. Carr to Elias Carr, Dec. 18, 1891, box 15, folder b, Carr Papers, ECU; W. K. Carr to Elias Carr, June 16, 192, box 17, folder a, Carr Papers, ECU; W. K. Carr to Father, Nov. 29, 1894, box 21, folder c, Carr Papers, ECU.

17. Lawrence Goodwyn and Bruce Palmer, among others, blamed North Carolina's Marion Butler and his attachment to silver for the failure of Populism. James Logan Hunt's fine biography and James Beeby's excellent study of state Populists show the limited range of Butler's options, but the debate over the true meaning of Populism endures, and the role of silver is at the forefront of it. For scholars in the tradition of John D. Hicks, C. Vann Woodward, Norman Pollack, Sheldon Hackney, Robert McMath, and Lawrence Goodwyn, Populists represent a lost radical opportunity, a native socialism, a precursor to the New Deal, or an inspiration for economic progressivism. For scholars more interested in a populist style than in the Populist

Party, like Michael Kazin, Thomas Sugrue, or Nancy MacLean, the influence of Richard Hofstadter still looms large, representing the party as a backward, irrational mass politics rooted in paranoia, anti-Semitism, and anxiety. During the 1990s, many scholars eschewed Populism for the populist style, especially the growth of a global reactionary populism. Recently, a new wave of Populist scholars, including Elizabeth Sanders, Charles Postel, Robert Johnston, Connie Lester, James Logan Hunt, James Beeby, and Matthew Hild have reestablished Populists as ideological innovators. At times the history of Southern Populism can seem wildly distinct from the portrayals of its Western variants. Populist scholars who emphasize the Great Plains, Midwest, and West — like Walter Nugent, Peter Argersinger, Robert Cherny, and Jeffrey Ostler — have avoided some of the excitement and the pitfalls of Southern arguments and have had more success incorporating Robert Darden's advice that Populism was not a debating society or a massed crowd but a political party, and that it was defined at the point of interaction between candidates and crowds. See Hicks, *Populist Revolt*; Pollack, *Populist Response*; Woodward, *Origins of the New South*; Goodwyn, *Democratic Promise*; Hackney, *Populism to Progressivism*; Palmer, *Man over Money*; Ayers, *Promise of the New South*; Johnston, *Radical Middle Class*, esp. xi; McMath, *American Populism*; McMath, *Populist Vanguard*; Sanders, *Roots of Reform*; Postel, *Populist Vision*; Lester, *Up from the Mudsills of Hell*; Hild, *Greenbackers*; Creech, *Righteous Indignation*; Hofstadter, *Age of Reform*; Hofstadter, *Paranoid Style*; Kazin, *Populist Persuasion*; MacLean, *Behind the Mask*; MacLean, "Leo Frank Case Reconsidered"; McGirr, *Suburban Warriors*; Sugrue, *Origins of the Urban Crisis*; Walter Nugent, *Tolerant Populists*; Cherny, *Populism*; Argersinger, *Limits of Agrarian Radicalism*; and Ostler, *Prairie Populism*.

For North Carolina Populism, see, particularly, Beeby, *Revolt of the Tar Heels*; Beckel, "Roots of Reform"; Hunt, *Marion Butler*; Redding, *Making Race*; Thurtell, "Fusion Insurgency"; Creech, *Righteous Indignation*; Anderson, "Populists and Capitalist America"; Durden, *Climax of Populism*; and Flynn, "Procrustean Bedfellows."

18. J. F. Tillman to Butler, n.d. [1892], subser. 1.1, folder 4, Marion Butler Papers, SHC; James H. Pou to Dear Sir, Sept. 15, 1894, box 3, Hawkins Papers, NCDAH; Pou to Dear Sir, Oct. 26, 1894, box 3, Hawkins Papers, NCDAH; "Buncombe" lists, box 2, folder 14, Pearson Papers #3647, SHC; Quarterly Reports, 1892, ser. 2.3.1, folder 705, Marion Butler Papers, SHC; R. F. Allison to Butler, Sept. 21, 1896, subser. 1.2, folder 31, Marion Butler Papers, SHC; *Elizabeth City North Carolinian*, June 5, 1895, p. 2; Ed. Chambers Smith to Hawkins, Oct. 22, 1890, Hawkins Papers, NCDAH; *Wilmington Messenger*, July 15, 1892, p. 2; W. S. Pearson to Vance, Oct. 18, 1893, reel 37, *Papers of Zebulon Vance*; *Elizabeth City North Carolinian*, May 23, 1872, p. 2; *Caucasian*, Oct. 18, 1894, p. 1; May 16, 1895, p. 1; J. C. Hazeley to William Coppinger, June 3, 5, 1879, ser. 1A, vol. 233, American Colonization Society Papers, LOC; *Harper's Weekly*, July 4, 1896, p. 649; Sept. 26, 1896; Oct. 17, 1896, p. 1017; June 2, 1900, p. 1; Sept. 22, 1900, p. 1; *Sound Money*, Apr. 15, 1896; *People's Advocate*,

July 16, 1896; *Judge*, July 25, 1896; *Rocky Mountain News*, Aug. 18, 1896; *Sound Money*, Aug. 20, 1896; *Los Angeles Times*, Aug. 20, 1896; *Judge*, Sept. 19, 1896; *Los Angeles Times*, Sept. 20, 1896; *Daily Inter-Ocean*, Sept. 25, 1896; *Saint Louis Post-Dispatch*, Oct. 11, 22, 1896; *Progressive Farmer*, Apr. 25, 1893, p. 2; *Wilmington Messenger*, July 26, 1892, p. 2; *Progressive Farmer*, July 18, 1893, p. 4; *Wilmington Morning Star*, Jul 3, 1892, p. 2. Many of the images referenced are available online either at the Harpweek's Explore History site at <http://www.harpweek.com> or the excellent collection designed by Rebecca Edwards and Sarah DeFeo at Vassar College, "1896: A Website of Political Cartoons," available at <http://projects.vassar.edu/1896>.

19. *Progressive Farmer*, Aug. 5, 1890, p. 1; Jan. 24, 1893, p. 8; May 30, 1893, p. 1; June 27, 1893, p. 1; July 11, 1893, p. 8; Sept. 12, 1893, p. 4; July 3, 1894, p. 1; Nov. 6, 1894, p. 6; Nov. 27, 1894, p. 4; May 31, 1898, p. 2; July 5, 1898, p. 5; Feb. 1, 1898, p. 6; Aug. 3, 1897, p. 2; Oct. 2, 1900, p. 1; *Caucasian*, Jan. 16, 1890, p. 1; Sept. 22, 1892, p. 2; Jan. 27, 1893, p. 3; Jan. 31, 1895, p. 2; May 16, 1895, p. 1; Aug. 8, 1895, p. 2; Aug. 15, 1895, p. 2; July 2, 1896, p. 1; July 21, 1898, p. 2; Mar. 29, 1900, p. 2; Chas. E. Taylor to Bailey, Dec. 2, 1893, box 2, Bailey Papers, SCL; D. S. Moss to Bailey, Dec. 31, 1893, box 2, Bailey Papers, SCL; *Raleigh News and Observer*, July 20, 1894, p. 2; Daniel McN. McKay to Polk, Mar. 13, 1886, box 6, folder 81, Polk Papers, SHC; Josiah Bailey to Kilgo, July 14, 1897, box 1, folder 3, Kilgo Papers, DUA; Chas. E. Taylor to Kilgo, July 6, 1896, box 1, folder 2, Kilgo Papers, DUA; A. R. Rudisill to Vance, Sept. 29, 1893, reel 37, *Papers of Zebulon Vance*; Speech, July 5, 1897, box 5, folder 58, William W. Kitchin Papers #4018, SHC; Leonidas L. Polk to Winston, Sept. 11, 1890, box 2, folder 22, Robert Watson Winston Papers, SHC; Sassfras Fork Alliance to Settle, Aug. 12, 1893, box 5, folder 72, Settle Papers, SHC; Resolutions, Caswell County Alliance, Aug. 25, 1893, reel 36, *Papers of Zebulon Vance*; W. T. McCulloch to Polk, Apr. 12, 1892, box 7, folder 103, Polk Papers, SHC.

20. Thos. J. Oldham to Augustus W. Graham, Oct. 17, 1894, box 3, folder 42, Graham Papers, SHC; W. D. Hightower to Graham, Aug. 18, 1894, box 3, folder 41, Graham Papers, SHC; T. Y. Holland to Thompson, n.d. [1896], box 1, folder 6, Thompson Papers, #715, SHC; C. McG. Dunn to Thompson, Dec. 1, 1896, box 1, folder 8, Thompson Papers, SHC; Hannibal N. Simpson to Russell, Apr. 26, 1897, GP 292, Russell Papers, NCDAH; S. T. Hinshaw to Butler, Nov. 17, 1896, subser. 1.2, folder 40, Marion Butler Papers, SHC; S. H. McElanny to Butler, Oct. 7, 1896, subser. 1.2, folder 35, Marion Butler Papers, SHC; C. McG. Dunn to Butler, Dec. 1, 1896, subser. 1.2, folder 42, Marion Butler Papers, SHC; Mrs. Henry Fryar to Butler, Dec. 11, 1896, subser. 1.2, folder 43, Marion Butler Papers, SHC; Thad Jones Jr. to Butler, Apr. 2, 1900, subser. 1.2, folder 148, Marion Butler Papers, SHC; W. M. Pearson to Butler, Apr. 23, 1897, subser. 1.2, folder 62, Marion Butler Papers, SHC; *Progressive Farmer*, Jan. 3, 1892, p. 2, Apr. 2, 1895, p. 1; *Contested-Election Case*, 283, 338; Testimony, R. I. Walder, Contested Election "Parker v. Peebles," box 21, Gen-

eral Assembly Session Records, 1895, NCDAH; Arthur T. Abernethy to Russell, n.d., GP 292, Russell Papers, NCDAH; Will E. Abernethy to Russell, Feb. 11, 1897, GP 291, Russell Papers, NCDAH.

21. W. E. White to Butler, May 5, 1896, subser. 1.2, folder 18, Marion Butler Papers, SHC; J. W. Flanigan to Settle, May 6, 1894, box 6, folder 95, Settle Papers, SHC; Osecca J. Spears to Olds, Apr. 23, 1894, box 6, folder 94, Settle Papers, SHC; J. A. C. Barkley to Olds, Apr. 18, 1894, box 6, folder 93, Settle Papers, SHC; T. F. Jones to Butler, May 19, 1896, subser. 1.2, folder 19, Marion Butler Papers, SHC; Hunt, *Marion Butler*, 47; B. F. White to Butler, June 28, 1896, subser. 1.2, folder 21, Marion Butler Papers, SHC.

22. A. E. Walters to Graham, May 4, 1894, box 4, folder 45, Graham Papers, SHC; R. B. Davis to Smith, Apr. 15, 1896, Smith Papers, SCL; Thos. J. Jarvis to Smith, Apr. 16, 1896, Smith Papers, SCL; Jarvis to Smith, May 28, 1896, Smith Papers, SCL; Jarvis to Smith, June 15, 1896, Smith Papers, SCL; *Wilmington Messenger*, July 1, 1896, p. 2; July 2, 1896, p. 2; Josephus Daniels to Bryan, May 9 1896, box 4, Bryan Papers, LOC; *Progressive Farmer*, July 14, 1896, p. 2; Daniels, *Editor in Politics*, 157, 166–70; Bryan and Bryan, *Memoirs*, 10, 105; Bryan, *First Battle*, 449–50; Bensel, *Passions and Preferences*.

23. Bryan, *First Battle*, 377, 447–48, 450, 456–58, 491, 522, 543, 548.

24. *Caucasian*, Nov. 5, 1896, p. 1; *Progressive Farmer*, Sept. 29, 1896, p. 3; Kazin, *Godly Hero*, 73–75; Mrs. Isaac Wolfe to Bryan, Feb. 18, 1896, box 43, Bryan Papers, LOC; T. D. Young to Bryan, Feb. 8, 1897, box 43, Bryan Papers, LOC; Mr. and Mrs. Thomas Rhodes to Bryan, Jan. 30, 1897, box 43, Bryan Papers, LOC; Anna B. Paul to Bryan, Jan. 19, 1898, box 43, Bryan Papers, LOC; A. D. Swindell to Bryan, Jan. 28, 1897, box 44, Bryan Papers, LOC; N. A. Nelson to Bryan, Oct. 12, 1897, box 44, Bryan Papers, LOC; Mr. and Mrs. W. E. G. Morris, May 24, 1897, box 44, Bryan Papers, LOC; Mrs. Paul Perry to Bryan, Oct. 24, 1897, box 44, Bryan Papers, LOC; Bryan and Bryan, *Memoirs*, 269.

25. Thomas Watson to Butler, Oct. 28, 1896, subser. 1.2, folder 38, Marion Butler Papers, SHC; W. H. Kitchin to Butler, June 5, 1896, subser. 1.2, folder 20, Marion Butler Papers, SHC; B. F. Keith to Butler, Sept. 19, 1896, subser. 1.2, folder 31, Marion Butler Papers, SHC.

26. Wm. E. Clark to Settle, June 26, 1896, box 9, folder 149, Settle Papers, SHC; Thomas Watkins to Settle, July 9, 1896, box 9, folder 150, Settle Papers, SHC; J. T. Hairston to Settle, Apr. 25, 1896, box 9, folder 146, Settle Papers, SHC; *Reidsville Weekly Review*, Jan. 26, 1894, p. 2; Feb. 7, 1896, p. 2; Mar. 27, 1896, p. 3.

27. Notebook, Sept. to Oct. 1894, box 28, folder 312, Graham Papers, SHC.

28. Corbett, *Harp of Ethiopia*, 6, 224; *Reidsville Weekly Review*, May 1, 1896, p. 3; M. N. Corbett to Settle, July 22, 1892, box 4, folder 55, Settle Papers, SHC; Corbett to Settle, July 26, 1892, box 4, folder 55, Settle Papers, SHC; Corbett to Settle,

Aug. 16, 1896, box 4, folder 56, Settle Papers, SHC; H. G. Tilley to Settle, Aug. 9, 1892, box 4, folder 56, Settle Papers, SHC.

29. Hahn, *Nation under Our Feet*, 364–411; Crow, " 'Fusion, Confusion and Negroism'"; H. G. Tilley to Settle, Aug. 9, 1892, box 4, folder 56, Settle Papers, SHC; M. N. Corbett to James F. Wray, Sept. 23, 1894, box 7, folder 106, Settle Papers, SHC; Wray to Settle, Oct. 3, 1894, box 7, folder 107, Settle Papers, SHC; Corbett to Wray, Oct. 26, 1894, box 7, folder 109, Settle Papers, SHC; J. O. Hoskins to Settle, Jan. 29, 1894, box 6, folder 87, Settle Papers, SHC; R. P. Hughes to Settle, May 11, 1894, box 6, folder 96, Settle Papers, SHC; Tilley to Settle, Oct. 16, 1894, box 7, folder 108, Settle Papers, SHC; Hughes to Settle, May 19, 1894, box 6, folder 96, Settle Papers, SHC; Hughes to Settle, Mar. 26, 1894, box 6, folder 91, Settle Papers, SHC; F. T. Greenlee to Settle, Sept. 25, 1894, box 7, folder 106, Settle Papers, SHC; Corbett to Settle, May 27, 1896, box 9, folder 148, Settle Papers, SHC; R. B. Russell et al. to The People of North Carolina, June 6, 1896, box 9, folder 149, Settle Papers, SHC; Jas. J. Kerner to Russell, July 7, 1896, box 2, folder 16, Russell Papers #645, SHC; Wm. A. Guthrie to Butler, Sept. 6, 1896, subser. 1.2, folder 28, Marion Butler Papers, SHC; *Caucasian*, Mar. 19, 1896, pp. 1, 2; Y. C. Morton to Butler, Apr. 30, 1896, subser. 1.2, folder 17, Marion Butler Papers, SHC; Alla W. McAlanham to Butler, Aug. 27, 1896, subser. 1.2, folder 26, Marion Butler Papers, SHC; M. Oliver to Butler, Sept. 24, 1896, folder 32, Marion Butler Papers, SHC; Wm. E. Clark to Settle, June 26, 1896, subser. 1.2, box 9, folder 149, Settle Papers, SHC; J. B. Eaves to Dear Sir, n.d., box 6, Hawkins Papers, NCDAH; E. J. Faison to Butler, Aug. 5, 1898, folder 109, Florence Faison Butler Papers, #115, SHC.

30. James H. Poe et al. to Settle, Aug. 6, 1894, box 7, folder 102, Settle Papers, SHC; *Charlotte Daily Observer*, July 19, 1898, p. 2; M. N. Corbett to Settle, Aug. 30, 1895, box 8, folder 120, Settle Papers, SHC.

31. *Reidsville Weekly Review*, Jan. 31, 1896, p. 2; Feb. 14, 1896, p. 2; Feb. 21, 1896, p. 2; Thomas D. Watkins to Settle, Aug. 23, 1896, box 10, folder 153, Settle Papers, SHC; Jno. F. Woody to Settle, Feb. 17, 1896, box 9, folder 135, Settle Papers, SHC; Samuel P. Satterfield to Settle, Feb. 7, 1896, box 9, folder 134, Settle Papers, SHC; Thos. W. Vincent to Settle, Feb. 12, 1896, box 9, folder 135, Settle Papers, SHC; Ed. Gravely to Settle, Apr. 16, 1896, box 9, folder 144, Settle Papers, SHC; E. P. McKissack to Settle, Feb. 6, 1896, box 9, folder 134, Settle Papers, SHC.

32. P. H. Hodson to Settle, Apr. 23, 1896, box 9, folder 145, Settle Papers, SHC; A. A. Parker to Settle, Apr. 17, 1896, box 9, folder 145, Settle Papers, SHC; *Reidsville Weekly Review*, Oct. 30, 1896, p. 4.

33. Wm. A. Guthrie to Butler, Oct. 16, 1896, subser. 1.2, folder 36, Marion Butler Papers, SHC; M. Oliver to Butler, Sept. 24, 1896, subser. 1.2, folder 32, Marion Butler Papers, SHC; *Reidsville Weekly Review*, Sept. 25, 1895, p. 2; Oct. 25, 1895, p. 2; Nov. 22, 1895, p. 2; Nov. 19, 1896, p. 2; William W. Kitchin to R. J. Oliver, June 29, 1897, box 1, folder 7, William W. Kitchin Papers, SHC.

Chapter Seven

1. Inaugural Address, Jan. 15, 1901, GLB 109, Aycock Papers, NCDAH.

2. Viewing white supremacy from the realm of campus debates seems peculiar next to the now-iconic images of the campaign drawn by scholars like Glenda Elizabeth Gilmore, Eric Anderson, and Helen Edmonds: jostling and then bloodshed on the streets of Wilmington, violent attacks at campaign canvasses in the eastern Black Second, and lurid and invented stories of rape in Josephus Daniels's newspaper. From Edmonds's pathbreaking 1951 *Negro and Fusion Politics*, through works by H. Leon Prather Sr., Eric Anderson, Janette Thomas Greenwood, Kent Redding, Paul Escott, Dwight B. Billings, and especially Glenda Elizabeth Gilmore, scholars have authoritatively toppled older, heroic accounts of white supremacy and replaced them with increasingly nuanced narratives of its leaders' tactics. Although Gilmore connects white supremacy to broad, if vaguely defined, intellectual trends, scholars have at times lost track of John Cell's comparatively driven insight that the state's segregationist movement was deeply modern and even liberal. Too easily, in less-nuanced accounts, white supremacy leaders become carriers of cultural prejudice or warriors for thwarted ambition. This personalizing historiographical strand reaches all the way back to Robert D. W. Connor, a UNC student in the fall of 1898 whose father helped lead the white supremacy campaign. Robert Connor, who studied under William Dunning at Columbia, served as a professor of history and government at the University of North Carolina until 1934, when Franklin Roosevelt named him the first archivist of the United States. Connor's 1929 *North Carolina: Rebuilding an Ancient Commonwealth* described white supremacy as a "small group" of leaders tied together by a "high civic duty" to drive the state toward their shared vision of its future. In overturning that judgment, and treating white supremacy not as honorable but as monstrous, scholars from Edmonds on have found themselves partly trapped in Robert Connor's own analysis, reversing his lens instead of replacing it. Instead of personal honor, white supremacy became in large part a story of personal failings. The role of ideas, and the role of the campus as the center of many of the social networks, is largely absent; without it, scholars have oddly defanged North Carolina's white supremacy, transforming a sweeping (and hardly anomalous) program for overhauling state and society into a vehicle for twisted or crass individuals. See R. D. W. Connor, *North Carolina*, 465, 479; Gilmore, *Gender and Jim Crow*, 61–66; Gilmore, "Murder, Memory, and the Flight of the Incubus"; Edmonds, *Negro and Fusion Politics*; Prather, *Resurgent Politics*; Prather, *We Have Taken a City*; Anderson, *Race and Politics*; Greenwood, *Bittersweet Legacy*; Billings, *Planters*; Redding, *Making Race*; Laura Edwards, "Captives of Wilmington"; Kantrowitz, "Two Faces of Domination"; Escott, *Many Excellent People*; Carlson, "White Man's Revolution"; Rivers, "Civilizing Tendencies"; Cell, *Highest Stage*; and Tindall, "Significance of Howard W. Odum," 289.

3. Edward Alsworth Ross, "Recent Tendencies," 441; Schneider, "Eugenics Movement in France," 69; Ellis, *Physician-Legislators*, 2–5, 180, 218; Lovett, *Conceiving the Future*, 11–12; Christine Rosen, *Preaching Eugenics*; Freeden, "Eugenics and Progressive Thought"; Kevles, *In the Name of Eugenics*, 64–77; Leonard, " 'More Merciful' "; Mark H. Haller, *Eugenics*; Pickens, *Eugenics and the Progressives*; Kline, *Building a Better Race*; Schneider, *Quality and Quantity*, 3–8, 28–48; Conklin, *Mission to Civilize*, 3–8; Rosenberg, "Albert Sarraut"; Andrew Zimmerman, *Anthropology and Antihumanism*, 57–87, 111–45, 215; Woodruff D. Smith, *Politics and the Science of Culture*, 91–103; Weiss, *Race Hygiene*, 86; Searle, *A New England?*, 305–85; Porter, *Karl Pearson*, 97–102, 267–92; Greta Jones, *Social Hygiene*, 2–45, 88.

4. Edwin Alderman to Connor, Nov. 18, 1898, box 40b, Henry Groves Connor Papers #175, SHC; "Negro in the South," 158; *The Hellenian* 10 (1899): 4; W. H. Carroll to Alderman, Nov. 23, 1898, box 20, University of North Carolina Papers, UA; Cornelia P. Spencer to June, Oct. 24, 1880, folder 11, Spencer Papers, #683, SHC; George T. Winston to Spencer, Apr. 9, 1895, box 2, Spencer Papers, P.C. 7, NCDAH; Beckert, *Monied Metropolis*, 8, 11, 13, 240; Haskell, *Emergence of Professional Social Science*. I develop these ideas in more detail in Downs, "University Men."

5. Although Joel Williamson defines Alderman as Conservative and Winston as Radical, their racial thought was closely related through the 1890s and early 1900s. See Williamson, *Crucible of Race*, 6, 274–75; Alderman to Woodrow Wilson, Apr. 21, 1908, box 2, Papers of Edwin Anderson Alderman, MSS 1001, UVA; McIver memoir, McIver Records, UNCG; Robert W. Winston, *It's a Far Cry*, 111; George T. Winston to Alderman, Apr. 21, 1908, box 12, Office Administrative Files 1902–14, President's Papers, University Archives, UVA; George T. Winston, "Relation of the White to the Negro," 115; George T. Winston, *Greek, the Roman, and the Teuton*, 3, 4, 6, 8, 18; John S. Haller, "Race and the Concept of Progress"; and Stocking, *Race, Culture, and Evolution*, 241–52.

6. Alderman, "Influence of Corporate Power," 100–103; Craig, "Wealth," 273–81; "Origin of Man," 54; Robert Watson Winston, "Chivalry," 27–31; McGee, "Science of Humanity," 262, 263, 269, 270; J. W. Powell, "From Barbarism to Civilization," 97–103, 122; J. W. Powell, "Competition as a Factor in Human Evolution," 319–21; McGee, "Trend of Human Progress," 411–14, 446; Harp, *Positivist Republic*, 121; Reed, *W. E. B. Du Bois*, 119; Warlick, "Race Problem," 14–16; Walser, "What Will the Harvest Be?," 295–96; Leloudis, *Schooling the New South*; Prather, *Resurgent Politics*; Alderman, "Historic Awakening in North Carolina," in *State Chronicle*, Mar. 7, 1892, clipping in box 1, folder 23, Alderman Papers, UVA; Untitled article about Edwin Alderman's May 1890 speech, *University Magazine*, June 1890, 259–61; "On Teaching History," 1886, box 1, folder 13, Alderman Papers, UVA; and Institute Statistics, 1888–90, box 1, folder 15, Alderman Papers, UVA. Although Michael Dennis did not include the University of North Carolina in his study of progressive Southern universities of this era, his analysis largely depends upon the conservatism

of Francis Venable, who succeeded Edwin Alderman and Winston as president. See Dennis, *Lessons in Progress*, 2.

7. Untitled article, *University Magazine*, July 1888, 280; Battle, *History of the University of North Carolina*, 450–51; Minutes, Feb. 11, 1890, volume S-8, Trustee Affairs #40001, UA; untitled article, *University Magazine*, 1891, 343; Samuel Lee Davis, "The Evolution of Nations," June 4, 1891, ser. 2, subser. 1, box 2, Dialectic Society Records, #40182, UA; Report of the Visiting Committee of 1894–1895, subgroup 1, vol. 9, Trustee Affairs, UA; George T. Winston to Spencer, Apr. 9, 1895, box 2, Spencer Papers, NCDAH; Bode, *Protestantism and the New South*. By emphasizing the "pathological vein" rather than the "pathological individual" in the construction of white supremacy, I follow Kathleen Blee's corrective to the overly personal and psychological studies on white supremacy by scholars like Gail Bederman and Joel Williamson. See Blee, "Evidence, Empathy, and Ethics," 601, 606; Bederman, *Manliness and Civilization*; and Williamson, *Crucible of Race*.

8. Samuel A'Court Ashe, "Concerning the Negro Race," Ashe Papers, P.C. 513, NCDAH; *Charlotte Daily Observer*, Aug. 18, 1898, p. 3. Kent Redding emphasizes the way Democrats imitated the organization innovations of the Populists they sought to defeat. For a reading that places the blame for the 1898 Populist-Republican defeat upon Populist internal division, rather than the Democratic effort, see James Beeby's fine study of the North Carolina Populist Party. See Redding, *Making Race, Making Power*; and Beeby, *Revolt of the Tar Heels*.

9. Claude Kitchin to Rodman, Oct. 17, 1898, box 71, folder h, Rodman Papers #329, ECU; Rippy, *F. M. Simmons*, 83–84; S. W. Freehan et al. to General Assembly, n.d., box 23, General Assembly Session Records, 1899–1900, NCDAH; Democratic Club Charter, Nov. 24, 1896, box 1, folder 6, Heriot Clarkson Papers #1313, SHC; Cotten to Gen W. G. Le Duc, Jan. 30, 1897, box 1, folder 1, Cotten Papers #2613, SHC; W. H. McFarland to Carr, Feb. 18, 1895, GP 284, Carr Papers, NCDAH; S. L. Gibson to Butler, July 17, 1900, subser. 1.2, folder 165, Marion Butler Papers, #114 SHC; J. T. B. Hoover to Butler, Mar. 14, 1900, subser. 1.2, folder 144, Marion Butler Papers, SHC; *Charlotte Daily Observer*, Aug. 24, 1898, p. 4; Sept. 16, 1898, p. 2; Sept. 27, 1898, p. 7; Oct. 22, 1898, p. 3; *Raleigh News and Observer*, Oct. 23, 1898, p. 4; Joseph Marion King to Butler, Oct. 25, 1898, subser. 1.2, folder 117, Marion Butler Papers, SHC; *Raleigh News and Observer*, July 21, 1898, p. 1; Sept. 11, 1898, p. 6; B. S. Graves to Jas. W. Somers, July 10, 1900, enclosed in W. E. Lowe to J. Southerland, July 20, 1900, box 1, folder 14, Coulter Papers #3579, SHC.

10. *Charlotte Daily Observer*, Aug. 18, 1898, p. 3; Sept. 13, 1898, p. 8; Oct. 7, 1898, p. 4; Oct. 22, 1898, p. 4; Oct. 23, 1898, p. 8; Nov. 1, 1898, p. 8; *Raleigh News and Observer*, Sept. 10, 1898, p. 5; Sept. 30, 1898, p. 2; Oct. 21, 1898, p. 3; Oct. 26, 1898, p. 1; Apr. 8, 1900, p. 2; Rippy, *F. M. Simmons*, 23–24, 83, 92; W. E. Lowe to H. Southerland, July 20, 1900, box 1, folder 14, Coulter Papers, SHC; E. J. Justice to Winston, Mar. 1, 1900, box 1, folder 10, Francis D. Winston Papers #2810, SHC; *Reidsville*

Weekly Review, May 18, 1900, p. 2; Speech Delivered in County Convention, June 1, 1900, box 1, Norwood Family Papers, P.C. 1219, NCDAH; white supremacy flyer, May 26, 1900, box 1, folder 9, London Papers #1561, SHC; May F. Jones, *Memoirs and Speeches*, 29.

11. 1912 speech, Craig Papers, SCL; *Wilmington Messenger*, July 23, 1898, p. 2; Sept. 27, 1898, p. 4; *Charlotte Daily Observer*, July 18, 1898, p. 4; Sept. 13, 1898, p. 8; Sept. 23, 1898, p. 4; Sept. 27, 1898, p. 3; Oct. 1, 1898, p. 6; Oct. 8, 1898, p. 4; Oct. 23, 1898, pp. 2, 8; July 5, 1900, p. 8; *Raleigh News and Observer*, Oct. 28, 1898, p. 4; Oct. 29, 1898, p. 1; Spruill, "Charles B. Aycock," 217–18; Alderman, "Southern Pioneers," 490; R. B. Davis to Clarkson, May 16, 1895, box 1, folder 6, Clarkson Papers, SHC; F. M. Simmons to My Dear Sir, May 27, 1900, box 74, folder a, Rodman Papers, ECU; W. H. Brown to Butler, July 5, 1900, subser. 1.2, folder 160, Marion Butler Papers, SHC; Page, *Southerner*, 229; Rippy, *F. M. Simmons*, 85–87; *Caucasian*, July 19, 1900, p. 4; July 26, 1900, p. 3; Address, [1899–1900], box 4, folder 21, Carr Papers #141, SHC; Fuller, *Twenty Years in Public Life*, 208.

12. Daniels, *Editor in Politics*, 254, 296; Page, *Southerner*, 241, 266; *Caucasian*, Sept. 22, 1898, p. 1; *Charlotte Daily Observer*, Sept. 17, 1898, p. 2; *Raleigh News and Observer*, Aug. 7, 1900, p. 5; Poland, *North Carolina's Glorious Victory*, 4; J. G. Newill to Butler, Jan. 29, 1900, subser. 1.2, folder 138, Marion Butler Papers, SHC; B. H. Tyson to Connor, Nov. 4, 1898, box 3, folder 40b, Henry Groves Connor Papers, SHC.

13. Daniels, *Editor in Politics*, 149–50, 254; *Raleigh News and Observer*, Aug. 6, 1898, p. 6; June 14, 1900, p. 4; J. F. Click to Butler, Mar. 8, 1900, subser. 1.2, folder 142, Marion Butler Papers, SHC; May F. Jones, *Memoirs and Speeches*, 29.

14. *Raleigh News and Observer*, Aug. 13 to Nov. 10, 1898.

15. *Charlotte Daily Observer*, Sept. 13, 1898, p. 8; July 1, 1900, p. 7; *Raleigh News and Observer*, Sept. 6, 1898, p. 4; July 14, 1900, p. 6; Samuel A'Court Ashe, "Concerning the Negro Race," Ashe Papers, P.C. 513, NCDAH; Daniels, *Editor in Politics*, 301; Page, *Southerner*, 241, 266, 291; Kilgo, "Inquiry," 8; Rebecca Cameron to My Dear Cousin, Oct. 26, 1898, box 1, folder 2b, Waddell Papers #743, SHC; May F. Jones, *Memoirs and Speeches*, 28–29.

16. *Raleigh News and Observer*, July 29, 1898, p. 4; Aug. 4, 1898, p. 1; Sept 23, 1898, p. 1; Nov. 8, 1898, p. 4; June 20, 1900, p. 4; July 14, 1900, p. 6; *Charlotte Daily Observer*, July 18, 1898, p. 4; Oct. 22, 1898, p. 3; Daniels, *Editor in Politics*, 254, 296.

17. In turn, Populists and Republicans responded within the framework of war discourse. Citing William Jennings Bryan's arguments against colonialism, they compared Democrats to the tyrannical Spaniards, and African Americans to sympathetic Cuban revolutionaries seeking "Civil Rights at home." This response failed not because it was logically less coherent than the Democratic arguments but because its practitioners lacked their opponents' force. See Carlson, "White Man's Revolution"; Gilmore, *Gender and Jim Crow*, 78–82; Thomas Dixon, *Leopard's Spots*, 412–19; *Reids-*

ville Weekly Review, Mar. 18, 1898, p. 2; *Wilmington Messenger*, Oct. 25, 1898, p. 2; Nov. 6, 1898, p. 1; *Charlotte Daily Observer*, Aug. 5, 1898, p. 2; Apr. 6, 1900, p. 4; *Raleigh News and Observer*, Apr. 27, 1898, p. 5; May 27, 1898, p. 1; Aug. 5, 1898, p. 2; Aug. 11, 1898, p. 5; Sept. 6, 1898, p. 4; Oct. 23, 1898, p. 4; Oct. 26, 1898, p. 2; Oct. 28, 1898, p. 5; Oct. 29, 1898, p. 3; Oct. 30, 1898, p. 5; Nov. 3, 1898, p. 3; Nov. 9, 1898, p. 4; June 10, 1898, p. 2; *Caucasian*, Sept. 13, 1900, p. 2; Oct. 4, 1900, p. 1; and Frank E. Emery to Butler, Apr. 2, 1898, subser. 1.2, folder 94, Marion Butler Papers, SHC.

18. John B. Tillinghast to Dear Frances, June 7, 1898, box 9, Tillinghast Family Papers, SCL; Tillinghast to My Dear Father, June 11, 1898, box 9, Tillinghast Family Papers, SCL; Tillinghast to Dear Father, Sept. 16, 1898, box 9, Tillinghast Family Papers, SCL; *Charlotte Daily Observer*, July 4, 1898, p. 7; Oct. 28, 1898, p. 4; Lorenzo Norvell to Butler, July 10, 1898, subser. 1.2, folder 104, Marion Butler Papers, SHC; MacKethan to My Dear Mother, May 11, 1898, box 8, folder 171, MacKethan Papers, #4298, SHC; White Man's Convention, May 29, 1900, box 15, folder 331, MacKethan Papers, SHC; Jos. M. Patton to Butler, Jan. 26, 1899, subser. 1.2, folder 123, Marion Butler Papers, SHC.

19. *Charlotte Daily Observer*, June 10, 1898, p. 3; June 22, 1898, p. 4; W. A. Blount to Jas. A Bryan, Apr. 11, 1898, folder 327, Bryan Family Papers, #96, SHC; Russell to J. C. L. Harris, Sept. 15, 1898, GP 300, Russell Papers, NCDAH; *Raleigh News and Observer*, June 28, 1898, p. 4; Bayliss Cade to S. D. Dill, Sept. 15, 1898, GP 300, Russell Papers, NCDAH.

20. *Raleigh News and Observer*, Sept. 16, 1898, p. 5; Sept. 20, 1898, p. 1; *Charlotte Daily Observer*, July 3, 1898, p. 4; Sept. 20, 1898, p. 8; Oct. 1, 1898, p. 1; Nov. 11, 1898, p. 3; John B. Tillinghast to Dear Father, Sept. 21, 1898, box 9, Tillinghast Family Papers, SCL; Journal, Aug. 6, Oct. 12, 1898, box 9, folder 114, vol. 2, Osborne Papers #567, SHC.

21. *Raleigh News and Observer*, Oct. 21, 1898, p. 3; June 27, 1900, p. 1; *Charlotte Daily Observer*, Oct. 2, 1898, p. 2; *Reidsville Weekly Review*, Aug. 3, 1900, p. 2; "Grand White Supremacy Rally and Ratification Meeting," Apr. 30, 1900, OP 4298.B, MacKethan Papers, SHC; "White Supremacy! Grand White Man's Rally!," May 26, 1900, box 1, folder 9, London Papers, SHC.

22. *Charlotte Daily Observer*, Aug. 2, 1900, p. 2; *Caucasian*, Sept. 20, 1900, p. 1; George T. Jones to Butler, Dec. 10, 1898, subser. 1.2, folder 118, Marion Butler Papers, SHC; "In Red Shirt Days," box 15, folder 115, Harris Papers #3804, SHC.

23. *Caucasian*, June 15, 1899, p. 2; *Caucasian*, Aug. 9, 1900, p. 1; Aug. 16, 1900, p. 1; Alex Parham to Butler, May 16, 1900, subser. 1.2, folder 154, Marion Butler Papers, SHC.

24. Thomas W. Clawson, "The Wilmington Race Riot of 1898," Clawson Papers, SCL; Desk Book, box 21, Cronly Family Papers, SCL; "Margaret Williams Neal," interview by Rhonda Mawhood, July 19, 1993, *Behind the Veil: Documenting African American Life in the Jim Crow South*, SCL; "William Childs," interview by Rhonda

Mawhood, July 12, 1993, *Behind the Veil: Documenting African American Life in the Jim Crow South*, SCL; Anonymous to William McKinley, Nov. 12, 1898, folder 1898-17743, box 1117A, entry 72, Department of Justice Central Files, Year Files, 1887–1903, RG 60, NA; Anonymous to McKinley, Nov. 13, 1898, folder 1898-17743, box 1117A, entry 72, Department of Justice Central Files, Year Files, 1887–1903, RG 60, NA.

25. J. A. Henry to William Coppinger, Mar. 16, 1899, ser. 1A, reel 149, vol. 296, American Colonization Society Papers, LOC; Anonymous to Hunter, June 1900, box 2, Hunter Papers, SCL; W. S. Key et al. to William McKinley, Nov. 13, 1898, folder 1898-17743, box 1117A, entry 72, Department of Justice Central Files, Year Files, 1887–1903, RG 60, NA; Anonymous to McKinley, n.d. (Document 68), folder 1898-17743, box 1117A, entry 72, Department of Justice Central Files, Year Files, 1887–1903, RG 60, NA; Della V. Johnson to McKinley, Nov. 14, 1898, folder 1898-17743, box 1117A, entry 72, Department of Justice Central Files, Year Files, 1887–1903, RG 60, NA; Anonymous to McKinley, Nov. 13, 1898, folder 1898-17743, box 1117A, entry 72, Department of Justice Central Files, Year Files, 1887–1903, RG 60, NA; Anna M. Johnson to McKinley, Nov. 11, 1898, folder 1898-17743, box 1117A, entry 72, Department of Justice Central Files, Year Files, 1887–1903, RG 60, NA.

26. *Caucasian*, Feb. 23, 1899, p. 1; George Rountree, "Memorandum of My Personal Recollection of the Election of 1898," box 3, folder 41, Henry Groves Connor Papers, SHC; McGee, "The Trend of Human Progress," 446; Keyssar, *Right to Vote*, 117–71; Lodge, *Speeches and Addresses*, 247, 251, 252, 263; Higham, *Strangers in the Land*, 142–54; Guterl, *Color of Race*, 95–109, 139–47; Gilmore, *Gender and Jim Crow*, 71.

27. To the Board of Trustees, Dec. 31, 1898, box 20, folder 674, University of North Carolina Papers, #40001, UA; Alderman, "University of Today," 288–90; "Obligations and Opportunities of Scholarship," box 1, folder 53, Alderman Papers, UVA; George T. Winston, "The Influence of Universities and Public Schools on National Life and Character," June 17, 1896, box 3, folder 23, Robert Watson Winston Papers, SHC; George T. Winston, "Industrial Training," 104–7; George T. Winston, "Relation of the Whites to the Negroes," 115–17; William A. Link, "Privies, Progressivism, and Public Schools"; William A. Link, *Paradox of Southern Progressivism*; Tindall, *Emergence of the New South*; Greenwood, *Bittersweet Legacy*, 230–36; Schoen, *Choice and Coercion*; Castles, "Quiet Eugenics."

28. "Rules Governing Applications for Pardons," July 20, 1901, GP 305, Aycock Papers, NCDAH; Charles B. Aycock Term, Records and Reasons for Granting Pardons, 135, 138, 144, 219, 226, 301, 326, 359, Aycock Papers, NCDAH; Governor's Message to the General Assembly of 1903, n.d. [Jan. 1903], GLB 109, Aycock Papers, NCDAH; Governor's Message to the General Assembly of 1905, n.d. [Jan. 1905], GLB 109, Aycock Papers, NCDAH; Inaugural Address, Jan. 11, 1905, GLB 113, Glenn Papers, NCDAH; Biennial Message to General Assembly, Jan. 10, 1907, GLB

113, Glenn Papers, NCDAH; Robert B. Glenn Term, Records and Reasons for Granting Pardons, 454, 466, 467, 529–30, 548, Glenn Papers, NCDAH; Glenn to E. B. Jones, Mar. 11, 1907, GP 315, Glenn Papers, NCDAH; W. L. Cunningham to Glenn, Mar. 12, 1907, GP 315, Glenn Papers, NCDAH; A. E. Dockery to Glenn, Mar. 20, 1907, GP 315, Glenn Papers, NCDAH; George Simmons to Glenn, Mar. 21, 1907, GP 315, Glenn Papers, NCDAH; Daniels, *Editor in Politics*, 390–91; *Caucasian*, Jan. 11, 1906, p. 2; Ashley Horne to James A. Lockhart, Feb. 21, 1908, Simms Papers, SCL; Message to the General Assembly of North Carolina of 1905, GLB 109, Aycock Papers, NCDAH; Inaugural Address, Jan. 11, 1905, GLB 113, Glenn Papers, NCDAH; To the Honorable the General Assembly of North Carolina, Feb. 4, 1905, Glenn Papers, NCDAH.

29. Inaugural Address, Jan. 15, 1901, GLB 109, Aycock Papers, NCDAH; Governor's Message to the General Assembly of 1903, n.d. [Jan. 1903], GLB 109, Aycock Papers, NCDAH; Governor's Message to the General Assembly of 1905, n.d. [Jan. 1905], GLB 109, Aycock Papers, NCDAH; Inaugural Address, Jan. 11, 1905, GLB 113, Glenn Papers, NCDAH; Biennial Message to the General Assembly, Jan. 10, 1907, GLB 113, Glenn Papers, NCDAH; Connor and Poe, *Life and Speeches*, 100–102; *Caucasian*, June 8, 1905, p. 2; June 7, 1906, p. 2; Aug. 16, 1906, p. 2; Aug. 23, 1906, p. 2.

30. Thomas J. Jarvis to Glenn, Jan. 15, 1908, GP 318, Glenn Papers, NCDAH; *Union Signal*, Feb. 20, 1908, p. 5; *Charlotte Daily News*, Feb. 23, 1908, p. 1; To the Honorable the General Assembly, Jan. 21, 1908, GLB 113, Glenn Papers, NCDAH; *Biblical Recorder*, June 8, 15, 1910, p. 4; Dec. 31, 1913, p. 3; "The Task of Wake Forest Alumni," box 1, folder 25, Oates Papers, WFU; "Law Enforcement," box 1, folder 25, Oates Papers, WFU; Smithfield speech, 1905, box 1, folder 32, Oates Papers, WFU; "Temperance and Law Enforcement," box 1, folder 48, Oates Papers, WFU; Mattingly, *Well-Tempered Women*; Blocker, *"Give to the Winds"*; Tyrrell, *Sobering Up*; Tyrrell, *Woman's World*; Szymanski, "Beyond Parochialism"; Bordin, *Frances Willard*; Whitener, *Prohibition in North Carolina*; Curtis, *Consuming Faith*; Ownby, *Subduing Satan*; Foster, *Moral Reconstruction*.

31. *Caucasian*, Feb. 4, 1904, p. 3; *Biblical Recorder*, Jan. 8, 1908, p. 7; Apr. 8, 1908, p. 1; Apr. 15, 1908, p. 12; Apr. 29, 1908, pp. 3, 4; May 20, 1908, p. 3; *Charlotte Daily News*, Feb. 22, 1908, p. 2; *Charlotte Daily Observer*, May 18, 1908, p. 5; *Raleigh News and Observer*, Apr. 3, 1908, p. 5; May 12, 1908, p. 6; May 20, 1908, p. 4; C. M. Anderson to Oates, n.d., box 2, folder 66, Oates Papers, WFU.

32. Aycock, *Why Prohibition Should Prevail*, 9–10; *Charlotte Daily Observer*, Apr. 29, 1908, p. 1; May 18, 1908, p. 5; *Biblical Recorder*, Feb. 26, 1908, p. 2; "Editor Oates Speaks," n.d., unidentified clipping, box 2, folder 57, Oates Papers, WFU; *Charlotte Daily News*, Feb. 23, 1908, p. 1; Proclamation, "Call Before Battle," May 20, 1908, box 2, folder 57, Oates Papers, WFU.

33. *Caucasian*, Aug. 30, 1906, p. 2; Clarkson, "The Drink Evil," July 13, 1904, box

1, folder 19, Clarkson Papers, SHC; Petition, Jas. P. Hyder et al., Dec. 10, 1902, box 17, General Assembly Session Records, 1903, NCDAH; *Progressive Farmer*, Aug. 13, 1895, p. 5; Rippy, *F. M. Simmons*, 120–22; Aycock, *Why Prohibition Should Prevail*, 5; T. Rolfe to Sallie Sue, July 6, 1908, Peebles Papers, SCL; *Charlotte Daily Observer*, May 3, 1908, p. 6; May 18, 1908, p. 5; *Raleigh News and Observer*, Apr. 5, 1908, p. 1.

34. *Raleigh News and Observer*, May 19, 1908, p. 4; May 24, 1908, p. 6; *Charlotte Daily Observer*, May 12, 1908, p. 6; May 18, 1908, p. 5; *Biblical Recorder*, May 20, 1908, p. 6; *North Carolina White Ribbon*, Feb. 1908, pp. 1, 2; June 1908, p. 1; Mattie Eaton to Peebles, Mar. 17, 1908, Peebles Papers, SCL; Elizabeth March to Oates, May 20, 1908, box 2, folder 74, Oates Papers, WFU; March to Oates, June 9, 1908, box 2, folder 74, Oates Papers, WFU; Mrs. S. F. Thompson to Oates, May 18, 1908, box 2, folder 79, Oates Papers, WFU.

35. *American Issue*, June 1908, p. 5; *Charlotte Daily News*, Jan. 5, 1908, p. 10; Feb. 23, 1908, p. 1; *Charlotte Daily Observer*, May 28, 1908, p. 1; Lectures, "Citizenship, the South and Other Subjects," box 11, folder 89, Kilgo Papers, DUA; *Caucasian*, July 23, 1908, p. 1; *Union Signal*, Jan. 23, 1908, p. 3; Charles B. Aycock to Connor, Apr. 17, 1908, box 8, folder 113, Henry Groves Connor Papers, SHC; Morone, *Hellfire Nation*, 11, 282–343; Ownby, *Subduing Satan*, 170–84; West, *From Yeomen to Redneck*. On the relationship between Southern Progressivism, localism, and prohibition, see William A. Link, *Paradox of Southern Progressivism*, 95–112; Grantham, *Southern Progressivism*; Pegram, "Temperance Politics"; Szymanski, "Beyond Parochialism"; Foster, *Moral Reconstruction*, 163–220.

36. J. W. Burkett to Aycock, Nov. 27, 1901, GP 305, Aycock Papers, NCDAH; Ney McNeely to Aycock, June 5, 1902, GP 307, Aycock Papers, NCDAH; Holly Johnston to Aycock, Sept. 20, 1904, GP 307, Aycock Papers, NCDAH; Hunter to Lee S. Overman, Dec. 12, 1903, box 2, Hunter Papers, SCL; W. M. Ross to F. M. Parker, Jan. 29, 1903, box 17, General Assembly Session Records, 1903, NCDAH; M. B. Strickley to Glenn, Apr. 9, 1907, GP 315, Glenn Papers, NCDAH; R. A. Morrow to William W. Kitchin, May 20, 1909, GP 323, William W. Kitchin Papers, NCDAH; W. R. Goodson to Locke Craig, Nov. 8, 1912, GP 347, Craig Papers, NCDAH; A. V. Craig to Locke Craig, Nov. 12, 1912, GP 347, Craig Papers, NCDAH; J. H. Fonville to Locke Craig, Nov. 12, 1912, GP 347, Craig Papers, NCDAH; A. M. Bennett to Locke Craig, Nov. 20, 1912, GP 348, Craig Papers, NCDAH; May F. Jones, *Memoirs and Speeches*, 197; Connor and Poe, *Life and Speeches*, 99–100.

Coda

1. By the time she was interviewed by the Federal Writers' Project, Rhodes had settled in St. Louis. However, by her account, she had lived in North Carolina until the 1910s, and most of her stories about power and the past reflected her memories of her experiences there. See Rawick, *American Slave*, supp., ser. 1, 11 (B) 283–89.

2. Roosevelt's upbringing around the most enduring bastion of agrarian privilege in the United States — the Hudson River estates — probably inspired his performance of the benevolent lord in his radio addresses and public appearances. Rather than adoring Roosevelt because he was like them, these North Carolinians seem to have been attracted to the ways he was unlike them but like their memory of the patronly pose of local "big men." Lawrence Levine argues that historians deal "rather poorly" with the relationship between "Franklin Roosevelt and his constituents," as they struggle with all questions of audience response and recreation. See Levine, "Folklore of Industrial Society," 1370. Although Lawrence and Cornelia Levine and Robert McElvaine have collected fascinating letters from "the forgotten man," the task of incorporating these epistles into grander political narratives is largely left undone, except in a few suggestive uses. See Levine and Levine, *People and the President*; McElvaine, *Down and Out*; Bryant Simon, *Fabric of Defeat*, 96; Hall et al., *Like a Family*, 293–94; Letter to the Clergy of America, Sept. 23, 1935, available at *The American Presidency Project*.

3. A. C. Herring to Roosevelt, Oct. 14, 1935, box 23, PPF 21 A, FDRL; J. W. Raynor to Roosevelt, Oct. 1, 1935, box 23, PPF 21 A, FDRL; John Smitherman to Roosevelt, Mar. 6, 1933, box 8, PPF 200 B, FDRL; Lena A. Barbour to Roosevelt, Apr. 29, 1935, box 20, PPF 200 B, FDRL; Fred Brown to Roosevelt, Apr. 28, 1935, box 20, PPF 200 B, FDRL; Ella Howell Keedon to Roosevelt, May 1, 1935, box 20, PPF 200 B, FDRL; G. G. Ludwig to Roosevelt, Apr. 30, 1935, box 21, PPF 200 B, FDRL; J. G. Phillips to Roosevelt, Jan. 3, 1936, box 27, folder 6, PPF 200 B, FDRL; Rawick, *American Slave*, 14 (A) 69, 131, 172, 178, 215, 277, 297, 326–27; 15 (A) 31, 53, 86–87, 104, 123, 182, 202, 358; 7 (A) 72; "I've Had Good Landlords," July 19, 1939, box 17, folder 453, Federal Writers' Project Papers #3709, SHC; Levine and Levine, *People and the President*, 365–66; "Never Weary on the Way," box 17, folder 452, Federal Writers' Project Papers, SHC; "Margaret Rogers," interview by Kara Miles, July 14, 1993, *Behind the Veil: Documenting African American Life in the Jim Crow South*, SCL.

4. Avril W. Icard to Roosevelt, June 24, 1935, box 44, folder 7, PPF 9, FDRL; Ransom Artis to Roosevelt, n.d., box 1, folder 4, PPF 9, FDRL; Oscar A. Abee to Roosevelt, Jan. 25, 1934, box 1, folder 1, PPF 15, FDRL; Mrs. Joe Osborne to Roosevelt, Nov. 25, 1933, box 9, folder 1, PPF 15, FDRL; Roosevelt Poole to Roosevelt, Nov. 17, 1933, box 9, folder 3, PPF 15, FDRL; Julius Delener Parrish to Roosevelt, July 19, 1938, box 9, folder 5, PPF 15, FDRL; L. H. Burns to Roosevelt, Oct. 20, 1935, box 23, PPF 21 A, FDRL; Blount Moore Jr. to Roosevelt, Oct. 12, 1935, box 23, PPF 21 A, FDRL; John Wilson Lafferty to Roosevelt, Oct. 11, 1935, box 23, PPF 21 A, FDRL; McElvaine, *Down and Out*, 158, 163, 219, 221, 223.

5. A. I. Hinson to Roosevelt, Oct. 1, 1935, box 23, PPF 21 A, FDRL; A. T. Parker to Roosevelt, Oct. 21, 1935, box 23, PPF 21 A, FDRL; W. I. Hughes to Roosevelt, Oct. 3, 1935, box 23, PPF 21 A, FDRL; McElvaine, *Down and Out*, 148.

6. Some of the most exciting scholarship in American political history is James

Terence Sparrow's and Meg Jacobs's recent work on the role of the state in World War II. See Sparrow, "Fighting over the American Soldier"; and Jacobs, *Pocketbook Politics*.

7. Increasingly scholars have begun to explore the notion of presidentialism, the idea that people view politics largely, even exclusively, through the lens of the presidency, a vision that narrows their capacity to imagine alternatives or to fight against the continued centralization of power in the White House. Although the premise is intriguing, it is equally possible that presidents occupy less, rather than more, of the popular imagination. Despite their ubiquitous presence in the media, they seem deeply diminished, even at times irrelevant or vulnerable. See Downs, "Hail to the Chief"; Dana D. Nelson, *Bad for Democracy*; McCann, *Pinnacle of Feeling*; Jeff Smith, *Presidents We Imagine*; Rubenstein, *This Is Not a President*; and Rogin, *Ronald Reagan, the Movie*.

Bibliography

Primary Sources

Manuscript Sources

Cambridge, Mass.
    Houghton Library, Harvard University
        Walter Hines Page Papers
    Schlesinger Library, Radcliffe Institute
        Charlotte Perkins Gilman Papers
Chapel Hill, N.C.
    North Carolina Collection, University of North Carolina
        Carr, Jas. O. "Philosophy Lectures by Prof. H. H. Williams '94–'95."
        Contested-Election Case of A. H. A. Williams vs. Thomas Settle from the Fifth
            Congressional District of North Carolina. Washington, D.C.: Government
            Printing Office, 1893.
        Woman's Christian Temperance Union of the State of North Carolina
            Convention Handbooks
    Southern Historical Collection, University of North Carolina
        Bagley Family Papers
        John Lancaster Bailey Papers
        Battle Family Papers
        Mary Jeffreys Bethell Diary
        John Grammar Broadnax Papers
        Bryan Family Papers
        Florence Faison Butler Papers
        Marion Butler Papers
        William P. Bynum Papers
        Bennehan Cameron Papers
        Cameron Family Papers
        Julian Shakespeare Carr Papers
        Joseph Blount Cheshire Papers
        Heriot Clarkson Papers

Cobb Family Papers
Octavius Coke Papers
Henry Groves Connor Papers
R. D. W. Connor Papers
Sallie Southall Cotten Papers
Cotten Family Papers
John E. Coulter Papers
Calvin J. Cowles Papers
Anna Cox Papers
Charles William Dabney Papers
William W. Davies Papers
Federal Writers' Project Papers
Augustus W. Graham Papers
Edward Joseph Hale Papers
Bernice Kelly Harris Papers
Harrison and Smith Family Papers
Archibald Henderson Papers
John Steele Henderson Papers
William A. Hoke Papers
Thomas Hume Papers
Benjamin Robinson Huske Papers
Norman E. Jennett Papers
James Yadkin Joyner Papers
Claude Kitchin Papers
William W. Kitchin Papers
Henry Mauger London Papers
James Lee Love Papers
Edwin Robeson MacKethan Papers
Alexander Worth McAlister Papers
Guthrie T. Meade Papers
Edgar Gardner Murphy Papers
Frank Nash Papers
Edwin August Osborne Papers
James W. Patton Papers
Richmond Pearson Papers
William Joseph Peele Papers
Leonidas Lafayette Polk Papers
Pope Family Papers
William Dorsey Pruden Papers
Matt Whitaker Ransom Papers
Reid-Scott Family Papers

Daniel Lindsay Russell Papers
Thomas Settle Papers
Southern Education Board Papers
Cornelia Phillips Spencer Papers
Cyrus Thompson Papers
University Baptist Church Papers
Alfred Moore Waddell Papers
Thomas E. Watson Papers
Edwin Yates Webb Papers
Weil Family Papers
Henry Horace Williams Papers
Henry Van Peters Wilson Papers
Francis D. Winston Papers
George T. Winston Papers
Robert Watson Winston Papers
University Archives, Wilson Library, University of North Carolina
Dialectic Society Records
Philanthropic Society Records
Trustee Affairs
University of North Carolina Papers
Charlottesville, Va.
Albert and Shirley Small Special Collections Library, University of Virginia
Papers of Edwin Anderson Alderman
President's Papers, University Archives
Chicago, Ill.
Special Collections Research Center, University of Chicago Library, University of Chicago
James E. O'Hara Papers
College Park, Md.
National Archives
General Records of the Department of Justice (RG 60) Department of Justice Central Files, Year Files, 1887–1903
Records of the Attorney General's Office Letters Received, North Carolina
Settled Case Files for Claims Approved by the Southern Claims Commission, 1871–1880, Records of the Accounting Officers of the Department of the Treasury, Records of the Land, Files, and Miscellaneous Division
Durham, N.C.
Duke University Archives
John Franklin Crowell Papers
William Preston Few Papers
John Franklin Heitman Papers

John Carlisle Kilgo Papers
W. H. Pegram Papers
Rare Books, Manuscripts, and Special Collections Library, Duke University
Herbert Baxter Adams Papers
Jonathan C. Angier Papers
Josiah William Bailey Papers
Behind the Veil: Documenting African American Life in the Jim Crow South
Major Bell Papers
Archibald H. Boyd Papers
John Heritage Bryan Papers
Bullock Family Papers
Julius Shakespeare Carr Papers
Thomas Carroll Papers
Thomas W. Clawson Papers
Albert L. Coble Letters
William Johnston Cocke Papers
Locke Craig Papers
Craven-Pegram Family Papers
Cronly Family Papers
Robert Paine Dick Papers
Benjamin Newton Duke Papers
Washington Duke Papers
Mary Sue Etheridge Papers
Paul Garrett Papers
James A. Goodman Papers
Frances Louisa Goodrich Papers
John C. Hackett Papers
Frank Armfield Hampton Papers
William D. Hardin Papers
John McLean Harrington Papers
Marmaduke Hawkins Papers
Hinsdale Family Papers
Charles N. Hunter Papers
Jamestown (N.C.) Branch of the Farmers' Alliance, Minutes, 1888–92
Hugh W. Johnson Papers
Joseph H. Johnson Papers
John N. Kelly Papers
Robert O. Linster Papers
Alice Lowrey Papers
William George Matton Memoirs
William Berry McKoy Papers

McRae Plantation Papers
William Henry Moore Papers
H. M. North Diary
Romulus Armistead Nunn Papers
Edward A. Oldham Papers
Pamphlet Collection
Edward S. Parker Sr. Papers
W. K. Parrish Papers
Sallie Sue (Ellis) Peebles Papers
Cornelius Miller Pickens Papers
James Price Papers
John R. Raine Papers
John Ramsay Papers
Records of the Proceedings of the Central Prohibition Club of Durham, N.C.
Rockingham County Public School Register District 58
Royal Cotton Mill Company Papers
Saint Paul's Church (Rockingham County) Record Book, 1909–59
Scarborough Family Papers
Furnifold M. Simmons Papers
Robert Nirwana Simms Papers
John Humphrey Small Papers
Edward C. Smith Papers
Alexander Sprunt & Sons Papers
Edward Alston Thorne Papers
Tillinghast Family Papers
Daniel Augustus Tompkins Papers
Zebulon Baird Vance Papers
Lewis Ward Papers
Hardy Whitford Papers
Worth Family Papers
Greensboro, N.C.
University Archives and Manuscripts, Walter C. Jackson Library, University of
North Carolina
Charles Duncan McIver Records
Greenville, N.C.
East Carolina Manuscript Collection, Joyner Library, East Carolina University
Elias Carr Papers
Frederick C. Douglass Papers
The End of the Century Book Club Papers
James L. Fleming Papers
Inglis Fletcher Papers

Flavel W. Foster Papers
William M. Hinton Papers
William L. Horner Collection
George Howard Papers
Thomas J. Jarvis Papers
Abraham G. Jones Papers
James Lewis Jones Manuscript
James Yadkin Joyner Papers
Hugh Harrison Mills Collection
William Blount Rodman Papers
William B. Shepard Papers
Clarence Leroy Shuping Papers
Albert R. Smith Collection
Harold G. Sugg Papers
Whitakers' Chapel Collection
Elihu A. White Papers
Hyde Park, N.Y.
　Franklin D. Roosevelt Library
　　Harry L. Hopkins Papers
　　President's Personal Files
　　Aubrey Williams Papers
Raleigh, N.C.
　State Archives, North Carolina Division of Archives and History
　　Albright-Dixon Papers
　　Samuel A'Court Ashe Papers
　　Charles B. Aycock Papers
　　E. H. Baker Papers
　　Thomas W. Bickett Papers
　　Curtis H. Brogden Papers
　　William Hyslop Sumner Burgwyn Papers
　　Tod R. Caldwell Papers
　　Elias Carr Papers
　　Walter Clark Papers
　　Heriot Clarkson Papers
　　Calvin J. Cowles Papers
　　Locke Craig Papers
　　Charles Christopher Crittenden Papers
　　Department of Justice Papers
　　Robert Martin Douglas Letters
　　Equal Suffrage Amendment Collection

John F. Flintoff Diary
Daniel G. Fowle Papers
General Assembly Session Records
Robert B. Glenn Papers
Hampton Family Papers
Marmaduke J. Hawkins Collection
William W. Holden Papers
Thomas H. Holt Papers
Thomas J. Jarvis Papers
William W. Kitchin Papers
Isaac S. London Papers
John F. Mitchell Papers
Norwood Family Papers
Clarence W. Poe Papers
Polk Family Papers
Records and Reasons for Granting Pardons, 1877–1901
William Blount Rodman Papers
Daniel L. Russell Papers
William Laurence Saunders Papers
Alfred M. Scales Papers
Charles Smallwood Papers
Cornelia Phillips Spencer Papers
Zebulon B. Vance Papers
Gertrude Weil Papers
Richard D. White Papers
Francis D. Winston Papers
Patrick Henry Winston Papers
Robert W. Winston Papers
Jonathan Worth Papers
Washington, D.C.
Library of Congress
American Colonization Society Papers
William Jennings Bryan Papers
Records of the U.S. Works Projects Administration
National Archives
Civil War Pension Claims Case Files
Records of the United States Senate (RG 46)
General Records of the Department of the Treasury (RG 56)
Records of the Adjutant General's Office (RG 94)
Records of the Bureau of Refugees, Freedmen, and Abandoned Lands (RG 105)

Records of the Office of the Secretary of War (RG 107)
War Department Collection of Confederate Records (RG 109)
Records of the Adjutant and Inspector General's Department (RG 94)
Records of the Office of the Secretary of War (RG 107)
Records of the United States House of Representatives (RG 233)
Winston-Salem, N.C.
   Z. Smith Reynolds Library, Wake Forest University
      John Alexander Oates Papers
      William Louis Poteat Papers

Published Primary Sources

MICROFILM

American Colonization Society Papers. Washington, D.C.: Library of Congress, 1970.
Grover Cleveland Papers. Washington, D.C.: Library of Congress, 1958.
Josephus Daniels Papers. Washington, D.C.: Library of Congress, 1982.
Benjamin Harrison Papers. Washington, D.C.: Library of Congress, 1964.
William McKinley Papers. Washington, D.C.: Library of Congress, 1961.
The Papers of Zebulon Vance. Edited by Gordon McKinney and Richard McMurry.
   From Research Collections in American Politics, Microforms from Major
   Archival and Manuscript Collections. Frederick, Md.: University Publications of
   America, 1987.
Records of the Assistant Commissioners of the State of North Carolina, Bureau of Refugees,
   Freedmen, and Abandoned Lands. Washington, D.C.: National Archives and
   Records Administration, 1972.
Theodore Roosevelt Papers. Washington, D.C.: Library of Congress, 1967.
Southern Women and Their Families in the 19th Century: Papers and Diaries. Bethesda,
   Md.: University Publications of America, 1993.
Temperance and Prohibition Papers. A Joint Microfilm Publication of the Ohio Historical
   Society, Michigan Historical Collections, and Woman's Christian Temperance Union.
   Columbus, Ohio: Ohio Historical Society, 1977.
Woodrow Wilson Papers. Washington, D.C.: Library of Congress, 1970.

WEBSITES

American Life Histories: Manuscripts from the Federal Writers' Project, 1936–1940,
   available at <http://rs6.loc.gov/ammem/wpaintro/nccat.html>
The American Presidency Project, available at <http://www.presidency.ucsb.edu>
Born in Slavery: Slave Narratives from the Federal Writers' Project, 1936–1938,
   available at <http://memory.loc.gov/ammem/snhtml/snhome.html>
Dear George Letters, available at <http://deargeorgeletters.blogspot.com/2004_
   06_13_deargeorgeletters_archive.html>

Documenting the American South, available at <http://docsouth.unc.edu/>

Edwards, Rebecca, and Sarah DeFeo, "1896: A Website of Political Cartoons," available at <http://projects.vassar.edu/1896>

"Explore History," Harpweek, available at <http://www.harpweek.com>

Historical Census Browser, University of Virginia, Geospatial and Statistical Data Center, available at <http://fisher.lib.virginia.edu/collections/stats/histcensus/index.html>

The Roanoke Island Freedmen's Colony, available at <http://.www.roanokefreedmens colony.com>

NEWSPAPERS

American Issue
Biblical Recorder
Caucasian
Charlotte Daily News
Charlotte Daily Observer
Charlotte News & Observer
Elizabeth City North Carolinian
New York Times
North Carolina White Ribbon
Philadelphia Inquirer
Progressive Farmer
Raleigh News
Raleigh News & Observer
Raleigh Weekly News
Reidsville Times
Reidsville Weekly Review
State Chronicle
Union Signal
Wilmington Messenger
Wilmington Morning Star

GOVERNMENT PUBLICATIONS

Biennial Report of the Superintendent of Public Instruction of North Carolina, 1881–1882. Raleigh: Ashe and Catling, 1883.

Congressional Record. Washington, D.C.: Government Printing Office.

Craig, Locke. "Presentation of the Portrait of Patrick Henry Winston to the Supreme Court of North Carolina by His Excellency, Locke Craig, March 31, 1914." In *North Carolina Reports*. Vol. 166. Raleigh: Mitchell Printing Company, 1914.

Executive Documents Published by the Order of the House of Representatives during the

First Session of the Thirty-ninth Congress, 1865–1866. Washington, D.C.: Government Printing Office, 1866.

Hannon v. Grizzard 89 N.C. 115.

Harris v. Scarborough 110 N.C. 232.

Howard, Oliver Otis. *Report of Brevet Major General O. O. Howard, Commissioner Bureau of Refugees, Freedmen, and Abandoned Lands to the Secretary of War, Oct. 20, 1869*. Washington, D.C.: Government Printing Office, 1869.

Kennedy, Joseph C. G., ed. *Population of the United States in 1860; Compiled from the Original Returns of the Eighth Census under the Secretary of the Interior*. Washington, D.C.: Government Printing Office, 1864.

Laws and Resolutions of the State of North Carolina, Passed by the General Assembly at Its Session of 1885, Begun and Held in the City of Raleigh on Wednesday, the Seventh Day of January A.D. 1885. Raleigh: P. M. Hale, 1885.

Laws and Resolutions of the State of North Carolina, Passed by the General Assembly at Its Session of 1889, Begun and Held in the City of Raleigh on Wednesday, the Ninth Day of January A.D. 1889. Raleigh: Josephus Daniels, 1889.

Papers and Documents in the Case of Jesse J. Yeates Vs. Joseph J. Martin, U.S. House of Representatives, 46th Cong., 2nd Session, Misc. Doc. #18. Washington, D.C.: Government Printing Office, 1880.

Polk, L. L. *Tabulated Statement of Industries & Resources of North Carolina*. Raleigh: North Carolina Department of Agriculture, 1878.

Public Documents of the General Assembly of North Carolina Session 1879. Document 8. Report of L. L. Polk, Commissioner of Agriculture. Raleigh: Farmer and Mechanic Print, 1879.

Public Laws and Resolutions of the State of North Carolina Passed by the General Assembly and at Its Session of 1901, Begun and Held in the City of Raleigh on Wednesday, the Ninth Day of January A.D. 1901. Raleigh: Edwards & Broughton and E. M. Uzzell, 1901.

Report and Testimony of the Select Committee of the United States Senate to Investigate the Causes of the Removal of the Negroes from the Southern States to the Northern States. Sen. Reports 46 (2) Report #693. Washington, D.C.: Government Printing Office, 1880.

Report of the Joint Committee on Reconstruction at the First Session Thirty-ninth Congress. Washington, D.C.: Government Printing Office, 1866.

Report of the Secretary of the Navy. Washington, D.C.: Government Printing Office, 1865.

Testimony Taken by the Joint Committee to Inquire into the Condition of Affairs in the Late Insurrectionary States. Vol. 2: North Carolina. Washington, D.C.: Government Printing Office, 1872.

U.S. Senate. *Select Committee of the Senate to Investigate Alleged Outrages in the*

Southern States. Testimony. Condition of Affairs in the Southern States. North Carolina. First Session of the Forty-Second Congress and the Special Session of the Senate. 1871. Washington, D.C.: Government Printing Office, 1871.

Views of the Minority. Condition of Affairs in the Southern States. North Carolina. Select Committee of the Senate to Investigate Alleged Outrages in the Southern States. 42nd Congress, 1st Session. Washington, D.C.: Government Printing Office, 1871.

The War of the Rebellion: A Compilation of the Official Records of the Union and Confederate Armies. 128 vols. Washington, D.C.: Government Printing Office, 1880–1901.

MAGAZINE ARTICLES

Adams, Charles Francis. "Mr. Cleveland's Tasks and Opportunities." *The Forum*, March–August 1893.

———. "What Mr. Cleveland Stands For." *The Forum*, March–August 1892.

Alderman, Edwin A. "The Influence of Corporate Power." *University Magazine*, 1882.

———. "Southern Pioneers in Social Interpretation: Charles Brantley Aycock." *Journal of Social Forces* 2 (1924): 487–91.

———. "The University of Today; Its Work and Needs." *University Magazine*, 1900.

Aycock, Charles B. "Vae Victis!" *University Magazine*, 1878.

Batchelor, O. D. "Social Ideas." *University Magazine*, 1888.

Bingham, Robert W. "Manifest Destiny and Manifest Duty." *University Magazine*, 1890.

Bookwalter, John W. "The Farmers' Isolation and the Remedy." *The Forum*, September 1891.

Brown, L. A. "Journalism in the University." *University Magazine*, 1910.

Colyer, Vincent. "Notes Among the Indians — I." *Putnam's*, September 1869.

"Commencement Exercises." *State Normal Magazine*, 1899.

Connor, George W. "The Nation's Law and the Nation's Life." *University Magazine*, 1891.

Craig, Locke. "Wealth — Its Unequal Distribution." *University Magazine*, 1885.

Kilgo, John Carlisle. "An Inquiry Concerning Lynchings." *South Atlantic Quarterly*, January 1902.

King, Clarence. "The Education of the Future." *The Forum*, March 1892.

Henderson, Archibald. "Francis Donnell Winston." *Alumni Review*, November 1942.

Howe, Louis McHenry. "The President's Mail Bag." *American Magazine*, 1934.

Laughlin, J. Laurence. "Coin's Food for the Gullible." *The Forum*, March–August 1895.

McGehee, Lucius P. "The Civilization of the Ancient Germans." *University Magazine*, 1886.

McIver, Charles. "Alumni Address." *University Magazine*, 1892.

Monroe, E. D. "The Influence of the Scientific Method of Thought." *University Magazine*, 1885.

"The Negro in the South." *University Magazine*, 1899.

Norton, Charles Eliot. "Some Aspects of Civilization in America." *The Forum*, February 1896.

"The Origin of Man." *University Magazine*, 1878.

Page, Walter Hines. "Address at the Inauguration of President Winston." *University Magazine*, 1891.

Pelton, Mabell Shippie Clark. "The Lucetta Election." *University Magazine*, 1906.

Pierce, Edward L. "The Contrabands of Fortress Monroe." *Atlantic Monthly*, November 1861.

"Priceless Heritage of Our English Blood." *University Magazine*, 1885.

Roosevelt, Theodore. "Degeneration and Evolution. Benjamin Kidd's *Social Evolution*." *North American Review*, July 1895.

Rupert. "Africa in America." *University Magazine*, 1882.

"Senior Speakings." *University Magazine*, 1885.

Shaler, Nathaniel Southgate. "Science and the African Problem." *Atlantic Monthly*, July 1890.

"Some Points on the Three Great Races as Gathered from Crawford's Lectures and Conversation." *University Magazine*, 1886.

Strayhorn, J. T. "The Patriot's Hope." *University Magazine*, 1883.

Tracy, Frank Basil. "Rise and Doom of the Populist Party." *The Forum*, September 1893–February 1894.

Untitled articles. *University Magazine*, 1890–95.

Walser, Zebulon Vance. "What Will the Harvest Be?" *University Magazine*, 1883.

Ward, Lester Frank. "The Transmission of Culture." *The Forum*, May 1891.

Warlick, Lee M. "The Race Problem in the United States." *University Magazine*, 1885.

Weeks, Stephen B. "The Religion of Our Saxon Forefathers." *University Magazine*, 1885.

Wickliffe, John C. "Negro Suffrage a Failure: Shall We Abolish It?" *The Forum*, February 1893.

Wilson, Woodrow. "A Calendar of Great Americans." *The Forum*, February 1894.

Winston, George T. "The University of To-Day." *University Magazine*, 1893–94.

Winston, Robert Watson. "Aycock: His People's Genius." *Alumni Review*, November 1933.

———. "Chivalry." *University Magazine*, 1878.

———. "The Greater United States." *University Magazine*, 1898.

Aycock, Charles B. *Why Prohibition Should Prevail. Indisputable Arguments Made by Ex-Gov. Chas. B. Aycock at the Academy of Music. Wilmington, N.C., Thursday, April 2nd, 1908.* Wilmington, N.C.: Wilmington Messenger, 1908.

Butler, Marion, and Cyrus Thompson. *Addresses of Marion Butler, President, and Cyrus Thompson, Lecturer, to the North Carolina Farmers' State Alliance, at Greensboro, N.C., Aug. 8, 9, and 10, 1893, at Its Seventh Annual Session.* Raleigh: Barnes Bros., 1893.

Campbell, Robert. *Don't Worry.* N.p.: n.d. (North Carolina Collection, UNC).

Connor, Henry G. *George Howard, 1829–1905. An Address by H. G. Connor, Presenting a Portrait of Judge George Howard to the Supreme Court of North Carolina, February 13, 1917.* Raleigh: Edwards & Broughton, 1917.

———. "A Saner Citizenship." In *Annual Publication of Historical Papers Published by the Historical Society of Trinity College,* 32–47. Durham: Department of History, 1900.

Dean, Sidney. *Eulogy Pronounced in the City Hall, Providence, April 19, 1865, on the Occasion of the Funeral Solemnities of Abraham Lincoln.* Providence, R.I.: H. H. Thomas & Co., 1865.

Dixon, Thomas. *An Open Letter from Rev. Thomas Dixon to J. C. Beam . . . Read It.* N.p., n.d.

Evans, P. S. *Funeral Elegy on Abraham Lincoln, Delivered before the Military Authorities in Norfolk, Va., Wednesday, April 19th, 1865.* Norfolk, Va: Office of the Old Dominion, 1865.

First Convention of the Woman's Christian Temperance Union of the State of North Carolina Held at Greensboro, Tuesday, November 27th, 1883 Containing Principles and Plan of Work, &C. Greensboro, N.C.: Thomas, Reece & Co., 1883.

James, Horace. *Our Duties to the Slave.* Worcester: Richardson & Filmer, 1847.

Jarvis, Thomas Jordan. *Schools Vs. Saloons: Governor Jarvis on the Eternal Conflict That Is Raging between the School-Room and the Bar-Room, That Is the Reason for the Election in May.* Raleigh: Edwards & Broughton, 1908.

Minutes of the Eighth Annual Convention of the Woman's Christian Temperance Union of the State of North Carolina Held at Concord, July 17th to 19th, 1890 in the Methodist Episcopal Church. Greensboro, N.C.: Thomas Brothers, 1890.

Minutes of the Eleventh Annual Convention of the Woman's Christian Temperance Union of the State of North Carolina Held at Waynesville, North Carolina, July 21st, 22nd, 23rd, 24th and 25th, 1893, in the Waynesville Academy. Greensboro, N.C.: C. F. Thomas, 1893.

Minutes of the Fifth Annual Convention of the Woman's Christian Temperance Union of the State of North Carolina Held at Goldsboro, in the Baptist Church, Oct. 31 to Nov. 2, 1887. Greensboro, N.C.: Thomas, Reece, 1887.

Minutes of the Fourth Annual Convention of the Woman's Christian Temperance Union of the State of North Carolina Held at Charlotte, in the M.E. Church, July 28–29, 1886. Greensboro, N.C.: Thomas, Reece, 1886.

Minutes of the Ninth Annual Convention of the Woman's Christian Temperance Union of the State of North Carolina Held at Durham, July 15th to 18th, 1891 in the Trinity Church. Greensboro, N.C.: Thomas Brothers, 1891.

Minutes of the Twelfth Annual Convention of the Woman's Christian Temperance Union of the State of North Carolina Held at High Point, North Carolina, August 6th and 7th, 1894 in the M.E. Church South. Greensboro, N.C.: C. F. Thomas, 1894.

Minutes of the Twentieth Annual Convention of the Woman's Christian Temperance Union of the State of North Carolina Held at Burlington, North Carolina, October 3–6, 1902 in the Christian Church. Greensboro, N.C.: C. F. Thomas, 1902.

Minutes of the Twenty-first Annual Session of the Woman's Christian Temperance Union of the State of North Carolina Held at Hickory, North Carolina, October 1–4, 1903. Concord, N.C.: Times Steam Book and Job Printers, 1903.

Polk, L. L. *Agricultural Depression. Its Causes — the Remedy. Speech of L. L. Polk, President of the National Farmers' Alliance with Industrial Union, before the Senate Committee on Agriculture and Forestry. April 22, 1890.* Raleigh: Edwards & Broughton, 1890.

Ramsay, David. *A Dissertation on the Manner of Acquiring the Character and Privileges of a Citizen of the United States.* Charleston, S.C.: n.p., 1789.

Second Convention of the Woman's Christian Temperance Union of the State of North Carolina Held in Asheville, Wednesday October 8th, 1884. Greensboro, N.C.: Thomas, Reece, 1884.

Spruill, F. S. "Charles B. Aycock." In *Proceedings of the Fourteenth Annual Session of the North Carolina Bar Association Held at the Atlantic Hotel, Morehead City, North Carolina, July 3, 4, and 5, 1912,* 215–19. Wilmington, N.C.: Jackson & Bell, 1912.

Third Annual Catalogue of the State Normal and Industrial School, Greensboro N.C. Greensboro, N.C.: The School, 1895.

Vance, Zebulon Baird. *The Inaugural Address of Gov. Z. B. Vance; Together with His First Message to the General Assembly of 1876–1877.* Raleigh: Raleigh News, 1877.

Watson, Alfred A. *Divine Worship: A Sermon Preached in St. James Church, Wilmington, N.C., the Second Sunday after Trinity, June 9th, 1872.* Wilmington, N.C.: n.p., 1872.

Winston, George T. *The Greek, the Roman, and the Teuton: An Address by Professor George T. Winston, of the University of North Carolina, Delivered before Several Classical Schools of the State.* Greensboro, N.C.: Thomas, Reece, 1884.

———. "Industrial Training in Relation to the Negro Problem." In *Proceedings of the Fourth Conference for Education in the South: Held at Winston-Salem, North Carolina April 18, 19 and 20, 1902,* 103–7. Harrisburg, Pa.: Committee, 1902.

Winston, Robert W. *Garland for Ashes: An Aspiration for the South; Address before the North Carolina Bar Association, June 28, 1934*. Raleigh: n.p., 1934.

———. *Judge Henry Groves Connor, Memorial Address by Judge Robert W. Winston before the North Carolina Bar Association, Asheville, N.C., July 2, 1925*. Asheville, N.C.: North Carolina Bar Association, 1925.

———. *Memorial Address for Frank Shepherd Spruill. Delivered before the Supreme Court of North Carolina*. Raleigh: n.p., 1938.

———. "Should the Color Line Go?" In *The Independent Church of God of the Juda Tribe of Israel: The Black Jews*, edited by Bishop A. W. Cook. N.p., 1925.

MEMOIRS, NOVELS, AND OTHER BOOK-LENGTH PUBLICATIONS

Andrews, Sidney. *The South since the War: As Shown by Fourteen Weeks of Travel and Observation in Georgia and the Carolinas*. Boston: Ticknor and Fields, 1866.

Baird, E. T., ed. *Hymns of the Voice of Praise*. Richmond: E. T. Baird, 1872.

Bonar, Horatio. *The Bible Hymn-Book*. New York: Robert Carter and Brothers, 1853.

Bryan, William Jennings. *The First Battle: A Story of the Campaign of 1896*. Chicago: W. B. Conkey, 1896.

Bryan, William Jennings, and Mary Baird Bryan. *The Memoirs of William Jennings Bryan*. Chicago: John C. Winston Company, 1925.

Clinton, George W. *Christianity under the Spotlight*. Nashville: National Baptist Publishing Board, 1909.

Colyer, Vincent. *Report of the Services Rendered by the Freed People to the United States Army, in North Carolina, in the Spring of 1862, after the Battle of Newbern*. New York: V. Colyer, 1864.

Connor, R. D. W., and Clarence Hamilton Poe. *The Life and Speeches of Charles Brantley Aycock*. Garden City, N.Y.: Doubleday, Page & Company, 1912.

Corbett, Maurice N. *The Harp of Ethiopia*. Nashville: National Baptist Publishing Board, 1914. Reprint, Freeport, N.Y.: Books for Libraries Press, 1971.

Crowell, John Franklin. *Personal Recollections of Trinity College North Carolina, 1887–1894*. Durham: Duke University Press, 1939.

Daniels, Josephus. *Editor in Politics*. Chapel Hill: University of North Carolina Press, 1941.

De Tocqueville, Alexis. *Democracy in America*. Translated by Henry Reeve. New York: D. Appleton, 1904.

Dennett, John Richard. *The South As It Is, 1865–1866*. Edited by Henry M. Christman. New York: Viking Press, 1965.

Diggins, John Patrick, ed. *The Portable John Adams*. New York: Penguin, 2004.

Dixon, Thomas. *The Clansman, an Historical Romance of the Ku Klux Klan*. New York: Doubleday, Page & Company, 1905.

———. *Dixon's Sermons: Delivered in the Grand Opera House, New York, 1898–1899*. New York: F. L. Bussey, 1899.

———. *The Leopard's Spots: A Romance of the White Man's Burden, 1896–1900.* New York: Doubleday, Page & Company, 1906.

———. *Living Problems in Religion and Social Science.* New York: Charles T. Dillingham, 1889.

Douglass, Frederick. *My Bondage and My Freedom.* New York: Miller, Orton, & Mulligan, 1855.

Elliott, Charlotte. *Hours of Sorrow Cheered and Comforted.* London: L. Booth, 1863.

Ferebee, L. R. *A Brief History of the Slave Life of Rev. L. R. Ferebee, and the Battles of Life, and Four Years of His Ministerial Life. Written from Memory. To 1882.* Raleigh: Edwards, Broughton, & Co., 1882.

Fiske, John. *Darwinism and Other Essays.* Boston: Houghton, Mifflin, 1885.

———. *The Destiny of Man Viewed in the Light of His Origin.* Boston: Houghton, Mifflin, 1884.

———. *Excursions of an Evolutionist.* Boston: Macmillan, 1884.

Fuller, Thomas Oscar. *Twenty Years in Public Life, 1890–1910: North Carolina–Tennessee.* Nashville: National Baptist Printing Board, 1910.

Gates, Merrill E., ed. *Men of Mark in America: Ideals of American Life Told in Biographies of Eminent Living Americans.* Vol. 2. Washington, D.C.: Men of Mark Publishing Company, 1906.

Graham, Billy. *Just as I Am: The Autobiography of Billy Graham.* San Francisco: HarperCollins, 1999.

Harris, Bernice Kelly. *Southern Savory.* Chapel Hill: University of North Carolina Press, 1964.

Harris, William C., ed. *"In the Country of the Enemy": The Civil War Reports of a Massachusetts Corporal.* Gainesville: University Press of Florida, 1999.

Holden, W. W. *Memoirs of W. W. Holden.* Durham: Sherman Printery, 1911.

Howard, Oliver Otis. *Autobiography of Oliver Otis Howard.* New York: Baker & Taylor Co., 1907.

James, Horace. *Annual Report of the Superintendent of Negro Affairs in North Carolina 1864. With an Appendix, Containing the History and Management of the Freedmen in the Department up to June 1st, 1865.* Boston: W. F. Brown & Co., 1865.

James, William. *Varieties of Religious Experience: A Study in Human Nature, Being the Gifford Lectures on Natural Religion Delivered at Edinburgh in 1901–1902.* New York: Modern Library, 1936.

Johnson, Frontis W., ed. *The Papers of Zebulon Vance.* Vol. 1: *1843–1862.* Raleigh: State Department of Archives History, 1963.

Jones, May F., ed. *Memoirs and Speeches of Locke Craig, Governor of North Carolina, 1913–1914. A History — Political and Otherwise. From Scrap Books and Old Manuscripts.* Asheville, N.C.: Hackney & Moale, 1923.

Kidd, Benjamin. *The Control of the Tropics.* New York: Macmillan, 1898.

———. *Social Evolution.* New York: Macmillan, 1895.

Latta, M. L. *The History of My Life and Work*. Raleigh: M. L. Latta, 1903.

Link, Arthur S. *The Papers of Woodrow Wilson*. Princeton: Princeton University Press, 1966.

Lodge, Henry Cabot. *Speeches and Addresses, 1884–1909*. Boston: Houghton Mifflin, 1909.

Manly, Basil, and B. Manly Jr. *The Baptist Psalmody: A Selection of Hymns for the Worship of God*. Charleston, S.C.: Southern Baptist Publication Society, 1850.

Marx, Karl. *Capital: A Critique of Political Economy*. Translated by Ben Fowkes. Vol. 1. New York: Random House, 1976.

———. *A Contribution to the Critique of Political Economy*. Translated by S. W. Ryazanskaya. New York: Lawrence & Wishart, 1970.

McElrath, Joseph R., Jr., ed. *Charles W. Chesnutt, Essays and Speeches*. Stanford: Stanford University Press, 1999.

McElvaine, Robert S., ed. *Down and Out in the Great Depression: Letters from the Forgotten Man*. Chapel Hill: University of North Carolina Press, 1983.

Melville, Herman. *Battle-Pieces and Aspects of War*. New York: Harper & Brothers, 1866.

Memoirs of General William T Sherman. Vol. 2. New York: D. Appleton, 1887.

Mobley, Joe A., ed., *The Papers of Zebulon Vance*. Vol. 2. Raleigh: State Department of Archives and History, 1995.

Moores, Charles W., ed., *Lincoln Addresses and Letters*. New York: American Book Company, 1914.

Nettleton, Asahel. *Village Hymns for Social Worship*. Hartford: Goodwin & Co., 1824.

Page, Walter Hines. *The Rebuilding of Old Commonwealths: Being Essays Towards the Training of the Forgotten Man in the Southern States*, 1–48. New York: Doubleday, Page & Company, 1902.

———. *The Southerner: A Novel, Being the Autobiography of Nicholas Worth*. New York: Doubleday, Page & Company, 1909.

Parker, Allen. *Recollections of Slavery Times*. Worcester, Mass.: Chas. W. Burbank & Co., 1895.

Pearson, R. G. *The Great Evangelist. Sermons of Rev. R. G. Pearson, Delivered in Centenary M.E. Church, Winston, N.C. during One of the Great Religious Revivals in the History of North Carolina*. Winston, N.C.: Lanier's Steam Print, 1888.

———. *Truth Applied or Bible Readings*. Nashville, Tenn.: Cumberland Presbyterian Publishing House, 1890.

Poland, C. Beauregard. *North Carolina's Glorious Victory, 1898. Sketches of Able Democratic Leaders and Statesmen*. Raleigh: n.p., 1898.

Poteat, William L. *Laboratory and Pulpit: The Relation of Biology to the Preacher and His Message. The Gay Lectures, 1900*. Philadelphia: Griffith & Rowland Press, 1901.

Private and Official Correspondence of Gen. Benjamin F. Butler during the Period of the Civil War. Vol. 1. Norwood, Mass.: Plimpton Press, 1917.

Raper, Horace W., and Thornton W. Mitchell, eds. *The Papers of William Woods Holden*. Raleigh: State Department of Archives and History, 2000.

Rawlinson, George. *The Origin of Nations: In Two Parts: On Early Civilisations; on Ethnic Affinities*. New York: Religious Tract Society, 1878.

Richardson, James D., ed. *A Compilation of the Messages and Papers of the Presidents, 1789–1907*. Vol. 6. Washington, D.C.: Bureau of National Literature and Art, 1908.

Riordan, William. *Plunkitt of Tammany Hall*. New York: Signet Classics, 1995.

Rippy, J. Fred, ed. *F. M. Simmons: Statesman of the New South: Memoirs and Addresses*. Durham: Duke University Press, 1936.

Simon, John Y., ed. *The Papers of Ulysses S. Grant*. 31 vols. Carbondale: Ulysses S. Grant Association, 1967–2009.

Singleton, William Henry. *Recollections of Slavery Days*. Peekskill, N.Y.: Highland Democrat, 1922.

Smith, Ira R. T., and Joe Alex Morris. *"Dear Mr. President . . .": The Story of Fifty Years in the White House Mail Room*. New York: J. Messner, 1949.

Taylor, John. *An Inquiry into the Principles and Polices of the Government of the United States*. Fredericksburg, Va.: Green and Caddy, 1814.

Welles, Gideon. *Diary of Gideon Welles, Secretary of the Navy under Lincoln and Johnson*. Vol. 2. Boston: Houghton Mifflin, 1911.

Wells, David Ames. *Our Burden and Our Strength*. Boston: Gould & Lincoln, 1864.

———. *The Theory and Practice of Taxation*. New York: D. Appleton, 1900.

White, Andrew Dickson. *A History of the Warfare of Science with Theology in Christendom*. New York: D. Appleton, 1898.

———. *Instruction in Social Science: Address of President White, 1890; Remarks of President White, 1891*. N.p.: American Social Science Association, 1891.

Williams, Henry Horace. *The Education of Henry Horace Williams*. Chapel Hill: University of North Carolina Press, 1936.

Winston, Carrie. "Cornelia Phillips Spencer." In *Biographical History of North Carolina from Colonial Times to the Present: "Old North State" Edition*, edited by Samuel A'Court Ashe, 400–405. Greensboro, N.C.: Charles L. Van Noppen, 1905.

Winston, George T. *A Builder of the New South: Being the Story of the Life Work of Daniel Augustus Tompkins*. New York: Doubleday, Page & Company 1920.

Winston, Robert W. *Horace Williams: The Gadfly of Chapel Hill*. Chapel Hill: University of North Carolina Press, 1942.

———. *It's a Far Cry*. New York: H. Holt, 1937.

Secondary Sources

Abbott, Martin. *The Freedmen's Bureau in South Carolina*. Chapel Hill: University of North Carolina Press, 1967.

Adam, Anthony J. *Black Populism in the United States: An Annotated Bibliography*. Westport, Conn.: Greenwood Press, 2004.

Alexander, Roberta Sue. *North Carolina Faces the Freedmen: Race Relations during Presidential Reconstruction, 1865–1867*. Durham: Duke University Press, 1985.

Ali, Omar H. "Black Populism in the New South, 1886–1898." Ph.D. diss., Columbia University, 2003.

Allswang, John M. *A House for All Peoples: Ethnic Politics in Chicago, 1890–1936*. Lexington: University Press of Kentucky, 1971.

Altschuler, Glenn C. *Andrew D. White, Educator, Historian, Diplomat*. Ithaca, N.Y.: Cornell University Press, 1979.

Altschuler, Glenn C., and Stuart M. Blumin. *Rude Republic: Americans and Their Politics in the Nineteenth Century*. Princeton: Princeton University Press, 2000.

Amin, Shahid. *Event, Metaphor, Memory: Chauri Chaura, 1922–1992*. Berkeley: University of California Press, 1995.

——. "Gandhi as Mahatma: Gorakhpur District, Eastern U.P., 1921–1922." *Subaltern Studies* 3 (1984): 1–61.

Anderson, Eric. "Black Responses to Darwinism, 1859–1915." In *Disseminating Darwinism: The Role of Race, Place, and Gender*, edited by Ronald L. Numbers and John Stenhouse, 247–66. New York: Cambridge University Press, 1999.

——. "The Populists and Capitalist America: The Case of Edgecombe County, North Carolina." In *Race, Class and Politics in Southern History: Essays in Honor of Robert F. Durden*, edited by Paul D. Escott, Jeffrey J. Crow, and Charles L. Flynn Jr., 106–25. Baton Rouge: Louisiana State University Press, 1989.

——. *Race and Politics in North Carolina, 1872–1901: The Black Second*. Baton Rouge: Louisiana State University Press, 1981.

Appleby, Joyce Oldham. *Liberalism and Republicanism in the Historical Imagination*. Cambridge, Mass.: Harvard University Press, 1992.

——. "Locke, Liberalism, and the Natural Law of Money." In *Liberalism and Republicanism in the Historical Imagination*, 58–89. Cambridge, Mass.: Harvard University Press, 1992.

Apter, Emily. *Feminizing the Fetish: Psychoanalysis and Narrative Obsession in Turn-of-the-Century France*. Ithaca, N.Y.: Cornell University Press, 1991.

Argersinger, Peter H. *The Limits of Agrarian Radicalism: Western Populism and American Politics*. Lawrence: University Press of Kansas, 1995.

Arnesen, Eric. "Whiteness and the Historian's Imagination." *International Labor and Working Class History* 60 (Fall 2001): 3–32.

Arnold, David. *Gandhi*. New York: Longman, 2001.

Aron, Cindy Sondik. *Ladies and Gentlemen of the Civil Service: Middle-Class Workers in Victorian America*. New York: Oxford University Press, 1987.

Arsenault, Raymond. *The Wild Ass of the Ozarks: Jeff Davis and the Social Bases of Southern Politics*. Philadelphia: Temple University Press, 1984.

Ash, Stephen V. *When the Yankees Came: Chaos and Conflict in the Occupied South*. Chapel Hill: University of North Carolina Press, 1995.

Ashworth, John. *Slavery, Capitalism, and Politics in the Antebellum Republic, 1850–1861*. New York: Cambridge University Press, 2008.

Ayers, Edward L. *The Promise of the New South: Life after Reconstruction*. New York: Oxford University Press, 1992.

——. *What Caused the Civil War?: Reflections on the South and Southern History*. New York: Norton, 2005.

Baker, Bruce. *This Mob Will Surely Take My Life: Lynching in the Carolinas, 1871–1947*. New York: Continuum, 2008.

Baker, Jean H. *Affairs of Party: The Political Culture of Northern Democrats in the Mid-Nineteenth Century*. Ithaca, N.Y.: Cornell University Press, 1983.

Baker, Paula C. *The Moral Frameworks of Public Life: Gender, Politics, and the State in Rural New York, 1870–1930*. New York: Oxford University Press, 1991.

Balogh, Brian. *A Government out of Sight: The Mystery of National Authority in Nineteenth-Century America*. New York: Cambridge University Press, 2009.

Bannister, Robert C. *Social Darwinism: Science and Myth in Anglo-American Social Thought*. Philadelphia: Temple University Press, 1979.

Baptist, Edward E. *Creating an Old South: Middle Florida's Plantation Frontier before the Civil War*. Chapel Hill: University of North Carolina Press, 2002.

——. " 'Cuffy,' 'Fancy Maids,' and 'One-Eyed Men': Rape, Commodification, and the Domestic Slave Trade in the United States." *American Historical Review* 106 (December 2001): 1619–50.

Bardaglio, Peter W. *Reconstructing the Household: Families, Sex and the Law in the Nineteenth-Century South*. Chapel Hill: University of North Carolina Press, 1995.

Barrett, John G. *The Civil War in North Carolina*. Chapel Hill: University of North Carolina Press, 1995.

Barrow, Clyde W. *Universities and the Capitalist State: Corporate Liberalism and the Reconstruction of American Higher Education, 1894–1928*. Madison: University of Wisconsin Press, 1989.

Barthelme, Marion K. *Women in the Texas Populist Movement: Letters to the Southern Mercury*. College Station: Texas A & M University Press, 1997.

Battle, Kemp. *History of the University of North Carolina*. Vol. 2. Raleigh: Edwards & Broughton, 1912.

Baudrillard, Jean. *For a Critique of the Political Economy of the Sign*. Translated by Charles Levin. St. Louis: Telos Press, 1981.

Bay, Mia. *The White Image in the Black Mind: African-American Ideas About White People, 1830–1925*. New York: Oxford University Press, 2000.

Beale, Howard K. *The Critical Year: A Study of Andrew Johnson and Reconstruction*. New York: Harcourt, Brace, 1930. Reprint, New York: F. Ungar, 1958.

Beckel, Deborah. "The Roots of Reform: The Origins of Populism and

Progressivism as Manifest in Relationships among Reformers in Raleigh, North Carolina, 1850–1905." Ph.D. diss., Emory University, 1998.

Beckert, Sven. "Democracy in the Age of Capital: Contesting Suffrage Rights in Gilded Age New York." In *The Democratic Experiment: New Directions in American Political History*, edited by William J. Novak, Meg Jacobs, and Julian E. Zelizer, 146–74. Princeton: Princeton University Press, 2003.

———. *Monied Metropolis: New York City and the Consolidation of the American Bourgeoisie, 1865–1896*. New York: Cambridge University Press, 2001.

Bederman, Gail. *Manliness and Civilization: A Cultural History of Gender and Race in the United States, 1880–1917*. Chicago: University of Chicago Press, 1995.

Beeby, James. *Revolt of the Tar Heels: The North Carolina Populist Movement, 1890–1901*. Jackson: University Press of Mississippi, 2008.

Bellah, Robert Neelly. *The Broken Covenant: American Civil Religion in Time of Trial*. Chicago: University of Chicago Press, 1992.

Bender, Thomas. *A Nation among Nations: America's Place in World History*. New York: Hill and Wang, 2006.

———, ed. *Rethinking American History in a Global Age*. Berkeley: University of California Press, 2002.

Bendix, Reinhard. *Kings or People: Power and the Mandate to Rule*. Berkeley: University of California Press, 1978.

Bennett, Jane. *The Enchantment of Modern Life: Attachments, Crossings, and Ethics*. Princeton: Princeton University Press, 2001.

Bensel, Richard Franklin. *The American Ballot Box in the Mid-Nineteenth Century*. New York: Cambridge University Press, 2004.

———. *Passions and Preferences: William Jennings Bryan and the 1896 Democratic National Convention*. New York: Cambridge University Press, 2008.

———. *The Political Economy of American Industrialization, 1877–1900*. New York: Cambridge University Press, 2000.

———. *Yankee Leviathan: The Origins of Central State Authority in America, 1859–1877*. New York: Cambridge University Press, 1990.

Bercaw, Nancy. *Gendered Freedoms: Race, Rights, and the Politics of Household in the Delta, 1861–1875*. Gainesville: University Press of Florida, 2003.

Berlant, Lauren. *The Anatomy of National Fantasy: Hawthorne, Utopia, and Everyday Life*. Chicago: University of Chicago Press, 1991.

———. *The Queen of America Goes to Washington City: Essays on Sex and Citizenship*. Durham: Duke University Press, 1997.

Berlin, Ira, Barbara J. Fields, Thavolia Glymph, Joseph P. Reidy, and Leslie S. Rowland, eds. *The Destruction of Slavery*. Ser. 1, vol. 1 of *Freedom: A Documentary History of Emancipation, 1861–1867*. New York: Cambridge University Press, 1985.

Berlin, Ira, Thavolia Glymph, Steven F. Miller, Joseph P. Reidy, Leslie S. Rowland,

and Julie Saville, eds. *The Wartime Genesis of Free Labor: The Lower South*. Ser. 1, vol. 3 of *Freedom: A Documentary History of Emancipation, 1861–1867*. New York: Cambridge University Press, 1990.

Berlin, Ira, Steven F. Miller, Joseph P. Reidy, and Leslie S. Rowland, eds. *The Wartime Genesis of Free Labor: The Upper South*. Ser. 1, vol. 2 of *Freedom: A Documentary History of Emancipation, 1861–1867*. New York: Cambridge University Press, 1993.

Berlin, Ira, Joseph P. Reidy, and Leslie S. Rowland, eds. *The Black Military Experience*. Ser. 2 of *Freedom: A Documentary History of Emancipation, 1861–1867*. New York: Cambridge University Press, 1982.

Berman, Milton. *John Fiske: The Evolution of a Popularizer*. Cambridge, Mass.: Harvard University Press, 1961.

Bernhardt, Kathryn. *Rents, Taxes, and Peasant Resistance: The Lower Yangzi Region, 1840–1950*. Stanford: Stanford University Press, 1992.

Billings, Dwight B. *Planters and the Making of a "New South": Class, Politics, and Development in North Carolina, 1865–1900*. Chapel Hill: University of North Carolina Press, 1979.

Bledstein, Burton J. *The Culture of Professionalism: The Middle Class and the Development of Higher Education in America*. New York: Norton, 1976.

Blee, Kathleen M. "Evidence, Empathy, and Ethics: Lessons from Oral History." *Journal of American History* 80 (September 1993): 596–606.

———. *Women of the Klan: Racism and Gender in the 1920s*. Berkeley: University of California Press, 1991.

Blight, David W. *Race and Reunion: The Civil War in American Memory*. Cambridge, Mass.: Harvard University Press, 2001.

Blocker, Jack S., Jr. *"Give to the Winds Thy Fears": The Women's Temperance Crusade*. Westport, Conn.: Greenwood Press, 1985.

———. *Retreat from Reform: The Prohibition Movement in the United States, 1890–1913*. Westport, Conn.: Greenwood Press, 1976.

Blum, Edward J. *Reforging the White Republic: Race, Religion, and American Nationalism, 1865–1898*. Baton Rouge: Louisiana State University Press, 2005.

Bode, Frederick A. *Protestantism and the New South: North Carolina Baptists and Methodists in Political Crisis, 1894–1903*. Charlottesville: University of Virginia Press, 1975.

Bolton, Charles C. *Poor Whites of the Antebellum South*. Durham: Duke University Press, 1994.

Bordin, Ruth Brigitta Anderson. *Frances Willard: A Biography*. Chapel Hill: University of North Carolina Press, 1986.

———. *Woman and Temperance: The Quest for Power and Liberty, 1873–1900*. Philadelphia: Temple University Press, 1981.

Boyer, Paul S. *Urban Masses and Moral Order in America, 1820–1920*. Cambridge, Mass.: Harvard University Press, 1978.

Bradley, Mark L. *Bluecoats and Tar Heels: Soldiers and Civilians in Reconstruction North Carolina*. Lexington: University Press of Kentucky, 2009.

———. *This Astounding Close: The Road to Bennett Place*. Chapel Hill: University of North Carolina Press, 2000.

Brantlinger, Patrick. *Fictions of State: Culture and Credit in Britain, 1694–1994*. Ithaca, N.Y.: Cornell University Press, 1996.

Bridges, Amy. *A City in the Republic: Antebellum New York and the Origins of Machine Politics*. New York: Cambridge University Press, 1984.

Brinkley, Alan. *Voices of Protest: Huey Long, Father Coughlin, and the Great Depression*. New York: Knopf, 1983.

Brock, W. R. *An American Crisis: Congress and Reconstruction 1865–1867*. New York: Harper and Row, 1963.

Bromberg, Alan Bruce. "Pure Democracy and White Supremacy: The Redeemer Period in North Carolina, 1876–1894." Ph.D. diss., University of Virginia, 1977.

Brown, Kathleen. *Good Wives, Nasty Wenches, and Anxious Patriarchs: Gender, Race, and Power in Colonial Virginia*. Chapel Hill: University of North Carolina Press, 1996.

Brown, R. Ben. "The Southern Range: A Study in Nineteenth-Century Law and Society." Ph.D. diss., University of Michigan, 1993.

Brown, Wendy. *States of Injury: Power and Freedom in Late Modernity*. Princeton: Princeton University Press, 1995.

Bruce, Dickson D. *Black American Writing from the Nadir: The Evolution of a Literary Tradition, 1877–1915*. Baton Rouge: Louisiana State University Press, 1989.

Brundage, W. Fitzhugh. *Lynching in the New South: Georgia and Virginia, 1880–1930*. Urbana: University of Illinois Press, 1993.

———. *Under Sentence of Death: Lynching in the South*. Chapel Hill: University of North Carolina Press, 1997.

Bruner, Jerome. *Acts of Meaning*. Cambridge, Mass.: Harvard University Press, 1990.

Bryson, W. Hamilton, and E. Lee Shepard. "The Virginia Bar, 1870–1900." In *The New High Priests: Lawyers in Post–Civil War America*, edited by Gerard W. Gawalt, 171–86. Westport, Conn.: Greenwood Press, 1984.

Buenker, John D. *Urban Liberalism and Progressive Reform*. New York: Scribner, 1973.

Buhle, Mari Jo. *Women and American Socialism, 1870–1920*. Urbana: University of Illinois Press, 1983.

Burkolter-Trachsel, Verena. *The Patronage System: Theoretical Remarks*. Basel, Switzerland: Social Strategies Publishers Co-operative Society, 1976.

Bynum, Victoria E. *Unruly Women: The Politics of Social and Sexual Control in the Old South*. Chapel Hill: University of North Carolina Press, 1992.

Campbell, Jacqueline Glass. *When Sherman Marched North from the Sea: Resistance on the Confederate Home Front*. Chapel Hill: University of North Carolina Press, 2003.

Campbell, James T. *Songs of Zion: The African Methodist Church in the United States and South Africa*. New York: Oxford University Press, 1995.

Carlson, Andrew James. "White Man's Revolution: North Carolina and the American Way of Race Politics, 1896–1901." Ph.D. diss., Brown University, 1993.

Carlton, David Lee. "The Revolution from Above: The National Market and the Beginnings of Industrialization in North Carolina." In *The South, the Nation, and the World: Perspectives on Southern Economic Development*, edited by David Lee Carlton and Peter A. Coclanis, 73–98. Charlottesville: University of Virginia Press, 2003.

Carpenter, Daniel P. *The Forging of Bureaucratic Autonomy: Reputations, Networks, and Policy Innovation in Executive Agencies, 1862–1928*. Princeton: Princeton University Press, 2001.

Carrington, Paul D. *Stewards of Democracy: Law as a Public Profession*. Boulder: University of Colorado Press, 1999.

Carter, Dan T. *When the War Was Over: The Failure of Self-Reconstruction in the South*. Baton Rouge: Louisiana State University Press, 1985.

Castles, Katherine. "Quiet Eugenics: Sterilization in North Carolina's Institutions for the Mentally Retarded." *Journal of Southern History* 68 (November 2002): 849–78.

Cell, John W. *The Highest Stage of White Supremacy: The Origins of Segregation in South Africa and the American South*. New York: Cambridge University Press, 1982.

Censer, Jane Turner. *The Reconstruction of White Southern Womanhood, 1865–1895*. Baton Rouge: Louisiana State University Press, 2003.

Chakrabarty, Dipesh. *Provincializing Europe: Postcolonial Thought and Historical Difference*. Princeton: Princeton University Press, 2000.

Chandler, Alfred D., Jr. *The Visible Hand: The Managerial Revolution in American Business*. Cambridge, Mass.: Harvard University Press, 1977.

Chappell, David L. *A Stone of Hope: Prophetic Religion and the Death of Jim Crow*. Chapel Hill: University of North Carolina Press, 2004.

Chatterjee, Partha. *The Politics of the Governed: Reflections on Popular Politics in Most of the World*. New York: Columbia University Press, 2004.

———. *A Princely Impostor?: The Strange and Universal History of the Kumar of Bhawal*. Princeton: Princeton University Press, 2002.

Chauncey, George. *Gay New York: Gender, Urban Culture, and the Making of the Gay Male World, 1890–1940*. New York: Basic Books, 1994.

Cheek, Roma Sawyer. "The Pardoning Power of the Governor of North Carolina." Ph.D. diss., Duke University, 1932.

Cherny, Robert W. *Populism, Progressivism, and the Transformation of Nebraska Politics, 1885–1915*. Lincoln: University of Nebraska Press, 1981.

Chesnutt, Charles W. *The Conjure Woman*. Ann Arbor: University of Michigan Press, 1969.

Chown, John F. *A History of Money: From A.D. 800*. New York: Routledge, 1994.

Cimbala, Paul A. *Under the Guardianship of the Nation: The Freedmen's Bureau and the Reconstruction of Georgia, 1865–1870*. Athens: University of Georgia Press, 1997.

Cimbala, Paul A., and Randall M. Miller, eds. *The Freedmen's Bureau and Reconstruction: Reconsiderations*. New York: Fordham University Press, 1999.

Clapham, Christopher. "Clientelism and the State." In *Private Patronage and Public Power*, edited by Christopher Clapham, 1–35. London: Frances Pinter, 1982.

Clark, John Spencer. *The Life and Letters of John Fiske*. Boston: Houghton Mifflin, 1917.

Clark, Norman H. *Deliver Us from Evil: An Interpretation of American Prohibition*. New York: Norton, 1976.

——. *The Dry Years: Prohibition and Social Change in Washington*. Seattle: University of Washington Press, 1988.

Clark, Terry Nichols. "Clientelism, U.S.A.: The Dynamics of Change." In *Democracy, Clientelism, and Civil Society*, edited by Luis Roniger and Ayse Gunes-Ayata, 121–44. Boulder: University of Colorado Press, 1994.

Clark, Walter, ed., *Histories of the Several Regiments and Battalions from North Carolina in the Great War, 1861–65*. Raleigh: E. M. Uzzell, 1901.

Click, Patricia C. *Time Full of Trial: The Roanoke Island Freedmen's Colony, 1862–1867*. Chapel Hill: University of North Carolina Press, 2001.

Cohen, Lizabeth. *Making a New Deal: Industrial Workers in Chicago, 1919–1939*. New York: Cambridge University Press, 1991.

Cohen, Nancy. *The Reconstruction of American Liberalism, 1865–1914*. Chapel Hill: University of North Carolina Press, 2002.

Cohn, Bernard S. "The Recruitment and Training of British Civil Servants in India, 1600–1800." In *An Anthropologist among the Historians and Other Essays*, 500–553. New York: Oxford University Press, 1987.

Conklin, Alice L. *A Mission to Civilize: The Republican Idea of Empire in France and West Africa, 1895–1930*. Stanford: Stanford University Press, 1997.

Connell, R. W. *Ruling Class, Ruling Culture: Studies of Conflict, Power, and Hegemony in Australian Life*. New York: Cambridge University Press, 1977.

Connelly, Mark Thomas. *The Response to Prostitution in the Progressive Era*. Chapel Hill: University of North Carolina Press, 1980.

Connolly, James J. *The Triumph of Ethnic Progressivism: Urban Political Culture in Boston, 1900–1925.* Cambridge, Mass.: Harvard University Press, 1998.

Connor, R. D. W. *North Carolina: Rebuilding an Ancient Commonwealth, 1584–1925.* Vol. 2. Chicago: American Historical Society, 1929.

———. *Race Elements in the White Population of North Carolina.* Greensboro, N.C.: The College, 1920.

Cook, James W. *The Arts of Deception: Playing with Fraud in the Age of Barnum.* Cambridge, Mass.: Harvard University Press, 2001.

Cooper, Frederick. "Conflict and Connection: Rethinking Colonial African History." *American Historical Review* 99 (December 1994): 1516–45.

Coronil, Fernando. "Listening to the Subaltern: The Poetics of Neocolonial States." *Poetics Today* 15 (Winter 1994): 643–58.

Cotten, Sallie Southall. *History of the North Carolina Federation of Women's Clubs.* Raleigh: Edwards & Broughton, 1925.

Cox, John H., and LaWanda Cox. "General O. O. Howard and the 'Misrepresented Bureau'." *Journal of Southern History* 19 (November 1953): 427–56.

Craig, Douglas B. *Fireside Politics: Radio and Political Culture in the United States, 1920–1940.* Baltimore: Johns Hopkins University Press, 2000.

Creech, Joe. *Righteous Indignation: Religion and the Populist Revolt.* Urbana: University of Illinois Press, 2006.

Critchlow, Donald T. *Phyllis Schlafly and Grassroots Conservatism: A Woman's Crusade.* Princeton: Princeton University Press, 2005.

Crook, D. P. *Benjamin Kidd: Portrait of a Social Darwinist.* New York: Cambridge University Press, 1984.

Crouch, Barry A. *The Freedmen's Bureau and Black Texans.* Austin: University of Texas Press, 1992.

Crow, Jeffrey J. " 'Fusion, Confusion and Negroism': Schisms among Negro Republicans in the North Carolina Elections of 1896." *North Carolina Historical Review* 53 (October 1976): 364–84.

———. "Thomas Settle Jr., Reconstruction, and the Memory of the Civil War." *Journal of Southern History* 62 (November 1996): 689–726.

Crow, Jeffrey J., and Robert F. Durden. *Maverick Republican in the Old North State: A Political Biography of Daniel L. Russell.* Baton Rouge: Louisiana State University Press, 1977.

Cruikshank, Barbara. *The Will to Empower: Democratic Citizens and Other Subjects.* Ithaca, N.Y.: Cornell University Press, 1999.

Curtis, Susan. *A Consuming Faith: The Social Gospel and Modern American Culture.* Baltimore: Johns Hopkins University Press, 1991. Reprint, Columbia: University of Missouri Press, 2001.

D'Emilio, John, and Estelle B. Freedman. *Intimate Matters: A History of Sexuality in America.* New York: Harper & Row, 1988.

Dailey, Jane. *Before Jim Crow: The Politics of Race in Postemancipation Virginia*. Chapel Hill: University of North Carolina Press, 2000.

———. "The Limits of Liberalism in the New South: The Politics of Race, Sex, and Patronage in Virginia, 1879–83." In *Jumpin' Jim Crow: Southern Politics from Civil War to Civil Rights*, edited by Jane Dailey, Glenda Elizabeth Gilmore, and Bryant Simon, 88–114. Princeton: Princeton University Press, 2000.

———. "Sex, Segregation and the Sacred after *Brown*." *Journal of American History* 91 (June 2004): 119–44.

Dannenbaum, Jed. *Drink and Disorder: Temperance Reform in Cincinnati from the Washingtonian Revival to the W.C.T.U.* Urbana: University of Illinois Press, 1984.

Davidoff, Leonore, and Catherine Hall. *Family Fortunes: Men and Women of the English Middle Class, 1780–1850*. Chicago: University of Chicago Press, 1987.

Davies, Glyn. *A History of Money: From Ancient Times to the Present Day*. Cardiff: University of Wales Press, 1994.

Davis, Susan G. *Parades and Power: Street Theatre in Mid-Nineteenth-Century Philadelphia*. Philadelphia: Temple University Press, 1986.

Dawley, Alan. *Changing the World: American Progressives in War and Revolution*. Princeton: Princeton University Press, 2005.

———. *Struggles for Justice: Social Responsibility and the Liberal State*. Cambridge, Mass.: Harvard University Press, 1991.

Degler, Carl N. *In Search of Human Nature: The Decline and Revival of Darwinism in American Social Thought*. New York: Oxford University Press, 1991.

Del Giudice, Luisa. "Mountains of Cheese and Rivers of Wine: Paesi Di Caccagna and Other Gastronomic Utopias." In *Imagined States: Nationalism, Utopia, and Longing in Oral Cultures*, edited by Luisa Del Giudice and Gerald Porter, 11–63. Logan: Utah State University Press, 2001.

Dennett, Daniel C. *Darwin's Dangerous Idea: Evolution and the Meanings of Life*. New York: Simon & Schuster, 1995.

Denning, Michael. *The Cultural Front: The Laboring of American Culture in the Twentieth Century*. New York: Verso, 1996.

Dennis, Michael. *Lessons in Progress: State Universities and Progressivism in the New South, 1880–1920*. Urbana: University of Illinois Press, 2001.

Desmonde, William H. *Magic, Myth, and Money: The Origin of Money in Religious Ritual*. New York: Free Press of Glencoe, 1962.

Dewey, David Rich. *Financial History of the United States*. New York: Longman, Green and Co., 1922.

Digeser, P. E. *Political Forgiveness*. Ithaca, N.Y.: Cornell University Press, 2001.

Dixon, Helen C. A. *A. C. Dixon: A Romance of Preaching*. New York: G. P. Putnam's Sons, 1931.

Donald, David Herbert. *Lincoln Reconsidered: Essays on the Civil War Era*. New York: Knopf, 1956.

Dowd, Clement. *Life of Zebulon Vance*. Charlotte, N.C.: Observer Print and Publishing House, 1897.

Downs, Gregory P. "Hail to the Chief and to the Thief: Fantasies, Fictions, and Fears about the United States Presidency." *American Quarterly* 61 (June 2009): 405–16.

———. "University Men, Social Science, and White Supremacy in North Carolina." *Journal of Southern History* 75 (May 2009): 267–304.

DuBois, Ellen Carol. *Woman Suffrage and Women's Rights*. New York: New York University Press, 1998.

DuBois, W. E. B. *Black Reconstruction in America*. New York: Harcourt Brace, 1935. Reprint, New York: Atheneum, 1992.

Dunning, William Archibald. *Essays on the Civil War and Reconstruction and Related Topics*. New York: Macmillan, 1910.

Durden, Robert F. *The Climax of Populism: The Election of 1896*. Lexington: University Press of Kentucky, 1965.

———. *The Dukes of Durham, 1865–1929*. Durham: Duke University Press, 1975.

During, Simon. *Modern Enchantments: The Cultural Power of Secular Magic*. Cambridge, Mass.: Harvard University Press, 2002.

Durrill, Wayne K. *War of Another Kind: A Southern Community in the Great Rebellion*. New York: Oxford University Press, 1990.

Eaton, Clement. "Professor James Woodrow and the Freedom of Teaching in the South." *Journal of Southern History* 28 (February 1962): 3–17.

Edmonds, Helen G. *The Negro and Fusion Politics in North Carolina*. Chapel Hill: University of North Carolina Press, 1951.

Edwards, Brent Hayes. *The Practice of Diaspora: Literature, Translation, and the Rise of Black Internationalism*. Cambridge, Mass.: Harvard University Press, 2003.

Edwards, Laura F. "Captives of Wilmington: The Riot and Historical Memories of Political Conflict." In *Democracy Betrayed: The Wilmington Race Riot of 1898 and Its Legacy*, edited by David S. Cecelski and Timothy B. Tyson, 113–35. Chapel Hill: University of North Carolina Press, 1998.

———. "Enslaved Women and the Law: Paradoxes of Subordination in the Post-Revolutionary Carolinas." *Slavery and Abolition* 26 (August 2005): 305–23.

———. *Gendered Strife and Confusion: The Political Culture of Reconstruction*. Urbana: University of Illinois Press, 1997.

———. *The People and Their Peace: Legal Culture and the Transformation of Inequality in the Post-Revolutionary South*. Chapel Hill: University of North Carolina Press, 2009.

———. "Southern History as U.S. History." *Journal of Southern History* 75 (August 2009): 1–28.

———. "Status without Rights: African Americans and the Tangled History of Law and Governance in the Nineteenth-Century U.S. South." *American Historical Review* 112 (April 2007): 365–93.

Edwards, Rebecca. *Angels in the Machinery: Gender in American Party Politics from the Civil War to the Progressive Era*. New York: Oxford University Press, 1997.

Einhorn, Robin. *Property Rules: Political Economy in Chicago, 1833–1872*. Chicago: University of Chicago Press, 1991.

Eisenach, Eldon J. *The Lost Promise of Progressivism*. Lawrence: University Press of Kansas, 1994.

———. "Progressive Internationalism." In *Progressivism and the New Democracy*, edited by Sidney M. Milkis and Jerome M. Mileur, 226–58. Amherst: University of Massachusetts Press, 1999.

Eisenstadt, S. N., and L. Roniger. *Patrons, Clients, and Friends: Interpersonal Relations and the Structure of Trust in Society*. New York: Cambridge University Press, 1984.

———. "Patron-Client Relations as a Model of Structuring Social Exchange." *Comparative Studies in Society and History* 22 (January 1980): 42–77.

Elkins, Stanley, and Eric McKitrick. *The Age of Federalism*. New York: Oxford University Press, 1993.

Ellis, Jack D. *The Physician-Legislators of France: Medicine and Politics in the Early Third Republic, 1870–1914*. New York: Cambridge University Press, 1990.

Ely, Melvin Patrick. *The Adventures of Amos 'n' Andy: A Social History of an American Phenomenon*. New York: Free Press, 1991.

———. *Israel on the Appomattox: A Southern Experiment in Black Freedom from the 1790s through the Civil War*. New York: Knopf, 2004.

Engs, Robert F. *Freedom's First Generation: Black Hampton, Virginia, 1861–1890*. Philadelphia: University of Pennsylvania Press, 1979.

Epstein, Barbara Leslie. *The Politics of Domesticity: Women, Evangelism, and Temperance in Nineteenth-Century America*. Middletown, Conn.: Wesleyan University Press, 1981.

Erie, Steven P. *Rainbow's End: Irish-Americans and the Dilemmas of Urban Machine Politics, 1840–1985*. Berkeley: University of California Press, 1988.

Escott, Paul D. *Many Excellent People: Power and Privilege in North Carolina, 1850–1900*. Chapel Hill: University of North Carolina Press, 1985.

———. "Poverty and Governmental Aid for the Poor in Confederate North Carolina." *North Carolina Historical Review* 61 (October 1984): 462–80.

Ethington, Philip J. *The Public City: The Political Construction of Urban Life in San Francisco, 1850–1900*. New York: Cambridge University Press, 1994.

Evans, William McKee. *Ballots and Fence Rails: Reconstruction on the Lower Cape Fear*. Chapel Hill: University of North Carolina Press, 1967.

———. *To Die Game: The Story of the Lowry Band, Indian Guerrillas of Reconstruction*. Baton Rouge: Louisiana State University Press, 1971.

Faulkner, Carol. *Women's Radical Reconstruction: The Freedmen's Aid Movement.* Philadelphia: University of Pennsylvania Press, 2004.

Faust, Drew Gilpin. *The Creation of Confederate Nationalism: Ideology and Identity in the Civil War South.* Baton Rouge: Louisiana State University Press, 1990.

———. *Mothers of Invention: Women of the Slaveholding South in the American Civil War.* Chapel Hill: University of North Carolina Press, 2004.

Feierman, Steven. *Peasant Intellectuals: Anthropology and History in Tanzania.* Madison: University of Wisconsin Press, 1990.

Feimster, Crystal Nicole. *Southern Horrors: Women and the Politics of Rape and Lynching.* Cambridge, Mass.: Harvard University Press, 2009.

Fellman, Michael. *Inside War: The Guerrilla Conflict in Missouri during the American Civil War.* New York: Oxford University Press, 1989.

Ferleger, Herbert Ronald. *David A. Wells and the American Revenue System, 1865–1870.* Philadelphia: Porcupine Press, 1977.

Ferrell, Henry C., Jr. "Prohibition, Reform, and Politics in Virginia, 1895–1916." In *Studies in the History of the South, 1875–1922,* 175–242. Greenville, N.C.: Department of History, East Carolina College, 1966.

Ferris, Charles J. "Southern Baptists in the 1920s: The Roles of Edgar Y. Mullins, J. Frank Norris, and William Louis Poteat." M.A. thesis, University of Louisville, 1973.

Field, Daniel. *Rebels in the Name of the Tsar.* Boston: Houghton Mifflin, 1976.

Fields, Barbara Jeanne. "Ideology and Race in American History." In *Region, Race, and Reconstruction: Essays in Honor of C. Vann Woodward,* edited by J. Morgan Kousser and James M. McPherson, 143–77. New York: Oxford University Press, 1982.

———. *Slavery and Freedom on the Middle Ground: Maryland during the Nineteenth Century.* New Haven: Yale University Press, 1985.

———. "Whiteness, Racism, and Identity." *International Labor and Working Class History* 60 (Fall 2001): 48–56.

Filene, Peter G. "An Obituary for 'the Progressive Movement'." *American Quarterly* 22 (Spring 1970): 20–34.

Fineman, Martha. *The Autonomy Myth: A Theory of Dependency.* New York: New Press, 2004.

Fink, Leon. *Workingmen's Democracy: The Knights of Labor and American Politics.* Urbana: University of Illinois Press, 1983.

Finkelman, Paul. *Dred Scott v. Sandford: A Brief History with Documents.* New York: Bedford Books, 1997.

Fiskesjo, Magnus. *The Thanksgiving Turkey Pardon, the Death of Teddy's Bear, and the Sovereign Exception of Guantanamo.* Chicago: Prickly Paradigm Books, 2003.

Fitzgerald, Michael W. "Emancipation and Military Pacification: The Freedmen's Bureau and Social Control in Alabama." In *The Freedmen's Bureau and*

Reconstruction: Reconsiderations, edited by Paul A. Cimbala and Randall M. Miller, 45–66. New York: Fordham University Press, 1999.

———. "Extralegal Violence and the Planter Class: The Ku Klux Klan in the Alabama Black Belt during Reconstruction." In *Local Matters: Race, Crime, and Justice in the Nineteenth-Century South*, edited by Christopher Waldrep and Donald G. Nieman, 155–71. Athens: University of Georgia Press, 2001.

———. "Reconstruction Politics and the Politics of Reconstruction." In *Reconstructions: New Perspectives on the Postbellum United States*, edited by Thomas J. Brown, 91–116. New York: Oxford University Press, 2006.

Flanagan, Maureen A. *Seeing with Their Hearts: Chicago Women and the Vision of the Good City, 1871–1933*. Princeton: Princeton University Press, 2002.

Flynn, Charles L., Jr. "Procrustean Bedfellows and Populists and Alternative Hypothesis." In *Race, Class, and Politics in Southern History: Essays in Honor of Robert F. Durden*, edited by Paul D. Escott, Jeffrey J. Crow, and Charles L. Flynn Jr., 81–105. Baton Rouge: Louisiana State University Press, 1989.

Foner, Eric. *Forever Free: The Story of Emancipation and Reconstruction*. New York: Knopf, 2005.

———. *Free Soil, Free Labor, Free Men: The Ideology of the Republican Party before the Civil War*. New York: Oxford University Press, 1970.

———. *Reconstruction: America's Unfinished Revolution, 1863–1877*. New York: Harper & Row, 1988.

———. *The Story of American Freedom*. New York: Norton, 1999.

Foner, Philip S. *The Spanish-Cuban-American War and the Birth of American Imperialism, 1895–1902*. New York: Monthly Review Press, 1972.

Formisano, Ronald P. *The Transformation of Political Culture: Massachusetts Parties, 1790s to 1840s*. New York: Oxford University Press, 1983.

Forsythe, Harold S. "African American Churches, Fusion Politics in Virginia, and the Republican Gubernatorial Campaign in 1889." In *Afro-Virginian History and Culture*, edited by John Saillant, 211–26. New York: Garland, 1999.

———. "But My Friends Are Poor: Ross Hamilton and Freedpeople's Politics in Mecklenburg County, Virginia, 1879–1901." *Virginia Magazine of History and Biography* 105 (October 1997): 409–38.

Foster, Gaines M. *Moral Reconstruction: Christian Lobbyists and the Federal Legislation of Morality, 1865–1920*. Chapel Hill: University of North Carolina Press, 2002.

Fowler, Dorothy Ganfield. *The Cabinet Politician: The Postmasters General, 1829–1909*. New York: Columbia University Press, 1943.

Fox-Genovese, Elizabeth. *Within the Plantation Household: Black and White Women of the Old South*. Chapel Hill: University of North Carolina Press, 1988.

Fox-Genovese, Elizabeth, and Eugene D. Genovese. *The Mind of the Master Class: History and Faith in the Southern Slaveholders' Worldview*. New York: Cambridge University Press, 2005.

Fraccia, Joseph, and R. C. Lewontin. "Does Culture Evolve?" *History and Theory* 38 (December 1999): 52–78.

Frank, Thomas. *What's the Matter with Kansas? How Conservatives Won the Heart of America*. New York: Metropolitan Books, 2004.

Franklin, John Hope. *The Militant South, 1800–1860*. Cambridge, Mass.: Harvard University Press, 1956.

Fraser, Nancy, and Linda Gordon. "A Genealogy of Dependence: Tracing a Keyword of the U.S. Welfare State." *Signs* 19 (Winter 1994): 309–36.

Fredrickson, George M. *The Black Image in the White Mind: The Debate on Afro-American Character and Destiny, 1817–1914*. New York: Harper & Row, 1971.

Freeden, Michael. "Eugenics and Progressive Thought: A Study in Ideological Affinity." *The Historical Journal* 22 (September 1979): 645–71.

Freehling, William W. *The Road to Disunion: Secessionists Triumphant, 1854–1861*. New York: Oxford University Press, 2007.

———. *The Road to Disunion: Southerners at Bay, 1776–1854*. New York: Oxford University Press, 1990.

———. *The South vs. the South: How Anti-Confederate Southerners Shaped the Course of the Civil War*. New York: Oxford University Press, 2001.

Freeman, Joanne B. *Affairs of Honor: National Politics in the New Republic*. New Haven: Yale University Press, 2001.

Friedman, Milton, and Anna Jacobson Schwartz. *A Monetary History of the United States, 1867–1960*. Princeton: Princeton University Press, 1963.

Gaither, Gerald. *Blacks and the Populist Revolt: Ballots and Bigotry in the "New South"*. Tuscaloosa: University of Alabama Press, 1977.

Gallagher, Gary W. *Confederate War: How Popular Will, Nationalism, and Military Strategy Could Not Stave off Defeat*. Cambridge, Mass.: Harvard University Press, 1997.

Gallarotti, Giulio M. "The Scramble for Gold: Monetary Regime Transformation in the 1870s." In *Monetary Regimes in Transition*, edited by Michael D. Bordo and Forrest Capie, 15–67. New York: Cambridge University Press, 1994.

Gatewood, Willard B., Jr. *Black Americans and the White Man's Burden, 1898–1903*. Urbana: University of Illinois Press, 1975.

———. *Preachers, Pedagogues, and Politicians: The Evolution Controversy in North Carolina, 1920–1927*. Chapel Hill: University of North Carolina Press, 1966.

Gawalt, Gerard W. Introduction to *The New High Priests: Lawyers in Post–Civil War America*, edited by Gerard W. Gawalt, vii–xiv. Westport, Conn.: Greenwood Press, 1984.

Genovese, Eugene D. *The Political Economy of Slavery: Studies in the Economy and Society of the Slave South*. New York: Pantheon Books, 1965.

———. *Roll, Jordan, Roll: The World the Slaves Made*. New York: Vintage Books, 1974.

——. *The Southern Tradition: The Achievements and Limitations of an American Conservatism*. Cambridge, Mass.: Harvard University Press, 1996.

——. *The World the Slaveholders Made: Two Essays in Interpretation*. New York: Pantheon Books, 1969.

Giangreco, D. M., and Kathryn Moore. *Dear Harry . . . Truman's Mailroom, 1945–1953: The Truman Administration through Correspondence with "Everyday Americans"*. Mechanicsburg, Pa.: Stackpole Books, 1999.

Gilfoyle, Timothy J. *City of Eros: New York City, Prostitution, and the Commercialization of Sex, 1790–1920*. New York: Norton, 1992.

Gillette, William. *Retreat from Reconstruction, 1869–1879*. Baton Rouge: Louisiana State University Press, 1979.

Gilmore, Glenda Elizabeth. *Gender and Jim Crow: Women and the Politics of White Supremacy in North Carolina, 1896–1920*. Chapel Hill: University of North Carolina Press, 1996.

——. "Murder, Memory, and the Flight of the Incubus." In *Democracy Betrayed: The Wilmington Race Riot of 1898 and Its Legacy*, edited by David S. Cecelski and Timothy B. Tyson, 73–94. Chapel Hill: University of North Carolina Press, 1998.

Ginzberg, Lori D. *Untidy Origins: A Story of Women's Rights in Antebellum New York*. Chapel Hill: University of North Carolina Press, 2005.

——. *Women and the Work of Benevolence: Morality, Politics, and Class in the Nineteenth-Century United States*. New Haven: Yale University Press, 1990.

Gladwell, Malcolm. *The Tipping Point: How Little Things Can Make a Big Difference*. Boston: Little, Brown, 2000.

Glymph, Thavolia. *Out of the House of Bondage: The Transformation of the Plantation Household*. New York: Cambridge University Press, 2008.

Gobbel, Luther L. *Church-State Relationships in Education in North Carolina since 1776*. Durham: Duke University Press, 1938.

Goldberg, Chad Alan. *Citizens and Paupers: Relief, Rights, and Race from the Freedmen's Bureau to Workfare*. Chicago: University of Chicago Press, 2007.

Goldberg, Michael L. *An Army of Women: Gender and Politics in Gilded Age Kansas*. Baltimore: Johns Hopkins University Press, 1997.

Goodman, James E. *Stories of Scottsboro*. New York: Pantheon, 1994.

Goodwyn, Lawrence. *Democratic Promise: The Populist Moment in America*. New York: Oxford University Press, 1976.

Gordon, Linda. *Pitied but Not Entitled: Single Mothers and the History of Welfare, 1890–1935*. New York: Free Press, 1994.

Gordon, Robert W. *The Ideal and the Actual in the Law: Fantasies and Practices of New York City Lawyers, 1870–1910*. In *The New High Priests: Lawyers in Post–Civil War America*, edited by Gerard W. Gawalt. Westport, Conn.: Greenwood Press, 1984.

Gould, Lewis L. *Progressives and Prohibitionists: Texas Democrats in the Wilson Era*. Austin: University of Texas Press, 1973.

Goux, Jean-Joseph. *Symbolic Economies: After Marx and Freud*. Translated by Jennifer Curtiss Gage. Ithaca, N.Y.: Cornell University Press, 1990.

Grantham, Dewey W. *Hoke Smith and the Politics of the New South*. Baton Rouge: Louisiana State University Press, 1958.

———. *Southern Progressivism: The Reconciliation of Progress and Tradition*. Knoxville: University of Tennessee Press, 1983.

Greenberg, Kenneth S. *Honor and Slavery: Lies, Duels, Noses, Masks, Dressing as a Woman, Gifts, Strangers, Humanitarianism, Death, Slave Rebellions, the Proslavery Argument, Baseball, Hunting, and Gambling in the Old South*. Princeton: Princeton University Press, 1996.

Greenwood, Janette Thomas. *Bittersweet Legacy: The Black and White "Better Classes" in Charlotte, 1850–1910*. Chapel Hill: University of North Carolina Press, 1994.

Gross, Ariela. "Beyond Black and White: Cultural Approaches to Race and Slavery." *Columbia Law Review* 101 (April 2001): 640–82.

———. *Double Character: Slavery and Mastery in the Antebellum Southern Courtroom*. Princeton: Princeton University Press, 2000.

Grossberg, Lawrence. "On Postmodernism and Articulation: An Interview with Stuart Hall." In *Stuart Hall: Critical Dialogues in Cultural Studies*, edited by David Morley and Kuan-Hsing Chen, 131–50. New York: Routledge, 1996.

Guha, Ranajit. *Elementary Aspects of Peasant Insurgency in Colonial India*. Delhi: Oxford University Press, 1983.

Gunes-Ayata, Ayse. "Clientelism: Premodern, Modern, Postmodern." In *Democracy, Clientelism, and Civil Society*, edited by Luis Roniger and Ayse Gunes-Ayata, 19–28. Boulder: University of Colorado Press, 1994.

Gusfield, Joseph R. *Symbolic Crusade: Status Politics and the American Temperance Movement*. Urbana: University of Illinois Press, 1986.

Guterl, Matthew Pratt. *The Color of Race in America, 1900–1940*. Cambridge, Mass.: Harvard University Press, 2001.

Hackney, Sheldon. *Populism to Progressivism in Alabama*. Princeton: Princeton University Press, 1969.

Hahn, Steven. "Class and State in Postemancipation Societies: Southern Planters in Comparative Perspective." *American Historical Review* 95 (February 1990): 75–98.

———. "Extravagant Expectations of Freedom: Rumour, Political Struggle, and the Christmas Insurrection Scare of 1865 in the American South." *Past and Present* 157 (November 1997): 122–58.

———. "Hunting, Fishing, and Foraging: Common Rights and Class Relations in the Postbellum South." *Radical History Review* 26 (October 1982): 37–64.

———. *A Nation under Our Feet: Black Political Struggles in the Rural South, from Slavery to the Great Migration*. Cambridge, Mass.: Harvard University Press, 2003.

———. *The Political Worlds of Slavery and Freedom*. Cambridge, Mass.: Harvard University Press, 2009.

———. "A Response: Common Cents or Historical Sense?" *Journal of Southern History* 59 (May 1993): 243–58.

———. *The Roots of Southern Populism: Yeoman Farmers and the Transformation of the Georgia Upcountry, 1850–1890*. Updated edition. New York: Oxford University Press, 2006.

Haley, John. *Charles N. Hunter and Race Relations in North Carolina*. Chapel Hill: University of North Carolina Press, 1987.

Hall, Jacquelyn Dowd, James L. Leloudis, Robert Rodgers Korstad, Mary Murphy, Lu Ann Jones, and Christopher B. Daly. *Like a Family: The Making of a Southern Cotton Mill World*. Chapel Hill: University of North Carolina Press, 1987.

Hall, Stuart. "The Problem of Ideology: Marxism without Guarantees." In *Stuart Hall: Critical Dialogues in Cultural Studies*, edited by David Morley and Kuan-Hsing Chen, 25–46. New York: Routledge, 1996.

———, ed. *Policing the Crisis: Mugging, the State, and Law and Order*. London: Macmillan, 1978.

Hall, Stuart, and Martin Jaques, eds. *The Politics of Thatcherism*. London: Lawrence and Wishart, 1983.

Haller, John S. "Race and the Concept of Progress in Nineteenth Century American Ethnology." *American Anthropologist* 73 (June 1971): 710–24.

Haller, Mark H. *Eugenics: Hereditarian Attitudes in American Thought*. New Brunswick, N.J.: Rutgers University Press, 1963.

Hambly, Alonzo L. "Progressivism: A Century of Change and Rebirth." In *Progressivism and the New Democracy*, edited by Sidney M. Milkis and Jerome M. Mileur, 40–80. Amherst: University of Massachusetts Press, 1999.

Hamm, Richard F. *Shaping the Eighteenth Amendment: Temperance Reform, Legal Culture, and the Polity, 1880–1920*. Chapel Hill: University of North Carolina Press, 1995.

Hanchett, Thomas W. *Sorting out the New South City: Race, Class, and Urban Development in Charlotte, 1875–1975*. Chapel Hill: University of North Carolina Press, 1998.

Harp, Gillis. *Positivist Republic: August Comte and the Reconstruction of American Liberalism, 1865–1920*. University Park, Pa.: Pennsylvania State University Press, 1990.

Harris, William C. *William Woods Holden: Firebrand of North Carolina Politics*. Baton Rouge: Louisiana State University Press, 1987.

Hartz, Louis. *The Liberal Tradition in America: An Interpretation of American Political Thought since the Revolution*. New York: Harcourt, Brace, 1955.

Harvey, David. *Consciousness and the Urban Experience: Studies in the History and Theory of Capitalist Urbanization*. Baltimore: Johns Hopkins University Press, 1985.

Harvey, Paul. *Freedom's Coming: Religious Culture and the Shaping of the South from the Civil War through the Civil Rights Era.* Chapel Hill: University of North Carolina Press, 2005.

———. *Redeeming the South: Religious Culture and Racial Identities among Southern Baptists, 1865–1925.* Chapel Hill: University of North Carolina Press, 1997.

Haskell, Thomas L. *The Emergence of Professional Social Science: The American Social Science Association with the Nineteenth-Century Crisis of Authority.* Urbana: University of Illinois Press, 1977.

Hawkins, Mike. *Social Darwinism in European and American Thought, 1860–1945.* New York: Cambridge University Press, 1997.

Hayden, René. "Root of Wrath: Political Culture and the Origins of the First Ku-Klux Klan in North Carolina, 1830–1875." Ph.D. diss., University of California, San Diego, 2003.

Hays, Samuel P. *The Response to Industrialism, 1885–1914.* Chicago: University of Chicago Press, 1957.

Hedrick, Burton J. *The Training of an American: The Earlier Life and Letters of Walter Hines Pages.* Boston: Houghton Mifflin, 1928.

Herbst, Susan. *Numbered Voices: How Opinion Polling Has Shaped American Politics.* Chicago: University of Chicago Press, 1993.

———. *Reading Public Opinion: How Political Actors View the Democratic Process.* Chicago: University of Chicago Press, 1998.

Hicks, John D. *The Populist Revolt: A History of the Farmers' Alliance and the People's Party.* Lincoln: University of Nebraska Press, 1961.

Higginbotham, Evelyn Brooks. "African-American Women's History and the Metalanguage of Race." *Signs* 17 (Winter 1992): 251–74.

Higham, John. *Strangers in the Land: Patterns in American Nativism, 1860–1925.* New York: Atheneum, 1963.

Hild, Matthew. *Greenbackers, Knights of Labor, and Populists: Farmer-Labor Insurgency in the Late-Nineteenth-Century South.* Athens: University of Georgia Press, 2007.

Hilderman, Walter C., III. *They Went into the Fight Cheering: Confederate Conscription in North Carolina.* Boone, N.C.: Parkway Publishers, 2005.

Hobsbawm, E. J. *Primitive Rebels: Studies in Archaic Forms of Social Movement in the 19th and 20th Centuries.* New York: Norton, 1965.

Hobsbawm, E. J., and George Rudé. *Captain Swing.* New York: Pantheon, 1968.

Hobson, Barbara Meil. *Uneasy Virtue: The Politics of Prostitution and the American Reform Tradition.* New York: Basic Books, 1987.

Hodes, Martha. *White Women, Black Men: Illicit Sex in the Nineteenth-Century South.* New Haven: Yale University Press, 1997.

Hoffman, Beatrix. "Scientific Racism, Insurance, and Opposition to the Welfare State: Frederick L. Hoffman's Transatlantic Journey." *Journal of the Gilded Age and Progressive Era* 2 (April 2003).

Hofstadter, Richard. *The Age of Reform: From Bryan to F.D.R.* New York: Knopf, 1955.

———. *The Paranoid Style in American Politics, and Other Essays.* New York: Knopf, 1965.

———. *Social Darwinism in American Thought.* Boston: Beacon Press, 1955.

Holland, Catherine A. *The Body Politic: Foundings, Citizenship, and Difference in the American Political Imagination.* New York: Routledge, 2001.

Holmes, William F. "The Southern Farmers' Alliance and the Georgia Senatorial Election of 1890." *Journal of Southern History* 50 (May 1984): 197–224.

———. *The White Chief: James Kimble Vardaman.* Baton Rouge: Louisiana State University Press, 1970.

Holt, Michael F. *Political Parties and American Political Development: From the Age of Jackson to the Age of Lincoln.* Baton Rouge: Louisiana State University Press, 1992.

Holt, Thomas C. "Marking: Race, Race-Making and the Writing of History." *American Historical Review* 100 (February 1995): 1–20.

———. *The Problem of Freedom: Race, Labor, and Politics in Jamaica and Britain, 1832–1938.* Baltimore: Johns Hopkins University Press, 1992.

Hoogenboom, Ari. *Outlawing the Spoils: A History of the Civil Service Reform Movement, 1865–1883.* Urbana: University of Illinois Press, 1961.

Hormats, Robert D. *The Price of Liberty: Paying for America's Wars.* New York: Times Books, 2007.

Horsman, Reginald. *Race and Manifest Destiny: The Origins of American Racial Anglo-Saxonism.* Cambridge, Mass.: Harvard University Press, 1982.

Hunt, James L. *Marion Butler and American Populism.* Chapel Hill: University of North Carolina Press, 2003.

Hutson, James H. "John Adams' Title Campaign." *New England Quarterly* 1 (March 1968): 30–39.

Isaac, Paul E. *Prohibition and Politics: Turbulent Decades in Tennessee, 1865–1920.* Knoxville: University of Tennessee Press, 1965.

Isenberg, Nancy. *Sex and Citizenship in Antebellum America.* Chapel Hill: University of North Carolina Press, 1998.

Israel, Charles A. *Before Scopes: Evangelicalism, Education, and Evolution in Tennessee, 1870–1925.* Athens: University of Georgia Press, 2004.

Ivy, James D. *No Saloon in the Valley: The Southern Strategy of Texas Prohibitionists in the 1880s.* Waco, Tex.: Baylor University Press, 2003.

Jacobs, Meg. *Pocketbook Politics: Economic Citizenship in Twentieth-Century America.* Princeton: Princeton University Press, 2005.

Jacobson, Matthew Frye. *Whiteness of a Different Color: European Immigrants and the Alchemy of Race.* Cambridge, Mass.: Harvard University Press, 1999.

Jacoby, Karl. *Crimes against Nature: Squatters, Poachers, Thieves, and the Hidden History of American Conservation.* Berkeley: University of California Press, 2001.

Jeffrey, Julie Roy. "Women in the Southern Farmers' Alliance: A Reconsideration of the Role and Status of Women in the Late Nineteenth-Century South." *Feminist Studies* 3 (Fall 1975): 72–91.

Jensen, Christen. *The Pardoning Power in the American States.* Chicago: University of Chicago Press, 1922.

John, Richard R. "Ruling Passions: Political Economy in Nineteenth-Century America." In *Ruling Passions: Political Economy in Nineteenth-Century America,* edited by Richard R. John, 1–20. University Park, Pa.: Pennsylvania State University Press, 2006.

———. *Spreading the News: The American Postal System from Franklin to Morse.* Cambridge, Mass.: Harvard University Press, 1995.

Johnson, Guion Griffis. *Ante-Bellum North Carolina: A Social History.* Chapel Hill: University of North Carolina Press, 1937.

Johnson, Ronald N., and Gary D. Libecap. *The Federal Civil Service System and the Problem of Bureaucracy: The Economics and Politics of Institutional Change.* Chicago: University of Chicago Press, 1994.

Johnson, Walter. "A Nettlesome Classic Turns Twenty-Five." *Common-Place* 4 (July 2001).

———. "On Agency." *Journal of Social History* 1 (Fall 2003): 113–24.

Johnston, Robert D. *The Radical Middle Class: Populist Democracy and the Question of Capitalism in Progressive Era Portland, Oregon.* Princeton: Princeton University Press, 2003.

Jones, Greta. *Social Hygiene in Twentieth Century Britain.* Wolfeboro, N.H.: Croom Helm, 1986.

Jordan, Winthrop D. *White over Black: American Attitudes toward the Negro, 1550– 1812.* Chapel Hill: University of North Carolina Press, 1968.

Joseph, Gilbert M., and Daniel Nugent. "Popular Culture and State Formation in Revolutionary Mexico." In *Everyday Forms of State Formation: Revolution and the Negotiation of Rule in Modern Mexico,* edited by Gilbert M. Joseph and Daniel Nugent, 3–23. Durham: Duke University Press, 1994.

Kantor, Shawn Everett, and J. Morgan Kousser. "Common Sense or Commonwealth? The Fence Law and Institutional Change in the Postbellum South." *Journal of Southern History* 59 (May 1993): 201–42.

Kantorowicz, Ernst H. *The King's Two Bodies: A Study in Medieval Political Theology.* Princeton: Princeton University Press, 1957.

Kantrowitz, Stephen David. *Ben Tillman and the Reconstruction of White Supremacy.* Chapel Hill: University of North Carolina Press, 2000.

———. "The Two Faces of Domination in North Carolina, 1800–1898." In *Democracy Betrayed: The Wilmington Race Riot of 1898 and Its Legacy,* edited by David S. Cecelski and Timothy B. Tyson, 95–112. Chapel Hill: University of North Carolina Press, 1998.

Katznelson, Ira. *City Trenches: Urban Politics and the Patterning of Class in the United States*. New York: Pantheon, 1981.

Kaye, Anthony E. *Joining Places: Slave Neighborhoods in the Old South*. Chapel Hill: University of North Carolina Press, 2007.

———. "Neighbourhoods and Solidarity in the Natchez District of Mississippi: Rethinking the Antebellum Slave Community." *Slavery and Abolition* 23 (April 2002): 1–24.

Kazin, Michael. *A Godly Hero: The Life of William Jennings Bryan*. New York: Knopf, 2006.

———. *The Populist Persuasion: An American History*. New York: Basic Books, 1995.

Keller, Morton. *Affairs of State: Public Life in Late-Nineteenth-Century America*. Cambridge, Mass.: Harvard University Press, 1977.

———. *Regulating a New Economy: Public Policy and Economic Change in America, 1900–1933*. Cambridge, Mass.: Harvard University Press, 1990.

———. *Regulating a New Society: Public Policy and Social Change in America, 1900–1933*. Cambridge, Mass.: Harvard University Press, 1994.

Kelley, Robin D. G. *Race Rebels: Culture, Politics, and the Black Working Class*. New York: Free Press, 1994.

Kenzer, Robert C. *Kinship and Neighborhood in a Southern Community: Orange County, North Carolina, 1849–1881*. Knoxville: University of Tennessee Press, 1987.

Kerber, Linda K. *No Constitutional Right to Be Ladies: Women and the Obligations of Citizenship*. New York: Hill and Wang, 1998.

Kerr, K. Austin. *Organized for Prohibition: A New History of the Anti-Saloon League*. New Haven: Yale University Press, 1985.

———. "Organizing for Reform: The Anti-Saloon League and Innovation in Politics." *American Quarterly* 32 (Spring 1980): 37–53.

Kesselring, K. J. *Mercy and Authority in the Tudor State*. New York: Cambridge University Press, 2003.

Kevles, Daniel J. *In the Name of Eugenics: Genetics and the Use of Human Heredity*. New York: Knopf, 1985.

Keyssar, Alexander. *The Right to Vote: The Contested History of Democracy in the United States*. New York: Basic Books, 2000.

King, William Eskridge. "The Era of Progressive Reform in Southern Education: The Growth of Public Schools in North Carolina, 1885–1910." Ph.D. diss., Duke University, 1970.

Kline, Wendy. *Building a Better Race: Gender, Sexuality, and Eugenics from the Turn of the Century to the Baby Boom*. Berkeley: University of California Press, 2001.

Kloppenberg, James. "From Hartz to Tocqueville: Shifting the Focus from Liberalism to Democracy in America." In *The Democratic Experiment: New Directions in American Political History*, edited by William J. Novak, Meg Jacobs, and Julian E. Zelizer, 350–80. Princeton: Princeton University Press, 2003.

———. *Uncertain Victory: Social Democracy and Progressivism in European and American Thought, 1870–1920*. New York: Oxford University Press, 1986.

Kitschelt, Herbert, and Steven Wilkinson. *Patrons, Clients, and Policies: Patterns of Democratic Accountability and Political Competition*. New York: Cambridge University Press, 2007.

Knox, Ronald Arbuthnott. *Enthusiasm: A Chapter in the History of Religion: With Special Reference to the XVII and XVIII Centuries*. New York: Oxford University Press, 1950.

Kohlstedt, Sally Gregory, and Mark R. Jorgensen. " 'The Irrepressible Woman Question': Women's Responses to Evolutionary Ideology." In *Disseminating Darwinism: The Role of Race, Place, and Gender*, edited by Ronald L. Numbers and John Stenhouse, 267–93. New York: Cambridge University Press, 1999.

Kolko, Gabriel. *Railroads and Regulation, 1877–1916*. Princeton: Princeton University Press, 1965.

———. *The Triumph of Conservatism: A Re-Interpretation of American History, 1900–1916*. New York: Free Press, 1963.

Korstad, Robert Rodgers. *Civil Rights Unionism: Tobacco Workers and the Struggle for Democracy in the Mid-Twentieth-Century South*. Chapel Hill: University of North Carolina Press, 2003.

Kousser, J. Morgan. *The Shaping of Southern Politics: Suffrage Restriction and the Establishment of the One-Party State*. New Haven: Yale University Press, 1974.

Koziol, Geoffrey. *Begging Pardon and Favor: Ritual and Political Order in Early Medieval France*. Ithaca, N.Y.: Cornell University Press, 1992.

Kramer, Larry D. *The People Themselves: Popular Constitutionalism and Judicial Review*. New York: Oxford University Press, 2004.

Kruse, Kevin Michael. *White Flight: Atlanta and the Making of Modern Conservatism*. Princeton: Princeton University Press, 2005.

Kuhn, Philip A. *Rebellion and Its Enemies in Late Imperial China: Militarization and Social Structure, 1796–1864*. Cambridge, Mass.: Harvard University Press, 1970.

Kyvig, David E. *Repealing National Prohibition*. Chicago: University of Chicago Press, 1979.

LaFeber, Walter. *The New Empire: An Interpretation of American Expansion, 1860–1898*. Twenty-Fifth Anniversary Edition with a New Preface. Ithaca, N.Y.: Cornell University Press, 1998.

Lakoff, George. *Moral Politics: How Liberals and Conservatives Think*. Chicago: University of Chicago Press, 2002.

Lakoff, George, and Mark Johnson. *Metaphors We Live By*. Chicago: University of Chicago Press, 1980.

Langum, David J. *Crossing over the Line: Legislating Morality and the Mann Act*. Chicago: University of Chicago Press, 1994.

Larson, Edward J. *Evolution: The Remarkable History of a Scientific Theory*. New York: Modern Library, 2004.

———. *Trial and Error: The American Controversy over Creation and Evolution*. New York: Oxford University Press, 1985.

Lassiter, Matthew D. *The Silent Majority: Suburban Politics in the Sunbelt South*. Princeton: Princeton University Press, 2006.

Lears, T. J. Jackson. *Something for Nothing: Luck in America*. New York: Viking, 2003.

Lee, Taeku. *Mobilizing Public Opinion: Black Insurgency and Racial Attitudes in the Civil Rights Era*. Chicago: University of Chicago Press, 2002.

Lefler, Hugh Talmage, ed. *North Carolina History Told by Contemporaries*. Chapel Hill: University of North Carolina Press, 1956.

Leloudis, James L. *Schooling the New South: Pedagogy, Self, and Society in North Carolina, 1880–1920*. Chapel Hill: University of North Carolina Press, 1996.

Leonard, Thomas C. " 'More Merciful and Not Less Effective': Eugenics and American Economics in the Progressive Era." *History of Political Economy* 35 (Winter 2003): 687–712.

Leslie, W. Bruce. *Gentlemen and Scholars: College and Community in the "Age of the University," 1865–1917*. University Park: Pennsylvania State University Press, 1992.

Lester, Connie. *Up from the Mudsills of Hell: The Farmers' Alliance, Populism, and Progressive Agriculture in Tennessee*. Athens: University of Georgia Press, 2006.

Leuchtenburg, William. *The F.D.R. Years: On Roosevelt and His Legacy*. New York: Columbia University Press, 1995.

———. *Franklin D. Roosevelt and the New Deal, 1932–1940*. New York: Harper and Row, 1963.

Levine, David O. *The American College and the Culture of Aspiration, 1915–1940*. Ithaca, N.Y.: Cornell University Press, 1986.

Levine, Lawrence W. "The Folklore of Industrial Society: Popular Culture and Its Audiences." *American Historical Review* 97 (December 1992): 1369–99.

Levine, Lawrence, and Cornelia R. Levine. *The People and the President: America's Conversation with F.D.R.* Boston: Beacon Press, 2002.

Lincoln, C. Eric, and Lawrence H. Mamiya. *The Black Church in the African American Experience*. Durham: Duke University Press, 1990.

Linderman, Gerald F. *The Mirror of War: American Society and the Spanish-American War*. Ann Arbor: University of Michigan Press, 1974.

Link, William A. *The Paradox of Southern Progressivism, 1880–1930*. Chapel Hill: University of North Carolina Press, 1992.

———. "Privies, Progressivism, and Public Schools: Health Reform and Education in the Rural South, 1909–1920." *Journal of Southern History* 54 (November 1988): 623–42.

Llobera, Josep R. *The Making of Totalitarian Thought*. New York: Berg, 2003.

Logue, Cal M., and Howard Dorgan, eds. *The Oratory of Southern Demagogues*. Baton Rouge: Louisiana State University Press, 1981.

Lonn, Ella. *Desertion during the Civil War*. Lincoln: University of Nebraska Press, 1998.

Lovett, Laura L. *Conceiving the Future: Pronatalism, Reproduction, and the Family in the United States, 1890–1938*. Chapel Hill: University of North Carolina Press, 2007.

Ludden, David. *An Agrarian History of South Asia*. New York: Cambridge University Press, 1999.

Lustig, R. Jeffrey. *Corporate Liberalism: The Origins of Modern American Political Theory, 1890–1920*. Berkeley: University of California Press, 1982.

MacLean, Nancy. *Behind the Mask of Chivalry: The Making of the Second Ku Klux Klan*. New York: Oxford University Press, 1994.

———. "The Leo Frank Case Reconsidered: Gender and Sexual Politics in the Making of Reactionary Politics." In *Jumpin' Jim Crow: Southern Politics from Civil War to Civil Rights*, edited by Jane Dailey, Glenda Elizabeth Gilmore, and Bryant Simon, 183–218. Princeton: Princeton University Press, 2000.

Magdol, Edward. *A Right to the Land: Essays on the Freedmen's Community*. Westport, Conn.: Greenwood Press, 1977.

Mallon, Florencia E. *The Defense of Community in Peru's Central Highlands: Peasant Struggle and Capitalist Tradition, 1860–1940*. Princeton: Princeton University Press, 1983.

———. *Peasant and Nation: The Making of a Postcolonial Mexico and Peru*. Berkeley: University of California Press, 1995.

Markoff, John. *Waves of Democracy: Social Movements and Political Change*. Thousand Oaks, Calif.: Pine Forge Press, 1996.

———. "Where and When Was Democracy Invented?" *Comparative Studies in Society and History* 41 (October 1999): 660–90.

Marsden, George M. "God and Man at Yale (1880)." *First Things* 42 (April 1994): 39–42.

———. *The Soul of the American University: From Protestant Establishment to Established Nonbelief*. New York: Oxford University Press, 1994.

Marsh, Charles. *The Beloved Community: How Faith Shapes Social Justice, from the Civil Rights Movement to Today*. New York: Basic Books, 2005.

———. *God's Long Summer: Stories of Faith and Civil Rights*. Princeton: Princeton University Press, 1999.

Martin, Donald L. "The Thought of Amzi Clarence Dixon." Ph.D. diss., Baylor University, 1989.

Martín-Aceña, Pablo. "Spain during the Classical Gold Standard Years, 1880–1914." In *Monetary Regimes in Transition*, edited by Michael D. Bordo and Forrest Capie, 135–72. New York: Cambridge University Press, 1994.

Martz, John D. *The Politics of Clientelism: Democracy and the State in Columbia*. New Brunswick: Transaction Publishers, 1996.

Masur, Kate. *An Example for All the Land: Emancipation and the Struggle over Equality in Washington, D.C.* Chapel Hill: University of North Carolina Press, 2010.

Mathews, Donald G. " 'Christianizing the South' — Sketching a Synthesis." In *New Directions in American Religious History*, edited by Harry Stout and D. G. Hart, 84–115. New York: Oxford University Press, 1997.

———. "The Southern Rite of Human Sacrifice." *Journal of Southern Religion* 3 (2000).

Mattingly, Carol. *Well-Tempered Women: Nineteenth-Century Temperance Rhetoric*. Carbondale: Southern Illinois University Press, 1998.

McCaffery, Peter. *When Bosses Ruled Philadelphia: The Emergence of the Republican Machine*. University Park: Pennsylvania State University Press, 1993.

McCann, Sean. *A Pinnacle of Feeling: American Literature and Presidential Government*. Princeton: Princeton University Press: 2008.

McClintock, Anne. *Imperial Leather: Race, Gender, and Sexuality in the Colonial Contest*. New York: Routledge, 1995.

McCormick, Richard L. *From Realignment to Reform: Political Change in New York State, 1893–1910*. Ithaca, N.Y.: Cornell University Press, 1981.

McCurry, Stephanie. *Confederate Reckoning: Power and Politics in the Civil War South*. Cambridge, Mass.: Harvard University Press, 2010.

———. *Masters of Small Worlds: Yeoman Households, Gender Relations, and the Political Culture of the Antebellum South Carolina Low Country*. New York: Oxford University Press, 1995.

———. "Women Numerous and Armed: Gender and the Politics of Subsistence in the Civil War South." In *Wars within a War: Controversy and Conflict over the American Civil War*, edited by Joan Waugh and Gary W. Gallagher, 1–26. Chapel Hill: University of North Carolina Press, 2009.

McElvaine, Robert S. *Franklin Delano Roosevelt*. Washington, D.C.: CQ Press, 2002.

———. *The Great Depression: America 1929–1941*. New York: Times Books, 1984.

McFeely, William. *Yankee Stepfather: General O. O. Howard and the Freedmen*. New York: Norton, 1970.

McGee, W. J. "The Science of Humanity." *American Anthropologist* 10 (August 1897): 241–72.

———. "The Trend of Human Progress." *American Anthropologist* 1 (July 1899): 401–47.

McGerr, Michael E. *A Fierce Discontent: The Rise and Fall of the Progressive Movement in America, 1870–1920*. New York: Free Press, 2003.

McGirr, Lisa. *Suburban Warriors: The Origins of the New American Right*. Princeton: Princeton University Press, 2001.

McKinney, Gordon B. *Southern Mountain Republicans, 1865–1900: Politics and the Appalachian Community*. Chapel Hill: University of North Carolina Press, 1978.

———. *Zeb Vance: North Carolina's Civil War Governor and Gilded Age Political Leader.* Chapel Hill: University of North Carolina Press, 2004.

McKitrick, Eric L. *Andrew Johnson and Reconstruction.* New York: Oxford University Press, 1960.

McLane, John A. *Land and Local Kingship in Eighteenth-Century Bengal.* New York: Cambridge University Press, 1993.

McMath, Robert C. *American Populism: A Social History.* New York: Hill and Wang, 1993.

———. *Populist Vanguard: A History of the Southern Farmers' Alliance.* Chapel Hill: University of North Carolina Press, 1975.

McMillen, Sally Gregory. *Seneca Falls and the Origins of the Women's Rights Movement.* New York: Oxford University Press, 2008.

McPherson, James Alan. *The Battle Cry of Freedom: The Civil War Era.* New York: Oxford University Press, 1989.

McSeveney, Samuel Thompson. *The Politics of Depression: Political Behavior in the Northeast, 1893–1896.* New York: Oxford University Press, 1972.

Merton, Robert King. *Social Theory and Social Structure.* Glencoe, Ill.: Free Press, 1949.

Meyerowitz, Joanne J. *Women Adrift: Independent Wage Earners in Chicago, 1880–1930.* Chicago: University of Chicago Press, 1988.

Mihm, Stephen, and Mark Peterson. "Introduction: Money Matters." *Common-Place* 6 (April 2006).

Milgram, Stanley. "The Small World Problem." *Psychology Today*, May 1967, 60–67.

Milkis, Sidney M., and Jerome M. Mileur, eds. *Progressivism and the New Democracy.* Amherst: University of Massachusetts Press, 1999.

Miller, Randall M. "Introduction. The Freedmen's Bureau and Reconstruction: An Overview." In *The Freedmen's Bureau and Reconstruction: Reconsiderations*, edited by Randall M. Miller and Paul A. Cimbala, xiii–xxxii. New York: Fordham University Press, 1999.

Miller, Zane L. *Boss Cox's Cincinnati: Urban Politics in the Progressive Era.* New York: Oxford University Press, 1968.

Mitchell, Memory. *Legal Aspects of Conscription and Exemption in North Carolina, 1861–1865.* Chapel Hill: University of North Carolina Press, 1965.

Mitchell, Theodore R. *Political Education in the Southern Farmers' Alliance, 1887–1900.* Madison: University of Wisconsin Press, 1987.

Mitchell, W. J. Thomas. *Iconology: Image, Text, Ideology.* Chicago: University of Chicago Press, 1986.

Mobley, Joe A. *James City: A Black Community in North Carolina, 1863–1900.* Raleigh: North Carolina Department of Cultural Resources, Division of Archives and History, 1981.

Moffitt, E. E. "The N.C. Society of the Daughters of the Revolution and Its

Objects." In *The North Carolina Booklet Great Events in North Carolina History*, 146–50. Raleigh: North Carolina Society of the Daughters of the Revolution, 1906.

Montgomery, David. *Citizen Worker: The Experience of Workers in the United States with Democracy and the Free Market during the Nineteenth Century*. New York: Cambridge University Press, 1993.

———. *The Fall of the House of Labor: The Workplace, the State, and American Labor Activism, 1865–1925*. New York: Cambridge University Press, 1987.

Moore, Albert Burton. *Conscription and Conflict in the Confederacy*. Columbia: University of South Carolina Press, 1996.

Moore, Kathleen Dean. *Pardons: Justice, Mercy, and the Public Interest*. New York: Oxford University Press, 1989.

Morgan, Edmund S. *Inventing the People: The Rise of Popular Sovereignty in England and America*. New York: Norton, 1988.

Morone, James A. *Hellfire Nation: The Politics of Sin in American History*. New Haven: Yale University Press, 2003.

Morris, Aldon. *Origins of the Civil Rights Movement: Black Communities Organizing for Change*. New York: Free Press, 1984.

Morris, Christopher. "The Articulation of Two Worlds: The Master-Slave Relationship Reconsidered." *Journal of American History* 85 (December 1998): 982–1007.

Mosher, Frederick C. *Democracy and the Public Service*. New York: Oxford University Press, 1968.

Mukherjee, Rudrangshu. *Awadh in Revolt, 1857–1858: A Study of Popular Resistance*. Delhi: Oxford University Press, 1984.

Mushkat, Jerome. *Tammany: The Evolution of a Political Machine*. Syracuse: Syracuse University Press, 1971.

Myrdal, Gunnar. *An American Dilemma: The Negro Problem and Modern Democracy*. Vol. 1. New York: Harper, 1944.

Naquin, Susan. *Millenarian Rebellion in China: The Eight Trigrams Uprising of 1813*. New Haven: Yale University Press, 1976.

Nelson, Dana D. *Bad for Democracy: How the Presidency Undermines the Power of the People*. Minneapolis: University of Minnesota Press, 2008.

Nelson, Scott Reynolds. *Iron Confederacies: Southern Railways, Klan Violence, and Reconstruction*. Chapel Hill: University of North Carolina Press, 1999.

———. "Red Strings and Half-Brothers: Civil Wars in Alamance County, North Carolina, 1861–1871." In *New Perspectives on Unionists in the Civil War South*, edited by John C. Inscoe and Robert C. Kenzer, 37–53. Athens: University of Georgia Press, 2001.

Newman, Simon P. *Parades and the Politics of the Street: Festive Culture in the Early American Republic*. Philadelphia: University of Pennsylvania Press, 1997.

Nicolay, John G., and John Hay. *Abraham Lincoln: A History*. New York: The Century, 1890.

Noble, David W. *The Paradox of Progressive Thought*. Minneapolis: University of Minnesota Press, 1958.

Noblin, Stuart. *Leonidas Lafayette Polk, Agrarian Crusader*. Chapel Hill: University of North Carolina Press, 1949.

Novak, William J. "The Myth of The 'Weak' American State." *American Historical Review* 113 (June 2008): 752–72.

——. *The People's Welfare: Law and Regulation in Nineteenth-Century America*. Chapel Hill: University of North Carolina Press, 1996.

Nugent, Daniel. "A Multiple Selective Tradition in Agrarian Reform and Agrarian Struggle: Popular Culture and State Formation in the *Ejido* of Namiquipa, Chihuahua." In *Everyday Forms of State Formation: Revolution and the Negotiation of Rule in Modern Mexico*, edited by Gilbert M. Joseph and Daniel Nugent, 209–46. Durham: Duke University Press, 1994.

Nugent, Walter K. *Money and American Society, 1865–1880*. New York: Free Press, 1968.

——. *The Tolerant Populists: Kansas Populists and Nativism*. Chicago: University of Chicago Press, 1963.

Numbers, Ronald L. *Darwinism Comes to America*. Cambridge, Mass.: Harvard University Press, 1998.

Numbers, Ronald L., and Lester D. Stephens. "Darwinism in the American South." In *Disseminating Darwinism: The Role of Place, Race, Religion, and Gender*, edited by Ronald L. Numbers and John Stenhouse, 123–44. New York: Cambridge University Press, 1999.

Oakes, James. "Radical Liberals, Liberal Radicals: The Dissenting Tradition in American Political Culture." *Reviews in American History* 27:3 (September 1999): 503–11.

——. *The Ruling Race: A History of American Slaveholders*. New York: Norton, 1998.

O'Brien, Gail Williams. *The Legal Fraternity and the Making of a New South Community, 1848–1882*. Athens: University of Georgia Press, 1986.

Odegard, Peter H. *Pressure Politics: The Story of the Anti-Saloon League*. New York: Columbia University Press, 1928.

O'Donovan, Susan. *Becoming Free in the Cotton South*. Cambridge, Mass.: Harvard University Press, 2007.

Oestreicher, Richard. "Urban Working-Class Political Behavior and Theories of American Electoral Politics, 1870–1940." *Journal of American History* 74 (March 1988): 1257–86.

O'Leary, Cecilia Elizabeth. *To Die For: The Paradox of American Patriotism*. Princeton: Princeton University Press, 2000.

O'Malley, Michael. "Free Silver and the Constitution of Man." *Common-Place* 6 (April 2006).

———. "Specie and Species: Race and the Money Question in Nineteenth-Century America." *American Historical Review* 99 (April 1994): 369–95.

Orren, Karen. *Belated Feudalism: Labor, the Law, and Liberal Development in the United States*. New York: Cambridge University Press, 1991.

Ostler, Jeffrey. *Prairie Populism: The Fate of Agrarian Radicalism in Kansas, Nebraska, and Iowa, 1880–1892*. Lawrence: University Press of Kansas, 1993.

Owen, Alex. *The Place of Enchantment: British Occultism and the Culture of the Modern*. Chicago: University of Chicago Press, 2004.

Ownby, Ted. *Subduing Satan: Religion, Recreation, and Manhood in the Rural South, 1865–1920*. Chapel Hill: University of North Carolina Press, 1990.

Painter, Nell Irvin. *Standing at Armageddon: The United States, 1877–1919*. New York: Norton, 1989.

———. "Thinking about the Language of Money and Race: A Response to Michael O'Malley, 'Specie and Species'," *American Historical Review* 99 (April 1994): 396–404.

Palmer, Bruce. *Man over Money: The Southern Populist Critique of American Capitalism*. Chapel Hill: University of North Carolina Press, 1980.

Pandian, M. S. S. "Culture and Subaltern Consciousness: An Aspect of the M.G.R. Phenomenon." In *State and Politics in India*, edited by Partha Chatterjee, 367–89. Delhi: Oxford University Press, 1997.

Pascoe, Peggy. "Miscegenation Law, Court Cases, and Ideologies of 'Race' in Twentieth-Century America." *Journal of American History* 83 (June 1996): 44–69.

Pasley, Jeffrey L. "The Cheese and the Words: Popular Political Culture and Participatory Democracy in the Early American Republic." In *Beyond the Founders: New Approaches to the Political History of the Early American Republic*, edited by Jeffrey L. Pasley, Andrew W. Robertson, and David Waldstreicher, 31–56. Chapel Hill: University of North Carolina Press, 2004.

Pasley, Jeffrey L., Andrew W. Robertson, and David Waldstreicher. "Introduction: Beyond the Founders." In *Beyond the Founders: New Approaches to the Political History of the Early American Republic*, edited by Jeffrey L. Pasley, Andrew W. Robertson, and David Waldstreicher, 1–28. Chapel Hill: University of North Carolina Press, 2004.

Pateman, Carol. *The Sexual Contract*. Stanford: Stanford University Press, 1988.

Patterson, Orlando. *Freedom in the Making of Western Culture*. New York: Basic Books, 1991.

———. *Rituals of Blood: Consequences of Slavery in Two American Centuries*. New York: Basic Civitas, 1998.

———. *Slavery and Social Death: A Comparative Study*. Cambridge, Mass.: Harvard University Press, 1982.

Paulson, Ross Evans. *Woman's Suffrage and Prohibition: A Comparative Study of Equality and Social Control*. Glenview, Ill.: Scott, Foresman, 1973.

Paxton, Robert O. *The Anatomy of Fascism*. New York: Knopf, 2004.

Payne, Charles. *I've Got the Light of Freedom: The Organizing Tradition and the Mississippi Freedom Struggle*. Berkeley: University of California Press, 1995.

Pearson, C. C., and J. Edwin Hendricks. *Liquor and Anti-Liquor in Virginia, 1619–1919*. Durham: Duke University Press, 1967.

Pegram, Thomas R. *Battling Demon Rum: The Struggle for a Dry America*. Chicago: Ivan R. Dee, 1998.

———. "Temperance Politics and Regional Political Culture: The Anti-Saloon League in Maryland and the South, 1907–1915." *Journal of Southern History* 63 (February 1997): 57–90.

Peirce, Paul Skeets. *The Freedmen's Bureau: A Chapter in the History of Reconstruction*. Iowa City: University of Iowa Press, 1904.

Peiss, Kathy. *Cheap Amusements: Working Women and Leisure in Turn-of-the-Century New York*. Philadelphia: Temple University Press, 1985.

Penningroth, Dylan. *The Claims of Kinfolk: African American Property and Community in the Nineteenth-Century South*. Chapel Hill: University of North Carolina Press, 2003.

Perman, Michael. *Reunion without Compromise: The South and Reconstruction: 1865–1868*. New York: Cambridge University Press, 1973.

———. *The Road to Redemption: Southern Politics, 1869–1879*. Chapel Hill: University of North Carolina Press, 1984.

———. *Struggle for Mastery: Disfranchisement in the South, 1888–1908*. Chapel Hill: University of North Carolina Press, 2001.

Perry, Elisabeth Israels. "Men Are from the Gilded Age, Women Are from the Progressive Era." *Journal of the Gilded Age and Progressive Era* 1 (January 2002): 25–48.

Petit, Jeanne. "Breeders, Workers, and Mothers: Gender and the Congressional Literacy Test Debate, 1896–1897." *Journal of the Gilded Age and Progressive Era* 3 (January 2004): 35–58.

Piattoni, Simona, ed. *Clientelism, Interests, and Democratic Representation: The European Experience in Historical and Comparative Perspective*. New York: Cambridge University Press, 2001.

Pick, Daniel. *Svengali's Web: The Alien Enchanter in Modern Culture*. New Haven: Yale University Press, 2000.

Pickens, Donald K. *Eugenics and the Progressives*. Nashville: Vanderbilt University Press, 1968.

Pietz, William. "Fetishism and Materialism: The Limits of Theory in Marx." In *Fetishism as Cultural Discourse*, edited by Emily Apter and William Pietz, 119–51. Ithaca, N.Y.: Cornell University Press, 1993.

———. "The Problem of the Fetish, 1." *Res* 9 (Spring 1985): 5–17.

———. "The Problem of the Fetish, 2." *Res* 13 (Spring 1987): 23–46.

Pleasants, Julian M. *Frank Porter Graham and the 1950 Senate Race in North Carolina*. Chapel Hill: University of North Carolina Press, 1990.

Pollack, Norman. *The Populist Response to Industrial America: Midwestern Populist Thought*. Cambridge, Mass.: Harvard University Press, 1976.

Portelli, Alessandro. *The Death of Luigi Trastulli and Other Stories: Form and Meaning in Oral History*. Albany: State University of New York Press, 1991.

———. "History-Telling and Time: An Example from Kentucky." *Oral History Review* 20 (Winter/Spring 1992): 51–66.

Porter, Theodore M. *Karl Pearson: The Scientific Life in a Statistical Age*. Princeton: Princeton University Press, 2004.

Postel, Charles. *The Populist Vision*. New York: Oxford University Press, 2007.

Poteat, R. Matthew. "Part 2: 'A Modest Estimate of His Own Abilities': Governor Henry Toole Clark and the Early Civil War Leadership of North Carolina." Pt. 2. *North Carolina Historical Review* 84 (April 2007): 127–55.

Potter, David Morris. *The Impending Crisis*. New York: Harper and Row, 1976.

Powell, J. W. "Competition as a Factor in Human Evolution." *American Anthropologist* 1 (October 1888): 297–323.

———. "From Barbarism to Civilization." *American Anthropologist* 1 (April 1888): 97–123.

Powell, Lawrence N. *New Masters: Northern Planters during the Civil War and Reconstruction*. New Haven: Yale University Press, 1980.

Prather, H. Leon, Sr. *Resurgent Politics and Educational Progressivism in the New South, North Carolina, 1890–1913*. Rutherford, N.J.: Fairleigh Dickinson University Press, 1979.

———. *We Have Taken a City: The Wilmington Racial Massacre and Coup of 1898*. Rutherford, N.J.: Fairleigh Dickinson University Press, 1984.

Prazniak, Roxann. *Of Camel Kings and Other Things: Rural Rebels against Modernity in Late Imperial China*. Lanham, Md.: Rowman & Littlefield, 1999.

Prince, Carl E. *The Federalists and the Origins of the U.S. Civil Service*. New York: New York University Press, 1977.

Pringle, Robert M. "To Educate the Head, the Hand, and the Soul: The Challenge to State-Supported Universities in the Post-Bellum South." Senior thesis, University of Pennsylvania, 2001.

Quarles, Benjamin. *Lincoln and the Negro*. New York: Oxford University Press, 1962.

Rable, George C. *But There Was No Peace: The Role of Violence in the Politics of Reconstruction*. Athens: University of Georgia Press, 1984.

———. *Civil Wars: Women and the Crisis of Southern Nationalism*. Urbana: University of Illinois Press, 1989.

———. *The Confederate Republic: A Revolution against Politics*. Chapel Hill: University of North Carolina Press, 1994.

Raboteau, Albert J. *Canaan Land: A Religious History of African Americans*. New York: Oxford University Press, 2001.

Randall, James Garfield. *The Confiscation of Property during the Civil War*. Indianapolis: Mutual Printing and Lithographing, 1913.

Ransby, Barbara. *Ella Baker and the Black Freedom Movement: A Radical Democratic Vision*. Chapel Hill: University of North Carolina Press, 2003.

Raper, Horace W. *William W. Holden: North Carolina's Political Enigma*. Chapel Hill: University of North Carolina Press, 1985.

Rauchway, Eric. *Blessed among Nations: How the World Made America*. New York: Hill and Wang, 2006.

———. *Murdering McKinley: The Making of Theodore Roosevelt's America*. New York: Hill and Wang, 2003.

Rawick, George P., ed. *The American Slave: A Composite Autobiography*. Westport, Conn.: Greenwood Press, 1972.

———. *The American Slave: A Composite Autobiography*. Supplement, Series 1. Westport, Conn.: Greenwood Press, 1977.

Redding, Kent. *Making Race, Making Power: North Carolina's Road to Disfranchisement*. Urbana: University of Illinois Press, 2003.

Reed, Adolph L., Jr. *Class Notes: Posing as Politics and Other Thoughts on the American Scene*. New York: New Press, 2001.

———. *W. E. B. Du Bois and American Political Thought: Fabianism and the Color Line*. New York: Oxford University Press, 1997.

Reid, Richard M. *Freedom for Themselves: North Carolina's Black Soldiers in the Civil War*. Chapel Hill: University of North Carolina Press, 2008.

Richardson, Heather Cox. *The Death of Reconstruction: Race, Labor, and Politics in the Post–Civil War North, 1865–1901*. Cambridge, Mass.: Harvard University Press, 2001.

———. "North and West of Reconstruction: Studies in Political Economy." In *Reconstructions: New Perspectives on the Postbellum United States*, edited by Thomas J. Brown, 66–90. New York: Oxford University Press, 2006.

———. *West from Appomattox: The Reconstruction of America after the Civil War*. New Haven: Yale University Press, 2007.

Ritter, Gretchen. *Goldbugs and Greenbacks: The Antimonopoly Tradition and the Politics of Finance in America*. New York: Cambridge University Press, 1997.

Rivers, Patrick Lynn. "Civilizing Tendencies: Miscegenation and Political Thought in North Carolina, 1889–1903." Ph.D. diss., University of North Carolina, 1998.

Roberts, Jon H. *Darwinism and the Divine in America: Protestant Intellectuals and Organic Evolution, 1859–1900*. Madison: University of Wisconsin Press, 1988.

———. *The Sacred and the Secular University*. Princeton: Princeton University Press, 2000.

Robertson, Andrew W. "Voting Rites and Voting Acts: Electioneering Ritual, 1790–1820." In *Beyond the Founders: New Approaches to the Political History of the Early American Republic*, edited by Jeffrey L. Pasley, Andrew W. Robertson, and David Waldstreicher, 57–78. Chapel Hill: University of North Carolina Press, 2004.

Rodgers, Daniel T. *Atlantic Crossings: Social Politics in a Progressive Age*. Cambridge, Mass.: Harvard University Press, 1998.

———. "In Search of Progressivism." *Reviews in American History* 10 (December 1982): 113–32.

Roediger, David R. *The Wages of Whiteness: Race and the Making of the American Working Class*. New York: Verso, 1991.

Rogers, Walter Pingrey. *Andrew D. White and the Modern University*. Ithaca, N.Y.: Cornell University Press, 1942.

Rogin, Michael Paul. *Ronald Reagan, the Movie: And Other Episodes in Political Demonology*. Berkeley: University of California Press, 1987.

Roller, David C. "The Republican Party of North Carolina 1900–1916." Ph.D. diss., Duke University, 1965.

Roniger, Luis. "Citizenship in Latin America: New Works and Debates." *Citizenship Studies* 10 (September 2006): 489–502.

———. "The Comparative Study of Clientelism and the Changing Nature of Civil Society in the Contemporary World." In *Democracy, Clientelism, and Civil Society*, edited by Luis Roniger and Ayse Gunes-Ayata, 1–18. Boulder: University of Colorado Press, 1994.

———. "Conclusions: The Transformation of Clientelism and Civil Society." In *Democracy, Clientelism, and Civil Society*, edited by Luis Roniger and Ayse Gunes-Ayata, 207–14. Boulder: University of Colorado Press, 1994.

———. *Hierarchy and Trust in Modern Mexico and Brazil*. New York: Praeger, 1990.

———. "Political Clientelism, Democracy and Market Economy." *Comparative Politics* 36:3 (April 2004): 353–75.

Rorabaugh, W. J. *The Alcoholic Republic, an American Tradition*. New York: Oxford University Press, 1979.

Rose, Jacqueline. *States of Fantasy*. New York: Oxford University Press, 1996.

Rose, Willie Lee. *Rehearsal for Reconstruction: The Port Royal Experiment*. New York: Vintage Books, 1964.

Rosen, Christine. *Preaching Eugenics: Religious Leaders and the American Eugenics Movement*. New York: Oxford University Press, 2004.

Rosen, Ruth. *The Lost Sisterhood: Prostitution in America, 1900–1918*. Baltimore: Johns Hopkins University Press, 1982.

Rosenberg, Clifford. "Albert Sarraut and Republican Racial Thought." *French Politics, Culture & Society* 20 (Fall 2002): 97–114.

Ross, Dorothy. *The Origins of American Social Science*. New York: Cambridge University Press, 1991.

Ross, Edward Alsworth. "Recent Tendencies in Sociology III." *The Quarterly Journal of Economics* 17 (May 1903): 438–55.

Rubenstein, Diane. *This Is Not a President: Sense, Nonsense, and the American Political Imaginary*. New York: New York University Press, 2008.

Rumbarger, John J. *Profits, Power, and Prohibition: Alcohol Reform and the Industrializing of America, 1800–1930*. Albany: State University of New York Press, 1989.

Ruse, Michael. *Darwin and Design: Does Evolution Have a Purpose?* Cambridge, Mass.: Harvard University Press, 2003.

———. *The Evolution-Creation Struggle*. Cambridge, Mass.: Harvard University Press, 2005.

———. Introduction to *Evolutionary Naturalism: Selected Essays*, 1–12. New York: Routledge, 1995.

———. *Monad to Man: The Concept of Progress in Evolutionary Biology*. Cambridge, Mass.: Harvard University Press, 1996.

———. *Taking Darwin Seriously: A Naturalistic Approach to Philosophy*. New York: Prometheus Books, 1986.

Russell, Phillips. *The Woman Who Rang the Bell: The Story of Cornelia Phillips Spencer*. Chapel Hill: University of North Carolina Press, 1949.

Ryan, Halford R. *Franklin D. Roosevelt's Rhetorical Presidency*. Westport, Conn.: Greenwood Press, 1988.

Ryan, Mary P. *Cradle of the Middle Class: The Family in Oneida County, New York, 1790–1865*. New York: Cambridge University Press, 1981.

———. *Women in Public: Between Banners and Ballots, 1825–1880*. Baltimore: Johns Hopkins University Press, 1990.

Sack, Robert David. *Human Territoriality: Its Theory and History*. New York: Cambridge University Press, 1986.

Saler, Michael. "Modernity and Enchantment: A Historiographical Review." *American Historical Review* 111 (June 2006): 692–716.

Sandage, Scott. *Born Losers: A History of Failure in America*. Cambridge, Mass.: Harvard University Press, 2005.

———. "The Gaze of Success: Failed Men and the Sentimental Marketplace, 1873–1893." In *Sentimental Men: Masculinity and the Politics of Affect in American Culture*, edited by Mary Chapman and Glenn Hendler, 181–201. Berkeley: University of California Press, 1999.

Sandel, Michael J. *Democracy's Discontent: America in Search of a Political Philosophy*. Cambridge, Mass.: Harvard University Press, 1996.

Sanders, Elizabeth. *Roots of Reform: Farmers, Workers, and the American State, 1877–1917*. Chicago: University of Chicago Press, 1999.

Savage, Barbara Dianne. *Broadcasting Freedom: Radio, War, and the Politics of War, 1938–1948*. Chapel Hill: University of North Carolina Press, 1999.

Saveth, Edward N. "Education of an Elite." *History of Education Quarterly* 28 (Fall 1988): 367–86.

Saville, Julie. *The Work of Reconstruction: From Slave to Wage Laborer in South Carolina, 1860–1870*. New York: Cambridge University Press, 1994.

Saxton, Alexander. *The Rise and Fall of the White Republic: Class Politics and Mass Culture in Nineteenth-Century America*. New York: Verso, 1990.

Schneider, William H. "The Eugenics Movement in France, 1890–1940." In *The Wellborn Science: Eugenics in Germany, France, Brazil, and Russia*, edited by Mark B. Adams, 69–109. New York: Oxford University Press, 1990.

———. *Quality and Quantity: The Quest for Biological Regeneration in Twentieth-Century France*. New York: Cambridge University Press, 1990.

Schneirov, Richard. *Labor and Urban Politics: Class Conflict and the Origin of Modern Liberalism in Chicago, 1864–1897*. Urbana: University of Illinois Press, 1998.

Schoen, Johanna. *Choice and Coercion: Birth Control, Sterilization, and Abortion in Public Health and Welfare*. Chapel Hill: University of North Carolina Press, 2005.

Schwartz, Michael. *Radical Protest and Social Structure: The Southern Farmers' Alliance and Cotton Tenancy, 1880–1890*. New York: Academic Press, 1976.

Schweiger, Beth Barton. *The Gospel Working Up: Progress and the Pulpit in Nineteenth-Century Virginia*. New York: Oxford University Press, 2000.

Schweiger, Beth Barton, and Donald G. Mathews, eds. *Religion in the American South: Protestants and Others in History and Culture*. Chapel Hill: University of North Carolina Press, 2004.

Scott, James C. *Domination and the Arts of Resistance: Hidden Transcripts*. New Haven: Yale University Press, 1990.

———. *The Moral Economy of the Peasant: Rebellion and Subsistence in Southeast Asia*. New Haven: Yale University Press, 1976.

———. *Seeing Like a State: How Certain Schemes to Improve the Human Condition Have Failed*. New Haven: Yale University Press, 1998.

Scott, Joan Wallach. "Fantasy Echo: History and the Construction of Identity." *Critical Inquiry* 27 (Winter 2001): 284–304.

———. "Women in the Making of the English Working Class." In *Gender and the Politics of History*, 68–92. New York: Columbia University Press, 1999.

Searle, G. R. *A New England?: Peace and War, 1886–1918*. New York: Oxford University Press, 2004.

Sefton, James E. *The United States Army and Reconstruction, 1865–1877*. Baton Rouge: Louisiana State University Press, 1967.

Selections from the Prison Notebooks of Antonio Gramsci. Translated by Quentin Hoare and Geoffrey Nowell Smith. New York: International Publishers, 1971.

Shain, Barry Alan. *The Myth of American Individualism: The Protestant Origins of American Political Thought*. Princeton: Princeton University Press, 1994.

Shalhope, Robert E. *The Roots of Democracy: American Thought and Culture, 1760–1800*. Boston: Twayne, 1990.

Shammas, Carole. *A History of Household Government in America*. Charlottesville: University of Virginia Press, 2002.

Sharkey, Robert P. *Money, Class, and Party: An Economic Study of Civil War and Reconstruction*. Baltimore: Johns Hopkins University Press, 1959.

Shefter, Martin. "The Emergence of the Political Machine: An Alternative View." In *Theoretical Perspectives on Urban Politics*, edited by Willis Hawley, 14–44. Englewood Cliffs, N.J.: Prentice-Hall, 1976.

———. *Political Parties and the State: The American Historical Experience*. Princeton: Princeton University Press, 1994.

Shell, Marc. *Art & Money*. Chicago: University of Chicago Press, 1995.

———. *Money, Language, and Thought: Literary and Philosophical Economies from the Medieval to the Modern Era*. Berkeley: University of California Press, 1982.

Shklar, Judith N. *Legalism: Law, Morals, and Political Trials*. Cambridge, Mass.: Harvard University Press, 1986.

Simon, Bryant. *A Fabric of Defeat: The Politics of South Carolina Millhands, 1910–1948*. Chapel Hill: University of North Carolina Press, 1998.

Simpson, Brooks D. *Let Us Have Peace: Ulysses S. Grant and the Politics of War and Reconstruction, 1861–1868*. Chapel Hill: University of North Carolina Press, 1991.

———. "Ulysses S. Grant and the Freedmen's Bureau." In *The Freedmen's Bureau and Reconstruction: Reconsiderations*, edited by Randall M. Miller and Paul A. Cimbala, 1–28. New York: Fordham University Press, 1999.

———. *Ulysses S Grant, Triumph over Adversity, 1822–1865*. New York: Houghton Mifflin, 2000.

Simpson, David. *Fetishism and Imagination: Dickens, Melville, Conrad*. Baltimore: Johns Hopkins University Press, 1982.

Sims, Anastatia. *The Power of Femininity in the New South: Women's Political Organizations in North Carolina, 1880–1930*. Columbia: University of South Carolina Press, 1997.

———. "'The Sword of the Spirit': The W.C.T.U. and Moral Reform in North Carolina, 1883–1933." *North Carolina Historical Review* 64 (October 1987): 394–415.

Sitterson, Joseph Carlyle. *The Secession Movement in North Carolina*. Chapel Hill: University of North Carolina Press, 1939.

Sklar, Kathryn Kish. *Florence Kelley and the Nations' Work*. New Haven: Yale University Press, 1995.

Sklar, Martin J. *The Corporate Reconstruction of American Capitalism, 1890–1916: The Market, the Law, and Politics*. New York: Cambridge University Press, 1988.

Skocpol, Theda. *Diminished Democracy: From Membership to Management in American Civic Life*. Norman: University of Oklahoma Press, 2003.

———. *Protecting Soldiers and Mothers: The Political Origins of Social Policy in the United States*. Cambridge, Mass.: Harvard University Press, 1992.

Skowronek, Stephen. *Building a New American State: The Expansion of National Administrative Capacities, 1877–1920*. New York: Cambridge University Press, 1982.

Slack, Jennifer Daryl. "The Theory and Method of Articulation in Cultural Studies." In *Stuart Hall: Critical Dialogues in Cultural Studies*, edited by David Morley and Kuan-Hsing Chen, 112–30. New York: Routledge, 1996.

Smith, Jay M. "No More Language Games: Words, Beliefs, and the Political Culture of Early Modern France." *American Historical Review* 102 (December 1997): 1413–40.

Smith, Jeff. *The Presidents We Imagine: Two Centuries of White House Fictions on the Page, on the Stage, Onscreen, and Online*. Madison: University of Wisconsin Press, 2009.

Smith, Rogers M. *Civic Ideals: Conflicting Visions of Citizenship in U.S. History*. New Haven: Yale University Press, 1997.

Smith, Woodruff D. *Politics and the Science of Culture in Germany, 1840–1920*. New York: Oxford University Press, 1991.

Snider, William D. *Light on the Hill: A History of the University of North Carolina at Chapel Hill*. Chapel Hill: University of North Carolina Press, 1992.

Sparrow, James Terence. "Fighting over the American Soldier: Moral Economy and National Citizenship in World War Two." Ph.D. diss., Brown University, 2002.

Staloff, Darren. *Hamilton, Adams, Jefferson: The Politics of Enlightenment and the American Founding*. New York: Hill and Wang, 2005.

Stanley, Amy Dru. *From Bondage to Contract: Wage Labor, Marriage, and the Market in the Era of Slave Emancipation*. New York: Cambridge University Press, 1998.

Stansell, Christine. *City of Women: Sex and Class in New York, 1789–1860*. Urbana: University of Illinois Press, 1987.

Stanton, Elizabeth Cady, Susan Brownell Anthony, and Matilda Joslyn Gage, eds. *History of Woman Suffrage*. 6 vols. Rochester, N.Y.: Mann, 1889–1922.

Steeples, Douglas W., and David O. Whitten. *Democracy in Desperation: The Depression of 1893*. Westport, Conn.: Greenwood Press, 1998.

Steinberg, Stephen. *Turning Back: The Retreat from Racial Justice in American Thought and Policy*. Boston: Beacon Press, 2001.

Stocking, George W. *Race, Culture, and Evolution: Essays in the History of Anthropology*. New York: Free Press, 1968.

Stout, Harry. "Rhetoric and Reality in the Early Republic: The Case of the Federalist Clergy." In *Religion and American Politics: From the Colonial Period to the 1980s*, edited by Mark A. Noll, 62–76. New York: Oxford University Press, 1990.

Stowell, Daniel W. *Rebuilding Zion: The Religious Reconstruction of the South, 1863–1877*. New York: Oxford University Press, 1998.

Sugrue, Thomas J. "All Politics Is Local: The Persistence of Localism in Twentieth-Century America." In *The Democratic Experiment: New Directions in American Political History*, edited by William J. Novak, Meg Jacobs, and Julian E. Zelizer, 301–26. Princeton: Princeton University Press, 2003.

———. "Crabgrass-Roots Politics: Race, Rights, and the Reaction against Liberalism in the Urban North, 1940–1964." *Journal of American History* 82 (September 1995): 551–78.

———. *The Origins of the Urban Crisis: Race and Inequality in Postwar Detroit*. Princeton: Princeton University Press, 1996.

Summers, Mark Wahlgren. *A Dangerous Stir: Fear, Paranoia, and the Making of Reconstruction*. Chapel Hill: University of North Carolina Press, 2009.

———. *Party Games: Getting, Keeping, and Using Power in Gilded Age Politics*. Chapel Hill: University of North Carolina Press, 2004.

———. *Rum, Romanism, and Rebellion: The Making of a President, 1884*. Chapel Hill: University of North Carolina Press, 2000.

Sussmann, Leila A. *Dear F.D.R.: A Study of Political Letter-Writing*. Totowa, N.J.: Bedminster Press, 1963.

Szymanski, Ann-Marie E. "Beyond Parochialism: Southern Progressivism, Prohibition, and State-Building." *Journal of Southern History* 69 (February 2003): 107–36.

———. *Pathways to Prohibition: Radicals, Moderates, and Social Movement Outcomes*. Durham: Duke University Press, 2003.

Tadmor, Naomi. *Family and Friends in Eighteenth-Century England: Household, Kinship, and Patronage*. New York: Cambridge University Press, 2001.

Takaki, Ronald. *Iron Cages: Race and Culture in Nineteenth-Century America*. New York: Knopf, 1979.

Tate, Adam L. *Conservatism and Southern Intellectuals, 1789–1861: Liberty, Tradition, and the Good Society*. Columbia: University of Missouri Press, 2005.

Tate, Cassandra. *Cigarette Wars: The Triumph of "The Little White Slaver"*. New York: Oxford University Press, 1999.

Taussig, Michael T. *The Devil and Commodity Fetishism in South America*. Chapel Hill: University of North Carolina Press, 1980.

———. *The Magic of the State*. New York: Routledge, 1997.

———. "*Maleficium*: State Fetishism." In *Fetishism as Cultural Discourse*, edited by Emily Apter and William Pietz, 217–47. Ithaca, N.Y.: Cornell University Press, 1993.

Teaford, Jon C. *The Unheralded Triumph: City Government in America, 1870–1900*. Baltimore: Johns Hopkins University Press, 1984.

Thelen, David P. *The New Citizenship: Origins of Progressivism in Wisconsin, 1885–1900.* Columbia: University of Missouri Press, 1962.

———. "Social Tensions and the Origins of Progressivism." *Journal of American History* 56 (1969): 323–41.

Thomas, Emory M. *The Confederacy as Revolutionary Experience.* Columbia: Englewood Cliffs, N.J.: Prentice-Hall, 1970.

———. *The Confederate Nation, 1861–1865.* New York: Harper & Row, 1979.

Thomas, William G. *Lawyering for the Railroad: Business, Law, and Power in the New South.* Baton Rouge: Louisiana State University Press, 1999.

Thompson, E. P. *Customs in Common.* New York: New Press, 1991.

Thurtell, Craig Martin. "The Fusion Insurgency in North Carolina: Origins to Ascendancy, 1876–1896." Ph.D. diss., Columbia University, 1998.

Timberlake, James H. *Prohibition and the Progressive Movement, 1900–1920.* Cambridge, Mass.: Harvard University Press, 1963.

Tindall, George Brown. *The Emergence of the New South, 1913–1945.* Baton Rouge: Louisiana State University Press, 1967.

———. "The Significance of Howard W. Odum to Southern History: A Preliminary Estimate." *Journal of Southern History* 24 (August 1958): 285–307.

Tolnay, Stewart, and E. M. Beck. *A Festival of Violence: An Analysis of Southern Lynchings, 1882–1930.* Urbana: University of Illinois Press, 1995.

Tomlins, Christopher. *Law, Labor, and Ideology in the Early American Republic.* New York: Cambridge University Press, 1993.

Tonkin, Elizabeth. *Narrating Our Pasts: The Social Construction of Oral History.* New York: Cambridge University Press, 1992.

Trachtenberg, Alan. *The Incorporation of America: Culture and Society in the Gilded Age.* New York: Hill and Wang, 1982.

Treitel, Corinna. *A Science for the Soul: Occultism and the Genesis of the German Modern.* Baltimore: Johns Hopkins University Press, 2004.

Trelease, Allen. *White Terror: The Ku Klux Klan Conspiracy and Southern Reconstruction.* Baton Rouge: Louisiana State University Press, 1971.

———. "The Fusion Legislatures of 1895 and 1897: A Roll-Call Analysis of the North Carolina House of Representatives." *North Carolina Historical Review* 57 (July 1980): 280–309.

Tyrrell, Ian R. *Sobering Up: From Temperance to Prohibition in Antebellum America, 1800-1860.* Westport, Conn.: Greenwood Press, 1979.

———. *Transnational Nation: United States History in Global Perspective since 1789.* New York: Palgrave Macmillan, 2007.

———. *Woman's World/Woman's Empire: The Woman's Christian Temperance Union in International Perspective, 1800–1930.* Chapel Hill: University of North Carolina Press, 1991.

Unger, Irwin. *The Greenback Era: A Social and Political History of American Finance, 1865–1879*. Princeton: Princeton University Press, 1964.

Van Riper, Paul P. *History of the United States Civil Service*. Evanston, Ill.: Row, Peterson, 1958.

Vansina, Jan. *Oral Tradition as History*. Madison: University of Wisconsin Press, 1985.

Varon, Elizabeth R. *We Mean to Be Counted: White Women and Politics in Antebellum Virginia*. Chapel Hill: University of North Carolina Press, 1998.

Veysey, Laurence R. *The Emergence of the American University*. Chicago: University of Chicago Press, 1970.

Wade, Richard C. *The Urban Frontier: Pioneer Life in Early Pittsburgh, Cincinnati, Lexington, Louisville, and St. Louis*. Cambridge, Mass.: Harvard University Press, 1959.

Waldrep, Christopher. *Night Riders: Defending Community in the Black Patch, 1890–1915*. Durham: Duke University Press, 1993.

——. *Roots of Disorder: Race and Criminal Justice in the American South*. Urbana: University of Illinois Press, 1998.

Waldrep, Christopher, and Donald G. Nieman, eds. *Local Matters: Race, Crime, and Justice in the Nineteenth-Century South*. Athens: University of Georgia Press, 2001.

Waldstreicher, David. *In the Midst of Perpetual Fetes: The Making of American Nationalism, 1776–1820*. Chapel Hill: University of North Carolina Press, 1997.

Walker, Clarence Earl. *A Rock in a Weary Land: The African Methodist Episcopal Church during the Civil War and Reconstruction*. Baton Rouge: Louisiana State University Press, 1982.

Walker, Vanessa Siddle. *Their Highest Potential: An African American School Community in the Segregated South*. Chapel Hill: University of North Carolina Press, 1996.

Waller, Altina L. *Feud: Hatfields, McCoys, and Social Change in Appalachia, 1860–1900*. Chapel Hill: University of North Carolina Press, 1988.

Watford, Christopher M., ed. *The Civil War in North Carolina: The Piedmont*. Jefferson, N.C.: McFarland, 2003.

Watts, Duncan J. *Six Degrees: The Science of a Connected Age*. New York: Norton, 2003.

——. *Small Worlds: The Dynamics of Networks between Order and Randomness*. Princeton: Princeton University Press, 1999.

Watts, Duncan J., and Steven H. Strogatz. "Collective Dynamics of 'Small-World' Networks." *Nature* 393 (June 1998): 440–42.

Weikart, Richard. *From Darwin to Hitler: Evolutionary Ethics, Eugenics, and Racism in Germany*. New York: Palgrave Macmillan, 2004.

Weinstein, Allen. *Prelude to Populism: Origins of the Silver Issue, 1867–1878*. New Haven: Yale University Press, 1970.

Weinstein, James. *Corporate Ideal in the Liberal State, 1900–1918*. Boston: Beacon Press, 1968.

Weiss, Sheila Faith. *Race Hygiene and National Efficiency: The Eugenics of Wilhelm Schallmeyer*. Berkeley: University of California Press, 1987.

West, Stephen A. *From Yeomen to Redneck in the South Carolina Upcountry, 1850–1915*. Charlottesville: University of Virginia Press, 2008.

Wexler, Laura. *Tender Violence: Domestic Visions in an Age of U.S. Imperialism*. Chapel Hill: University of North Carolina Press, 2000.

Whitener, Daniel Jay. *Prohibition in North Carolina, 1715–1945*. Chapel Hill: University of North Carolina Press, 1945.

Wiebe, Robert H. *The Search for Order, 1877–1920*. New York: Hill and Wang, 1967.

——. *Self-Rule: A Cultural History of American Democracy*. Chicago: University of Chicago Press, 1995.

Wiener, Jonathan M. *Social Origins of the New South, 1860–1885*. Baton Rouge: Louisiana State University Press, 1978.

Wiener, Philip P. *Evolution and the Founders of Pragmatism*. Cambridge, Mass.: Harvard University Press, 1949.

Wilentz, Sean. *Chants Democratic: New York City and the Rise of the American Working Class, 1788–1850*. New York: Oxford University Press, 1984.

——. *The Rise of American Democracy: Jefferson to Lincoln*. New York: Norton, 2005.

Williamson, Joel. *After Slavery: The Negro in South Carolina during Reconstruction*. Chapel Hill: University of North Carolina Press, 1965.

——. *The Crucible of Race: Black-White Relations in the American South since Emancipation*. New York: Oxford University Press, 1984.

Wilson, Charles Reagan. *Baptized in Blood: The Religion of the Lost Cause, 1865–1920*. Athens: University of Georgia Press, 1980.

Wilson, Louis R. *The University of North Carolina, 1900–1930: The Making of a Modern University*. Chapel Hill: University of North Carolina Press, 1957.

Wilson, Mark R. *The Business of Civil War: Military Mobilization and the State, 1861–1865*. Baltimore: Johns Hopkins University Press, 2008.

Wilson, R. Jackson. *Darwinism and the American Intellectual: An Anthology*. Chicago: Dorsey Press, 1989.

Winfield, Betty Houchin. *F.D.R. and the News Media*. Urbana: University of Illinois Press, 1990.

Winston, George Parsons. *John Fiske*. New York: Twayne, 1972.

Winston, George T. "The Relation of the Whites to the Negroes." *Publications of the American Academy of Political and Social Science* 18 (July to December 1901): 105–18.

Winston, Robert Watson. "An Unconsidered Aspect of the Negro Question." *South Atlantic Quarterly* 1 (July 1902): 265–68.

Winter, Alison. *Mesmerized: Powers of Mind in Victorian Britain*. Chicago: University of Chicago Press, 1998.

Winterer, Caroline. *The Culture of Classicism: Ancient Greece and Rome in American Intellectual Life, 1780–1910*. Baltimore: Johns Hopkins University Press, 2002.

Wolin, Sheldon S. *The Presence of the Past: Essays on the State and the Constitution*. Baltimore: Johns Hopkins University Press, 1989.

———. *Tocqueville between Two Worlds: The Making of a Political and Theoretical Life*. Princeton: Princeton University Press, 2001.

Wood, Gordon S. *The Creation of the American Republic, 1776–1787*. Chapel Hill: University of North Carolina Press, 1998.

———. *Empire of Liberty: A History of the Early Republic, 1789–1815*. New York: Oxford University Press, 2009.

———. *The Radicalism of the American Revolution*. New York: Vintage Books, 1993.

Wood, Philip J. *Southern Capitalism: The Political Economy of North Carolina, 1880–1980*. Durham: Duke University Press, 1986.

Woodward, C. Vann. *The Future of the Past*. New York: Oxford University Press, 1989.

———. *Origins of the New South, 1877–1913*. Baton Rouge: Louisiana State University Press, 1971.

Wyatt-Brown, Bertram. *The Shaping of Southern Culture: Honor, Grace, and War, 1760s–1880s*. Chapel Hill: University of North Carolina Press, 2001.

———. *Southern Honor: Ethics and Behavior in the Old South*. New York: Oxford University Press, 1982.

Yates, Richard E. "Zebulon B. Vance as War Governor of North Carolina, 1862–1865." *Journal of Southern History* 3 (February 1937): 43–75.

Yeager, Gertrude M. "Elite Education in Nineteenth-Century Chile." *The Hispanic American Historical Review* 71 (February 1991): 73–105.

Zaeske, Susan. *Signatures of Citizenship: Petitioning, Antislavery, and Women's Political Identity*. Chapel Hill: University of North Carolina Press, 2003.

Zelizer, Viviana A. *The Social Meaning of Money*. New York: BasicBooks, 1994.

Zimmerman, Andrew. *Anthropology and Antihumanism in Imperial Germany*. Chicago: University of Chicago Press, 2001.

Zimmerman, Jonathan. *Distilling Democracy: Alcohol Education in America's Public Schools, 1880–1925*. Lawrence: University Press of Kansas, 1999.

Zundel, Alan F. *Declarations of Dependency: The Civic Republican Tradition in U.S. Poverty Policy*. Albany: State University of New York Press, 2000.

Index

sacralization of silver, 177–78; and
pleas after Wilmington massacre,
204–5; and alcohol prohibition, 208–
11; and appeals to Franklin Roosevelt,
215–16; in modern politics, 218
Bigelow, Albert, 181
Birdsall, S. H., 95–96
Black Code, 84
Blaine, James, 152
Bollinger, Michael: asks for bread for
family, 32
Boner, Johnson: asks for help from
Vance, 37
Booth, John Wilkes, 81
Bowe, William B., 93, 94, 124
Boyle, A. H., request for discharge for,
37
Boyle, Richard: petition to Lincoln, 67–
69
Bread riots, 27–28
Brogden, Curtis H., 128
Brown, Joseph, 105
Brown, Michael: and Salisbury bread
riots, 27
Bryan, Frederick J., request for dis-
charge for, 35–36
Bryan, William Jennings: popular calls
upon, 4, 5; and 1896 election, 168,
176–78; popular views of, 176–78,
214; and evangelical language, 177–
78; and namesakes, 178
Buck, Williamson, 7, 11, 112, 122–23,
126, 128–29
Bureaucrats: as obstacles to assistance,
26, 67
Burnside, Ambrose: invasion of North
Carolina, 18, 51, 56, 57; and William
Henry Singleton, 53
Butler, Benjamin: devises policy for contraband, 18, 47–51; defines freedom,
61; receives petition, 66–67

Butler, Marion: and management of
Populism, 173, 176, 178, 261 (n. 17)

Caldwell, Franklin: and geography of
power, 127
Caldwell, Tod, 7, 126–29
Cameron, Simon, 48
Carnegie, Andrew: as site for fantasy,
171
Carr, Elias: pardons, 146–47; as celebrity, 157; and Farmers' Alliance, 170–
71, 173
Carr, Julian S., 157
Chase, Salmon, 82
Cheshire, Joseph Blount, 140–41
Chesnut, James, 15
Citizenship: compatibility of subjecthood and, 1, 2, 9, 33–34, 98, 114, 129,
134, 137, 156
Civil service reform, 4, 147–56, 253
(n. 24)
Civil War: impact of, 1, 2, 4, 5, 10–11,
17, 232 (n. 13); relief programs and, 4,
17, 25; coming of, 15–16; North Carolina's role in, 16–17; Union invasion
of North Carolina in, 17, 18, 51; conscription policies during, 17, 19–20;
and breakdown of slave control, 19,
20, 21, 24; prompts Confederate appeals for help, 22–40; and conflicts
between state and Confederate government, 23; shortages and, 25; desertion during, 29–30; popular visions of
the Confederacy during, 35–37; impact of Union actions upon slaves, 44,
45, 50, 74; and veterans' benefits,
157–58
Clark, Charles, 150
Clark, Henry Toole: and the limits of
state government, 22
Clark, Walter: as celebrity endorser, 157

Cleveland, Grover: popular calls upon, 4, 214; and civil service, 147–56; and silver standard, 166

Clinton, Bill, 219

Clopton, William H.: and former slaves, 62

Cobb, R. A.: asks for governor's friend-ship, 128

Coin's Financial School (pamphlet), 174

Colyer, Vincent: supervision of contra-bands, 56–59

Condescension, pleas for, 27, 33–34

Confederacy, popular vision of, 37

Conklin, John, 109

Connor, Henry G.: and university men, 188–91

Corbett, Maurice N.: and African Amer-ican politics, 180–84

Corliss, Alonzo B., 122, 128–29

Cotton, Sallie, 192

Craig, Locke: and university men, 188–91

Crandell, Sallie C.: and Vance's conde-scension, 27

Crasson, Hannah: recalls Lincoln as "Medicine man," 71

Curlee, Archibald: sends dime to Vance for answer, 29

Curtis, Silas, 114

Cutter, William A.: and Republican Re-construction, 111

Daniels, Josephus, 152; and university men, 188–91; and propaganda cam-paign, 194–95; and centrality of ex-clusion to democracy, 197

Davidson, William: and request for furlough, 35

Davis, Anabella: and skepticism of Vance's aid, 27

Davis, Jefferson: and conflict with Zebulon Vance, 23; popular appeals to, 35–37; and fantasy of wrestling match with Abraham Lincoln, 73

Davis, John F., 117

Dawes, Harriet Ann: recalls Lincoln, 74

Dependence: political utility of, 1, 2, 4, 6, 7, 8, 228 (n. 2); stigma of, 3, 4, 7, 9, 47, 57–59, 217–18; centrality of to politics, 9; relation to equality, 10; Civil War's role in fostering claims of, 17, 37; uses for free people of color, 33; as form of access, 40; as lens into emancipation, 45–46; as strategy for ex-slaves, 67–70; during Reconstruction, 77, 101, 102, 132; compatibility with economic transformation, 138–39; as the right to beg, 155; compatibility with bureau-cratic programs, 157; and fight over currency standard, 166–67; transfor-mation in prohibition campaign, 211; transformation during New Deal, 215–20; and fantasy of autonomy, 219–20; inevitability of, 219–20

Disenfranchisement, 185–86, 197

Divorce: as favor, 7, 11, 112, 122–23, 126, 128–29; and reform, 206–7

Dixon, Thomas Jr., 133, 153

Douglas, Stephen: and importance of in-formal slave control, 20

Douglass, Ambrose: celebrates eman-cipation twelve times, 56

Dowd, Squire: educated to love the Yankees, 54

Duke family: as site for fantasies of help, 171–72; and Tom Settle III, 179, 182

Durham, Plato, 124

Elliott, Charlotte, 121, 248 (n. 34)

Enthusiasm, power of, 165, 172

Exceptionalism, American, limits of, 229 (n. 5)

Ex Parte Milligan, impact of, 91

bate, 167–68; and white supremacy, 192, 195–99; and pictorial campaign, 194–95; and New Deal, 214–20; amnesia about, 219–20

Pearsall, Jere: and the problem of slave control, 21

Pearson, R. G., 141

Pearson, Richmond M., 125

Pendleton Act, 151–52

Penny, Amy, 73

People's Party. *See* Populism

Pierce, Edward L.: and contrabands, 48

Ploetz, Alfred, 187

Plummer, Hannah: and love for Franklin Roosevelt, 215

Plunkitt, George Washington, urban patronalism of, 12

Political, definition of line between personal and, 11, 114, 204, 219–20, 232 (n. 13)

Polk, Leonidas L., 168–73

Pope, N. P.: and the problem of slave control, 21

Popular politics, 1, 2, 3, 8, 151, 167, 191–92; definition of, 3

Populism: importance of, 163–65, 168; and emergence from Farmers' Alliance, 173–76; and patronage, 175–76; and fusion, 176–78, 261 (n. 17); and race, 180–84. *See also* Farmers' Alliance

Porfiriato: and contemporary state-building projects, 13

Porter, Otis: asks Vance to be "soldier's friend," 31

Powell, John Wesley, 190

Prayer: similarity to forms of petition, 139

Presidency, popular visions of, 4, 44, 70–74, 115, 126–27, 150–52, 176–78, 204–5, 213–20, 274 (n. 2); 275 (n. 7)

Presidential elections: 1868, 113, 115, 116; 1896, 176–78

Price, Peter: and personalization of Freedmen's Bureau power, 94–95

Progressivism, 164–65, 184; as movement that ends Reconstruction, 14, 185–87, 205–6; and white supremacy, 186–87, 266 (n. 2); North Carolina as exemplar of, 206; and education, 206; and alcohol prohibition, 211; continued influence on modern politics, 218–19

Race: and patronage fights, 149–50, 154–55, 180–84, 192; and democratic competition, 159–60, 180–84, 192–206, 268 (n. 7); remade within local geographies, 182; as fetish, 182–84; and soft eugenics, 186; and Spanish-American War, 201–2; and alcohol prohibition, 209–11

Ramsour, A. K., 119–20

Ransom, Matt, 149

Rations, conflicts over, 45, 48–49, 57–59, 63–70

Reconstruction: patronalism and, 12, 101; concept of long, 13, 77, 131–32, 233 (n. 16); violence during, 76, 77, 112, 114, 116, 118, 119, 122–29, 135, 161–62, 241 (n. 2), 245 (n. 2); problem of continuity of government during, 80–81; Southern response to defeat during, 81, 83–85, 95, 112; competing plans for, 81–82, 91; problem of legitimacy during, 102–4, 106, 111–12, 125; Redemption as pivot in, 131–33; economic transformations of, 138–39; religion and, 139

Reform: as effort to excise dependence, 132, 143–46, 147–56, 164, 206–7; and Darwinism, 188–91

Religion. *See* Biblical language, political uses of

Soft eugenics: international movement for, 187–88; and alcohol prohibition, 208–11

Sorrell, Ria: recalls Lincoln stories, 73

South, relationship between the nation and, 7, 12, 46–47, 231 (n. 8)

Spanish-American War: and white supremacy campaign, 188, 197, 200–202, 269 (n. 17); and formation of white familialism, 200

Speaks, Nancy: asks Vance for help, 32

Spencer, Cornelia P.: pleas for Vance's pardon, 41

Spikes, Tanner, 56

Stanly, Edward, 59

State: power of nineteenth-century American, 1, 12, 150, 233 (n. 16); vision of as light, 107, 135, 185; strange growth spurts of, 149, 168, 184, 211; vision of as social organism, 185, 189; autonomy and myth of weakness of, 219–20

Stephens, John W., assassination of, 124

Stevens, Thaddeus, 106

Stricklen, James W., 30

Subtreasury plan, 170–71

Suffrage: and dependence, 9, 231 (n. 11)

Sumner, Charles: appeals to Lincoln, 59; worries over Reconstruction, 83; explains the need for the Freedmen's Bureau, 85

Swain, David, 81

Tammany Hall, 12

Tender mercy, pleas for, 39

Territorialism: definition of, 103–4, 159–62, 245 (n. 3); and localism, 103. *See also* Geography of power

Third Republic, French: and contemporaneous state-building projects, 13

Thomas, Elias: fears Yankees, 54

Thomas, Eliza A.: asks Vance to hear cry of poor, 34–35

Tillman, Benjamin, 191

Tocqueville, Alexis de: and the relationship between equality and dependence, 10

Toland, John, 9

Trent River. *See* James City

Twain, Mark, 13

Tyranny: access and definition of, 174–75

Union: and impermanence of control over Confederate territory, 56, 65–66; hopes for loyalist awakening in the South, 59; demobilization, 75, 77–81, 88, 89, 90, 108, 111, 128; financial retrenchment, 79–80, 242 (n. 7)

Union Leagues, 11, 112–14, 117

University of North Carolina: Zebulon Vance's rise through, 22–23; as central site in white supremacy movement, 186, 188–91, 266 (n. 2)

Vance, Zebulon Baird: central role of in North Carolina politics, 4; popular claims upon, 5; and state-sponsored relief, 11, 17, 25, 26; and Confederate conscription, 20; and expansion of state government, 22; background of, 22–23; and exemptions, 23; and conflict with Jefferson Davis, 23, 35–37; wartime appeals to, 24–40; surrenders, 41, 81; and second term as governor, 131, 136–38, 140, 142–45; and campaign of 1876, 133–35; and freedpeople, 135–36; postwar appeals to, 136–38, 142–45, 148–49; religious appeals of, 140; and civil service fight, 147–56; as celebrity, 157; and sacralization of silver, 165–66,

177; and fight over subtreasury, 170–71

Vernacular vocabularies of politics, 1, 95, 164, 216–17, 219–20

Waddell, Alfred M., 203
Ward, Lester Frank, 190
Washington School of ethnology, 190
Watauga Club, 153
Watkins, Susie H.: plea for help, 172
Watson, H. L., 95
Weaver James B., 173
Wells, David Ames, 80
White supremacy campaign, 185–206; and international currents, 187–88, 205–6; as rural movement, 196–97, 203–5; and white familialism, 202, 204; and violence, 202–5; and education, 206
Whittlesey, Eliphalet, 69, 75, 83, 85, 86, 87, 88, 89, 107
Wiggins, M. S., 38

Wild, Edward A.: oversees black regiments, 61–62
Williams, Nancy, 15, 16
Wilmington massacre: relationship of to white supremacy, 203–5; and appeals to Washington, D.C., 204–5
Wilson, Henry, 93
Windsor, Mary: begs Vance's tender mercy, 38–39
Winston, Francis D.: and university men, 188–91
Winston, George T.: and university men, 188–91; and education, 206
Woman's Christian Temperance Union (WCTU), 208–11
Works Progress Administration, 213
World War II: and decline of patronalism, 217–18, 275 (n. 6)
Worth, Jonathan, 84, 94, 106

Yellady, Dilly, 54, 70, 73
Young, James, 194, 195, 201